Writing the World of Policing

Writing the World of Policing

The Difference Ethnography Makes

EDITED BY DIDIER FASSIN

The University of Chicago Press
Chicago and London

The University of Chicago Press, Chicago 60637
The University of Chicago Press, Ltd., London
© 2017 by The University of Chicago
Published 2017

26 25 24 23 22 21 20 19 18 17   1 2 3 4 5

ISBN-13: 978-0-226-49750-1 (cloth)
ISBN-13: 978-0-226-49764-8 (paper)
ISBN-13: 978-0-226-49778-5 (e-book)
DOI: 10.7208/chicago/9780226497785.001.0001

Library of Congress Cataloging-in-Publication Data

Names: Fassin, Didier, editor.
Title: Writing the world of policing : the difference ethnography makes / edited by Didier Fassin.
Description: Chicago : The University of Chicago Press, 2017. | Includes index.
Identifiers: LCCN 2017005978 | ISBN 9780226497501 (cloth : alk. paper) | ISBN 9780226497648 (pbk. : alk. paper) | ISBN 9780226497785 (e-book)
Subjects: LCSH: Police. | Law enforcement—Fieldwork. | Law enforcement—Research—Methodology. | Social sciences—Research—Methodology. | Law and the social sciences.
Classification: LCC HV7897.W75 2017 | DDC 363.2—dc23 LC record available at https://lccn.loc.gov/2017005978

CONTENTS

DIDIER FASSIN
INTRODUCTION / Ethnographying the Police / 1

PART I : POSITION

STEVE HERBERT
ONE / Accountability:
Ethnographic Engagement and the Ethics of
the Police (United States) / 23

JULIA HORNBERGER
TWO / Complicity:
Becoming the Police (South Africa) / 42

BEATRICE JAUREGUI
THREE / Intimacy:
Personal Policing, Ethnographic Kinship, and
Critical Empathy (India) / 62

JEFFREY T. MARTIN
FOUR / Affect:
The Virtual Force of Policing (Taiwan) / 91

PART II : OBSERVATION

HELENE MARIA KYED
FIVE / Predicament:
Interpreting Police Violence (Mozambique) / 113

ELIF BABÜL
SIX / Morality:
Understanding Police Training on Human Rights (Turkey) / 139

CLARA HAN
SEVEN / Experience:
Being Policed as a Condition of Life (Chile) / 162

DANIEL M. GOLDSTEIN
EIGHT / Aspiration:
Hoping for a Public Policing (Bolivia) / 184

PART III : DESCRIPTION

DUNCAN McCARGO
NINE / Sense and Sensibility:
Crafting Tales about the Police (Thailand) / 207

SUSANA DURÃO
TEN / Detention:
Police Discretion Revisited (Portugal) / 225

LAURENCE RALPH
ELEVEN / Alibi:
The Extralegal Force Embedded in the Law (United States) / 248

DIDIER FASSIN
TWELVE / Boredom:
Accounting for the Ordinary in the Work of Policing (France) / 269

Index / 293

Ethnographying the Police

DIDIER FASSIN

> Law and order arise out of the very processes which they govern.
>
> —Bronislaw Malinowski, *Crime and Custom in Savage Society* (1926)

The police have for a long time been an object of interest—and passions—within society. For more than half a century, they have also been a subject of research—and debates—within the social sciences, significantly contributing to the renewal of criminology. In recent years, however, this dual trend has become more pronounced, and policing has come to occupy an increasing place in the public sphere as well as in the scientific field: new issues have called for new approaches.

On the one hand, there has been a growing concern regarding law enforcement practices, particularly in poor neighborhoods and toward racial and ethnic minorities. The implication of the police in the death of young men of color in Aulnay-sous-Bois in 2005, Tottenham in 2011, and Ferguson in 2014, among many others, and the impunity from which they have benefitted, have caused major urban unrest in France, the United Kingdom, and the United States, respectively, revealing the moral gap between the law enforcement institution and the population that it is supposed to protect.[1] However, these incidents have not been limited to Western countries, and, although they have received less international attention, tragic encounters with the police resulting in killings have become an increasing source of preoccupation in the global South, from Brazil to South Africa, from Egypt to India. Yet, more than the novelty of these phenomena—or even their aggravation, for which little evidence can be provided in the absence of continuous statistics and homogenous data—it is their rising visibility through traditional and social media as well as political discourses on law and order and social mobilizations of citizens protesting abuses that explain contemporary anxiety. The shooting, beating, or harassing by the police of people belonging to underprivileged classes and groups has long been a common fact without turning into a public concern. It has become one when the experience of those affected has been exposed, thus rendering denial no longer possible.[2] But simultaneously, beyond these tragic episodes, law enforcement has exercised an increasing fascination within society, as is manifest in the media with the multiplication of news reports, reality shows, television series, documentaries, and films dedicated to all aspects—actual or fictional—of policing, from patrol work to criminal investigation, from the war on drugs to the paramilitarization of special units.[3] Whether criticized or praised, respected or feared, the police have become a major controversial figure in the contemporary world, while law and order policies have tended to disseminate globally.

On the other hand, there has recently been a renewal in research on policing, both within the field of criminology, via the contestation of the dominant classical and positivist paradigms by critical, cultural, and feminist approaches, and within the humanities and the social sciences, through novel theoretical as well as empirical inquiry. An interesting trend of this renewal has been what could be called the reinvention of police ethnography. Indeed, there exists an important tradition of qualitative and observational approach in research on law enforcement.[4] One could even argue that most classics in criminology have been nourished by the intimate knowledge of the field acquired by their authors, which allowed for their deeply informed interpretation of police work and organization.[5] However, in their writings, accounts of fieldwork were often limited and illustrative, as is the case with the sociological literature of symbolic interactionism, which exercised a significant influence on this approach in criminology. Vignettes and excerpts served to exemplify general points.[6] Rarely were they the matter of a specific reflection on the conditions of their collection, the modalities of their restitution, and their various epistemological, ethical, and political implications.[7] Furthermore, in later studies, the expanding prominence of quantitative surveys and experimental studies contributed to the marginalization of qualitative and observational works while at the same time theoretical elaborations on policing tended to be more valued than empirical research on the ground. Ethnography was often ignored or even disqualified as deceptive since it relied on a limited number of cases reflecting a specific setting and subjectively assessed by the researcher.[8] Over the past decade, however, things have begun to change as criminologists have rediscovered the merits of participant observation and ethnographers have showed interest in the study of policing. Anthropology in particular, which had remained almost absent from this field since Michael Banton's seminal study of the British policeman fifty years ago, has significantly invested it anew.[9] Today, in different parts of the world, anthropologists are conducting fieldwork on policing and bringing an ethnographic gaze to the study of law enforcement.[10] But they do not have the monopoly of police ethnography: other scholars are also part of this scientific move, which increasingly finds a legitimate place within criminology.[11] The most important implication of the ethnographic shift is that, far from being a mere empirical addition to existing methodological procedures, it obliges social scientists to reevaluate both the theoretical self-evidence of their object (policing) and their very relation to their subjects (the police).

The present volume is a collective attempt to link these two major trends: the increasing significance of policing issues in contemporary society and the growing salience of police ethnography for their comprehension.

So, what difference does police ethnography make? This interrogation can be understood from three complementary perspectives: What difference does it make for the study of the police? What difference does it make for the practice of ethnography? Finally, what difference does it make for the societies where it is conducted? In our chapters, we propose various answers to these questions, highlighting the relevance of ethnographic insight for the analysis of law enforcement and the contribution of the inquiry into policing to ethnographic practice as well as the pertinence of this approach for contemporary societies. But before going further, two *prefatory comments* may be necessary.

First, what is ethnography is generally taken for granted, namely as an equivalent, more or less, to fieldwork, participant observation, or qualitative approach. It is, however, much richer and more complex a practice than these self-evident equivalences imply.[12] I suggest it has three dimensions. It is a method of scientific research, requiring our long-term presence, an intimate knowledge of people and places, the acquisition of the local language and the identification of the local codes: more than being there, as is often said, it involves living with, at least for certain periods of time, talking to, learning from. It is also an experience of social worlds, resulting from an encounter with people generally different from us and with a culture foreign to us, but developing into a familiarization through a combination of reciprocal trust and mutual recognition: as time goes by, we do not only get to know our interlocutors better but we also realize that we have much more in common with them than what we had initially imagined. Finally, it is an operation of singular writing, that is, of transcription and translation, of putting into words and ideas what has been seen and heard, of giving a meaningful order to a succession of facts and events that may seem completely disparate at first sight: it all starts with a blank sheet or a black screen. These three aspects—method, experience, writing— radically contrast with approaches relying on statistics, questionnaires, or interviews: ethnographers do not look at figures, but are interested in what is going on; they do not delegate their production of data to assistants, but are themselves present in the field; they do not ask standardized questions, but observe scenes and converse with their protagonists; they do not know in advance what they look for, but try to make sense of what people do, and how, and why; their mode of thinking is not deductive but inductive. All these elements differentiate ethnography from other procedures commonly used in studies on policing, particularly in the field of criminology, and pose specific epistemological, political, and ethical problems.

Second, policing also needs to be delimited, if not defined. It can refer to two quite different kinds of activities. In the usual sense, it corresponds to law enforcement and peacekeeping, in other words, what police officers and agencies do: it encompasses a remarkable diversity of practices, from arresting criminals to containing demonstrations, from ticketing drivers to assisting accident victims, with the sole common ground that they may at some point require the recourse to force, as pointed out by Egon Bittner.[13] In its older meaning, it comprises a much wider range of human interventions in the regulation of society, from public health to child welfare, from the maintenance of order to the control of morals: this utopic project of normalization of life initially imagined in the eighteenth century embraces what Michel Foucault called biopolitics.[14] In fact, the contrast between these two extremes has been reduced in recent years with the expansion of the spectrum of police activities and the development of new technologies of surveillance. In the following pages, we focus on the more restrictive meaning, in other words, on policing as it appears through the presence and activity of officers as well as other actors involved in issues related to crime and security, law and order, social control and legitimate violence. This delimitation is often contested on the ground, as the police can be absent or inactive, their intervention can be deemed illegal or disproportionate, and the distinction between official and informal agents can be blurred. This is even truer since we chose to concentrate our observations on the policing of poor neighborhoods, underprivileged populations, and marginalized minorities. Our choice can easily be justified on the grounds that it represents the most common and often the most problematic activity of law enforcement in peace times all over the world. It is also where the control of the public order and the reproduction of the social order get the most confused, where the distance from professional norms is the most obvious, and where the indulgence of the authorities with respect to the deviance of their personnel is the highest. In sum, our decision to focus on this type of policing was not only guided by theoretical issues of possible comparisons and generalizations of our findings in various settings, but also by practical considerations with regard to its social relevance and political implications.

These preliminaries being made, we can now address the two questions of the contribution of ethnography to the understanding of policing and of the benefits of studying policing for the practice of ethnography.

What can we learn from an *ethnography of policing*? Under which conditions? With which limits? If we consider the two essential characters of ethnography, namely its reliance on observation and induction, we can infer two heuristic properties: first, observation confronts discursive propositions with actual facts, thus allowing for the unveiling of discrepancies between what is said and what is done, what is presumed to be and what really is; second, induction restrains preconceived ideas or preformed judgments, since it does not suppose hypotheses to test or questions to answer, but proceeds by progressive elaboration of knowledge through the emergence of meanings. To account for these two properties, let us call the former uncovering and the latter discovery.

The first heuristic property—*uncovering*—is of course not specific to the study of policing. But it is particularly crucial in this case, since policing is an activity in which legal and normative constraints are important, whereas discretionary power is the rule in the street. This tension results in potential irregularity or deviance that officers are not inclined to mention in questionnaires or interviews but which do not escape observation. Of course, one can retort that the presence of the ethnographer constitutes a bias as the agents are on their guard, that it consequently reduces the chances of witnessing unorthodox practices, and that it allows for the presentation a portrait of law enforcement more flattering than it would be if the officers had been on their own. Surprisingly, however, all ethnographic accounts of policing reveal illegal and abnormal practices such as violent gestures, racist words, and unlawful acts in much greater quantity than one could have expected. There are two reasons for this: on the one hand, with time, relations of trust develop between observer and observed, and the officers' control over themselves diminishes, giving free rein to spontaneous attitudes; but on the other, and even more interestingly, much of what the outsiders might find shocking or inappropriate does not seem so to the insiders and therefore is not censured. Thus, while it is certain that what ethnographers see and hear is an attenuated and softened version of what would occur in their absence, it is still instructive in terms of both the deviance that is left to be witnessed and the implicit norms thus revealed about what can be shown without precaution to a stranger. Actually, so blurred is the line between the normal and the deviant, in practice, that one may even start to reconsider the relevance of such distinction.

Moreover, ethnography does not only give access to ordinary facts related to policing, including wrongdoing, it also provides essential elements of their justifications by the officers as well as their possible interpretation by the researcher. With respect to justifications, social agents often feel the need to account a posteriori for their actions, especially when those might be viewed as illegal or illegitimate. Ethnographic work facilitates the expression of such justifications in two ways: the fact that the social scientist has witnessed such deviant practices calls for explanation, which would probably not be formulated otherwise; the sort of interaction between the researcher and the officers in this context consists of informal conversations, which are more propitious than formal interviews to genuine confidence or simply straight talk. Regarding interpretation, the observed scene generally makes sense within its immediate setting as well as its broader background, with which the researcher has become familiar over the months or years of his ethnography. The interpretation may therefore include the specific circumstances of the scene and its relation with previous similar events, the role of the various protagonists and its link with their biographical trajectory, but also general aspects such as the habitus of the profession, the expectations of the superiors, the constraints of the organization, the local and national political contexts. In the end, not only does ethnography render visible practices of abuse, violence, discrimination, and provocation that are usually denied by the institution and overlooked by other methods, but it also makes it possible to account for the police's view on these practices while embedding them in a larger picture.

The second heuristic property—*discovery*—is the logical consequence of the inductive approach that characterizes ethnography. Whereas most quantitative studies of the police start with hypotheses that the research will test, for instance whether the differences in the racial distribution of the stops or the arrests are due to the officers' racial prejudices or to other factors, ethnographic work proceeds through the slow combination of sedimentation and decantation of empirical materials that progressively make sense and possibly lead to hypotheses. Of course, the researchers' minds are not free from implicit theories or questions when they are in the field, but one could go as far as saying that the success of their work can be measured by their capacity to get rid of their old ideas and let new ones emerge. Such a process implies that they remain attentive to what may be hidden in plain sight and acknowledge, for example, that patrolling is not the intense and breathtaking activity generally depicted but an overwhelmingly tedious and repetitive work. It also entails that they have the ability to be surprised by what is buried in the routine of the institution and recognize, for instance, that most car chases may have for function not arresting criminals but producing excitement. Like any profession the police present and represent themselves in a way that does not correspond to what they are and what they do, but in their case, this tendency is particularly pronounced due to the mythology that films, series, novels, and officers themselves produce about them. It may thus take time for the ethnographer to remove this fictional cover that shrouds law enforcement. Thus, the commonplace according to which officers commit deviant acts because just ends justify bad means is often a sheer sociological excuse to cover up reprehensible practices. A temporal and epistemic tension exists here. While researchers need a long period to become acquainted with the activity of the police and start demystifying their world, this process simultaneously tends to make them share the habits, norms, and values of their subjects and, as a result, lose their distance and even lucidity. With time, their critical sense with regard to their object tends to become blunted.

Not unexpectedly considering the positivism that dominates criminological studies, the inductive approach is subject to criticism. Ethnographic findings are often discredited as intuitive and unverifiable, in other words, unscientific. Since they are so dependent on the ethnographers and the interpretation they make of what they observe, it is said that their results cannot be generalized, all the more so because they usually conduct their fieldwork at a single site and sometimes even focus on a small number of events or individuals, which cannot be deemed representative of the entire activity or population of officers. Such criticism makes it possible to contest their conclusions, especially when they have a critical content. The intellectual as well as political risk is real. Indeed, this disqualification implies that what cannot be established via deductive methods and can only be known through inductive approaches is deemed unreliable. If it were accepted, such contest could thus leave whole aspects of police practices—probably the most problematic—beyond the empirical gaze. But the reluctance to acknowledge the validity of the ethnographic method can—and certainly should—be countered. As such, it is no less rigorous than the analytical method; it is simply differently so. Both have their specific weaknesses and flaws, which can be partially controlled and corrected, and if they are epistemologically symmetrical, they can be practically complementary. There is indeed something irreplaceable in the contribution of ethnography to the understanding of policing, whether it concerns facts that cannot be measured, for example the qualitative dimension of racial discrimination, which is systematically ignored in studies about stop and frisk encounters, or facts that may not even be identified unless through long-term observation, such as the paradox of the reversal of the charge, according to which the offense of resisting the police is often the sign of the officer's aggressiveness rather than that of the suspect as is alleged in court. Once sufficiently established and relevantly explained, such phenomena may even be generalizable. This generalization is, however, distinct from that of quantitative studies. It does not imply that the processes that have been identified are to be found everywhere, but that they can be evidenced anywhere: they correspond to logics and mechanisms of general signification in police practices.

By its distinct characteristics—observation as opposed to survey and induction as opposed to deduction—ethnography thus offers an original perspective on police work, exploring dimensions that would not be accessible otherwise. It is as open to the singular and the unforeseen as it is to the routine and its regularities. Instead of focusing on spectacular aspects, whether heroic or tragic, as commentators and journalists in particular often do, ethnographers are attentive to the ordinary and the mundane, to the uncertain and the ambiguous, to meaningful details and significant variations. The links they develop with the officers make them aware of and sensitive to their personal history, their doubts and dilemmas, their values and affects. The duration of their presence combined with their interest in the diverse dimensions of life in the social space they study make them conscious of the broader network of human relations and cultural signs in which policing is embedded. Even obvious notions such as violence and racism are apprehended in a novel way, taking into account how they are experienced by the victims as well as the perpetrators. Through the ethnographic lenses, policing becomes a more complex universe. But while it is important to discuss the merits of ethnography for the understanding of police work, it is equally pertinent to ask if the reverse is true and wonder whether ethnography can benefit from such police studies.

How can police ethnography thus contribute to enriching our comprehension of *ethnography as such*? How does the specificity of this object recently regained by anthropologists enlighten general questions regarding a method they have been using for a hundred years in so many contexts? To address these interrogations, we must recall that ethnography is precisely more than just a method: it is also, as suggested earlier, an experience of social worlds and a practice of singular writing. For both these dimensions, police ethnography offers interesting challenges.

The *experience* of social worlds that are initially foreign to the ethnographer is the rule. The sense of otherness that results from it is prima facie much less pronounced when working on law enforcement than it is when studying headhunters in the Philippines, shamanism in Siberia, possession in Madagascar, or cosmologies in Brazil. Indeed, the police are familiar figures of both our real and virtual environment: we see them in the streets and on screen; they are involved in actual events recounted in newspapers and fictional stories narrated in crime novels; some of us may even have relatives or friends who are officers. Yet, for the ethnographers, the distance they feel with their subjects might sometimes be greater with the police than it is with remote ethnic groups. The paradox can be explained by the fact that this distance is not so much cultural as it is moral and affective. In fact, once past the excitement of a few car chases or red-handed catches, there is not much exoticism in law enforcement, especially when it consists of patrol or paperwork. Conversely, unlawful, abusive, and racist practices, which are not uncommon especially within certain units and toward certain populations, generate reprobation and unease. Sometimes this moral and affective distance has developed before entering the field through personal experiences or mere prejudgment, as the police often provoke contrasted images and emotional reactions. Furthermore, whereas social scientists using quantitative methods or theoretical approaches only deal with the officers or their institution at a safe distance from the field with the only risk that of being exposed to the canteen culture of racist jokes, ethnographers are confronted with actual practices, which can be deeply disturbing. It should be noted that this moral and affective distance is not specific to the ethnography of the police: it is similarly experienced by researchers who study groups or professions with which they feel little sympathy or even profound antipathy, be it because of their political affinities, ideological stances, or social practices.

As a result, both the attitude to adopt in the field and the analysis of the situations encountered pose singular problems and raise delicate issues. A first tension exists between duplicity and complicity. On the one hand, even if the ethnographers do not work undercover and overtly state that they are doing research, they generally do not express their disapproval or even opinion about what they witness. To comment and criticize would jeopardize their inquiry. Consequently, they tend to conceal what they think and feel. On the other hand, by their mere presence in the field with the officers, they participate in their activity. The public often mistakes them for law enforcement agents and even takes them on, asking for their assistance or condemning their silence. The researchers themselves may be troubled by the role they come to play. A second tension arises from the conflict between the viewpoint of the police and the perspective of the ethnographers. The former produce a rationalization of their acts that may substantially differ from the latter's assessment. How to account simultaneously for the justifications of the agents and their own interpretation can be a complicated challenge for social scientists. Yet the crucial point is that they do not substitute one for the other, merely endorsing the arguments of their interlocutors or, symmetrically, ignoring them and imposing their reading. There is much to learn from what officers have to say about the reasons why they act in the way they do, but their discourse cannot be taken for granted and must be questioned.

The transition to *writing* is also a crucial test for ethnographers working on policing. First, the material that they have recorded on tapes and in field notes translates into narratives and dialogues that must be inserted into descriptions. This complex operation supposes a selection of relevant scenes and interactions that reflects what they have witnessed, while with respect to police work it is often more tempting and more rewarding to focus on thrilling episodes, deviant practices, or disparaging attitudes. Since ethnography does not include technical procedures of control comparable to what quantitative studies have in terms of both sample representativeness and statistical significance, it is the sole responsibility of the researcher to present cases and provide descriptions that give a reliable picture of the reality as they have witnessed it. Second, this picture does not speak for itself and calls for an interpretation of some kind. Such an interpretation can be limited to what is immediately intelligible within the perimeter of the observation or relate the observed facts with their broader historical, political, cultural, and social contexts. The choice of one option or the other will give very different outcomes. Whether one restricts the analysis of stop and frisk encounters to what officers do in the street or links their activity to legacies and policies of the institution will provide a quite distinct comprehension of racial discrimination in law enforcement. Third, rhetorical decisions are also critical. The general tone of the writing can suggest benevolence or indignation with respect to police actions. On the one hand, neutralizing the emotional and moral involvement of the author leads to a more factual account, which may, however, lose some essential dimensions. On the other, letting affects or norms filter through between the lines provides more faithful depictions of the scenes as they were experienced, but may disqualify the description as partial. Moreover, whereas the objective restitution of an event is an elusive goal, the multiplication of subjective perspectives with the confrontation of different versions of the same story may offer an alternative to the usual univocal view presented in narratives. More generally all these "tales of the fields" involve rhetorical strategies that have important implications for the way the world of policing is represented.

Thus, more than would be the case with most other topics, policing exposes the ethnographers to difficult epistemological as well as ethical ordeals. The challenges posed by the negotiation of their *position* in the field are the object of the first part of this volume. How do researchers react to the discourses and practices that they witness? How do they become morally and emotionally involved with the protagonists of their research? These are the questions discussed in the first four chapters, whose authors analyze their perplexity as they observe the interactions of the police with their public, among themselves, and even with the ethnographer.

Relating three brief banal episodes of law enforcement in Seattle, Steve Herbert puts to the test the notion of accountability by displacing it from the police to the ethnographer. When the latter observes unlawful or immoral acts committed by the former, they both become accountable. What attitude should the researcher adopt? If he remains silent while disapproving, is he not deceiving the officers and betraying their public? Before answering these questions, Herbert proposes three portraits of the ethnographer as a distanced professional, as an engaged public actor, and as an ethical human being. Facing the dilemma of having to choose between these three positions, he explains that he opted for the duplicity of silence so as to continue his observation of the business of policing as usual and to complete his critical analysis of newly implemented policies of social control.

While she is also troubled by the ambiguous role she comes to play during her fieldwork, it is through the eyes of the public that Julia Hornberger becomes herself the police as she accompanies officers involved in the repression of intellectual property law violations in the inner city of Johannesburg. The situation is made even more disturbing as she realizes that her sentiment of complicity resonates with the embarrassment of the agents at the scene, who are confronted as she is by the distress of the suspects. But this moment is heuristic since it allows for a deeper understanding of the predicament of law enforcement and a more insightful reflection on the paradoxical place occupied by the ethnographer as she is simultaneously impotent and on the side of the powerful.

During her fieldwork in a small town of Uttar Pradesh, Beatrice Jauregui also developed an ambivalent relationship with her interlocutors, but it is of a different kind. Indeed, it derives from a sentiment of closeness she associates with her own family background and therefore coins ethnographic kinship. The intimacy thus created with the police does not prevent her, however, from analyzing critically the abuses exerted by superiors over rank-and-file officers. It makes her even more receptive to the often-ignored vulnerability of the latter, who may endure injustice and violence from their management almost similar to those suffered by their public from the police.

Far from this empathetic attachment, the disconcerting story narrated by Jeffrey Martin about his early interactions with a high-ranking law enforcement official in Taiwan reveals a method of intimidation used to inculcate a lesson: the ethnographer experiences fear at the same time as he learns how social control works. Policing, he is made to understand, operates not only through the use of physical force but also via the resort to immaterial power. The interaction between the official and the ethnographer can thus be assimilated to a literal incorporation of empirical knowledge: it is through his body that the researcher profoundly grasps the cultural meaning of this idiosyncratic form of policing.

But positioning oneself in relation with law enforcement agents is not the only challenge ethnographers face in the field. Events, situations, discourses, and practices that they witness need to be rendered intelligible by taking into account their interlocutors' perspective, be they the police or the policed. The issues raised by the *observation* of these facts form the matter of the second part of the book. The first two chapters adopt the viewpoint of the officers and their institution as they are either perpetrating or preventing violence. Symmetrically, the last two take the standpoint of the population regarding law enforcement. In each case study apprehending the local configurations and their meaning needs an intellectual move away from self-evident considerations about policing.

While the scenes of police brutality recounted by Helene Maria Kyed in Maputo may seem all too common, their interpretation poses a series of interesting problems. As the agents are members of a community law enforcement group officially appointed to replace the infamous national police deemed too cruel, this delegation of power questions the supposed monopoly of the legitimate use of violence by the state. Moreover, as these agents also seem to abuse physically and verbally both suspects and innocents, their behavior calls for explanations that resort to a variety of practical and moral reasons, from the instrumental utilization of beatings to obtain information to the retributive function of harsh treatments. The irony is that this community policing was conceived by international agencies as part of the democratization process after the civil war.

Apparently similar pressures led the government in Turkey to develop human rights programs for the police, which Elif Babül spent two years studying. These programs had been designed to harmonize law enforcement practices with those supposedly in effect in the European Union, which, at the time, the country hoped to enter. Participant observation of the training sessions uncover how officers as well as their educators distort the meaning of the instructions they receive and display cynicism with respect to their relevance. Although they were expected to enhance professionalization and expertise among police forces, it appears that the programs tend in large part to strengthen and legitimate their power, simply rendering it more acceptable by international norms.

The fact that under these conditions the experience of the inhabitants of poor urban areas incorporates police violence as usual practice should therefore not be a surprise, but Clara Han, in her study of a neighborhood in Santiago under police occupation for several years, goes further when she describes this experience as a condition of life. The presence of officers and military buses form part of the habitual landscape in the same way as occasional gunfire and drug raids punctuate the ordinary rhythm of the days. Through this normalization of state violence, policing differentiates territories and discriminates populations within the city, allowing for the marginalization of already vulnerable groups.

The account provided by Daniel Goldstein of a meeting he organized in Cochabamba with market vendors to discuss insecurity problems seems to offer a remarkable contrast since his interlocutors do not complain about the presence of the police but about their absence. It is not the excess of the power of state that they fear: on the contrary, they deplore its withdrawal. However, such expectations for more law enforcement may not be the exception in disadvantaged neighborhoods. Indeed, what their residents often suffer from is that the police are never present when needed and generally abusive when they come, as they say. In this sense, by revealing these aspirations for better policing, the ethnographer challenges common views about the rejection of law enforcement by the poor, which ultimately justifies the conjunction of state indifference and repressive policies.

In the end, ethnography translates into an act of writing. Books and essays transform observations collected in the field into a text that communicates them to various audiences. *Description*, which is crucial to this process, is the common thread of the third part of this collection. Often presumed to be a neutral activity of mere transcription of empirical data into legible form, it is on the contrary a delicate exercise and a sensitive practice. It involves choices regarding what to retain and what to discard, how to tell and how to depict. It implies that one has to decide about the place granted to emotions and the way to avoid normative stances.

Not without humor, Duncan McCargo takes his fieldwork with the police in Bangkok as a pretext to discuss the way ethnographers think, including about themselves, and write, sometimes featuring themselves. He opposes sense and sensibility in ethnographic practice, preferring the intellectual detachment of the former to the moral superiority of the latter, as he says. Advancing his argument still further, he suggests that description should be self-sufficient and that the author should get rid of academic habits, theoretical references, and critical reflections in order to simply immerse the reader into the social world he studies, an objective that he admits not having achieved in his own inaugural vignette.

Taking a different posture, Susana Durão demonstrates in her meticulous account of the arrest and detention of a man accused of drug dealing in Lisbon that thorough descriptions can support strong theoretical claims as long as they are contextualized within the broader picture. The officers' discretionary power, which allows them to file charges against the man for something they know he has not committed, can only be interpreted in light of the institutional norms, political incentives, and historical legacies of abuses. At the same time, by the zeal they display in applying these norms, implementing these policies, and reproducing these historical tropes, the police demonstrate that discretion is not only a question of power but also of personal desire and professional fulfillment.

But abusive behavior is taken to its limits in the case related by Laurence Ralph about the Chicago police. Although the events date back forty years, the acts of torture perpetrated by a commander remain vivid for the victims who endured them as well as the other officers who covered them up. To account for such infamous practices, description takes the form of a narrative where not only stories and dialogues occupy a major place but also senses and affects are mobilized. Such an account displaces the gaze from the rogue agent to those who suffered at his hands as well as it renders problematic the complicity of his colleagues who saw and heard but, to protect their career, did not speak out.

An extreme case of description is finally proposed on the basis of my ethnography of policing in the outskirts of Paris. Whereas most novels, series, and films about the police depict their work as thrilling and exhilarating, the most obvious characteristic of being on patrol is in general the lack of activity. Both because of the persistence of the traditional image of action and danger attached to the profession and because of the challenge posed by the depiction of eventless days and nights, little has been written on boredom within law enforcement. Yet this experience is essential to interpret police practices, including deviant ones, as the dearth of incidents leads to harassment of vulnerable groups in order to reach the quota of arrests and as minor affairs give rise to spectacular overreaction. The relative absence of tedium in criminological literature invites a wider reflection on what remains invisible or untold in studies on law enforcement.

The initial intention of convening the twelve authors of this volume was to account for the remarkable development of police ethnographies in the past decade and to demonstrate their significant contribution to the renewal of the studies on law enforcement. An international workshop, which brought together scholars from various disciplines working on five continents, was held at the Institute for Advanced Study in Princeton in May 2014. It generated intense discussions, which resulted in the project of a collective book exploring both what ethnography adds to the understanding of policing and what observing the police involves for ethnographic practice. In order to benefit from this fruitful exchange, the present essays were entirely written after the meeting and thoroughly revised on the basis of reciprocal comments made on early versions.

Hardly more than a month after our workshop Eric Garner was killed by a police officer in Staten Island, and a few weeks later Michael Brown was shot dead by a law enforcement agent in Ferguson; both were unarmed; both were African Americans. These two events, followed by the decisions by the respective grand juries not to indict the two perpetrators, were the starting point of a national surge of awareness regarding violent and discriminatory policing practices toward minorities belonging to lower-income groups in the United States. The public discovered that, instead of being exceptional, these two tragic incidents were part of a long series of similar events until then ignored or hidden: as established by the *Guardian*, more than a thousand persons die each year in the country as a result of an interaction with the police, and there were more individuals killed by law enforcement officers during the first twenty-four days of 2015 in the United States than in the past twenty-four years in England and Wales.

However, two categories of individuals were not surprised by these revelations. What others discovered they already knew. African Americans living in disadvantaged neighborhoods knew by experience. Ethnographers who had studied police practices in these environments knew by observation. Of course the latter group was considerably smaller than the former one. Some of these social scientists had even acquired their knowledge working with these local populations.

This leads to the third question initially posed: What difference does the ethnography of police make for the societies where it is conducted? To be sure, it should not be credited with the power to provide easy solutions to the complex issues raised by law enforcement in these contexts of deeply entrenched inequality. But it does two things. First, because it is grounded in a permanent dialogue between the empirical material and the theoretical stakes, it can make these issues more intelligible in a way that journalistic approaches cannot. Second, because it is based on the relation of trust and indebtedness that derives from long-term presence, it can make audible the voices of those who experience them in a way that positivist approaches cannot. In this dual sense of rendering issues intelligible and voices audible, the ethnography of policing is a modest but necessary contribution to democracy.

Acknowledgments

The workshop convened in Princeton benefited from a grant of the Fritz Thyssen Foundation. The authors express their gratitude to Donne Petito, Patrick Brown, and Laura McCune, in the School of Social Science of the Institute for Advanced Study, for their assistance at various stages of the preparation of the meeting and of the book. The editor is also indebted to the anonymous reviewers of the manuscript for their insightful comments and helpful suggestions.

Notes

1. A comparison of French and British riots has been proposed by David Waddington, Fabien Jobard, and Mike King (2009) and a discussion of urban unrest in France and the United States is found in Cathy Lisa Schneider's book (2014). In both cases, the authors focus on the role of the police.

2. In the United States, while grassroots organizations and social mobilizations such as the Black Lives Matter movement as well as the media have played a major role in the publicization of the issues related to interactions between the police and the African American population, several books that came out in the aftermath of the Ferguson events received unprecedented attention, in particular *On the Run*, a study of the everyday life in the poor neighborhoods of Philadelphia by sociologist Alice Goffman (2014), and *Between the World and Me*, a memoir about the experience of growing up as a black adolescent in Baltimore by journalist Ta-Nehisi Coates (2015).

3. From the 1958 police drama series *The Naked City* on the New York Police Department to the 2002 *The Shield* on the Los Angeles Police Department, from the ninety-minute documentary *The Police Tapes* by Alan and Susan Raymond in 1977 to the twenty-five seasons of the reality series *COPS* initially broadcast by Fox, the interest of television audiences in both fictional and real police has been unfailing.

4. A comprehensive review of the classical works in English-speaking criminology using the "observational method" can be found in the third chapter of Eugene McLaughlin's *The New Policing* (2007).

5. This is the case of the works of William Westley (1970 [1950]), Egon Bittner (1980 [1970]), Jerome Skolnick (1994 [1966]), Peter Manning (1997 [1977]), and Richard Ericson (1982), to name a few. Significantly, the task of meticulously accounting for observation was sometimes left to research assistants, as in Albert Reiss's book (1971, 20–45). Not valued as such, ethnography could even be delegated.

6. An example of this way of dealing with ethnographic research can be found in the classic collection of studies edited by Peter Manning and John Van Maanen, *Policing: A View From the Street* (1978, viii). Claiming the influence of symbolic interactionism, it emphasizes "empirical work based upon the fieldwork tradition in sociology" that conveys "the richness of any investigated social sphere in a more lively and telling fashion than reports grounded upon survey or archival material." But with few exceptions in the volume, the authors do not develop descriptions and narratives, nor do they discuss the way their fieldwork was conducted.

7. The obvious exception is John Van Maanen's much-celebrated *Tales of the Field* (1986). But there are other examples, such as Maurice Punch's (1979) classic monograph in Amsterdam.

8. As an indication of this trend, a search conducted in the leading journal of the field, *Criminology* (http://onlinelibrary.wiley.com/advanced/search/results), shows that citations appearing with the keywords "police ethnography" refer to either to large surveys through questionnaires or small samples via interviews, in other words standardized quantitative or semi-quantitative studies rather than participant observation allowing for the collection of qualitative information.

9. After Michael Banton's study (1964), several decades pass with hardly any anthropological research on the police, with very few exceptions such as that of Michael Young (1991), a former officer turned social scientist. Recently, however, anthropological studies have multiplied. Some of them rely on direct observation of police

work, such as Julia Hornberger (2011) in South Africa, Beatrice Jauregui (2013) in India, Jeffrey Martin (2014) in Taiwan, William Garriott (2011) in the United States, and Didier Fassin (2013 [2011]) in France. Others consider policing through the experience of the population, like Teresa Caldeira (2000) and Ben Penglase (2014) in Brazil, David Goldstein (2012) in Bolivia, and Philippe Bourgois and Jeff Schonberg (2009) and Lawrence Ralph (2014) in the United States. An article by Kevin Karpiak (2010) proposes a review of the figure of the policeman in classic urban ethnographies. A collective volume on the anthropology of the police has been edited by William Garriott (2013). The website Anthropoliteia provides a panorama of current research in this field: http://anthropoliteia.net.

10. The importance of this ethnographic revival is certainly underestimated by the fact that most relevant works come out in languages other than English and are often overlooked in international reviews. See, for instance, Geneviève Pruvost (2007) in France, Susana Durão (2008) in Portugal, Merlijn van Hulst (2013) in the Netherlands, and Sabina Frederic et al. (2014) in Argentina.

11. Let us mention, among others, geographer Steve Herbert (1997) in Los Angeles, sociologist Andreas Glaeser (1999) in Berlin, political scientist Peter Moskos (2008) in Baltimore, journalist writer Jonny Steinberg (2008) in Johannesburg, and urban planning scholar Graham Denyer Willis (2015) in Rio de Janeiro.

12. The literature on ethnography is considerable. For an overview of some of the classic texts and contemporary discussions as well as of the different uses and presentations across disciplines, one can refer to the edited volumes by Daniel Cefaï (2010) and by Mitchell Duneier, Philip Kasinitz, and Alexandra Murphy (2014), for sociology, and by Antonius Robben and Jeffrey Sluka (2007) and by Didier Fassin and Alban Bensa (2008), for anthropology.

13. According to his famous formulation of what makes policing specific, "whether it involves protection against an undesired imposition, caring for those who cannot care for themselves, attempting to solve a crime, helping to save a life, abating a nuisance, or settling an explosive dispute, police intervention means above all making use of the capacity and authority to overpower resistance to an attempted solution in the native habitat of the problem" (Bittner 1980 [1970], 40). One of the oldest activities of the police that is not included in this definition is the secret police, going back to medieval Italian cities, of which recent research essentially based on archives has been conducted in Romania (Verdery 2013) and Gaza (Feldman 2015).

14. Biopolitics, as "the regulations of the population," and anatomopolitics, as "the disciplines of the body," compose the bio-power, "the organization of power over life" (Foucault 1978 [1976], 139).

References

Alves de Araújo, Fábio. 2014. *Das "técnicas" de fazer desaparecer corpos*. Rio de Janeiro: Lamparina.

Banton, Michael. 1964. *The Policeman in the Community*. New York: Basic Books.

Bittner, Egon. 1980 [1970]. *The Functions of the Police in Modern Society*. Cambridge, MA: Oelgeschlager, Gunn & Hain Publishers.

Bourgois, Philippe, and Jeff Schonberg. 2009. *Righteous Dopefiend*. Berkeley: University of California Press.

Caldeira, Teresa. 2000. *City of Walls: Crime, Segregation, and Citizenship in São Paulo*. Berkeley: University of California Press.

Cefaï, Daniel, ed. 2010. *L'engagement ethnographique*. Paris: Éditions de l'École des Hautes Études en Sciences Sociales.

Coates, Ta-Nehisi. 2015. *Between the World and Me*. New York: Spiegel & Grau.

Denyer Willis, Graham. 2015. *The Killing Consensus: Police, Organized Crime, and the Regulation of Life and Death in Urban Brazil*. Berkeley: University of California Press.

Duneier, Mitchell, Philip Kasinitz, and Alexandra Murphy, eds. 2014. *The Urban Ethnography Reader*. Oxford: Oxford University Press.

Durão, Susana. 2008. *Patrulha e proximidade. Uma etnografia da polícia em Lisboa*. Coimbra: Almedina.

Ericson, Richard. 1982. *Reproducing Order: A Study of Police Patrol Work*. Toronto: University of Toronto Press.

Fassin, Didier. 2013 [2011]. *Enforcing Order: An Ethnography of Urban Policing*. Cambridge: Polity Press.

Fassin, Didier, and Alban Bensa. 2008. *Les politiques de l'enquête: Épreuves ethnographiques*. Paris: La Découverte.

Feldman, Ilana. 2015. *Police Encounters: Security and Surveillance in Gaza under Egyptian Rule*. Stanford: Stanford University Press.

Foucault, Michel. 1978 [1976]. *The History of Sexuality, Volume 1*. New York: Random House.

Frederic Sabina, Mariana Galvani, José Garriga Zucal, and Brigida Renoldi, eds. 2014. *De armas llevar: Estudios sobre los quehaceres socio-antropológicos de policías y de las fuerzas de seguridad*. La Plata: Ediciones EPC.

Garriott, William. 2011. *Policing Methamphetamine: Narcopolitics in Rural America*. New York: New York University Press.

Garriott, William, ed. 2013. *Policing and Contemporary Governance: The Anthropology of Police in Practice*. New York: Palgrave Macmillan.

Glaeser, Andreas. 1999. *Divided in Unity: Identity, Germany, and the Berlin Police*. Chicago: University of Chicago Press.

Goffman, Alice. 2014. *On the Run: Fugitive Life in an American City*. Chicago: University of Chicago Press.

Goldstein, Daniel. 2012. *Outlawed: Between Security and Rights in a Bolivian City*. Durham: Duke University Press.

Herbert, Steve. 1997. *Policing Space: Territoriality and the Los Angeles Police Department*. Minneapolis: University of Minnesota Press.

Hornberger, Julia. 2011. *Policing and Human Rights: The Meaning of Violence and Justice in the Everyday Policing of Johannesburg*. New York: Routledge.

Jauregui, Beatrice. 2013. "Beatings, Beacons, and Big Men: Police Disempowerment and Deligitimation in India." *Law and Social Inquiry* 38 (3): 643–69.

Karpiak, Kevin. 2010. "Of Heroes and Polemics: 'The Policeman' in Urban Ethnography." *Political and Legal Anthropology Review* 33:7–31.

Manning, Peter. 1997 [1977]. *Police Work: The Social Organization of Policing*. Long Grove: Waveland Press.

Manning, Peter, and John Van Maanen, eds. 1978. *Policing: A View from the Street*. Santa Monica, CA: Goodyear Publishing Company.

Martin, Jeffrey. 2014. "The Confucian Ethic and the Spirit of East Asian Police: A Comparative Study in the Ideology of Democratic Policing." *Crime, Law & Social Change* 61 (4): 461–90.

McLaughlin, Eugene. 2007. *The New Policing*. London: Sage.

Moskos, Peter. 2008. *Cop in the Hood: My Year Policing Baltimore's Eastern District*. Princeton: Princeton University Press.

Penglase, Ben. 2014. *Living with Insecurity in a Brazilian Favela: Urban Violence and Daily Life*. New Brunswick: Rutgers University Press.

Pruvost, Geneviève. 2007. *Profession: policier: Sexe: féminin*. Paris: Editions de la Maison des Sciences de l'Homme.

Punch, Maurice. 1979. *Policing the Inner City: A Study of Amsterdam's Warmoesstraat*. London: Macmillan.

Ralph, Laurence. 2014. *Renegade Dreams: Living Through Injury in Gangland Chicago*. Chicago: University of Chicago Press.

Reiss, Albert. 1971. *The Police and the Public*. New Haven: Yale University Press.

Robben, Antonius, and Jeffrey Sluka. 2007. *Ethnographic Fieldwork: An Anthropological Reader*. Malden, MA: Blackwell Publishing.

Schneider, Cathy Lisa. 2014. *Police Power and Race Riots: Urban Unrest in Paris and New York*. Philadelphia: University of Pennsylvania Press.

Skolnick, Jerome. 1994 [1966]. *Justice without Trial; Law Enforcement in Democratic Society*. New York: John Wiley and Sons.

Steinberg, Jonny. 2008. *Thin Blue: The Unwritten Rules of Policing in South Africa*. Johannesburg: Jonathan Ball Publishers.

van Hulst, Merlijn. 2013. *Politieverhalen: Een etnografie van een belangrijk aspect van politieculturen*. The Hague: Reed Business.

Van Maanen, John. 1988. *Tales of the Field: On Writing Ethnography*. Chicago: University of Chicago Press.

Verdery, Katherine. 2013. *Secrets and Truth: Ethnography in the Archive of Romania's Secret Police*. Budapest: Central European University Press.

Waddington, David, Fabien Jobard, and Mike King, eds. 2009. *Rioting in the UK and France: A Comparative Analysis*. Cullompton, UK: Willan Publishing.

Westley, William. 1970 [1950]. *Violence and the Police: A Sociological Study of Law, Custom, and Morality*. Cambridge, MA: MIT Press.

Young, Malcolm. 1991. *An Inside Job: Policing and Police Culture in Britain*. Oxford: Oxford University Press.

PART ONE

Position

ONE

Accountability:
Ethnographic Engagement and the
Ethics of the Police (United States)

STEVE HERBERT

The uniformed police are the most socially obvious manifestation of the state's capacity for violence. Other institutions, such as the military and the prison, also perform state-sanctioned violence, but they are less visible than the police. The police's capacity for violence, of course, is justified as integral to the rule of law and the need for social order. Yet police violence must be constrained, lest the power of the state exceed legitimate bounds. In other words, the police must be held accountable in some fashion to the public, to best ensure necessary limits on their coercive power.

I use this chapter to consider what it might mean for ethnographies of the police to be oriented toward ensuring greater police accountability. I am particularly interested in how a focus on accountability might impact the ethical conduct of fieldwork. I illustrate my discussion with reference to fieldwork conducted as part of a project with my colleague, Katherine Beckett. That project sought to investigate and critique social control tools in Seattle that criminalize the presence of individuals in spaces from which they are banned.[1]

I use three vignettes from one day of fieldwork to focus my analysis. After describing those vignettes, I outline three different roles that a police ethnographer commonly plays—as professional, as public actor, and as ethical human. As professionals, ethnographers must adhere to common standards of inquiry, ones that typically emphasize some degree of neutral, analytic detachment from the milieu under study. As public actors, ethnographers should arguably inform the populace about police practice, particularly when it eclipses lawful or ethical bounds. As ethical humans, ethnographers must treat the officers they encounter with consistent respect and honesty.

As it turns out, these are roles that the police also commonly play. I thus consider the variant roles of the ethnographer alongside the analogous roles for the police, and consider how these roles can vary across both groups and how they can conflict. I seek to show how these conflicts create intractable dilemmas for the police ethnographer, particularly anyone who pursues the project of police accountability.

I offer no easy resolutions to these conflicts here. My more modest hope is to gain greater clarity on the nature of these tensions and how one might proceed in the face of them. In the end, it seems clear that an ethnographer focused on police accountability cannot escape some degree of ethically questionable behavior. If Eric Gable is correct that fieldwork "is an intrinsically guilty act," then this is especially true for those who study the police.[2]

Ethnographic Encounters: Three Moments

It is 5 a.m., my earliest arrival ever for a ride-along. The police station is eerily quiet, but I am expected, and thus I am quickly escorted inside by a young officer. He seems inexperienced with the concept of a ride-along. His awkwardness combines with my sleepiness to make our initial conversations halting. I fear it could be a trying day.

That fear is quickly dispelled, because this is not the usual ride-along. I am with a special unit, part of the "Neighborhood Corrections Initiative." The NCI is a joint operation of the Seattle Police Department (SPD) and the Washington State Department of Corrections (DOC). It partners an SPD officer with a DOC community corrections officer. The SPD officer possesses all of the powers of those on patrol: he can respond to presumed violations of criminal law, intervene in troublesome situations to restore order, and use legally sanctioned violence when justifiable. The DOC officer possesses even more robust powers, at least with respect to those recently released from prison. Such "DOC active" individuals must submit to searches of their bodies, cars, or homes whenever requested by community corrections officers. Placed together, the officers can reinforce each other's power and can intervene intrusively into the lives of many citizens they encounter.

Three moments during this ride-along can help focus my analysis of the ethical dilemmas that accompany fieldwork that is explicitly oriented toward enabling greater accountability for police actions.

Moment One: As we leave the station, the SPD officer responds eagerly to questions about the NCI. A garrulous contrast to his younger colleague, the SPD officer evinces much enthusiasm for his partnership. He emphasizes the DOC officer's ability to override some restrictions on police actions, including those created by the Fourth Amendment to the US Constitution, which should prohibit searches and seizures of individuals without "probable cause" of a crime. The SPD officer expresses envy that his partner can ignore such restrictions with anyone who is "DOC active." Says the SPD officer, gesturing to his colleague: "The power this guy possesses is awesome."

Moment Two: The SPD officer steers toward Seattle's Aurora Avenue for their first task. A state highway, Aurora was once Seattle's main north-south thoroughfare. The construction in the 1960s of a federal interstate highway running parallel to Aurora led to the latter's decline, evidenced in part by numerous run-down motels notorious for hosting sales of drugs and sexual services. The NCI vehicle heads to one of those motels. The officers wish to check on a registered sex offender, whose pariah and financial statuses deny him access to any tonier lodgings. The officers want to ensure he is complying with various DOC-imposed restrictions.

They never make it to his room. Instead, their attention is captivated by two men in the parking lot who flee when the police van arrives. Like hunting dogs, the officers bolt from the van and give chase. I follow more languidly but soon encounter the officers and their quarry. The now-suspects have their hands on a car while the SPD officer calls in their names on his shoulder-mounted radio device. What he learns leads him to handcuff each of them. Each falls victim to an innovative use of criminal trespass law. Via a program created by the SPD, business owners can sign agreements that essentially transfer their trespass authority to the police. If an officer sees an individual on any such business's property without "any legitimate purpose," the officer can "admonish" that individual. That means that the individual cannot return to that business for a year. Any such return leaves the individual susceptible to arrest. As he closes the handcuffs, the officer makes his intentions plain. "We have a zero tolerance policy here on Aurora," he says. "I don't care where else you go, but you must be any place other than Aurora."

Moment Three: The officers spend much of their day cruising the street looking for anything suspicious. On a break, they park in front of another motel, a sagging one-story affair that runs perpendicular to the highway. They are approached by two individuals about a nonemergency matter: they cannot convince their elderly mother to leave one of the motel's units. The SPD officer, bored by such matters, leaves the conversation to his DOC colleague and walks down the row of motel units. He pauses by a sight he considers anomalous: a late-model BMW parked in front of one unit. What, he wonders, is such a nice car doing at a dilapidated motel? He considers it his duty to find out. He goes to the unit fronting the car and bangs the door, announcing himself as an SPD officer. He waits a few seconds. Greeted by no response, he repeats his pounding and announcement. A third such outburst proves necessary before the door opens. Inside, the officer finds a man and a presumed sex worker; there is also a recently used crack pipe on the bedside table. When I enter, the officer is hectoring the man, whose head droops under the resulting guilt. Turning to the woman, the officer tosses a coin in the air and asks her to call heads or tails. Her choice is a lucky one, he says: she wins, and thus he will not arrest her. Each pledges to disperse immediately, and the officers and I return to the car.

The Position of the Police and of the Ethnographer

Each of these incidents troubled me; each illustrated a police interest and willingness to intrude rather brusquely into citizens' lives. The early conversation reveals an SPD officer distressingly unbothered by the US Constitution, whose strictures he arguably later ignores. Although he does not physically enter the motel room for an unauthorized search, his loud remonstrations undoubtedly left the occupants feeling compelled to allow him inside. And although his arrests for criminal trespass are legal, his actions reproduce a program that criminalizes the mere presence of unwanted individuals in particular places.

My unease raises several questions. Am I obligated to inform the officers of my condemnation of their actions? If so, why? If not, what must I say to them about my presence in their workday lives? As I consider these questions, should it matter that these officers are representatives of the state? That they can exercise coercive force? Should I play a role in ensuring accountability for police actions? Or should I be beholden to the norms of professional social science? If so, what do such norms dictate that I do? Should I prioritize any ethical obligations I arguably possess to the police as research subjects? If so, what are those obligations? Or are any such obligations obviated by an arguable need for me to render transparent police practices that might otherwise escape public scrutiny? Should I pursue the project of police accountability and, if so, does that compromise my ethical relationship to officers I observe?

That fieldworkers exist in complicated ethical relations with those they study is hardly a novel realization; ethnographers are commonly vexed about how to situate themselves toward those they observe.[3] Such questions, I contend, are heightened if one's focus is the police. As Egon Bittner long ago argued, the capacity to exercise legitimate state violence makes the police unique and deeply structures what they do.[4] The police ethnographer may see such violence and will likely wonder if it is justified. As Beatrice Jauregui and John Van Maanen note, it is particularly challenging to position oneself ethically vis-à-vis officers who commit acts of violence that are themselves ethically questionable.[5] What must a fieldworker do in response? Is there any obligation to help hold the police accountable for questionable acts of violence?[6]

Certainly, the capacity for violence is precisely why police accountability is so important; without it, officers might too easily abuse their power. Accountability measures are thus those that help check potential police excesses. Many such measures are focused on responses to alleged instances of police misbehavior. As a result, much of the literature on police accountability addresses how best to construct formalized review procedures when citizens allege officer misconduct.[7]

Yet rarely does a police action lead to public discussion of any sort. At this writing, the United States is witnessing an effusion of public conversation about excessive police force; Michael Brown and Eric Garner are now household names and symbolize race-inflected and unnecessary lethal police violence. Despite these robust conversations—aided by public commentary from the US Attorney General and the Director of the Federal Bureau of Investigation—it remains the case that the vast majority of police-citizen contacts occur in front of only one or a handful of individuals and receive little to no attention when the encounter ends. This is particularly true for those individuals who concerned me on Aurora: the housing-challenged and otherwise destitute, the street-level sex worker, the previously incarcerated. Police intrusions into the lives of such people are routine and rarely documented.

Thus, just as lethal police violence must undergo scrutiny, so must more commonplace and seemingly banal encounters with the impoverished. The extent of physical violence I observed on Aurora involved handcuffing and arresting. Yet the significant power of the police was still readily on display. Indeed, the book to which my fieldwork contributed demonstrated the consequential complications that enhanced social control creates for the lives of many poor people in Seattle.[8] We intended to question these social control practices. In other words, we sought to hold the police and other social actors accountable for how their power was being exercised against disadvantaged Seattleites.

However, in consciously choosing to emphasize police accountability, I arguably placed myself in an awkward, and even ethically compromised, relation to the officers I observed. The ethnographer does need to develop an analytic distance from his/her research subjects and to evaluate the milieu in terms of broader conceptual frameworks. For that reason, there is always a disjuncture between the ethnographer and ethnographic subjects. But when an ethnographer takes an avowedly political stance to provide critical assessments of police practice, then the research will likely run counter to the officers' interests as they would define them. For instance, I doubt the officers on Aurora would have cooperated with me very much had they known that my subsequent analysis would strongly critique their practices.

All ethnographers, of course, are critical of the practices they observe. They necessarily step outside the immediate frames of references used by their subjects. In these practices of critique, ethnographers seek to explicate subjects' actions within wider frameworks of understanding. Yet the project that led me to Aurora that day was quite explicitly critical in the more common sense of that term: I sought evidence of particular police practices so that I could more legitimately condemn them. My coauthor and I sought to write an accessible manuscript that would generate public scrutiny of social control mechanisms that we believed needed review and reform.

This more critical stance toward the police rendered me incapable of various maneuvers that many ethnographers deploy to address potential disjunctures between themselves and those they study. Aware of the power imbalance inherent in the relation between fieldworkers and subjects, some ethnographers seek to collaborate or otherwise find common cause with their subjects. Whether developed as collaborative ethnography,[9] embedded ethnography,[10] participatory action research,[11] or activist ethnography,[12] such projects allow the fieldworker to work to close the analytic and interpersonal distance between themselves and their subjects. Such projects necessarily trouble any suggestions that there is a common or correct way to structure the ethnographer-subject relation. In my case, however, I had limited options for how to construct that relation. I could not participate actively in police work, nor did I wish to identify closely with their role. I was thus much more an observer of their actions than a participant in them.

This more detached approach, however, hardly obviated the tensions that I felt during my time on Aurora and at my computer afterward. These tensions deserve further exploration. Toward that end, I explore below three key roles that police ethnographers play. Instructively, these roles find mirror images within the world of the police. It is thus productive to consider the roles of the ethnographer and the police together. It soon becomes clear that each must be held accountable, although just how and to whom remain open questions.

The Professional

Ethnography is not an archly scientific enterprise. It involves direct engagement with research subjects and hence contravenes the norm of scientific detachment. This direct engagement involves the full humanness of the researcher, including his/her emotional reactions to the milieu under study.[13] The centrality of these emotions to the research enterprise also lies in tension with scientific ideals that trumpet rational thought. In addition, the data that the ethnographer gathers are diffuse and rarely anticipated in advance. It is thus nonsensical to construct ethnography, as a professional practice, in the strictly deductive, hypothesis-testing model that many scientists idolize.[14]

That said, ethnographers always analyze the data they gather. Closeness to subjects may be required, but so is analytic detachment. Ultimately, ethnographic analysis must be situated within theoretical or conceptual frameworks that are recognizable to other academic analysts. So, just as ethnographers must draw near to their subjects, so must they also pull back, so they can discuss their data within academic conversations.[15] Even if an ethnographer wishes to work in close collaboration with the subjects under study, their interests rarely will align perfectly. This is particularly true for ethnographers motivated by advancement in their academic careers. The requirements for publications in esteemed journals force academics to frame their work in terms that will commonly be alien to their research subjects.

Further, professional ethnographers commonly work to understand their subjects as social actors who are beset and buffeted by various forces. In terms of the police, this means recognizing that officers' actions are influenced by a range of social dynamics, ones that derive from legal, bureaucratic, and cultural systems.[16] Further, the police regularly enter into troublesome social situations that are disproportionately concentrated in neighborhoods riven by various forms of social inequality. It is not the police's fault, for instance, that extensive impoverishment and racial segregation create multiple pockets of disadvantage in cities. Yet the police are called regularly to such locales, and their resultant actions cannot stanch, and may even magnify, the tensions generated by inequality. But officers neither generate those tensions nor can they remedy them.[17]

Viewed in this way, the officers on Aurora are not so culpable for the actions that disturbed me. They did not themselves create the trespass admonishment program that they enforce, nor the police culture that values catching "bad guys" regardless of constitutional restrictions. They cannot change the legal regimes that criminalize prostitution, just as they cannot control the social forces that lead a woman into that vocation. To see the police as fully social actors, then, might diminish any emphasis on accountability, at least at the level of the individual officer. This realization perhaps should thereby quell my condemnatory stance.

Indeed, my predilection for such a stance is arguably a problem. If I enter the field with an explicit intent to hold the police accountable, might it cloud my subsequent judgment? Might I focus overmuch on incidents that I believe provide evidence of police overreaching? Might I misinterpret any such incidents in ways that are unfairly unflattering to the officers? On the other hand, if I strive too ardently to be a detached, presumptively scientific observer, might I neglect to call out troublesome police behavior? Might I use a comprehensive analysis of the police's legal, bureaucratic, and cultural structures to absolve officers of boorish behavior that merits strong critique?

Thus, the role of the professional both highlights and fails to resolve the ethical dilemmas I felt on Aurora Avenue that day, and later when I constructed my analysis. If I hold myself accountable to the norms of professionalism, then I presumably will craft work that mostly speaks to my academic peers, and I will situate the officers in terms of the various forces that shape their actions. These professional norms might thus be ignored or at least diminished when I foreground a need to hold the police publicly accountable for questionable behavior.

Interestingly, the norms of professionalism are no less significant in the world of the police. Indeed, one of the greatest reform movements in modern police history was crafted in exactly these terms. The professional movement was seen in much of the twentieth century as the best means to curb excessive police corruption and to otherwise gain widespread legitimacy.[18] This meant creating more standardized means by which officers were hired and promoted; constructing a more rigid chain of command; and adopting technology wherever possible. Although the professional movement was ultimately supplanted by subsequent reform movements, most notably community policing, its ideology remains regnant in police culture, with notable implications for police accountability. Indeed, officers often use the mantle of professionalism to assert that they alone can properly assess police actions. Their unique training and experience, they assert, leaves them solely equipped to evaluate police behavior properly; outsiders simply cannot fully comprehend officers' decisions.[19] This line of argument is regularly mobilized in postmortems after uses of force, especially if the officer(s) in question reacted to a quickly unfolding situation. In such a scenario, officers' decisions are commonly legitimated with reference to how they are trained to make split-second decisions with imperfect information.

Looked at this way, the norms of professionalism, if adopted too ardently by both ethnographers and officers, might inhibit the pursuit of greater police accountability. For that reason, perhaps other roles that ethnographers and police play deserve our attention. I turn now to the role of public actor.

The Public Actor

It is not a requirement that police ethnographers consciously seek to hold the police accountable. As noted, career advancement generally requires an analyst to be primarily accountable to other academics, and hence to frame work in conceptual schemes that are au courant within relevant literatures. Whether such work reaches a wider audience is usually a quite secondary concern. Indeed, work that is consciously written for a narrow audience might enhance one's status. For these reasons, it is hardly typical for an analyst to try to influence a more public conversation about police practice.

The day on Aurora was part of a research project that resulted in a book with a deliberately provocative title—*Banished*.[20] We strove from the outset to document and critique practices that criminalized the mere presence of individuals in particular places. We sought to understand those practices as exhaustively as possible. We also sought to construct the book in accessible prose, the better to help prompt a public conversation about practices that we hoped to see scrutinized.

Our approach was a self-consciously political one, and thus I entered the field at a more pronounced critical remove from the officers. The fieldwork consisted of days like the one on Aurora, that is, encounters with officers who were most likely to enact the social control regime that we sought to critique. That meant observing officers who patrolled in high-crime areas or units that were more proactive. For instance, I conducted five ride-alongs with NCI units as part of this work. The ethnographic components of the *Banished* project were thus composed of targeted observations of officers most likely to engage in specific practices. Other data components included interviews with judges, lawyers, social service providers, police commanders, private security officers, anticrime activists, and the banished themselves; police and court records; and a wide range of legal and archival materials. The ethnographic component was thus just part of a larger data collection enterprise and was itself constrained. I was not, for example, interested more broadly in police culture or the nature of the police-community relation, as in earlier works.[21] Instead, I drew on that earlier work and my familiarity with the Seattle Police Department to construct an ethnographic approach that was strategically targeted to investigate a clearly drawn phenomenon.

We also identified the city and the police department we were studying. We thus sought to contravene a practice sometimes adopted by police ethnographers, namely to avoid identifying the department in question. Such an avoidance is common, for at least two reasons. One is that it accentuates the norm of social scientific analysis to describe the processes under study in broad, generalizable terms. If the social scientist seeks to make general claims about police processes, then the particular location is of little interest. Secondly, some departments will make disguising their name a condition of granting ethnographic access. For an academic interested solely in academic publications, this condition is unproblematic.

For an analyst focused on accountability, however, this restriction may not be acceptable. For the *Banished* project, the story had to be set in Seattle. Although we recognized that other cities were enacting similar social control programs, we wished to tell the Seattle story in detail. We were convinced that Seattle was a notable pioneer in the use of these programs, and we sought to explain their underpinnings fully. Although we never identified any individual by name, we did note their institutional status. This was necessary for us to explain how different actors helped to create and reproduce social control practices that we found questionable.

Banished was thus a project that emerged from a desire to accentuate the ethnographer's role as public actor. It required revealing the city under study, and it required something less than full disclosure in conversations with officers. It mandated accepting some risk that my preexisting critical stance clouded my analysis. It meant writing an accessible work that minimized or ignored academic debates, and hence accepting some condemnation in reviews of the book in academic journals. Whether the resultant analysis was worth these sacrifices depends entirely on how one wishes to balance the role of public actor against other roles the ethnographer might play.

The police are also public actors. As noted previously, they are a quite consequential component of the state. Their capacity for violence is both the core of their unique status and the reason why accountability measures are necessary. If the ethnographer wishes to emphasize a role as a public actor it is precisely because the police are public actors themselves. In this way, both the ethnographer and the police can be seen as accountable to the same audience—the wider public. The police must thereby strive to exercise violence within appropriate bounds and to accept investigations of their practices to ensure respect for such bounds. Ethnographers must embrace their role as investigators and use their close observations of the police to provide descriptions and assessments of police practice.

Again, we must consider just which role both the ethnographer and the police should play, to ask to whom they should be principally accountable. This vexing question is all the harder when we realize that they also have some obligations to be accountable to each other in the very human interactions that transpire within the fieldwork encounter. Here, they should arguably be guided by the need to treat each other ethically and humanely. I turn now to that critical dimension of fieldwork with the police.

The Ethical Human

It is no small matter for subjects of an ethnography to allow a researcher into their midst. Beyond the potential inconveniences of dealing with an outsider, research subjects withstand a scrutiny of their lifestyles that most people happily shun. Further, subjects rarely possess much if any control over the resulting analysis. They cannot thus avert potentially embarrassing disclosures from emerging, just as they cannot modify anything they believe the ethnographer incorrectly characterizes or interprets. The capacity to interpret and to author are bestowed uniquely on the ethnographer, and that generates a fraught power imbalance.

So, the ethnographer benefits to a unique and likely asymmetric degree from the research relationship. Because of this, the ethnographer possesses an ethical obligation to treat the research subjects with as much care and respect as possible. This can mean many things, but at the very least it requires the need to be honest, open-minded, and fair. Hard to disagree with that, but such a sensible assertion is far from sufficiently specific.

Take the prescription to be honest. At a minimum, this means never saying anything false to a research subject. For this reason, Richard Leo was perhaps rightly castigated for deliberately misleading the police detectives whose interrogations he wished to observe.[22] The critique of Kai Erickson of this stance is fairly straightforward and sensible.[23]

Like Erickson, I find Leo's approach questionable at best; deliberate misrepresentation is indefensible. Yet maybe I should not be so smug. While I do not think I have ever provided a distinctly false impression of myself to a police officer, neither have I ever been truly forthcoming with any of them. When asked about the ultimate purposes of my analysis—a question one commonly gets in the early stage of a ride-along—I am accustomed to saying something vague about the needs of academics to publish in journals with small readerships. This is not incorrect, but neither is it fully transparent. This was particularly true of the project that motivated the day on Aurora. My coauthor and I were opposed to the practices we analyzed, and we sought data to demonstrate why our opposition was justified; we had made a prior decision to be more accountable to our roles as public actors than as professional academics. This is a truth I would not have revealed to the NCI team, even under the most persistent questioning.

So, my ethical distance from Richard Leo may not be so far. I say this, in part, because he and I would justify our practices via the same logic: unstinting honesty would have prevented us from observing police practices that commonly escape scrutiny. Thus, if we are intent in pursuing police accountability, then perhaps some sacrifices in honesty are the price we must pay.

And what does it mean to be open-minded? In general terms, I believe this means heeding the expectation that the ethnographer try to adopt the worldview of the researched so as to better understand it. But this is not so simple, either. How does one balance the danger of overidentifying with the subjects (the "going native" problem) versus the need to remain analytically detached? If my focus is on police accountability, might I remain a little too critical, a little too removed? If I am too open-minded and seek to fully adopt the officers' viewpoint, might I lose sight of my potential role in ensuring greater oversight of police behavior?

And what might it mean to be fair? Such a goal would seem consistent with the mandate to understand officers' actions on their own terms and to situate those actions within the broader social dynamics that structure the police role. Matters get trickier when an analyst foregrounds accountability. If one subjects police behavior to critique, this could compromise the goal of being fair to the officers as research subjects. Further, if the ethnographer does not come clean with the critical nature of the enterprise, then officers will be less able to provide any counterarguments that might bear consideration.

For their part, officers are also likely conflicted and constrained as to how to approach the academic ride-along. For starters, they typically must simply accept the ride-along as part of the job; it is something imposed on them by their superiors. Of course, officers vary in how receptive they are to having company, but all of them know that outright hostility might displease their superiors. Further, officers are as beholden to common norms of social interaction as anyone else. Most of us seek to be friendly rather than hostile to those we encounter. For the police, this norm is accentuated by the fact that the ride-along is entering the somewhat private sphere of the officer's car. Common norms of hospitality dictate the need for cordiality. This can thus mean that officers feel obliged both to answer any questions the ethnographer poses and to provide after-action accounts following any incidents that occur. How forthright officers might be in such accounts is always difficult to gauge, and I have always suspected that some officers exaggerate just as others obfuscate. On balance, however, I have found officers willing to be patient and forthright, in part because many of them are deeply proud of their work.

Given their inability to refuse a ride-along and their tendency to adhere to common norms of cordiality, officers commonly provide insights into their work that benefit the ethnographer to a disproportionate degree. In short, if officers choose to be accountable to the ride-along, they can heighten the preexisting imbalance in power.

At the same time, patrol officers are likely to be somewhat suspicious of an academic ride-along. Sometimes this is explicit; prior to one ride-along, as part of an earlier project with the SPD, an officer asked me, "Are you a liberal or a conservative?" Taken aback by the directness of his question, I struggled to find a good and truthful answer. Luckily, I consider myself well to the left of the American mainstream, so I could honestly say, "Neither," which he likely interpreted as a commitment to a moderate position between the two. More commonly, officers will ask a few questions about why I am doing a ride-along and what I intend to publish. I have a ready answer to those questions, but I rarely volunteer a full account of my purposes. In the case of the NCI ride-along, I explained that I was interested in this unique law enforcement partnership. I said nothing about my interest in critiquing spatial restrictions.

My experience thus illustrates the dance between the complicity and duplicity that is characteristic of all ethnographic encounters but is perhaps especially regnant in fieldwork with the police. As Julia Hornberger (this volume) notes, ethnographers are inherently complicit with the police they observe; they are part of the police social world, and they invariably remain silent when the police intervene into the lives of others. And some of this complicity is certainly strategic;[24] I always seek to find some common ground between myself and officers to enable productive conversations and to make them feel less awkward in my presence. Officers commonly seek to reciprocate. At the same time, neither I nor they reveal all of what we are thinking and may direct attention away from uncomfortable thoughts or actions.

Officers and I thus enter an interpersonal space that Didier Fassin describes as ambiguous; our relationships resist full disclosure and clarity even as we comply with norms of respectful interaction.[25] In my experience, some officers remain wary throughout and only tersely respond to questions. Others are warmer and eagerly answer questions. In those instances, one's questions can become more direct. Even so, I have learned from extensive exposure to officers that they are wary of those who might critique them. As noted above, officers commonly see outside critics as ill-informed and disrespectful of the professional status of contemporary police organizations. I thus avoid any questions or comments that evince critique of their practice, for fear that it will stifle the conversation and lead officers to tell their colleagues to approach me warily.

But even if conversations never become as open as I might like, I believe I commonly exploit the human decency of the police. The discomfort generated by this reality is compounded when, as with the *Banished* project, I wish to subject the police to public scrutiny. Even if my role as a professional requires me to see each individual officer as a member of a social group, and even if my role as a public actor requires me to expose typically unseen police practices, my capacity to act as an ethical human arguably suffers when my approach is consciously critical.

Roles, Disjunctures, Challenges

The roles of professional, public actor, and ethical human are not the only ones enacted by police ethnographers and the police. But they are largely unavoidable, and they do not sit in easy relations to one another; accentuating one role likely complicates how one plays another. It is always true that the ethnographer faces a fraught challenge in relating oneself to one's research subjects. This challenge is especially troublesome when the subjects are the police, given the prominent, and frequently violent, role that officers play in daily life.

The need to situate one's research subjects is a requirement of a good ethnography. Even if the worldview of one's subjects is initially alien, the process of ethnographic engagement generates greater familiarity and understanding. The full humanness of the research subjects can thereby emerge. It is the great privilege of ethnographers that they get to know their subjects well enough to make them more comprehensible to outsiders. This privilege bequeaths responsibilities, however, and bestows a need to be accountable to the demand for ethical treatment of our research subjects.

Yet ethnographers possess multiple responsibilities; like the police, they are accountable in multiple ways and to multiple audiences. Some of those responsibilities are to themselves. Most notably, academic ethnographers want to advance their careers. Others of those responsibilities are to one's readers, who deserve a comprehensive and insightful analysis and an opportunity to gain some new perspective. Those readers might also deserve to understand how government processes actually occur, particularly with agents capable of exercising coercive force.

Police ethnographers must thus decide how to best balance the sometimes-conflicting roles that they must play, just as they must decide which police role to accentuate in their fieldwork encounters and their subsequent analysis. And in those fieldwork encounters, the ethnographer must decide just what to say to the police about who one is and what one is doing. As I indicated, I cannot boast of complete honesty on this score. Part of that is due to the difficulty of explaining the world of academic publishing. But just as much stems from a desire to ensure the continued flow of information. Without that information, one's career will stall, and one's ability to influence public policy will wither. So, a minimalist narrative often emerges; one says just enough to stanch the flow of questions, and then one switches topics as quickly as possible. This is not dishonest, but it may not be fair.

One way to avoid, or at least partially minimize, my ethical dilemma is to foreground the police's role as state agents of coercive force. In adopting this role, the police must accept that they will be observed. Further, those observations should include some critical assessments of their practice. The ethnographer can thus be seen primarily as an agent acting legitimately on behalf of the wider public, who must do all that is necessary to see police practice as it would commonly occur. If this requires limits on one's honesty, so be it.

The police ethnographer must thus make some difficult decisions. Which role does one accentuate? Which set of responsibilities—to one's career, to the norms of social scientific inquiry, to one's integrity, to the wider public—deserve greatest priority? As should be clear, there is no easy resolution to these questions. Choices must occur, and the resultant trade-offs accepted. The interests of the police and of the ethnographer, particularly one inclined to be critical, will never exactly align. Any efforts to earn the police's trust will thus always smack of at least a little duplicity.

Conclusion

That day on Aurora was one component of a wider research project that sought to explain the emergence and implications of a novel social control scheme in Seattle. Through a series of policies and practices, many citizens in Seattle were susceptible to arrest for their mere presence in spaces from which they had been banned. The ethnographic components of that project sought to understand how these practices were implemented on the ground.

The analysis that resulted was not a blanket condemnation of the police. We worked to understand the actions of the police and other officials, such as prosecutors, as manifestations of wider processes. Some of those processes were ones that generated widespread homelessness (paucities of low-skilled jobs and affordable housing) and ones that prompted concern about urban "disorder" (extensive gentrification and tourism development). These latter concerns prompted elected officials to create new laws to enable banishment and motivated the police and other criminal justice actors to enforce those laws. We identified our location, and we identified the institutional role of those individuals whose opinions we quoted or whose practices we described. We allowed the book to be distributed by a public defense organization that was interested in changing the social control regime in Seattle. Members of the Seattle City Council and other key actors in city politics received a copy of the book, although we ourselves did not purchase or distribute those. We were pleased to learn that the resulting public conversation led to a decrease in the use of criminal trespass in Seattle.

I fully expect members of the Seattle Police Department who read *Banished* will likely object to it. Part of their critique, I imagine, will focus on their missions to reduce crime and increase order. From that perspective, it is a benefit to the police to possess more tools to address "disorder." If nothing else, the practices of banishment give the police something to point to when citizens complain about the homeless. The police may further object to my interpretations of those police actions I recount in the book, just as they may object to my not disclosing my point of view.

These are only speculations, but my extensive ethnographic contact with officers leaves me confident I am correct. I am thereby troubled that in seeking to make officers accountable I sacrificed some degree of accountability to ethical norms of honesty and fairness. If this is true, then the key question is whether my unhesitating interest in holding the police accountable for their role in the practices of banishment justifies any possible ethical lapses.

My view is that any such lapses are justified. While I do not believe I encouraged the police to act in any particular way, my unwillingness to fully disclose my motivations prevented officers from altering their behavior accordingly. Had I been more forthcoming, they likely would have acted differently. If my silence was a failure to be ethically accountable, then it was simultaneously necessary to ensure that they proceeded with business as usual. Without witnessing how officers typically act, I could not fully understand and critique the policies of banishment.

Of course, my confidence in this position rests on my belief that my condemnation of police practice is justified. Those who disagree with my critical stance toward the NCI team might find my ethical position untenable; for them, I arguably abused the police's trust to advance a questionable politics. I have no sacrosanct defense to such an argument, because I did do some abuse to the officers' trust, and my political position was a strong one. But my analysis had the virtue of highlighting police practices that might otherwise have escaped public attention. Even if banishment can be justified, such justification should occur through open public conversation. In presumptively democratic societies, state action—particularly if coercive—must undergo regular checks.

I therefore think it best to see police ethnography as a potential means to advance the project of police accountability. To use ethnography in this fashion, however, seems unavoidably to intensify rather than resolve some of the ethical dilemmas inherent in fieldwork relations. Whether this trade-off is acceptable is a matter much like police practice: subject to ongoing debate.

Notes

1. Beckett and Herbert 2009.
2. Gable 2014, 239.
3. Armbruster and Laerke 2008; Caplan 2003.
4. Bittner 1970.
5. Jauregui 2013; Van Maanen 1973.
6. Jauregui's contribution to this volume (chapter 3) poignantly describes her responses

to police interactions outside the context of violence. Although I did not develop any kin-like relations with officers like those she describes, her interrogation of the notion of "critical empathy" fruitfully describes a means to construct the ethnographer-police relation.

7. See Walker 2001; 2014.
8. Beckett and Herbert 2010.
9. Rappaport 2008.
10. Lewis and Russell 2008.
11. Kemmis and McTaggart 2000; McIntyre 2008.
12. Goldstein 2014.
13. Herbert 2000.
14. Lederman 2007.
15. Herbert 2010.
16. Fassin 2013.
17. Stuart and Herbert 2016.
18. Fogelson 1977.
19. Herbert 2006.
20. Beckett and Herbert 2010.
21. Herbert 1997; Herbert 2006.
22. Leo 1995.
23. Erikson 1995; cf. Leo's response (1996).
24. Jauregui 2013.
25. Fassin 2013.

References

Armbruster, Heidi, and Anna Laerke. 2008. *Taking Sides: Ethics, Politics, and Fieldwork in Anthropology.* New York: Berghahn.

Beckett, Katherine, and Steve Herbert. 2010. *Banished: The New Social Control in Urban America.* New York and Oxford: Oxford University Press.

Bittner, Egon. 1970. *The Functions of the Police in Modern Society.* Chevy Chase, MD: National Institute of Mental Health.

Caplan, Pat. 2003. *The Ethics of Anthropology: Debates and Dilemmas.* London: Routledge.

Erikson, Kai. 1995. "Commentary." *American Sociologist* 26 (2): 4–11.

Fassin, Didier. 2013. *Enforcing Order: An Ethnography of Urban Policing.* Cambridge, UK: Polity Press.

Fogelson, Robert. 1977. *Big-City Police.* Cambridge, MA.: Harvard University Press.

Gable, Eric. 2014. "The Anthropology of Guilt and Rapport." *Journal of Ethnographic Theory* 4:237–58.

Goldstein, Daniel. 2014. "Laying the Body on the Line: Activist Anthropology and the Deportation of the Undocumented." *American Anthropologist* 116:839–42.

Herbert, Steve. 1997. *Policing Space: Territoriality and the Los Angeles Police Department.* Minneapolis: University of Minnesota Press.

———. 2000. "For Ethnography." *Progress in Human Geography* 24:550–68.

———. 2006. *Citizens, Cops, and Power: Recognizing the Limits to Community.* Chicago: University of Chicago Press.

———. 2010. "A Taut Rubber Band: Theory and Empirics in Qualitative Field Research."

In *Sage Handbook of Qualitative Geography*, edited by D. Delyser, S. Herbert, S. Aitkin, M. Crang, and L. McDowell, 77–96. London: Sage.

Jauregui, Beatrice. 2013. "Dirty Anthropology: Epistemologies of Violence and Ethical Entanglements in Police Ethnography." In *Policing and Contemporary Governance: The Anthropology of Police in Practice*, edited by William Garriott, 125–53. New York: Palgrave.

Kemmis, Stephen, and Robin McTaggart. 2000. "Participatory Action Research." In *Handbook of Qualitative Research*, edited by N. K. Denzin and Y. S. Lincoln, 2nd ed., 567–605. Thousand Oaks, CA: Sage Publications.

Lederman, Rena. 2007. "Comparative 'Research': A Modest Proposal Concerning the Object of Ethics Regulation." *Political and Legal Anthropology Review* 30 (2): 305–27.

Leo, Richard. 1995. "Trial and Tribulations: Courts, Ethnography, and the Need for an Evidentiary Privilege for Academic Researchers." *American Sociologist* 26 (1): 113–34.

———. 1996. "The Ethics of Deceptive Research Roles Reconsidered: A Response to Kai Erikson." *American Sociologist* 27 (1): 122–28.

Lewis, Sue, and Andrew Russell. 2008. "Being Embedded: A Way Forward for Ethnographic Research." *Ethnography* 12:398–416.

McIntyre, Alice. 2008. *Participatory Action Research*. Thousand Oaks, CA: Sage Publications.

Rappaport, Joanne. 2008. "Beyond Participant Observation: Collaborative Ethnography as Theoretical Innovation." *Collaborative Ethnographies* 1:1–31.

Stuart, Forrest, and Steve Herbert. 2016. "The Police and Inequality: Tales from Two Cities." In *The Sage Handbook of Global Policing*, edited by B. Bradford, B. Jauregui, I. Loader and J. Steinberg, 193-210. London: Sage.

Van Maanen, John. 1978. "On Watching the Watchers." In *Policing: A View from the Street*, edited by P. Manning and J. Van Maanen, 309–49. Santa Monica, CA: Goodyear Publishing.

Walker, Samuel. 2001. *Police Accountability: The Role of Citizen Oversight*. Belmont, CA: Wadsworth.

———. 2014. *The New World of Police Accountability*. Thousand Oaks, CA: Sage Publications.

TWO

Complicity:
Becoming the Police (South Africa)

JULIA HORNBERGER

Being mistaken for a police officer is one of the most awkward, challenging moments of doing ethnographic fieldwork with the police. It is one thing to do work with the police as an empathetic but ultimately critical observer, but to actually *be* a police officer—in the eyes of others—seems to produce an implication of complicity that is much harder to resolve. But since I have been working with nonuniformed detectives, such mistaken identification has happened to me quite often. Once the uniforms are gone, only a limited spectrum of symbolic acts is available to a researcher in situations of police practice to indicate that he or she is not one of them. One can stand aside when the arrest is happening, or when somebody gets interrogated. If there is time and space for it, one can even explain to those being policed that one is a researcher. But this has to be balanced against a pact of solidarity with the officers one is working with, either to not disrupt their work or to not make one's moral distancing felt to them as they are going about their work. This is especially the case as ethnographic work with the police is a long-term commitment toward the police and depends on the cultivation of a good relationship and even, at times, the emergence of friendship.

More important, such attempts at distancing might in fact fail. A figure such as a researcher might not make much sense to people who find themselves in the existential situation of their lives being (violently) disrupted by the intervention of the police. Even if police are wearing uniform and I am not, to arrive with them in the same marked car makes it hard to understand how I am not one of them. And so it has often happened that my claims to noncomplicity are simply overridden by the people being policed. What has happened instead is that people assume because of my hands-off role at the scene that I must be an even more senior official—or worse—that I could somehow influence the situation. And because I lack the no-nonsense demeanor of seasoned officers, I have often become the addressee of pleas and bargains. This has left me helpless and even more at a loss as to my complicity.

What this points to, as I would like to argue in this chapter, is the fact that there is a form of complicity that has less to do with questions of our own consciousness and responsibility (subjective complicity), or with our factual involvement or not in actual acts of police violence (objective complicity)—instead, it is a complicity that exists foremost in the eyes of the beholder, in how people being policed see us and see what we do and represent as we observe and participate in policing. It is a complicity in which we have no power or say over judgments of us. It is a form of complicity that can best be understood as fundamentally intersubjective. It is, I argue, a residual act of complicity that remains to haunt us even as a form of tactical[1] or strategic complicity[2] can be justified as the precondition to actually produce a certain kind of critical writing.

I will develop this argument by presenting in the first section following this introduction a case of everyday policing of intellectual property (IP), or to be more specific, of DVD piracy in Johannesburg, South Africa. This presentation of ethnographic material serves two purposes. First, it is an instance in which I was (mis)taken as police. Second, it demonstrates the virtue of ethnographic research, namely to produce critical insights about, in this case, the stealthy workings of new property (here, IP) regimes and the role of policing within them. With this ethnographic case I demonstrate that weighted against the outcome of insight a certain level of complicity is a small price to pay and might actually even be desirable.

In the second section, however, I show that no matter how much one takes up the ethical challenge of complicity and converts one's own involvement into the basis of critical writing, a deeply uncomfortable, unproductive sense of complicity stubbornly remains. Here I start by showing that, within the South African context where I work both as a researcher and as a teacher, questions of complicity have produced particular attitudes toward the discipline of anthropology. In the past, anthropologists' anxieties about complicity nearly led to total retreat from the ethnographic project, but more recently, calls to "studying up," and thus seeking ethnographic complicity with the powerful, have been launched as critical intervention within the discipline. While in other parts of the world "studying up" might have become a given, in the South African context "studying up" still carries a particular yet only minimally executed critical relevance. It serves as a way to confronting what some have called the blind spots of anthropology, namely to study those who might think they are beyond being studied.[3] This leads me to revisit some of the propositions George Marcus[4] articulated in the late nineties regarding questions of carrying out multisited research and what this means in terms of complicity. In his work he identifies as primary ethnographic locations not a single site, but a site always already connected with somewhere/something else. This somewhere else is often said to be the place of power, but like a hall of mirrors, as we enter this site of power, again "real power" seems to be lying somewhere else. Thinking about power (or whatever makes the world turn) like this and following these sites of said power ethnographically helps, so Marcus argues, to refigure questions of complicity. I agree with this proposition in that it firstly diffuses forms of subjective complicity, especially with regard to representation. And indeed we might not have to worry too much about our own positionality, and about misrepresenting the police, as their own representations of themselves are robust enough. Thus the issue of epistemological violence, and our broad, ultimately inescapable complicity in "the system as such," might move to the background. Secondly, this allows our work with the police to assume a level of tactical complicity that can be used in analytically enhancing and generative ways, rather than morally paralyzing ones. We then quickly learn about those in power, and as they allow us into their world we end up realizing that they themselves are both inside and outside of power and that they are trying to make sense of this positionality in a way that is not much different from the efforts of the anthropologist of grasping the world. Still, such complicity as affinity[5] is precisely what appears to the onlooker as that very concrete complicity where we become part of the exercising of overt forms of power over others, with an uncanny immediacy. Complicity then is not a monolithic phenomenon. Rather it is a relational issue with different temporalities. Some dimensions of it can be morally confronted, and as we are able to reflect on it, and as our creative and ethical agency create a (temporal) distance between ourselves and our experiences, this can even become analytically generative. But other parts remain stubbornly traumatic and disabling, subsisting as they do in other people's experiences of our own immediate presence in our work.

I conclude with the assertion that the issue of complicity helps us to understand policing better. On the one hand it shows how policing can be a fragile undertaking, where police officers themselves hardly feel that they are in charge. This is particularly pronounced if policing is being used to stabilize unstable economic categories—in the case at hand here, the category of intellectual property. On the other hand, policing always comes down onto people's lives and subjects them in concretely disruptive ways, in which such instabilities and the wider contexts and agencies involved are being obscured. While power might be multisited and dispersed, policing has a very sharp edge. It creates an experience of power being insistently immediate and personal. These insights can also be taken to other ethnographic situations where the lines between subjecting and being subjected might not be as clear cut as they seem to be in the case of policing. Even here we have to learn to live with the fact that people we encounter during ethnographic research, and yet who are not our primary interlocutors, will inscribe on us identities and associations with which we may not be comfortable but over which we have no influence, since doing ethnographic work is choosing sides, and each side does have some form of a sharp edge for its others.

Policing Media Piracy in Johannesburg

While I have long defended the virtues of ethnographic fieldwork, the engagement I shall now describe has made me rethink the limits of turning ethnographic virtues into fruitful scholarly gains. At the time I was doing fieldwork with the Counterfeit Unit of the Commercial Crime Unit of the South African Police Service. This unit dealt with all kinds of cases of counterfeiting, piracy, and copyright infringement. A small unit, but responsible for the whole of Johannesburg, they were housed in a separate building and had direct access to the commercial crime court. This made their work relatively manageable. The unit shot to fame in 2010, during the FIFA Soccer World Cup, when they arrested a group of blonde Dutch women. The latter were involved in ambush marketing for the beer brand Bavaria, wearing skimpy orange dresses and attracting the attention of TV cameras during matches. Already sensitised to the fierce IP regime that FIFA had unilaterally imposed on South Africa during the World Cup, international media jumped on the case. They stormed the offices of the Counterfeit Unit to get a glimpse of the naïve young women now in the hands of the overzealous South African police. Generally, however, the unit's work took place with little attention from the outside world. And even within the overall Commercial Crime Unit, the Counterfeit Unit worked in the shadow of much more prominent and well-staffed sister units whose responsibility it was to fight ever-prevalent credit card fraud and other financial crimes. The unit's staple diet of cases was also far less sensational, focusing mainly on fake Adidas T-shirts, Nike sneakers, and of course media piracy.

The case that made me stumble and brought my attention to the question of complicity was a raid on manufacturers of pirated DVDs. It was supposed to be the case where the police officers with whom I was working were finally to prove me, as they liked to say, that "they were not just dealing with small fish"—DVD street traders—but "tackling the crime at its very roots"—namely where the pirated goods were being produced. They were making a claim that their work was worthy in terms of fighting crime. It was also a case where crime intelligence was going to be applied, instead of just going out onto the street and chasing after some poor but clever street hustler (of which there were many). But as we arrived at the site that had been identified by informers and private investigators with the South African Federation against Copyright Theft (SAFAC), the image of the grand bust and heroic police action quickly crumbled away. The allegedly "big manufacturing plant" was a small run-down private house in one of the low-income inner city neighbourhoods of Johannesburg. And the "dangerous gang of DVD pirates" was a young South African Indian Muslim couple with three adorable small children. Instead of storming the house the police just demanded access, to which the man and women submitted obediently. While I still thought this must be a mistake, the police officers searched the first room of the house and immediately found what they had been looking for. There were heaps of DVDs packed into bags and piling up on the bed together with the plastic sleeves and photocopied covers, in the midst of which, to the humming noise of the DVD burning towers, a baby was sleeping. The piles were made up of a mixture of then-current American blockbusters (*Planet of the Apes, X-Men, Transformers, The Matchmaker*), Islamic DVDs (*The Complete Quran, The Renewal*), and then stacks of pornography. As the police moved from room to room and started seizing both the copying equipment and every pile of DVDs they could find, I could see how the young woman in particular was becoming more and more distraught. She started pleading with some of the police officers—as well as with me. While the officers quickly brushed her off, I was not able to do the same. And so she told me that she had previously worked for a supermarket but lost the job after staying home once too often with a sick child. That is why she had taken up this recent occupation. She insisted that the burning of DVDs was also work, but that she could do it while staying at home. And she did not understand why they were being targeted when there were so many shops out there that openly sold the copied goods. Please, could I at least not arrest her and her husband? I tried to tell her that it was not in my power as I wasn't police. But she clearly thought that that wasn't true and kept holding my arm and pleading.

We then moved to the porch of the house where the police did an inventory of all the DVDs. They had to be counted and written down one by one while being packed into carefully sealed plastic bags. These long inventory lists then had to be signed by the suspects. This took a long time, and it even created something of a mundane interface. As all of us sat there involved in the tedious labour, the police and suspects even shared some jokes.

During this time I could also feel the woman's eyes on me, silently asking how we could do this to her and to her family. At one point her parents arrived, called to look after the children in case the woman and her husband would be taken into custody. There was no overt violence involved, and even the police felt somewhat awkward doing their job. Their behavior lacked the pompous performance of victory that I had witnessed at other moments when an arrested far better fitted the image of "a real criminal." In this case, it seemed, far too little separated their own sense of doing good work and making a living from the sense of making ends meet that the young couple presented. In fact, the making of the long inventory list of seized goods came to mirror the packaging and labelling that was part of producing the pirated DVDs. Both were laborious efforts at singularizing and counting what was in principle an unquantifiable good. But when all the tedious work was done, the police asserted their power again. They loaded the seized DVDs and the equipment onto the back of a pickup van, shoved the young couple into the back of one of the passenger cars, and took them off to the nearest police station. The small children until then had seemingly thought of the police more as visitors to their house, and obliviously continued their play in the midst of it all. But as they saw their parents disappear into the unknown car, they caught on to the gravity of the situation and started to cry, with the grandparents trying in vain to console them. I went back to the station with one of the detectives, with the desperate weeping of the children still ringing in my ears, with the eyes of the woman looking at me burning themselves into my memory, and with a nauseous feeling in my belly.

I could present other, more crass, ethnographic material here of cases in which I felt that people looked at me and thought of me as being part of a group of police officers and where there was also nothing I could do about this. For example, when the police I accompanied were raiding and turning people's houses upside down in the middle of the night. The fragility and humiliation of somebody just being pulled out of bed by an outside intruder remains with me so strongly, and with it my implication in it. But the case I have chosen to present in more detail here is significant in a different way. It is a case of where the police were actually just going about their work. It was not about violent coercion or extralegal activity, and it wasn't even about being particularly rude or insensitive. Thus, the complicity that was at stake here for me was not so much in a crime or an abuse of power but rather in the policing of a particular social order: in this case, the expansion of a new property regime.

Moral Laundering

What is so confusing about the case I have just described is that even the police felt uncomfortable and unsatisfied about it. As I was driving back to town, my companion confirmed a discomfort that surely had its own police-specific dimensions but for all that was not entirely different from what I felt in my belly. At least it allowed us to relate to each other in commiserating about the futility of the case. Admitting that these had hardly been hardened criminals they had arrested, he said, "This was hardly a successful case—what a waste of a Saturday morning this has been." And indeed, I had noticed how the police had struggled to keep up the justification and motivation for the raid once the image of the big crime bust had crumbled. At one point, for instance, the husband had tried to plead with one of the officers to at least leave some DVDs with them so they could make ends meet for the next few days. And at first the officer had actually indulged him, but then, becoming aware of the blurring of boundaries such indulgence produced, he suddenly changed his attitude and held up the pornography DVDs and said: "What kind of family man are you, leaving these lying around in the presence of the kids?" Then he pointed to some of the religious DVDs, such as the Koran, and accused the husband of throwing them together with the pornography. What was so telling about the moment was that the police had to revert to a moralizing rather than legal justification to put the husband back in place and to mark his doings as wrong. Yet the officers also knew that this moralistic argument would not hold up for long as the overriding motivation guiding their actions. In fact, it would produce an untenable irony for them as it made them into protectors of the intellectual property rights of pornographers. Yet again, therefore, other kinds of arguments were required to restore the meaningfulness of the case.

On our drive home, the same officer also complained about the private investigators who had come along from SAFAC. They had been, so he lamented, very arrogant, and unwilling to treat the police with proper respect. Instead they had withheld important information, like the exact address of the house where the raid was to take place. The police officers were only to find this out as they followed the private investigators in their cars. The officer explained to me: "They don't trust us, but they want us to do the dirty work of opening the doors and arresting people, while they get paid double what we earn by the brand-holders, like Sony and Warner Brothers, whose films they are protecting." He made it clear how public-private partnerships in the field of law enforcement around intellectual property were actually working out. Most intellectual property policing is supposed to be carried out through public-private partnerships in order to expand the capacity and expertise of the police. What becomes evident here, to the contrary, is that the police are only involved as far as they have coercive force, rather than in the field of intelligence. This means they do not get to decide in which cases to intervene and what criteria beyond commercial interest might be applied to prioritize cases. It is then only the private interest of the companies that is expanded here, with the help of free public resources. This leaves the police quite begrudging with regard to their private counterparts but without much choice but to swallow the arrogant treatment, as they depend on them for receiving expert reports from the industry confirming the inauthenticity of the goods that they have seized.

Resignedly concluding his lament about the wasted case, the officer added: "But . . . well . . . it will look good in the arrest statistics. Two arrests and bags of seized goods." Here then we seemingly end with a reduction of the case to mere numbers, but these are very meaningful and effective as performance indicators internal to the institution. And indeed, DVD raids are lucrative in upping the numbers, so much so that the Counterfeit Unit was given the trophy for most arrests among the various subunits of the Commercial Crime Unit in the previous year. Still, even that, as I was able to gather from my previous conversations with the officers, can leave a cynical emptiness regarding the felt legitimacy, meaning, and motivation of their work. Many of them are quite able to see through the game of performance statistics and actually joined the police with a sincere sense of doing something for society. This empty void that the number gain leaves they then try to fill again with claims about fighting *real* crime and using crime intelligence methods—just as they had done advertising the upcoming raid to me: "We'll show you that we fight real crime." This then brings them full circle in their efforts to make sense of what they were doing. Thus while for me my discomfort about the case strengthened my resolve to write about the policing of IP, the officer had his own way of undoing the experience of indeterminacy in his role in policing IP. In order not to have to stare into an abyss of meaninglessness and the lack of felt legitimacy in his work, he resorted to a form of reasoning that I would like to call *moral laundering*.

Moral laundering here means constantly moving and shifting from one justification to the next—from real crime fighting to moralizing and hanging
on to nonlegal social norms, from moralizing to the number game, from
the number game to real crime fighting—so that the fallibility and instability of each of these justifications do not become apparent.

The irony of course is that the instability of the notion of meaningful
and legitimate work, and therewith work in general, even more so erases
the clear line of difference separating police from the pirates they target. It
is not that the young family was not aware that what they were doing was
illegal. But that formal and distant reality competed with another in which
they saw DVD reproduction as a way to build up a sense of familial dignity through income-generating work—a reality that the woman tried to
evoke when she pleaded with me and when she compared the burning of
DVDs to her work at the supermarket. And police officers are quite able to
recognize such argumentation. One day, for example, the head of the unit,
sitting in the hall and smoking a cigarette, recounted to me how he had
made a living as child by "buying and reselling cheap things like cigarettes,
peanuts, fruits, and vegetables. I worked hard." He even managed to put
himself and his sister through school with this business. He then said: "If I
were a youngster today these cheap things would be counterfeit goods and
it would be me selling them." Such empathy with the people they police is
noteworthy. It speaks to how easily piracy can be considered a permissible,
earnest activity. Many have argued that IP creates a crisis because it is not
really property. It is not based on finite resources like water or land or gold,
but instead it is without limits as it can be reproduced endlessly with little
effort and few to no costs, thanks to technological advances. It therefore
resists enclosure.[6] Here, in this case of the police fretting over the meaningfulness of policing IP, we do have a crisis indeed, but a crisis centered
on, or, rather, expressed through the expansive meaning of work. While
the officers' own sense of meaningful work relies on the idea that what
they police is not work but crime, the people they police are able to build
up a sense of dignity on the basis of taking copying as work. So the crisis
of property takes shape not by pointing toward an outside to the capitalist
logic of property altogether but rather by being folded back into a common
language of work as the source of value. In one version, police and DVD
pirates of the kind described here are supposed to be on different sides of
the law. This is partly enacted, though tellingly in an imaginary form, when
for example police were enthusiastically telling me of the big bust that lay
ahead of us. In a different version, where economic volatility creates ambiguities with regard to right and wrong, this all seems to falter and the space

between legality and morality becomes harder to bridge. Suddenly police themselves feel subjected to, if not violated by, the imposed logic of the law enforcement of IP.

Ethnographic Virtue

These are insights about how the law enforcement of intellectual property takes place. They are enabled through ethnography, and ethnography alone. None of these would have become discernable to me without my being there with the police. Some of them are outright counterintuitive, such as the officers' own sense of existential crisis. Police are often depicted as the handmaiden of the regime they serve. This is clearly the case here, but we also see that there is a strange in-between space made up of the kind of human, professional (however unprofessional these might be at times), and institutional expectations police have of themselves. These do not change the course of things, but they show how much the police themselves can be outsiders to the logic they produce. And they produce interesting and telling instabilities—instabilities that might mean that a capillary policing is not stabilizing intellectual property as a common sense crime, and that a measure of crude force will always be required to keep turning intellectual property into private property if one wants to prevent it from asserting its ambivalent character as work. It is then also not surprising that, as this research further shows, justifications for the enclosure of intellectual property always draw from sources outside of the law. This can be either an exaggerated sense of morality, such as a hysterical contempt for pornography, or a reduced version of an abstract number game, such as arrest statistics. Interestingly this is exactly what we see in all the public relations campaigns to convince people that their theft of intellectual property is wrong. These campaigns do not state the message of the law but are always appealing to a dramatic moralistic sense and require references to highly obvious and dramatic cases. These ask us to "imagine what would happen if you took counterfeit antibiotics to treat pneumonia or a plane flew with counterfeit spare parts." The immediacy of the moral outrage these examples evoke is then transferred to also discredit the faking of T-shirts, which hardly hurt the person wearing them but represent lost profits for private companies. One of the reasons why the legal regulations carry no explanatory or inhibitive power might then be exactly that intellectual property itself is at crisis by upsetting logics of work, as we have seen in this case. Finally, carrying out participant observation with the Counterfeit Unit has also enabled me to see the way that public-private partnerships unfold in practice, namely with the public resources being put in the service of private interests instead of the other way around. It is these kinds of insights that ethnography can provide. It can form the base of a more outspoken critique of the policing of IP, or it can motivate further scholarship on the social life of IP law and law enforcement. What this indirectly shows is that complicity can be highly generative. Complicity in fact might be a small price to pay for what one gets in return.

What is more, to come back to a point made earlier, this was not a case in which the police acted violently or beyond the law. This "legal legitimacy" allows one to highlight how far a certain complicity with the police can go. A complicit alignment with the police, which might even include a sense of common ground, can bring out both their own struggles with what they do and a view onto the threads of things, meanings, and practices in which they are caught up. In cases where police act outside of the law in full view of the researcher, for example when extralegal violence is meted out, the analysis is almost necessarily overshadowed by the stark ethical dilemmas that this raises. Here assumptions of common ground might be much harder to find, as the witnessing of policing produces a sense of repulsion and a visceral retreat from empathy. The point, however, remains that working with the police can be immensely fruitful even though highly compromising at times.

"Studying Up" and the Question of Complicity in South Africa and Elsewhere

For reasons like this I have argued very much in favour of doing ethnographic work, particularly with institutions of the state and the law. My aim is to contribute to building this as a strong tradition in the anthropology of South Africa, where I carry out most of my research, and where I am also based as a scholar and a teacher. But South African anthropology has a complicated relationship with the question of ethnography and complicity. In fact, during late apartheid, ethnography and its related methods of participant observation was seen as the ultimate form of colonial complicity. *Volkekunde*, the branch of anthropology that more or less explicitly worked in the service of apartheid, had contaminated the very idea of ethnography. This wasn't actually justified, as *volkekunde* scholars did very little long-term fieldwork. They spoke to interpreters, but living in the field in black communities was not considered acceptable. Even so, *volkekunde* made "difference" and "otherness" programmatic to such an extent that a critical anthropology could only take an opposed position.

A programmatic assumption of ignoring difference and stressing political comradeship, together with a strong Marxist theoretical influence, shifted the focus away from everyday life to fundamental structures that could be discerned by macro- rather than microanalysis. Ethnography was more or less discredited and discarded as a critical epistemological tool and as a form of representation.[7] Postapartheid anthropology, however, has been recovering a sense of the essential importance of ethnographic work to the anthropological project. Even if it involves some form of methodological and theoretical othering, it is assumed that it actually does better justice to people's intricate imbrications in structures of inequality and injustice. In fact, fieldwork can be constructed as a powerful way of bearing witness and as a form of solidarity—or as an "ethics of mutuality," as was put forward for discussion in the keynote address to the 2012 Anthropology Southern Africa conference.[8] At the same time an internationally familiar call to "study up"[9] or to study "here and there"[10] has been uttered with renewed vigor. It has challenged South African researchers and researchers of South Africa to also study those who think they are beyond being studied. This call responds to a trend to exclusively focusing on the poor and to seeing anthropology as lending voice to those who lack the means to make themselves heard. As Francis Nyamnjoh[11] says, this doubles in problematic ways with white people studying black people and leaves African anthropologists somehow suspended between the role of researcher and research subject. At the same time it has created a blind spot with regard to studying white people, whose societal position has been entirely normalized. Thus questions of studying the morally ambiguous life worlds of those who inhabit institutions of power or spaces of taken-for-granted privilege acquire new relevance in the context of stark postapartheid racial and institutional inequalities. Some such work has already been carried out, even before such calls were pronounced. Vincent Crapanzano published *Waiting: The Whites of South Africa* in 1985, and more recently there have been studies of institutions such as prisons,[12] the Department of Home Affairs,[13] the Truth and Reconciliation Commission (TRC),[14] and even forays into the world of private business, like the study of insurance companies.[15] I would firmly locate my own[16] and others'[17] ethnographic work on the study of the police in South Africa within this trend.

It is in this light of my own and these other studies that I want to revisit the now-classic 1997 article in which George Marcus explored what multisited studies do to questions of complicity. In that article he makes the argument that studying the various sites through which power and cultural production are dispersed—as opposed to bounded localities that are seen as merely subject to external power relations—transforms questions of complicity. Previously questions of representation have nearly brought an end to the ethnographic project. Here it was the complicity with the institutions of knowledge production and the realization that "speaking for" also produces "doing violence to" the very people whose lives we deem so interesting and worthy studying. Marcus argues that this dead-lock can be diffused. As we reconceptualize "the system" and the working of global power and the making of culture in a less monolithic and given form, but as unbounded and dispersed, this turns the global into the local and the forces, actors, and dynamics beyond the local into the potentially ethnographic particular. With regard to these "global" localities, inhabited by actors who mostly can powerfully speak for themselves, questions of representation become less sensitive and make the ethnographic endeavor less morally loaded. For some, this then reopens the possibility to fully assume some form of tactical complicity with those being researched, as Clifford Geertz[18] has always argued. For Marcus, however, this moment has passed. With the reconceptualization of the field-site as a multisited assemblage, the field-site has lost its inside-outside divide. The outside is always yet another local site that at best points to yet another elusive (out)site. What then remains for researchers and research subjects, as Marcus argues in the character of the postmodernist moment in which he was writing, is the complicity between these interlocutors (the researcher and the research participants), shaped by a shared sense of the sheer difficulty of trying to make sense of things, each with as much of a guess as good as the other.

Here then, be it in the Geertzian manner of tactical complicity or in Marcus's way by affinity through a shared epistemological predicament—of never quite being able to understand the outside—complicity is being turned into something utterly productive. For the one complicity is a question of method, while for the other it is even an analytical approach. Very much like Beatrice Jauregui[19] I find it convincing and helpful to employ this to my experience with the police. Jauregui in "Dirty Anthropology" makes clear that the anthropologist in fact needs to go along with if not mirror the experience of the police of marginality rather than centrality to power. This allows for a description of the police in all its nonlinear complexity of being both subject to and subject of power/violence, which she describes as the "simultaneous sensibilities of hyper-vulnerability and hyper-vigilance."[20] For me, particularly, it speaks to my experience with the police, where I share their difficult search for the meaning of their work, which constantly resists being pinned down and stabilized.

The Relationality and Temporality of Complicity

Still, there is something that remains unresolved. When it comes to being seen by others as being police, there is something of an uncanny immediacy that utterly resists being made productive. Often when we do work with the police, our focus is on the relationship we have with the police and how we position ourselves toward them. But what about the people whose lives we encounter as we go along with the police? This is an experience unavoidable for anyone studying the police in an ethnographic way, sometimes simply accepted, sometimes explicitly mentioned. Didier Fassin[21] describes such an occurrence in the introduction to *Enforcing Order*, saying how this identification came with the impossibility of "absent[ing] myself mentally" from it. In a similar vein, as I recall these moments, they bring my thoughts and feelings right back to the field, as if no time had passed since then. There are traces here of trauma's uncanny ability to compress time and space, causing one to relive things without allowing for a sense of reflective distance to grow between oneself and the event. What kind of complicity is this then that somehow fails to give up its immediacy? And where does this leave us with the possibility to turn complicity into understanding and critical writing as argued by Nyamnjoh, Geertz, and Marcus?

To try to understand this stubborn residue of complicity, I would like to take another theoretical loop that will highlight both the relationality of complicity—who is involved, who gets to judge, and who gets to do what about it—and the kind of temporality this produces. While for some complicity and responsibility might be an either-or question, Mark Sanders[22] entirely turns this assumption around and proposes that there is no responsibility without complicity, and that even more so, complicity precedes responsibility. He uses this insight to compose an interesting account of the complicities of intellectuals during the times of apartheid South Africa. He suggests that one key way in which intellectuals assumed responsibility was not just by identifying with the victims of apartheid's injustice but, in the first instance, by considering their own imbrication in the system of apartheid. Even if they were not the brute oppressors they were still part of the system, and whatever one was doing within it was also then contaminated by it. Drawing further from the way in which the TRC Report[23] conceptualized responsibility, which in turn drew inspiration from Hannah Arendt's[24] account of the "banality of evil," Sanders states that identifying with the "little perpetrator" within each and every person would "make one act to stop or prevent those deeds."[25] He continues that "when opposition takes the form of demarcation from something, it cannot, it follows, be untouched by that to which it opposes itself. Opposition takes its first steps from a footing of complicity."[26] This is a powerful claim. The realization of being implicated is what compels action: the idea that one cannot ever wash one's hands of complicity, that as one makes universal claims to justice one also becomes part of humanity's deeds, compels responsibility. With regard to the ethnographic case that I presented, one could say that the discomfort I felt about the case—which very much was compounded by my being there with the police, witnessing the legal violence of the intervention—strengthened my resolve to write about it and to expose the absurdity of IP policing. The more I realize I find myself entangled with the police, the more I am indeed compelled to write about it. Complicity here is a powerful spell, creating responsibility beyond ourselves.

As we act upon complicity, however, we are also in the act of transforming it. The focus in Sanders's account lies with the action—advocacy, refusal, critical scholarship—that follows the recognition of complicity and contamination with all-surrounding evil. This allows us, as we assume complicity, to put a reflective distance between ourselves and the experience of complicity, and with that, to make complicity less immediate. Such a perspective is enabled, so I would argue, as long as we remain in the realm of the overridingly subjective, with imagination being a powerful subjective force. Implicitly or explicitly, in every statement in Sanders's account about complicity there is an expression of a very wilful assertion acted out in the realm of the imaginative. For example he states: "*Actively* assuming a role in a moral drama, one is making sure that one does not unwittingly become an instrument of someone else's agenda" (my emphasis). He talks of "*Contemplating* an intricate play of perpetrator-figures . . ." and says that "In this *fable*, as in all *fables*, one identifies in order to dis-identify"[27] (my emphasis). Further on he even says explicitly "A major difference [when people acknowledge their complicity] . . . lies in the will."[28] This indicates a voluntarist perspective where the imaginative act of identifying with the perpetrator already serves as the catalyst for further action. In other words, complicity is not imposed as a judgment from outside by a third party but is being very much self-imposed. It is asserted by mobilizing a creative imaginative force, which in itself already carries the force of dignity and righteousness of some sort. This means one cannot simply be annihilated morally by the assertion of complicity. As one's contamination increases and one's moral high ground diminishes, one's sense of self as responsible moral subject, acknowledging the contamination and acting upon it, grows. In fact, my wilfully seeking out the company of the police for research purposes is a deliberate concretization of this imaginative act, followed then by the compulsion to write about it in order to pay my dues. Yet this very act of writing also undoes the complicity through creating a distance in time and by turning my being with the police into knowledge about them. We all know how, as we write, the reality on paper becomes more proximate than our less mediated memories of the moment. Material and argument become intertwined, holding within them the time spent on reflecting, writing, editing, rewriting, rethinking, and building the person up as scholar rather than researcher—creating its own momentum and reality.

I would like to contrast this deliberate identification by the researcher with the police with the researcher being identified as police by others. To be mistaken for a police officer, I would like to argue, turns the assertive imaginative act of complicity, which in Sanders's account remains a subjective act, into a fundamentally intersubjective act. After all, I know that I am not a police officer, and I know what I am writing and why I am writing it, but it is the others whom I encounter with the police—people who are unwilling to accept this, or to even ever know this—who now come to the fore. This means that it is not my own imagination that is at stake here but the imagination of the person who sees me with the police, as police. It is that young couple's image and experience of me as I walked into their house by virtue of the power of the police, stood by and watched as their DVDs were confiscated and as they were arrested and taken off to a police station. To think with Michael Jackson[29]—who has nothing much to say about complicity but who has thought through the idea of intersubjectivity as it pertains to the practice of ethnography—this is an act of entirely external inscription. According to Jackson, ethnographic work does not only look into social life as "a field of inter-experience, inter-action, and inter-locution" but also describes the relationship between observer and research subjects as one in which "analytically, inter-existence is given precedence over individual essence."[30] He further makes clear that this is not a romantic notion of shared experience. In contrast, intersubjectivity holds both understanding and conflict. The inscription upon the researcher of apparently being police can then be seen as one of these conflicts. While the research asserts distance through the project of writing, the people being policed, and looking upon the researcher tagging along with the police, refuse the distancing and affirm the indistinction. Jackson talks about the integral ambiguities and instabilities that come with intersubjectivity. One of them he describes as follows: "Intersubjectivity reflects the instability of human consciousness—the way our awareness continually drifts or oscillates between a retracted, substantive, and ontologically secure sense of self and a comparatively expanded and unstable sense of self in which one is sometimes fulfilled in being with another, at other times overwhelmed and engulfed."[31] It is the sense of being overwhelmed and engulfed that overlaps with the experience of complicity being inscribed upon the merely observing researcher. It is a moment beyond one's own imaginative control or intellectual activity. It is a moment and an identity that will not be undone by the insight into the complexity of the role of the police in IP law enforcement that fieldwork has afforded me. The fact that police might have been instrumentalized by the SAFAC private investigators, that there are actually different actors at the scene that might be grudgingly at odds with each other, that the police officers' sense of work had been compromised by the case, even that my writing would put the family into a favorable light and question their criminal liability: all that remains invisible and inconsequential to the people who were subject to the raid, in the moment in which it takes place, and with that my role as researcher rather than as police officer.

This is something that cannot and should not be undone, as with undoing it one would also in principle lose the insights gained by being with the police. One could argue I could go to the same house afterward and explain myself. But while I could do it with one family, how could I do this with everyone I encountered with the police during the long-term process that ethnographic fieldwork represents? Would this not be a different study, then, namely one with the people being raided rather than with those who carry out raids? And again I have to ask, what are the chances that I would find these people at the time of the raid, other than by working with the police? What all this implies is that doing ethnographic research with the police is choosing sides. The moment in which my identity as police is frozen represents the hard edge with which police come down on people's lives even though the power that compels police to act might lie somewhere else. By choosing sides I become part of the kind of reified form state power takes, and by which it becomes a reality in people's own experiences.

Thus whatever reflective and critical act follows from such experience (emerging from one's own subjective awareness of complicity), there will always remain the *other* person involved in the encounter; the impression that one has left with another person, in another person's imagination.

And it is purely up to this person what to do with this impression. It is not for us to turn it into something else. It can also thus only be revisited in this frozen state, in its temporal immediacy, without the act of reflection having created an intellectual and temporal distance between that moment and the now. It is a complicity that will never leave us off the hook.

Conclusion

Doing ethnographic work on powerful institutions and with people in power might lessen the burden of older questions of representation and power, but it brings with it a new form of complicity. It brings with it complicity in the hard edge of power. It brings with it a complicity in the reified image of state power as it appears to people who are subjected to it and into whose lives these institutions intervene with very real, concrete, and immediate consequences. Complicity here is based on the fact that by doing ethnographic research with the police we choose sides. To choose the side of the police can partly be rationalized. The subjective side of the complicity this involves, our deliberate choice to be touched by what the police do and are, can be turned into a productive process of complex understanding and critical writing. In fact, if we take seriously the idea that complicity actually precedes responsibility, it means that the deeper we become entangled with the police and reflect upon our complicity with the police, the more we might be compelled to do something about it and to write about it. What this also means is that with the choosing of sides our creative and imaginative agency increases and allows us to partly undo or at least put a distance between ourselves and the moment of contagion. On the other hand, choosing sides also means that we have to accept that we cannot surpass every aspect of what—and, especially, who—we encounter *with* the police. It is here that our agency has to pay its dues and has to surrender to the fact that we might very much be damned in the minds of those who we in our research with the police probably, ironically, care about the most: the people being policed. Here we are in the intersubjective realm. The encounter remains frozen in the moment of the encounter and can only be accessed in its immediacy as its authorship, so to speak, lies beyond our reach. That is also where its discomfort originates. This is a corollary of ethnographic research, one that studying with the police (and studying up in general) brings out in an accentuated form since these institutions have a very hard edge by which they intervene in people's lives.

These insights can also be taken to doing ethnography more generally, even to cases where we think we are not choosing the side of any particular powerful group as such. Still we will and have to learn to live with the fact that people whom we encounter during ethnographic research and yet who are not our primary interlocutors will inscribe on us identities and associations with which we are not comfortable but over which we have no influence, since doing ethnographic work is choosing sides and each side does have some form of a sharp edge for those on the other side.

Notes

1. Geertz 1973.
2. Jauregui 2013.
3. Nyamnjoh 2012.
4. Marcus 1997; Marcus 1998.
5. Marcus 1998.
6. Boyle 2013.
7. Hammond-Tooke 1997.
8. Morreira 2012.
9. Nader 1972.
10. Marcus 1998.
11. Nyamnjoh 2012.
12. Gillespie 2008.
13. Hoag 2011; Hoag 2014.
14. Buur 2002.
15. Bähre 2012.
16. Hornberger 2011.
17. I.e., Jensen 2005.
18. Geertz 1973.
19. Jauregui 2013.
20. Jauregui 2013, 142.
21. Fassin 2013, 23.
22. Sanders 2002.
23. The Truth and Reconciliation Commission 1998.
24. Arendt 2006.
25. Sanders 2002, 3–4.
26. Ibid., 9.
27. Ibid., 3.
28. Ibid., 9.
29. Jackson 1998.
30. Ibid., 3.
31. Ibid., 9–10.

References

Arendt, H. 2006. *Eichmann in Jerusalem: A Report on the Banality of Evil*. New York: Penguin Classics.

Bähre, Erik. 2012. "The Janus Face of Insurance in South Africa: From Costs to Risk, from Networks to Bureaucracies." *Africa* 82 (1): 150–67.

Boyle, James. 2013. *The Public Domain: Enclosing the Commons of the Mind*. New Haven: Yale University Press.

Buur, Lars. 2002. "Institutionalising the Past: Information Management and Other Methods of Ordering the Truth in the Work of the South African Truth and Reconciliation Commission." *Folk* 44:117–44.

Fassin, Didier. 2013. *Enforcing Order: An Ethnography of Urban Policing*, translated by Rachel Gomme. Cambridge: Polity.

Geertz, Clifford. 1973. *Interpretation of Cultures*. New York: Basic Books.

Gillespie, Kelly. 2008. "Moralizing Security: 'Corrections' and the Post-Apartheid Prison." *Race/Ethnicity* 2 (1): 69–87.

Hammond-Tooke, David. 1997. *Imperfect Interpreters: South African Anthropologists, 1920–1990*. Johannesburg: Wits University Press.

Hoag, Colin. 2011. "Assembling Partial Perspectives: Thoughts on the Anthropology of Bureaucracy." *PoLAR: Political and Legal Anthropology Review* 34 (1): 81–94.

———— 2014. "Dereliction at the South African Department of Home Affairs: Time for the Anthropology of Bureaucracy." *Critique of Anthropology* 34 (4): 410–28.

Hornberger, Julia. 2011. *Policing and Human Rights: The Meaning of Violence and Justice in Everyday Policing in Johannesburg*. London: Routledge.

Jackson, Michael. 1998. *Minima Ethnographica: Intersubjectivity and the Anthropological Project*. Chicago: University of Chicago Press.

Jauregui, Beatrice. 2013. "Dirty Anthropology: Epistemologies of Violence and Ethical Entanglements in Police Ethnography." In *Policing and Contemporary Violence: The Anthropology of Police in Practice*, edited by William Garriot, 125–53. New York: Palgrave Macmillan.

Jensen, Steffen. 2005. "Above the Law: Practices of Sovereignty in Surrey Estate, Cape Town." In *Sovereign Bodies: Citizens, Migrants, and States in the Postcolonial World*, edited by Thomas Blom Hansen and Finn Stepputat, 218–38. Princeton: Princeton University Press.

Marcus, George E. 1997. "The Uses of Complicity in the Changing Mise-En-Scène of Anthropological Fieldwork." *Representations*, no. 59 (July): 85–108. doi:10.2307/2928816.

————. 1998. "Ethnography In/of World System: The Emergence of Multi-Sited Ethnography." In *Ethnography through Thick and Thin*, 79–104. Princeton: Princeton University Press.

Morreira, Shannon. 2012. "'Anthropological Futures'? Thoughts on Social Research and the Ethics of Engagement." *Anthropology Southern Africa* 35 (3&4): 100–104.

Nader, Laura. 1972. "Up the Anthropologist: Perspectives Gained from Studying Up." In *Reinventing Anthropology*, 284–311. New York: Pantheon Books.

Nyamnjoh, Francis B. 2012. "Blinded by Sight: Divining the Future of Anthropology in Africa." *Africa Spectrum* 47 (2–3): 63–92.

Randeria, Shalini. 2007. "The State of Globalization: Legal Plurality, Overlapping Sovereignties and Ambigious Alliances between Civil Society and the Cunning State in India." *Theory, Culture and Society* 24 (1): 1–33.

Sanders, Mark. 2002. *Complicities: The Intellectual and Apartheid*. Durham: Duke University Press.

The Truth and Reconciliation Commission. 1998. *The Truth and Reconciliation Commission of South Africa Report*. http://www.justice.gov.za/trc/report/index.htm.

THREE

Intimacy:
Personal Policing, Ethnographic Kinship, and Critical Empathy (India)

BEATRICE JAUREGUI

An ethnographic account of a "day in the life" of police can tell us many things about how personal relationships, intersubjective identifications, and affective networks configure institutional praxis and knowledge production.[1] As part of an ethnography of state police in northern India that I have been conducting for a more than a decade,[2] I here recount moments of tension and connection between senior officers and subordinates; a local "big man"'s ability to influence a criminal investigation; extralegal police responses to citizen complaints; and my own responses to observing these interactions, as well as my being benignly coerced by a station chief to sponsor a police banquet. This recounting theorizes how policing may be more personalized than not in everyday practice and also how what I call "ethnographic kinship" and "critical empathy" work together as peculiar forms of intimacy that may help us to understand both personal policing and anthropological fieldwork as processes marked by fragile social bonds, fractured forms of affect, and fluctuations in power.

Ethnographic kinship took two primary forms over the course of my fieldwork. The first form, which I call "interlocutor ethnographic kinship," developed during my everyday interactions with police in Uttar Pradesh (UP) as an enacted but unnamed form of exchange that positioned me as simultaneously empowered and subordinated in relation to my interlocutors. The second form, which I call "biographical ethnographic kinship," involved the way my experience as the immediate family member of US Army personnel unexpectedly resonated with some of the status positions and expressions of the police with whom I worked. This latter form of ethnographic kinship became salient to me when I began conducting a side project with US combat veterans several years into my fieldwork in India. This second project was inspired by an interest in better understanding the experiences and actions of my father and younger brother, who deployed as enlisted-rank infantry soldiers to Vietnam in 1969 and to Iraq in 2009, respectively. Although I had long been studying and producing scholarly writing on the historical and philosophical codevelopment of military and policing institutions,[3] it had not occurred to me that my familial connections with the US Army may have constituted a significant motivating force for my fieldwork with police in India, or played a crucial role in shaping my analytical frames.

This is not to say that I was completely unaware of the links between my personal background and my scholarly interests. When police in UP (and others) would inquire about what inspired me to want to study their life world, one of the answers that first came to me and which I repeated often was, "my father and brother are in the army." I began telling people this because I knew not only that the Indian police organizational hierarchy had retained its military structure from the colonial period[4] but also that many people who join the police in India have family members already working for the force. Many police would reply, "ah yes, okay . . . that makes sense," and I simply thought I was being a savvy ethnographer, strategically utilizing biographical and historical accidents to access what are otherwise mostly impenetrable social institutions and individual lives. What I did not fully understand at the time was that I was also building a shared sense of identification with the people I was studying, and revealing a feeling of being called to do this work to explain not only the subjectivities and representations of police in India but also those of persons with whom I had lifelong blood ties.

Once I began to realize that my anthropological work constituted a kind of Weberian vocation that was not only political or scientific but also personal and affective,[5] I found myself returning to my written notes, unwritten memories, and recorded images of fieldwork in India to analyze anew the disturbing bonds I often felt with police who expressed ideologies or engaged in practices that I found repulsive or conflicting with my own moral and ethical beliefs. As elaborated below, I believe that this peculiar form of intimacy worked to foster what I call critical empathy, the ability to approximately understand and explain the perceptions and practices of others while simultaneously maintaining a measure of distance that allows—indeed, demands—questioning and critiquing of these same perceptions and practices.[6] I argue that a sensibility of critical empathy—cultivated through ethnographic kinship relations or otherwise—

may allow nuanced ethnographic analysis of unpalatable perceptions and practices more ably than other conceptual tools of anthropological engagement like "rapport" or "complicity" or "being affected."[7]

Rapport as a kind of intimacy between ethnographers and interlocutors who are often presumed to be powerful, physically violent, or corrupt—like police or soldiers—has been theorized previously through a sensualized lens with terms like "ethnographic seduction," an ethically questionable "we feeling" with immoral actors that allegedly "trades our critical stance as observers for an illusion of congeniality with cultural insiders . . . subverts our understanding of social and cultural phenomena by dissuading an inquiry beyond their appearance . . . [and] disarms our critical detachment."[8] In response to this normative understanding, which may stymie critical ethnography with particular persons and institutions, I have theorized concepts of "dirty anthropology" and "strategic complicity" as means to continue and encourage such work.[9] These concepts together suggest that the ethnographer may conduct her work with ethical integrity and professional responsibility even though she can never be morally "pure" or fully "detached" from the forces and relations being observed and analyzed. She does this by maintaining an awareness of, and continually questioning, her complicity with her interlocutors' problematic perceptions and practices while cultivating an empirically grounded and nuanced understanding of the relationships among what they themselves say they are doing, what they are observably doing, and what other people say about why and how they are doing what they are doing.[10]

Building on these ideas, I argue here that a vital component of the ethnographer's responsibility involves critically interrogating and triangulating not only what she observes among her interlocutors, but also how she herself may be implicated in a palimpsest of affective engagements that configure the knowledge she produces. More than a rehashing of the "Writing Culture" moment of anthropological self-reflexivity[11] this analysis launches from Ruth Behar's concept of "the vulnerable observer," the individual ethnographer in the field who is confronted with her own subjective "tenderminded toughmindedness" and thus becomes uncertain about, and unexpectedly interdependent with, a variety of interlocutors with whom she has a complex "intellectual *and* emotional engagement."[12] The constellation of emotions I experienced during fieldwork with the UP Police ranged from humor and appreciation to ennui and irritation to disgust and horror. Most often, my fieldwork experience with police was laced with negative feelings of compulsion, guilt, resentment, and anxiety regarding what I witnessed of their life world. That said, I also felt compassion and even admiration for some of my interlocutors. And over time I came to believe that many of them expressed ideas and behaviors that, in context, seemed perhaps "reasonable" or oriented toward an alternative sense of "justice," whereas previously, I might have perceived them as utterly unreasonable or unjust.[13]

While I previously theorized my shifting responses to interlocutors and their practices as a process of desensitization that put me on ethically "shaky ground" or sliding down a "slippery slope" of some sort,[14] especially with regard to police violence, I now believe that a deeper understanding of ethnographic kinship and critical empathy may better account for the changes I experienced over time, and for the subsequent forms of social knowledge that I now produce and disseminate about policing in India and about police more generally as a global social institution.[15] Importantly, I have chosen here to discuss interactions that did *not* involve physical violence perpetrated by police. Many critical analyses of police focus on such violence.[16] While grounded research on police violence is necessary and important, as I discuss in depth elsewhere,[17] the theoretical and pragmatic applications of such analysis are constricted by a narrow concentration on harm to human bodies and violations of legality, at the expense of recognizing and analyzing other types of relationships, dilemmas, and transgressions configuring police work. The vast majority of the time, police are not engaging in categorically extralegal or physically violent acts, and their raison d'être must not be reduced to such acts, lest we understand only a small part of the puzzle of police and policing and become trapped in simplistic and polarized debates regarding what is right and what is to be done.

In my observations, the majority of everyday police practices involved the interpretation and management of personal relationships characterized by power inequalities, both among police themselves and among police and the various persons with whom they interacted on a daily basis. As an anthropologist studying these police practices in situ, my own relationships and interactions with them took on some of the structural qualities of their relationships and interactions with others. Moreover, as I spent more time in the field and my connections with interlocutors deepened, my responses to them changed and often surprised me, especially when I felt something like compassion for persons who would often do and say things that I found intensely disagreeable. In what follows, I examine these interactions and responses in order to demonstrate how both policing and ethnography as social practices not only may reflect a variety of power inequalities, but also may be grounded in peculiar forms of personalized and gendered intimacy—specifically kinship and empathy—that demand ongoing recognition and interrogation. Through fieldwork with biological kin in the US Army[18] and fictive kin in the Indian police, I have gained a new understanding of how emotionally charged relationships of obligation figure both police and ethnographers as simultaneously powerful *and* vulnerable subjects producing consequential knowledge.

A Christmas Story with the Uttar Pradesh Police

After my research assistant and I arrive at the police station called Chakkar Rasta Thana (CRT) on Christmas morning we watch as the station staff— who on paper number approximately thirty-five, though most days only five or six are present and active—meet with local village *pradhan* (elected headmen) and gather information about the almost sixty villages falling within the station jurisdiction, an area of approximately 100 square miles with more than 100,000 inhabitants. The police conduct this review process annually to make sure that they have a record of things like population estimates, births and deaths, updated records of gun licenses, reported criminal activities, and the names and addresses of local political party leaders. While the review proceeds, a woman and several male relatives arrive to lodge a complaint that her husband's family is harassing her for more dowry, a crime under sections 304B and 498A of the Indian Penal Code. They make their case to the CRT chief station officer (SO), a sub-inspector named Y. K. Yadav, who calls their village *pradhan* and orders him to tell the accused persons to come to CRT for questioning.[19] Meanwhile, several drunken men who have been engaged in some kind of physical conflict bring their dispute to the station. As these goings on proceed, I feel like my participant-observation of policing for the day has "officially" begun.

After some time, one of the CRT constables with whom we are most familiar, Prithvi, calls my research assistant's mobile phone from his own to tell us to hurry up and come to the annual party of a local "big man," named Arjun Trivedi, an event to which we were all invited earlier in the week. On my direction, my assistant says we are observing work at the station and will try to come by later, but Prithvi insists that we come immediately. When we appear uninterested, Prithvi calls his boss, SO Yadav, who tells us to go to the party and that he will join us there very soon. I protest, saying I would rather observe the goings on at the station, but Yadav says somewhat forcefully, "No, go to the party." I am annoyed, imagining this event as an unwanted distraction from doing my job as an ethnographer of policing, but I feel compelled by the SO to go, and so oblige.

My assistant and I ride our motorbikes about fifteen kilometers up the highway to a defunct but still grand bungalow dating back to the height of the British Raj in 1927, and by the time we arrive the grounds are swarming with several hundred party guests, mostly journalists since the host, Trivedi, is a well-known media mogul and owner of several widely read Hindi language newspapers. There are also significant numbers of police officers, civil servants, and politicians. When the mayor of Lucknow arrives, surrounded by a gaggle of armed police protectors and peons, Trivedi greets him warmly and servants literally trip over each other to swiftly offer up the most comfortable chair available and provide snacks and *chai*. As per custom, the guest of honor eats, shakes hands and smiles for the clicking cameras and clucking beseechers for a few minutes, then departs with his entourage. Following these formal public exchanges, the crowds move a short distance away to Trivedi's personal house and indulge in an enormous feast of fine locally grown vegetables and spices, rich *lassi* (yogurt drink), and sumptuous sweets. My assistant and I quickly take our meals at the long table in assembly line fashion, then thank our host and leave with full bellies.

Upon returning to the police station, we see SO Yadav sitting like a village elder before two groups of about half a dozen people each: the opposing sides in the alleged dowry violence case that arose earlier. I hear the station chief say he does not believe the woman's story because it keeps changing. This visibly embarrasses her father, who asks for ten days to try to settle the matter. The SO gives him five days to "get the story straight" and return if he wishes, then everyone leaves. Immediately following their departure, the SO arbitrates the other dispute that has led to the aforementioned bloody physical fighting among four visibly and odorously drunken men. When Yadav recommends a compromise, which he indicates he will broker and put into writing, the men seem to lose interest and wander off. Following this, Yadav hears the case of a different group of men regarding a land dispute that they are in with none other than Mr. Trivedi, the host of the party we have all just attended. Yadav comports himself more formally and seriously with this group than he did with the others, and in response to their pleas that he file a first information report (FIR) against Trivedi, he tells them that he first will have to consider the stack of documentary evidence they are presenting and make some inquiries, which he does by phone after they leave. Unlike with the previous cases, the SO is clearly reluctant to get involved in this last dispute, and he ultimately decides not to file the FIR.[20] When I ask Yadav if his reticence has anything to do with Trivedi's status and influence, he answers with a Hindi proverb: *"paani mein reha kar magar se bair nahin karthe"* (when you live in the water, you don't make an enemy of the crocodile).[21]

Yadav then shifts the focus of the conversation and asks what I thought of Trivedi's party. Before I can answer, my assistant chimes in relating a joke that I had made to him about the *barda khaanaa* (feast) at Trivedi's house being my Christmas dinner. The SO's face lights up and he says, "ah yes, Christmas, this is your holiday, no? You should throw us a Christmas party. We will have our own *barda khaanaa* right here at CRT!" I initially think that he is also joking. But no: Yadav has decided that I will host a holiday party for the *thana* staff and that it will happen the following day. I feel an awkward pressure, especially when he says, "I'll make the arrangements and you can give the money." But, I do not protest, as his decisive tone makes it a fait accompli.

When the SO retires to his room for a rest before night patrol, my assistant and I go to the CRT front yard, where we observe a couple of constables returning from duty out-of-station, greeting their colleagues who stayed behind with laughter and handshakes. One of the returning constables, a mustachioed man in his early thirties named Virendra, whips out a thick stack of small bills from his pocket, mostly ten-, twenty-, and fifty-rupee notes. Another constable who has remained at the station for the day does the same, revealing a much thinner pile. They do a count of their *kaalaa daan* (black money) earnings from petty bribes and then, to my astonishment, engage in a kind of redistributive division of spoils, with Virendra giving the station-bound constable some of his cash. When I ask why they are exchanging their black money earnings like this, one of the constables explains that they have no control over which duties they are assigned by the SO, and some people therefore have a greater opportunity to extract money from people—so they will sometimes divvy it up to settle small debts amongst themselves, or simply with the understanding that this is more "fair" to everyone in the long run. This redistribution is especially important because constables are often expected to pay their boss, the SO, regular sums in order to be assigned to duties that have more black money earning potential. Moreover, SOs often have to pay what is known as *thana hafta/monthly* (weekly or monthly payments) to *their* superiors, the district senior superintendents of police (SSPs), in order to keep their station chief posts.[22]

Constable Virendra then says to us, "one day, I'll show you how we take money . . . but no photos, and no names." We agree to the promissory note, then the constable adds with a giggle, "actually, maybe you *should* take photos . . . then the culprits will think we are with the press, capturing them in the act of trying to bribe us, and they'll have to give us even more money to keep quiet!" Eventually, the SO comes outside and we accompany him on an overnight patrol that, excepting stopping to investigate a fatal car accident near a local truck stop, is mostly uneventful. We return to CRT at about 3 a.m. and catch a few hours of sleep in the barracks.

The next morning, I wake and emerge from my temporary sleeping quarters to see more paperwork flurry happening outside: signing of orders that came overnight from the district SSP, continuation of the annual review process, checking of the station general diary and inventory in the armory, and so forth. As I watch, a constable approaches the tired-looking SO with a handwritten application requesting several days of leave from work. Yadav looks at it somewhat disdainfully, then refuses saying too many people are already on leave. He turns to me and explains that everyone is trying to take the remainder of their annual allotment of leave now, because it is almost January and whatever entitled leave may remain on someone's account will not roll over into the new year.[23]

The constable begins to plead, saying he needs three days to go to his faraway home village and retrieve a personal motorcycle that he can use for work since CRT only has one jeep.[24] Upon hearing this, Yadav relents a bit and says, "Okay, I'll give you two days if you like, but not three. I can only give you three when there are not so many people already away." The constable becomes angry and rips his application up in front of the SO before stomping off.

Yadav becomes visibly angry himself and shouts after the constable, "Have you gone crazy!? Don't you know what power I have? I don't need a *lathi* (truncheon), I can use my pen to punish you if you become undisciplined . . ."

The SO then turns to the group milling around outside CRT and continues his rant.

"What's wrong with all you people wanting leave now? If I give leave to everyone who wants it at the same time, I'll have to shut down the station!"

As the morning wears on, I hear continued grumblings among constables about how they are on call 24/7 and can never get leave when they request it. As I watch, at least five more CRT staff approach the SO to request leave. They are all rebuffed, including a woman constable in her mid-fifties who took over the post when her son was killed in the line of duty. (She is the only female personnel member I've met at CRT, except for a

sub-inspector trainee stationed there for a few months of in-field training.) I understand the SO's logic but find myself increasingly offended by
his seemingly dismissive demeanor. My indignation mixes with exhaus-
tion and boredom in a way that seems to mirror the expressions of the
police themselves.[25] This malaise intensifies when I learn that the *barda
khaanaa* that I have been "voluntold" to host will happen later in the day
than I expected.[26] This displeases me greatly, both because I am already
very hungry—a common occurrence when I'm with CRT police, who tend
to snack on small bits of junk food on a catch-as-catch-can basis for lack of
time and money for full meals—and also because I want to take my own
leave and make the long journey home before dark since the roads can be
dangerous, especially at night. But Yadav says he has told "the men" that
the feast will happen around 5–6 p.m.

I become increasingly ill-tempered as morning turns into afternoon,
which eventually compels my assistant to suggest that he ride the ten kilometers into town to grab us some snacks. He brings back some overripe
bananas and bottled water and tells Chhottu, the station chief's personal
servant, to make us some lunch. I immediately feel guilty, like a pompous *memsaheb* (colonial era madam) ordering servants around. My remorse
and self-loathing are compounded when Yadav later relates that the CRT
staff are expressing great pleasure about the forthcoming party, delighted
that they will have the unusual privilege of a full meal just prior to evening patrol.

After a lunch of rice and *daal*, my assistant and I head back toward the
nearby market. We have agreed to deliver some of the SO's money to a
bank there and think the errand might afford an opportunity talk to some
CRT police who are on what is known as "picket duty," serving as sentries
along the roadside at strategic spots that may be specially subject to highway robbery. Across the road from a State Bank of India outpost, we begin
chatting up a constable named Vikram, who is in his early twenties and
about six months out of training.[27] We learn that at least half a dozen other
people in Vikram's family are in the police: three uncles, two cousins, and
his brother. When I ask how he likes the job, I note that unlike many of
his more seasoned colleagues he still carries a somewhat hopeful tone, although he indicates that he is becoming more disillusioned day by day.
Despite his expressed childhood dreams of being a hero nabbing criminals, he indicates that in less than one year, he has found the job trying and
disappointing and had the all-too-common experience of superiors taking
credit for his own good work of catching a thief.

"Now, I have to be practical," he sighs. He says his wife is "in poor health" and has already lost two babies. Their home villages are far away, and they are struggling with rent payments, having been unable to secure the much in-demand subsidized police housing. "Now, I want to learn one thing only," he says. "I want to learn how to make [black] money." We tell him how his older colleague, Virendra, promised yesterday to show us how he takes money, and say, "Maybe he can show you as well." Vikram expresses hope that this will come to pass. "People will exploit you," he continues, "so, you have to survive. It is good that there are so many criminals out there . . . people who are doing something wrong will always give money—we [police] don't even need to ask."

As if the gods hear him and want to give us an illustration, just a few minutes later an ox-drawn cart with an obviously oversized (and therefore illegal) load of grain approaches on the main road, slowly moving in the direction of the city. A middle-aged farmer sitting next to the driver leaps off of the raggedy makeshift seat, runs up to Vikram, and surreptitiously tries to shove a Rs.20 note (worth less than US$0.50) into the constable's hand, muttering, "*le lijiye, saheb, le lijiye*" (please, sir, take this [and let us pass without botheration]). Vikram seems embarrassed, probably because two anthropologists are present and watching, and pushes the man away, not looking in his eyes. But, eventually, he takes the money, saying to us somewhat sheepishly as the cart trundles by, "Why not? See, he is giving it . . . this is how it is . . . it's part of 'the system.'"

As we continue talking, Vikram expresses great respect for SO Yadav, calling him "guru" (mentor). He relates how Yadav took care of him when he had a bad accident on his motorbike and how one day, when he made a rookie mistake, the SO shouted at him but did not write a negative note in his annual confidential roll, a professional record that follows each individual officer for his entire career. When I ask him about the problem of taking leave witnessed earlier, he says that the SO knows who is malingering and who is truly in need of leave and that all three times he has requested leave he really needed, his boss granted it. Vikram speaks of the SO admiringly, saying that he is like a father.

"Your real family is at the *thana*," he concludes.

I tell him that I hope he will return to CRT for the *barda khaanaa* we are planning, and that we have to head back since it will start soon.

The winter sun is setting as we return to the station, and the police community is bustling with activity. The CRT grounds contain not only the station proper but also several dozen units of police family housing, all painted the same pastel yellow as the station office and shaded by a few sparse trees. Most of the living quarters are one-room flats reserved for families of constables, and there are a few two-room units for sub-inspectors' families, which altogether form a kind of police village. During the day, I often witness police wives walking around, hanging clothes to dry, tossing rice in baskets, shelling peas or preparing other vegetables for dinner, gossiping with each other about mundane things, complaining about (or relaxing and delighting in) not seeing their husbands for weeks because the men are on duty out-of-station. In many ways, it is like any other village, except that the ostensible calm is routinely interrupted by things like complainants arriving to report alleged crimes or demand resolution of disputes; visits by persons trying to demonstrate or acquire social influence (over police themselves, or over others by virtue of being friendly with police); and the audible or even visible beating or coercion of suspected criminals or their associates inside or outside of the station.[28]

The CRT police village is also brimming with dozens of children of all ages. They run around playing games, climbing trees or any other available structure. Sometimes they sit on the station steps or even the chairs and other furniture when not occupied by officers and visitors. Occasionally they steal into the newly built but unused "interrogation room" during games of hide and seek. Every so often, a uniformed cop on duty will bark at them to get down off the high boundary wall or not eat those berries off the bush, or just to scram, as Bollywood pop songs blare over someone's radio. This evening, the CRT village is quite lively, and kids keep trying to peek into the station mess room to watch the constable Prithvi, Chhottu, and a third man that has been hired from outside preparing food for the police officer feast. The kids are especially intrigued by me, a foreign woman speaking Hindi, and they do things like ask for my autograph and photograph.

After sundown, around 6 p.m., the food is finally ready. Prithvi and crew have cooked a tasty variety of rich vegetarian fare—*matar paneer* (peas and cheese cubes), mixed vegetables, *chana dal* (chickpeas), *puuri* (deep fried bread), *pullao* (fried rice vegetable mix), and *gulab jaman* (balls of baked cream slathered in sugar cane syrup) for dessert—and laid out a gorgeous spread. It all cost me approximately Rs. 1300 (US$20). About thirty CRT staff come to eat, and in an unusual and purposeful role reversal, SO Yadav makes it a point to serve his subordinates from one of the dishes. The CRT police eat while engaging in unusually demure conversation, standing up in the yard in front of the station rather than sitting down. When they finish their meals most of them make it a point to fold their hands in my direction in an obliging *namaste* gesture before returning to duty. I feel pleased, secretly wishing that I had come up with the idea to provide the feast myself rather than feeling compelled to sponsor it by one of my most important interlocutors.

Personal Policing and Fictive Kinship

The above recounting of a day (and a half) in the life of a small police station in northern India shows how everyday police work and institutional decision making are shaped by, and productive of, many social forms other than violence, governmentality or official-legal proceduralism. Most of the daily interactions I observed at CRT were configured by extralegal, unofficial, or quasi-official forces and relations, things like calculations of personal or professional interest; compulsions of ordinary life like wage earnings and domestic upkeep; and ad hoc decisions based less on formal laws and more on hunches, experiences, biases, and dynamics specific to a local context. The everyday goings on at CRT—only a small snapshot of which are related here—show how personal considerations, especially status position and range of influence, shape everything from evidence production and case investigation to professional policies and fellow feeling among police officers. It thus becomes clear how, *pace* Max Weber's figuration of the ideal typical rule-following "impersonal bureaucrat"[29]—which is certainly present at CRT and in most other sites of policing in UP, in various manifestations—policing is in fact intensely "personal." And while none of the personal forces and relations related here are necessarily or exclusively linked with kinship networks or sensibilities, they were often expressed more or less explicitly in some version of this social idiom. In tandem with an examination of some of the sources and implications of personal policing in northern India, I explore here how the idiom of kinship—and its attendant experiences and expressions of mutual obligation, faltering compassion, guilt, and resentment—may take various forms: actual blood ties, fictive familial bonds, professional membership, and also a peculiar form that I am calling "ethnographic kinship" between the anthropologist and (some of) her interlocutors.

As demonstrated in his arbitrations of local disputes and requests for leave from subordinates, the CRT station chief's standards of evidence often had little to do with legal documentation or forensic science. They tended instead to rest on things like the immediately apparent credibility and internal consistency of peoples' stories, the personal reputation of the subjects or their representatives, and his own gut feelings based on fifteen years of experience. "It is a common thing to do," Yadav says when I inquire about his acting as arbiter in the three cases described. "In fact, both the police and the people usually find it much more efficient than going to court. It is not a legal process, but much of our work is done this way."

Of course another "standard of evidence" is his own self-interest. Returning to the Trivedi land dispute case, Yadav suggests that it would be foolish of him to incur the ire of this local big man and patron of many who, if insulted, might then wield his influence to punish the SO in some way, perhaps by sabotaging his police work, smearing his reputation, or even working to have him removed from his leadership post. The problem of outside influence on and politicization of bureaucratic postings is often claimed as the bête noire of the police profession in India (and among the civil services more generally), especially among officers at the rank of sub-inspector and above.[30] If an appointed official offends someone with *pahunch* (influence or "reach" in the social field), then he is likely to be punished in some way, usually a transfer to an undesirable or even dangerous post.

Such conditions index a social field in which personal relationships and reputations, shifting status positions, ongoing resource exchange, and forces of mutual obligation fundamentally constitute order and authority. Analysis of these forms of sociality mark a well-worn path in anthropological research, which has only recently begun to focus directly on the life worlds of police. One of the insights ethnography of police produces is an understanding that their relationships and acts may not be reduced to purely instrumental or coercive exchanges, nor to simple patron-client interactions between powerful state representatives and hapless citizens, nor to dominance and violent oppression writ large. As my observations show, the authority of public police in India is as fractured and fraught as it is among many other imagined or represented communities. This social fact relates to other sources of authority and influence, such as that of Trivedi in this context. It is also manifest among police themselves, as we can see in the tense interactions around subordinates requesting leave from work.

It is crucial to understand that police engagements with one another may be just as compassionate, convivial, detached, distrustful, or exploitative as they may be with individual members or communal sections of the broader public. The more negative side of this relational spectrum is clearly visible in what has been called the "market for public office"[31] and the institution of *thana hafta/monthly*, the paying of an illegal tariff up the ladder of the police hierarchy in order to obtain or maintain a particular position that may allow some kind of personal or professional advancement, such as earning black money or making connections with powerful persons.[32] The potentially positive side of this spectrum is evidenced by the

CRT constables' evening redistribution of black money earnings. In relation to the public, this exchange seems to be little more than fallout from systemic corruption. But this simple reading is belied by the exchange with Vikram the "rookie" constable on picket duty, who first passively receives then actively accepts a petty bribe from persons knowingly breaking the law and actively trying to pacify him, a common interaction that he and others describe as "part of 'the system.'"[33]

A less normative and perhaps more empathetic reading of the black money redistribution exercise is the way it indexes, if not a shadowy side of police esprit de corps, then certainly some kind of communal identification or fellow feeling among subordinate police. This feeling may be especially strong and durable among police who have worked together in the field or are members of the same caste, religious, or regional community. And it is often quite robust among police who occupy comparable positions in the official rank hierarchy of four levels among which there is little to no upward mobility, especially when one occupies the lowest rung of the ladder as a constable.

There is a tacit understanding among police across India that the subordinate ranks, especially the constables who comprise more than 90 percent of the force, "serve" their senior officers personally as well as professionally.[34] This generally involuntary and unofficial or quasi-official servility results in a normalization of what I observed to be the parallel positions of Constable Prithvi and SO Yadav's personal servant, Chhottu, in organizing the exceptional CRT *barda khaanaa*, and in other more ordinary elements of daily life around the police station and its area of jurisdiction. Such conflation of official and unofficial duties has inspired among some subordinate police negative charges of indignity and even slavery.[35] But the other more positive side of this coin entails an experience of such relationships through idioms of mutually obliged donor-servant and even familial bonds.[36]

Constable Prithvi is actually well known among CRT police as one of SO Yadav's favorite *hamraahi* (traveling companion) associates, someone whom the station chief entrusts with the most important tasks and with whom he feels an observable fraternal connection. The constable was at once like a brother and a servant to the SO. A crucial reason for the development of this relationship was that Prithvi had been posted at CRT longer than any other staff member, including and especially Yadav himself. Prithvi therefore had the most well-entrenched relationships with local authority figures and the most wide ranging network of confidential informants, and so he was most likely to be able to "get the job done" whatever said job entailed, officially or unofficially. His special *hamraahi* status in relation to the station chief hinged largely on his professional aptitude as a function of personal capabilities and avenues of access. Another kind of bond between police of different ranks combining a fictive familial relationship with professional membership was a mapping of official rank onto kinship categories of descent. Recall constable Vikram's claim that he looks up to Yadav as a father figure who, while sometimes harsh with his disciplinary measures, is also a fair, knowledgeable, and supportive caretaker. Vikram further claims the CRT staff and the police organization more generally as his "family."

These relations of kinship and intimacy among some CRT police are not necessarily present at every station or among all police coworkers. But over many years of fieldwork, I have observed such bonds expressed among police commonly enough to feel confident in saying they are not an aberration. And they are in keeping with the village-like spatial and social organization of police stations like CRT—with its aforementioned family housing units immediately juxtaposed to the station office. Importantly, due to the aforementioned shortage of available subsidized housing for police families, people would receive—and usually quickly accept—offers of housing on station grounds other than those where the officer was actually posted. This meant that the police posted at CRT and most other stations like it were routinely in contact with, and often watching over, the family members of colleagues posted elsewhere, extending the idea of the police "as family" across a wide geospatial area.

Such expressions of kinship and community are also in keeping with modes of everyday sociality in India more broadly. It is worth noting that even some Hindi slang terms for police draw on kinship idioms: police station chiefs like Yadav are often referred to informally as *mama* (maternal uncle) or *dada* (paternal grandfather), specifically indexing their authoritative status buttressed by the potential to use coercion.[37] Many Hindi speakers also refer to jail as *sasu-raal*, or the home of one's in-laws, more or less ironically. But even more generally, people unrelated by blood or descent routinely refer to each other using kinship terms like *baba* (grandfather), *beta* (son), or *bhai* (brother). Even as an American researcher, when I am in the field I am often immediately likened to someone's *beti* (daughter) or *didi* (sister) or *mausi* (aunt), depending on their age and our relationship, and I am not infrequently addressed with such terms by personal friends, friends of friends, shop owners, or even occasional strangers on the street. Some of the CRT and other UP police that I have come to know well, especially SO Yadav, seemed to relate to me in this way also. However, the police never addressed me directly using kinship terms. There was something more unusual and unnamed about the forms of kinship that developed between my interlocutors and me. What I call our "ethnographic kinship" manifested in a variety of ways and most often involved a kind of paternalism by police claiming that I need to be "protected" from dangerous situations, or "taught" like a student, or given what seemed like unofficial "orders." In the next section, I will examine how this peculiar, if not unique, set of kinship forms configured both our day-to-day interactions in the field—especially the seemingly odd fluctuations in our affective and power relations—and also the configurations of my ethnographic foci and analyses.

Ethnographic Kinship and Critical Empathy

My relationship to SO Yadav in particular, and to the CRT and other UP police more generally, occasionally may have borne some similarities to other anthropologists, especially women, who have been "adopted" by families in the field.[38] But my relationships with police interlocutors were also distinct from these types of fictive kinship relations in at least two ways. First, we never explicitly referred to one another or to our relationships in kin terms: I did not call them "uncle" or "brother" and they did not address me directly as an inter- or intragenerational female relative. Whatever the character and quality of our kinship, it went unspoken and unnamed. Second, the police organization itself generally is not structured around familial and genealogical bonds but rather based on very different kinds of exchange relationships and purposes related to social order, boundary maintenance, security, surveillance and knowledge production. Still, considering my (and perhaps others') relationships with people associated with this public institution in terms of "ethnographic kinship" may help us think critically not only about vital forces and relations constituting the worlds of policing but also about the history and dynamics of conducting ethnographic research in and of said worlds.

When I felt compelled by SO Yadav to go to Trivedi's lavish party, I experienced a host of feelings that seemed to resonate with subordinate police officers when they were disallowed things they desired or needed (like taking leave from work), or forced to do things they would rather not do (like carrying out assignments that do not earn them much black money). I ultimately found the party attendance worthwhile since it allowed me to observe the demonstration of power and influence by a nonstate actor over police and other government officials. But because I initially thought it would comprise little but a diversion from what I felt I really needed to be doing as an ethnographer of police in the field—i.e., observing the goings on at the CRT police station—I felt irritated and restricted, like a powerless child being pushed by their parent to do something that seemed arbitrary and unfair and in conflict with my personal desires and professional goals as an anthropologist. At the same time, I felt grateful to be given access to this world of policing and invited along as "one of the gang" not only to events like Trivedi's party but also to crime scene investigations and raids and other spaces of both official police work and unofficial engagement.[39] In other words, I also felt empowered as an ethnographer in the field, at least somewhat. The tension wrought by my feeling simultaneously empowered and disempowered made me more sensitive to the possibility of this experience among my interlocutors themselves, especially subordinate ranking police.

Following my obligation to attend Trivedi's party, the next time I experienced a kind of forced participation in the more "personal" side of policing was less than twenty-four hours later, when Yadav decided I was going to throw CRT a Christmas party. This placed me in a rather different kind of awkward position, that of compelled feast sponsor rather than compelled feast guest. Again, while I felt disempowered in a way, benignly coerced to pay for the party, in the end I also felt empowered as a kind of gift giver, as someone not just "taking" things from my interlocutors but also participating in a productive and positively charged exchange with them.[40] Ironically, my sponsorship of the feast seemed to constitute me as a kind of minor patron in a way I did not expect. I wondered: Did this gift of a communal meal make my interlocutors feel obliged to serve or defer to me, by giving me access to their life worlds, or in other ways? Was it a sign of some other kind of bond(age)? How did CRT police understand and relate to me, a foreign female scholar who was so extraordinarily "other" in their world? Did the police perceive me as somehow similar to Trivedi, the local big man known as a potentially benevolent ally but also as a generally coercive and corrupt figure?[41]

In the final analysis, I would answer the last question with a resounding "no" even if there were some substantial resemblances between myself and the local big man. My potential likeness to Trivedi in relation to the CRT police was strongly countered not only by my extreme Other-ness as a non-local American anthropologist, but also by the peculiar form that my ethnographic kinship with them took, primarily as a function of the initiation of my relationship with CRT, my age, and my gender. I was introduced to the CRT station chief by a junior relative of his, someone from a descendant generation in his family, and this was a fact known to all of the SO's subordinates. For this reason, our relationship was understood to be not only relatively informal and personal, even familial if fictively so, but also one in which Yadav was explicitly constituted as a kind of authority figure in relation to me as a younger person. No such relationship existed between Yadav and other CRT police, or between the CRT police and Trivedi. So the only way in which Trivedi and I might have been seen as similar would be as sometimes patrons of police who are also potentially subject to criminal legal penalties if the latter decided to exercise their legal authority over us (which in relation to Trivedi, recall, Yadav deemed it prudent not to do, and there was no comparable case of a criminal allegation levied against me). In any case, I was no "big man" to them, and never would be.

Gender also played a significant role in configuring my ethnographic kinship with my interlocutors. SO Yadav, and by association many of his subordinates, seemed to view me as something like an oddball daughter or niece, or (if the officers were younger in age) as analogous to a sister or cousin, from an exotic faraway land. As already indicated, the SO sometimes treated me the way elders treat their children, telling me what/not to do, where/not to go, with whom/not to interact. My interactions with police were also gendered in a broader sense, arguably barring my access from certain types of interactions. The fact that I was a younger woman and could never fully be "one of the boys" as some other police ethnographers have explicitly claimed or implicitly expressed themselves to be[42] meant that I could not always "participate" as a man of comparable status and age might be able to do. While some might see this as a platform to raise questions about how "deep" my access actually was, or even how "valid" my ethnography is, I would turn the question around and ask: How has a historically masculinist bias in ethnographies of policing, and in policing studies more generally, shaped this field of study?[43] Addressing this question comprehensively would reach far beyond the scope of this chapter, but it is a worthy endeavor that I hope will begin in earnest sooner than later. It is also worth noting that more women are now doing ethnographic fieldwork on policing than ever before, as evidenced in part by the demographic composition of the contributors to this volume.[44]

The fact that I am a woman meant that in the context of doing ethnography of police life in northern India—where women are widely positioned as the "weaker sex" or "second class citizens" and subordinated to men in various ways—I was probably not taken very seriously or seen as a threat by most of my interlocutors. While this lack of authority-cum-fear was sometimes frustrating for me, the likelihood that it made the police let down their guard around me was arguably a crucial component, if not the very foundation, of my unusually deep and sustained access to everyday life at CRT, and in other sites of policing throughout the course of my fieldwork in UP. Though the feminist in me detested it, I accepted the lack of agency that my subordinate gendered status often made me feel as a kind of strategic trade-off. I would venture to claim that had I had a more "official" license to observe police as a man, or had I had a more formally distant relationship with the CRT police, divorced from a sense of fictive kinship with them, then I may have had *more* access to their world in certain instances—like perhaps being permitted to accompany police on potentially "dangerous" missions, which they often refused claiming they wanted to "protect" me[45]—but *less* access in other ways, like being able to come and go as I pleased; residing on station grounds for extensive periods (not unlike the family members of police living in CRT housing); being invited to officers' homes to meet their spouses and children; reading whatever CRT registers and files I wished; and observing and questioning the best and worst of everyday life both inside and outside of the police station. The gendered, quasi-familial, mostly unofficial form that my ethnographic kinship with the police took on opened a space for tagging along and being taught about everyday ways and means.

Even though I experienced this peculiar kind of kinship with police—which included the acquisition of humorous or even quasi-affectionate nicknames like "*baijayanthi*" (a kind of flower associated with the garland of Lord Vishnu) or "*chaaval pito*" (literally: the imperative to "beat rice," a joke formulated by an officer when he learned how to spell my first name in English)—there is no doubt that I always remained distinctly foreign and outside of what might be understood as the police community, especially in relation to subordinate CRT police and to those police that I did not see on a regular basis at the station or in the areas under its jurisdiction. Some police even continued to call me "Madam" or to address me with other formal honorifics like adding "ji" to the end of my name throughout my fieldwork tenure (and who knows what names and words were used out of my earshot). I heard rumors that other people never let go of a suspicion that I might be some sort of spy for a foreign government or intelligence agency, or for the media, or for a human rights or some other watchdog organization. The symbolism of my sponsorship of the CRT *barda khaanaa* may have even reinforced my potentially suspicious otherness, for various reasons: the unprecedented character of the feast itself; the resemblance and proximity in time it held to the exclusive and elite gathering hosted by

Trivedi; and the sheer fact that my contribution was primarily a monetary sum, which generates both a "rational economic" and hierarchical type of social distance.

That said, as indicated above I feel confident that the Christmas party also shrunk or changed, even if it could not foreclose, the social distance between my police interlocutors and me. It created a sense of mutual provision and cooperation that, while often still marked by reservation and a critical or even mistrustful regard for "the other," paved the way for a productive exchange of information and mutual, if not perfectly reciprocal, access to life worlds. Such a simultaneously productive and apprehensive connection may be a product of many extensive ethnographic encounters.[46] In this context it may also have been related to the fact that while acts of sharing provisions and eating together are some of the most fundamental modes of producing and reinforcing intimate relations, concepts of consumption are also associated explicitly with corruption, greed, and other negative relations. Indeed, one of the most commonly used Hindi phrases for taking a bribe is *ghuus khaanaa*, literally to "eat" a bribe. In any case, I experienced a palpable increase in informal exchanges of knowledge and access to the CRT police world following the feast I sponsored and attended.

It was only later that I realized how the *barda khaanaa* experience resonated strongly with my childhood participation along with members of my own family in similar kinds of communal gatherings among current or former military personnel in Midwestern and mid-Atlantic America. When I was in primary school in Cincinnati, Ohio, each year my family would make it a point to attend my father's official US Army reserve unit annual Christmas party and summer picnic. In 2012, following my brother's deployment to Iraq several years earlier, I also attended a similar gathering with his unit in Philadelphia, Pennsylvania. These types of gatherings would be officially sponsored by the military institution as a means of building cohesion and fellow feeling among soldiers and their families. And my engagements with other unofficial types of gatherings of current or former military personnel in other places, like veterans reunions across the country or social media sites for soldiers online, have also raised my consciousness of the dynamics of ethnographic kinship across time and space and shaped my analysis of it and of things like personal policing in profound ways that I did not anticipate.

Since 2001, my father has been traveling to the American Midwest for annual reunions with members of his US Army company who deployed to Vietnam between 1968 and 1971. These meetings of former combat veterans are self-organized rather than officially sponsored by the army, but some of the general effects are the same: exchange of resources and knowledge and the production and reinforcement of social bonds amidst consumption of food and drink. In 2008, the year my brother deployed to Iraq, I began accompanying my father to ethnographically study and film the dynamics of these reunions as a kind of "native anthropologist."[47] These gatherings can be extremely emotional for many of the men, especially for those veterans who may be attending and reuniting with their former co-soldiers for the first time. Similar to—though more explicitly than—some of the CRT police with whom I spend many months in the field, many of the veterans who attend these reunions have expressed strong feelings of kinship with one another, some even saying aloud that my father is their brother, and by association I am like their daughter/niece. This more explicit experience of "biographical ethnographic kinship" with US combat veterans made salient my more implicit experience of "interlocutor ethnographic kinship" with UP police such that I began to consider in new ways how my unusual position in relation to my interlocutors configured both my and their experiences in the field, as well as my modes and objects of analysis of data gathered during fieldwork.

In addition to deepening the bonds of ethnographic kinship with my interlocutors, the Christmas feast I sponsored also seemed to affect relationships among the police themselves, allowing for things like the unusual role reversal of the station chief serving the rank and file. SO Yadav indicated that he enjoyed the rare opportunity to provide such a treat to his "men," and though we never discussed it, I later wondered if our being able to cooperatively offer a small pleasure to CRT subaltern staff allowed Yadav and I to share a kind of relief of guilt (for very different reasons) regarding our everyday relationships with our interlocutors. For me, it offered an exceptional chance to provide something to persons who had been allowing me to enter their life world for several months, and would continue to do so for many more months; for the station chief, it may have been a way to bolster morale and compensate for, among other causes of disaffection, the day's earlier frustrations regarding many peoples' failed efforts to request leave from work.

Such tense interactions between officers and subordinates were not unique to CRT; they were echoed multiple times during my fieldwork. In one case I witnessed, the officer disallowing subordinates to take leave was extremely abusive, calling them lazy, lying cheats and alleging that they were fabricating stories in order to evade work. While Yadav's response was not so extreme, there was a resemblance to the former case in the way many of the constables trembled and pleaded, or fell silent and sullen, as they foresaw their failure to obtain leave. This visible and audible discomfort resonated with other instances I had witnessed of both public and private humiliation of police, which took various forms including defiance, insult, or even physical abuse of police—especially, though not exclusively, low-ranking police—by well-connected persons or suspects. I also saw many other instances of senior officials not taking subordinates seriously, to say nothing of the abysmal living and working conditions I knew many of the latter suffered from my visits to their barracks or home villages or places of work.[48]

While anyone might find this sort of thing depressing or upsetting, I found it acutely so. Though it was only subconscious at the time, I later realized that such interactions probably reminded me of when I would see my father come home from the US Army recruiting office where he worked as a low-level functionary, dejected at being abused by his superior officers for having trouble meeting his quotas—or when I would not see him at all for an extended duration because he was posted away from home, in central America or on some other US military base. Amidst these challenging or humiliating experiences, my father would still express a kind of pride in his identity as an army soldier, which was explicitly linked with both his deployment to Vietnam and his intergenerational ties to the military institution (his father was also in the US Navy, and his son, my brother, would later join the US Army as well).

These childhood memories of mine were recalled with a force I did not anticipate in many of my observations of and interactions with CRT constables in UP, especially Vikram. My interaction with him also reminded me in unexpected ways of my father enduring things like low pay resulting in financial struggles at home, and his experience of a lack of avenues, or being unceremoniously and inexplicably passed over, for promotion, which resulted in low morale and professional frustration. This intersection of biographical kinship with interlocutor kinship as interwoven forms of "ethnographic kinship" led me to identify and empathize with UP police in disconcerting ways that I did not expect. I had to reconcile this unnamed complex of identification and empathy with police with my observations of them doing things like extorting money or other resources from crime victims, neglecting people in need of help, or even actively abusing people in ways that might involve physical violence. The concomitant pathos that developed was only partly voluntary and often caused me great discomfort and anxiety, especially considering the fact that the persons with whom I shared it were notorious for brutal, corrupt, discriminatory, and neglectful behavior as public servants.

In an attempt to navigate and understand my ongoing disquiet as an ethnographer of police, I developed in my analysis a sensibility of critical empathy: the ability to approximately understand and explain the perceptions and practices of others while simultaneously maintaining a measure of distance that allows for critique or even active intervention or obstruction if needed. Some might consider this a contradiction in terms, or argue that it is an impossible balance to strike, claiming that one cannot be sufficiently critical of the affiliations, actions, and expressions of one's interlocutors (to say nothing of the conditions in which they operate) while also being genuinely empathetic with said interlocutors. Such a dismissal assumes a problematic, and arguably positivist, ideal of "objectivity" as either the illusion of moral or political neutrality or the removal of the self from scientific analysis, an assumption that has long been outmoded in anthropological inquiry and has arguably begun to spread among other more "qualitatively" oriented fields or subfields of social science that have taken up ethnographic methods. Further explication of the contours of critical empathy, and perhaps some pragmatic guidelines for its conscious deployment in ethnographic fieldwork and writing about the world of policing, will be a crucial part of the continued development of this field of inquiry.

Conclusion

Critical empathy developed in fieldwork encounters—especially though not exclusively through forms of biographical and interlocutor ethnographic kinship—may serve as an important tool for building and refining analytical frameworks like that discussed here as "personal policing" and like the concept of "provisional authority" that I develop elsewhere.[49] Understanding and active utilization of these fraught forms of intimacy and identification may be especially productive for anthropologists and other ethnographers who choose to answer the call of studying less savory subjects, social institutions, and interlocutors, like police, military, intelligence or other security-oriented agents. More than "critical detachment" as an index of so-called objectivity,[50] and as much as the "combination of presence and distance,"[51] critical empathy is crucial to crafting any ethnography worth its salt, no matter who one's interlocutors may be. It seems an internally contradictory concept, involving both sharing in another's experience while being separated from it enough to interrogate and critique it.

And it is not without its limits or drawbacks: it may lead to various forms of "missing the forest for the trees," or preclude the ethnographer from asking certain kinds of questions of herself or her interlocutors, or even place one in morally or physically dangerous situations one would not otherwise enter or remain within.

For all of these possible pitfalls, critical empathy also opens analytical and ethical doors that might otherwise remain locked or even hidden to ethnographers, and it offers vital opportunities for creating new knowledge about the worlds of policing and other human worlds. While I feel it is my job as an anthropologist to analyze how things like physical violence, structural violence, discriminatory othering, and social inequality work *through* "the police" *on* and *against* "the policed," I also cannot abide abstract, overdetermined, or polarized views of police as embodying nothing but the "ignoble" force of law, the originary violence of state sovereignty who "make law" through coercion and the suspension of an idealized distinction between the norm and the exception.[52] I am unable and unwilling to ignore—or, spun more positively, I am able and willing to attend to—how violence and inequality subjectivize the police as vulnerable humans, too. This remains one of many under-researched and controversial theses related to police, which I hope that my own work, and the work of others including many of the contributors to this volume, will help begin to rectify.

Notes

1. I thank participants in the Ethnography and Policing Workshop at the Institute for Advanced Studies, especially Susana Durão and Didier Fassin, for comments on earlier drafts of this chapter. I would also like to thank an anonymous reviewer for questions and comments that helped push me to clarify the concepts explored herein.
2. I have been conducting research on the political and legal history of India generally since 2000 and began scholarly research on police practice in northern India in 2004. The longest period of sustained fieldwork with police in Uttar Pradesh occurred over eighteen months in 2006 and 2007, with follow-up field trips to India in 2009, 2010, and 2013. While back in the United States in 2008, I began an ongoing research project on the subjectivities and figurations of American combat veterans. The two projects are not directly related, though there is some overlap in the motivations and questions.
3. Jauregui 2010a; Jauregui 2010b; Jauregui 2010c.
4. Police organizations in India are still modeled on the 1861 Police Act, which was constructed by a commission consisting of both military leaders and civilian administrators.
5. Weber 1991 (1918)b; Weber 1991 (1918)c.

6.   Cf. McCargo, chapter 9, this volume.
7.   Cf. Geertz 1973; Marcus 1997; and Favret-Saada 2012, respectively.
8.   Robben 1995, 85–86. See also Robben 1996; McNamara and Rubenstein 2011.
9.   Jauregui 2013b.
10. Cf. Fosher 2010.
11. Clifford and Marcus 1986.
12. Behar 1996, 20.
13. Cf. Roitman 2005; Roitman 2006.
14. Jauregui 2013b.
15. Bradford et al., 2016.
16. See Bittner 1970; Muir 1977; Benjamin 1978 (1922); Klockars 1980; Westmarland 2001; Derrida 2002; Jauregui 2013b.
17. Jauregui, 2016.
18. Jauregui 2015.
19. Names of persons and local places have been changed.
20. See Jauregui 2014a and Jauregui 2016 for further detailed accounts of the Trivedi land dispute case and the dowry and drunken conflict cases.
21. Almost all of our verbal interactions occur in Hindi, which I have translated into English for readability, occasionally including the original Hindi phrasing if I feel it has linguistic or lyrical value.
22. Cf. Gupta 1995; Wade 1982; Wade 1985.
23. See HRW 2009, 35 and *passim*, regarding widespread stress among constables around the inability to take leave.
24. As a rule, subordinate police personnel are not allowed to be posted in their home district, in order to prevent the corruption that many presume comes with personal or vested interests. So, most constables and sub-inspectors live and work quite far from home and apart from their families.
25. On policing and boredom see Fassin 2013.
26. I first learned from my father the term "voluntold," derived from military slang indicating being forcibly volunteered for a task by a superior.
27. For further details of this exchange see Jauregui 2016.
28. Jauregui 2013b.
29. Weber 1991 (1918)a.
30. Jauregui, 2016. See also Singh 2000; Verma 2005; Dhillon 2005.
31. For more on the "market for public office" in India, see Wade 1982 and Wade 1985.
32. Importantly, bribes for posts and nonmaterial exchanges of favors do not simply flow up the police chain of command (cf. Gupta 1995); they also flow out and around among a variety of provisional power holders both within and outside of the police institution. See Jauregui 2016.
33. For further reading on the social legitimation of corruption see Jauregui 2014b. See also Roitman 2006.
34. Jauregui 2016.
35. Ghosh 1981; Baxi 1982; Subramanian 1988; Chande 1997.
36. See Piliavsky 2014.
37. *Dadagiri* is a Hindi slang term for bullying or generally coercive behavior, character-istic of *goondas* (from which the term "goon" is derived), hoodlums, or gangsters. *Dada*, paternal grandfather, also signifies a "big man" in general; when combined with "*-giri*" (or "*-gari*"), a noun formant that means "one who practices," the word

harbors connotations of one whose practice exhibits the often coercive authority of an elder male, for better or worse.

38. See Briggs 1970; Golde 1970; Kan 2001; High 2010.
39. Early on in my days of participant observation at CRT, SO Yadav actually organized a party at a local resort for *me* as an honored guest and a few members of the station staff. He was friendly with the resort owner and apparently wanted to impress me with a sumptuous meal in a posh setting, even going so far as to procure the "forbidden fruit" of alcohol, which is not only banned among on duty police but also, like meat, viewed as morally corrupt among many Hindus and Muslims. There was no alcohol or meat at the CRT Christmas feast I sponsored.
40. For a provocative analysis of dynamics of exposure, exchange, and expectation between anthropologists and interlocutors, with a focus on "the 'spectral return' of that which gifts and other kindnesses [especially those offered by the anthropologist to her interlocutors] seek to repress," see High 2010, 308.
41. Besides SO Yadav's expressed reticence to offend this man, many months later, I learned from another constable that he had been defied and severely beaten by Trivedi and some of his brothers. See Jauregui 2013a and 2016.
42. Cf. Martin 2013; Moskos 2008; Hobbs 1998; Young 1991; Van Maanen and Manning 1978; Muir 1977; Bittner 1970.
43. I thank an anonymous reviewer for comments inspiring me to foreground this question.
44. See also Eckert 2005; Hautzinger 2007 and 2016; Westmarland 2001; Robb Larkins 2015.
45. Cf. Willis 2015.
46. Geertz 1968; Crapanzano 1977; Marcus 1997; High 2010.
47. Narayan 1993.
48. Jauregui 2013a. Even with recent pay raises, most constables in Uttar Pradesh have a monthly base salary of less than Rs.5000 (approximately US$80), which is barely above the national poverty line and extremely low in comparison with what some have called "working class standards" in India (Parry 2000).
49. Jauregui 2016.
50. Robben 1995, 86.
51. Fassin 2013, 5.
52. Das 2004; Derrida 2002; Agamben 1998 (1995); Benjamin 1978 (1922).

References

Agamben, Giorgio. 1998 [1995]. *Homo Sacer: Sovereign Power and Bare Life.* Palo Alto: Stanford University Press.

Baxi, Upendra. 1982. *The Crisis of the Indian Legal System.* Alternatives in Development Series: Law. New Delhi: Vikas Publishing House Pvt., Ltd.

Behar, Ruth. 1996. *The Vulnerable Observer: Anthropology That Breaks Your Heart.* Boston: Beacon Press.

Benjamin, Walter. 1978 [1922]. "Critique of Violence." In *Reflections: Essays, Aphorisms, Autobiographical Writings,* edited by Peter Demetz, 277–300. New York: Schocken.

Bittner, Egon. 1970. *The Functions of the Police in Modern Society.* Chevy Chase, MD: National Institute of Mental Health.

Bradford, Ben, Beatrice Jauregui, Ian Loader, and Jonny Steinberg. 2016. *The Handbook of Global Policing*. Sage.

Briggs, Jean L. 1970. "Kapluna Daughter." In *Women in the Field: Anthropological Experiences*, edited by Peggy Golde, 19–44. Berkeley: University of California Press.

Chande, M. B. 1997. *The Police in India*. New Delhi: Atlantic Publishers and Distributors.

Clifford, James, and George Marcus. 1986. *Writing Culture: The Poetics and Politics of Ethnography*. Berkeley: University of California Press.

Crapanzano, Vincent. 1977. "The Life History in Anthropological Field Work." *Anthropology and Humanism Quarterly* 2–3:3–17.

Das, Veena. 2004. "The Signature of the State: The Paradox of Illegibility." In *Anthropology in the Margins of the State*, edited by Veena Das and Deborah Poole, 225–52. Oxford, UK: Oxford University Press.

Derrida, Jacques. 2002. "Force of Law: The 'Mystical Foundation of Authority.'" In *Acts of Religion*, edited by Gil Anidjar, 228–98. New York: Routledge.

Dhillon, Kirpal. 2005. *Police and Politics in India: Colonial Concepts, Democratic Compulsions*. New Delhi: Manohar.

Eckert, Julia. 2005. "The *Trimurti* of the State: State Violence and the Promises of Order and Destruction." *Sociologus* 55 (2):181–217.

Fassin, Didier. 2013. "The Moral World of Law Enforcement." Occasional Paper no. 49. School of Social Science, Institute of Advanced Study, Princeton University.

Favret-Saada, Jeanne. 2012. "Being Affected." *HAU: Journal of Ethnographic Theory* 2 (1): 435–45.

Fosher, Kerry. 2010. "Yes, Both, Absolutely: A Personal and Professional Commentary on Anthropological Engagement with Military and Intelligence Organizations." In *Anthropology and Global Counterinsurgency*, edited by John D. Kelly, Beatrice Jauregui, Sean T. Mitchell, and Jeremy Walton, 261–72. Chicago: University of Chicago Press.

Geertz, Clifford. 1968. "Thinking as a Moral Act: Ethical Dimensions of Anthropological Fieldwork in the New States." *Antioch Review* 28(2): 139–59.

———. 1973. "Deep Play: Notes on the Balinese Cockfight." In *The Interpretation of Cultures*. New York: Basic Books.

Ghosh, S. K. 1981. *Police in Ferment*. New Delhi: Light and Life Publishers.

Golde, Peggy, ed. 1970. *Women in the Field: Anthropological Experiences*. Berkeley: University of California Press.

Gupta, Akhil. 1995. "Blurred Boundaries: The Discourse of Corruption, the Culture of Politics, and the Imagined State." *American Ethnologist* 22 (2): 375–402.

Hautzinger, Sarah. 2007. *Violence in the City of Women: Police and Batterers in Bahia, Brazil*. Berkeley: University of California Press.

———. 2016. "Policing by and for Women in Brazil and Beyond." In *The Handbook of Global Policing*, edited by Ben Bradford, Beatrice Jauregui, Ian Loader, and Jonny Steinberg. Sage.

High, Holly. 2010. "Ethnographic Exposures: Motivations for Donation in the South of Laos (and Beyond)." *American Ethnologist* 37 (2): 308–22.

Hobbs, Dick. 1998). *Doing the Business: Entrepreneurship, the Working Class, and Detectives in the East End of London*. Oxford, UK: Oxford University Press.

Human Rights Watch (HRW). 2009. *Broken System: Dysfunction, Abuse, and Impunity in the Indian Police*. Human Rights Watch no. 1-56432-518-0. August.

Jauregui, Beatrice. 2010a. "Bluing Green in the Maldives: Countering Insurgency by 'Civil'-izing Security." In *Anthropology and Global Counterinsurgency*, edited by John D.

Kelly, Beatrice Jauregui, Sean T. Mitchell, and Jeremy Walton, 23–38. Chicago: University of Chicago Press.

———. 2010b. "Categories of Conflict and Coercion: The Blue in Green and the Other." In *Anthropology and Global Counterinsurgency*, edited by John D. Kelly, Beatrice Jauregui, Sean T. Mitchell, and Jeremy Walton, 17–22. Chicago: University of Chicago Press.

———. 2010c. "Civilised Coercion, Militarised Law and Order: Security in Colonial South Asia and the Blue in Green Global Order." In *Blurring Military and Police Roles*, edited by Marleen Easton et al., 57–77. The Hague: Eleven International Publishing.

———. 2013a. "Beatings, Beacons, and Big Men: Police Disempowerment and Delegitimation in India." *Law and Social Inquiry* 38 (3): 643–69.

———. 2013b. "Dirty Anthropology: Epistemologies of Violence and Ethical Entanglements in Police Ethnography." In *Policing and Contemporary Governance: The Anthropology of Police in Practice*, edited by William Garriott, 125–43. New York: Palgrave.

———. 2014a. "Police and Legal Patronage in Northern India." In *Patronage as Politics in South Asia*, edited by Anastasia Piliavsky. Cambridge, UK: Cambridge University Press.

———. 2014b. "Provisional Agency in India: Jugaad and Legitimation of Corruption." *American Ethnologist* 41(1): 76–91.

———. 2015. "World Fitness: The US Army Family and the Positive Science of Persistent War." *Public Culture* 27 (3): 449–85.

———. 2016. *Provisional Authority: Police, Order, and Security in India*. Chicago: University of Chicago Press.

Kan, Sergei, ed. 2001. *Strangers to Relatives: The Adoption and Naming of Anthropologists in Native North America*. Lincoln: University of Nebraska Press.

Klockars, Carl B. 1980. "The Dirty Harry Problem." *Annals of the American Academy of Political and Social Science* 452:33–47.

Marcus, George E. 1997. "The Uses of Complicity in the Changing Mise-en-Scène of Anthropological Fieldwork, " in "The Fate of 'Culture': Geertz and Beyond," special issue of *Representations* 59 (Summer): 85–108.

Martin, Jeffrey. 2013. "Legitimate Force in a Particularistic Democracy: Street Police and Outlaw Legislators in the Republic of China on Taiwan." *Law and Social Inquiry* 38(3): 615–42.

McNamara, Laura, and Robert Rubinstein. 2011. *Dangerous Liaisons: Anthropologists and the National Security State*. Santa Fe: School for Advanced Research Press.

Moskos, Peter. 2008. *Cop in the Hood: My Year Policing Baltimore's Eastern District*. Princeton: Princeton University Press.

Muir, William Ker. 1977. *Police: Streetcorner Politicians*. Chicago: University of Chicago Press.

Narayan, Kirin. 1993. "How Native is a 'Native Anthropologist'?" *American Anthropologist* 95 (3): 671–86.

Parry, Jonathan. 2000. "The 'Crisis of Corruption' and 'The Idea of India': A Worm's Eye View." In *Morals of Legitimacy: Between Agency and System*, edited by Italo Pardo, 27–56. New York: Berghahn Books.

Piliavsky, Anastasia, ed. 2014. *Patronage as Politics in South Asia*. Cambridge, UK: Cambridge University Press.

Robben, Antonius C. G. M. 1995. "The Politics of Truth and Emotion among Victims and Perpetrators of Violence." In *Fieldwork under Fire: Contemporary Studies of Violence and Survival*, edited by Carolyn Nordstrom and Antonius C. G. M. Robben, 81–104. Berkeley: University of California Press.

———. 1996. "Ethnographic Seduction, Transference, and Resistance in Dialogues about Terror and Violence in Argentina." *Ethos* 24 (1): 71–106.

Robb Larkins, Erika. 2015. *The Spectacular Favela: Violence in Modern Brazil*. Oakland: University of California Press.

Roitman, Janet. 2005. *Fiscal Disobedience: An Anthropology of Economic Regulation in Central Africa*. Princeton: Princeton University Press.

———. 2006. "The Ethics of Illegality in the Chad Basin." In *Law and Disorder in the Postcolony*, edited by Jean Comaroff and John L. Comaroff, 247–72. Chicago: University of Chicago Press.

Singh, Prakash. 2000. "All-India Services: Dilemmas of Change." In *The Changing Role of the All-India Services: An Assessment and Agenda for Future Research on Federalism and the All India Services*, edited by Balveer Arora and Beryl Radin. Center for the Advanced Study of India and Center for Policy Research, University of Pennsylvania.

Subramanian, K. S. 1988. "Police Unrest in India: Notes Toward an Understanding." *Occasional Papers on History and Society*. Second Series, no. 10. November. Nehru Memorial Library. Microfiche.

Van Maanen, John, and Peter Manning, eds. 1978. *Policing: A View from the Streets*. New York: Random House.

Verma, Arvind. 2005. *The Indian Police: A Critical Evaluation*. New Delhi: Regency Publications.

Wade, Robert. 1982. "The System of Administrative and Political Corruption: Canal Irrigation in South India." *Journal of Development Studies* 18 (3): 287–328.

———. 1985. "The Market for Public Office: Why the Indian State Is Not Better at Development." *World Development* 13 (4): 467–97.

Weber, Max. 1991 [1918]a. "Bureaucracy." In *From Max Weber: Essays in Sociology*, edited by Hans Gerth and C. Wright Mills, 196–244. Oxford, UK: Oxford University Press.

———. 1991 [1918]b. "Politics as a Vocation." In *From Max Weber: Essays in Sociology*, edited by Hans Gerth and C. Wright Mills, 77–128. Oxford, UK: Oxford University Press.

———. 1991 [1918]c. "Science as a Vocation." In *From Max Weber: Essays in Sociology*, edited by Hans Gerth and C. Wright Mills, 129–56. Oxford, UK: Oxford University Press.

Westmarland, Louise. 2001. "Blowing the Whistle on Police Violence." *British Journal of Criminology* 41:523–35.

Willis, Graham Denyer. 2015. *The Killing Consensus: Police, Organized Crime, and the Regulation of Life and Death in Urban Brazil*. Oakland: University of California Press.

Young, Malcolm. 1991. *An Inside Job: Policing and Police Culture in Britain*. Oxford, UK: Oxford University Press.

FOUR

Affect:
The Virtual Force of Policing (Taiwan)

JEFFREY T. MARTIN

Affect is the whole world: from the precise angle of its differential emergence.

—Brian Massumi, *Parables of the Virtual: Movement, Affect, Sensation* (2002)

How should we understand the "force" in police force? The convention is to think in terms of physical violence. Indeed, the most widely accepted definition of the police institution defines it by its capacity for legitimate physical violence.[1] I write here from a different perspective, taking the *non-physical* dimension of police force as no less fundamental. I do this in an attempt to explain my ethnographic experience with police action organized through a discourse of *qing*, or "affect." *Qing* is a Chinese idiom for thinking about interpersonal relationships. This idiom plays an important role in policing in the Republic of China on Taiwan. The role of *qing* in Taiwanese policing is a result of a distinctive historical understanding of the police as a political institution dedicated to the task of cultivating the moral order of society. This ideal is operationalized at street level by institutional arrangements that situate a population registry at the core of police operations. Registry-based police techniques utilize the virtual power of record keeping to channel the virtual force of affect into a bureaucratic apparatus of state control. I argue that this fusion of two immaterial modes of force—writing and feeling—supplies the primary mechanism by which Taiwanese society is policed. The state registry orders society at the level of relationships. Legible affect *is* the "force" in Taiwanese policing.

A Banquet Toast

One wall of our private room was glass. Outside, in the darkness beneath us, the city's lights sparkled through a driving rain. The city was unsettled. Radical students had seized the national legislature a month earlier, and citizens came into the streets by the hundreds of thousands to support them. The whole police force was mobilized. Regular patrolmen from every corner of the island were called to Taipei to hold the lines guarding government offices. The students remained in the legislature for three weeks, leaving in victory after the speaker of parliament guaranteed he would personally ensure that the president's controversial policies were not implemented. The night the students left and the crowd outside the legislature dispersed, several thousand people spontaneously gathered around a police station a block away: the command center that coordinated police response to the occupation. The police inside dropped steel shutters over their doors and windows and waited while the crowd covered their station with paint and posters, shouting slogans from the earlier protest: "Unconstitutional Police," "State Violence," "Yingning [the name of the precinct commander] Resign!" After several hours, the commanding officer finally came out to address the crowd. As the nation watched on live television, he offered his resignation.[2] The constituted authority of the state seemed to be in free fall, upset by a convulsion of constituent power working its way up from the streets. The police on those streets were left in an awkward position. Their political backing was uncertain, yet they remained on high alert, responsible for managing sporadic eruptions of dissent that seemed increasingly to focus on little beyond challenging the legitimacy of the repression they provoked.

Inside the private room of the restaurant, I was attending an informal banquet with a number of high-ranking policemen. The table in front of us was laden with shark fin soup, fresh sashimi, aged red wine, single-malt scotch, and the like. A dynamic company was consuming the opulent feast, people from various walks of life coming and going throughout the evening. Our host was owner and CEO of a firm that manufactured computer parts in factories around Taiwan and a half-dozen other countries. He, along with a couple of his executive officers who happened to be in town, was reconnecting with old friends at top levels of command in the police. It was a banquet of a sort that features centrally in the ethnography of modern China, an arena for cultivating the *ganqing* ("affective feelings"; see below) that consolidates clientage networks organized by the idiom of *guanxi* (a hybrid fusion of instrumental and affective social "connections").[3] Like many in attendance I was there as a friend-of-a-friend, the guest of a patron who was in turn a client of one of the principals. And, like everyone else, I was there to mix business with pleasure. In my case business was ethnography and pleasure was the frisson of access, of being in the company of people who trusted me enough to share an intimate sphere of their lives. One of the pretexts for the get-together was the host's intention to make a financial donation to the police. The civic unrest had compelled the largest sustained public order management operation since the old standing antiriot brigades were dissolved by the democratic transition. There were no longer any facilities to house police posted to Taipei from other jurisdictions. They were sleeping in buses or on the street. That, the businessman and police officers agreed, was a shameful hardship to impose on those who have already sacrificed so much in service to the public good. The businessman proposed to buy them all mattresses and blankets. It was a welcome gesture.

Taiwanese police have an institutionalized system for managing such private donations. An hour or so into the banquet, a man near the top of that system arrived. It was Tiehan, a retired policeman that I knew. He came around the table and sat next to me. We made small talk and drank a few toasts. "And how is Achun?" Tiehan inquired, raising a glass of scotch. "Does he still work at the Highland Station, where he was back in 1999, when you were doing that first research project?" Tiehan and I had met more than a decade earlier. I quickly learned he was a dangerous man. He was in his late sixties. His policing career had begun before the end of martial law. His first appointment was with the "Garrison Command," the military agency at the heart of the martial law apparatus, which administered the criminal justice system under a national security mandate before it was dissolved in 1992. Officers of the Garrison Command were trained in something called "political warfare," the Leninist art of steering social forces to realize party objectives. Tiehan's career was built on skill with this kind of work.

Tiehan took an interest in my research. His inquiry about Achun was an example of the form that interest took. Every time I saw him, Tiehan would find an opportunity to politely inquire about the welfare of some informant of mine whose identity he had managed to learn. "And how is so-and-so, who worked in such-and-such a station, from year X to year Y?" I never told him any of this information. He uncovered it on his own, a demonstration of surveillant prowess. Tiehan's collection of intelligence regarding my network was a consequence of my movement through his social and bureaucratic world. He was habituated to the power of intelligence within that world. The inquiry made in the form of a banquet toast, for example, projected a kind of interpersonal soft power, an ostentatiously polite gesture with a shocking effect. The shock is produced by the invocation of individuals who, Tiehan implied, are complicit in and thus accountable for the consequences of my research. Tiehan wants me to know he knows, to know that the quality of my relationship with those people is at stake in the content of what I write. If I want to be true to the promises I make that warrant the trust of those who trust me, Tiehan politely reminds me, I should think seriously about what I do.

Such messages shock and worry me. But I cannot discern Tiehan's agenda for delivering them. He could be acting from paternal concern, warning me I am being watched, not just by him but by others as well. He could be trying to impose his political agenda on what I publish. Or he could simply, habitually, be lording the dominance of his position over mine. It is impossible to clarify any content to the message beyond its inducement to vigilance. This is characteristic of the performative attentions of state security agents more generally; they secure the state by producing insecurity in those on whom they act.[4] This securitizing inducement to vigilance is the logic of *qing*-work in Taiwanese policing. A student active in the protest movement told me a story about attending a protest with a group of his friends a year earlier. They had rented a bus to go to Taipei (he lived in the south of the island). The day before they were to leave, a local policeman paid a visit to his parents' house and beseeched them to keep their son from going up north and getting into trouble. The state is watching you, the policeman's visit said. It knows what you are doing and it knows who cares about what happens to you. A politically activist lawyer told me a different kind of story about the spooky discipline of surveillant attention. In his case, the message came in the form of a newspaper's description of his marital indiscretion. He had been studying the state his whole life and had a clearer understanding than most people of the workings of the intelligence apparatus that exposed his infidelity. What he couldn't figure out was any coherent political intention behind revealing that particular secret at that particular moment. He concluded there was no political message to be found. The newspaper had probably bought the secret to sell papers.

These are examples of how the force of *qing*—affect—can serve the interests of police. At issue in these stories is something called *ganqing*. Etymologically, this word reads as the sensation (*gan*) of affect (*qing*), an intersection of consciousness and energy. The standard government dictionary defines *ganqing* as "an emotional response produced by external stimulus;

an emotional relationship between people; to move a subject emotion-ally."[5] *Ganqing* is a profound concept. It is at the heart of the way those who use it to talk about human relationships understand the ethical quali-ties of human life. To feel *qing* defines what it means to be human: we are subjects embedded in a "magnetic field" of *qing*, and people individuate as selves through cultivation of the relationships in which those selves are embedded.[6] This is an idiom of social subjectivity that does not situ-ate affect inside an individual. *Qing* is, rather, a field of *mutuality* within which individuals are embedded. To cultivate *ganqing* is to produce social value and a self, simultaneously. This situates the focal point of ethical self-consciousness in contextual appropriateness rather than authentic interior-ity. As Kipnis describes it:

> *Ganqing* is not primarily an individual matter. Rather it is a type of feeling that must be conceived of more socially than psychologically (i.e., that is held to exist between and among people as much as in individual's heads). Furthermore, sincerity—at least a notion of sincerity that requires one's words and facial expressions to accurately represent the "inner" feelings of one's heart—is usually absent from *ganqing*. To be "sincere" with one's *ganqing* is to be serious about and to live up to the obligations incurred in [relationships].[7]

The significance of *qing* in Taiwan's police apparatus foregrounds the sig-nificance of cosmology to policing more generally. While covert surveil-lance and attention to social relationships are part of every policing regime, the distinctive objectification of *qing* provided by Taiwanese political cul-ture allows coercion to be organized without reducing it to the terms of a crude materialism. In other places, where affect is thought to be contained in the flesh of individual bodies (rather than being understood as the field of social energies in which selves individuate), social outcomes are seen as the effect of individual behaviors. These behaviors are understood as the effect of inner affective processes, and these processes are thought to be materially grounded in physiology. Coercion is thus visualized as a con-tinuum that moves from verbal action into the flesh, culminating in the destruction of an individual body. By contrast to this materialism, the im-material force of *qing* does not anchor in individual bodies. It is anchored in the connections between people. Police technologies based on *qing* objectify human mutuality: the fact that certain people are so profoundly connected to one another that they "live each other's lives and die each other's deaths."[8]

Qing-based policing is organized through a lexicon of "feelings" and "compassion." Yet it is ultimately no more pacific than policing based on bodies. Violence and brutality remain potentials in the field of social control. What cosmology changes is not the fact of material destruction but the way instrumental violence is articulated through a social field. Consider, for example, the following comment made to me by a Chinese human rights lawyer living in de facto exile in Hong Kong, far from his job, his wife, and his child. He explained his experience as an object of political persecution in terms of the traditional Chinese judicial principle of "mutual culpability" (*lianzuo*) as it is practiced in China's contemporary system of *qingzhi* (literally "*qing*-control," a Chinese term for the political police apparatus): "I have known many dissidents who have been kidnapped [by the secret police] and tortured, and who did not give up their cause. They are very courageous people. They do not even fear death. But when the authorities target their families, then they give up. Nobody can bear that." The use of *qing*-based techniques in policing resembles covert "intelligence" operations of the sort that liberal democratic countries reserve to military use (or ban altogether). This, I would argue, expresses another facet of the cosmological contrast between the *qing*-based idea of police and a materialist model. They have different ways of framing the decoupage between civil and military concerns. The materialist force-continuum ideal conceives of technology as apolitical: a technique is a pure instrument and acquires its political significance entirely through the end to which it is put. The ends of police work are defined by contrast to military operations as "nonpolitical" in the sense that they uphold the consent-based values of the civic order.[9] Police work is to military action as civil is to political power, and there is a clear line to be drawn between the routine operations of a local constabulary and the political intrigue of "high policing."[10]

The line between political intervention and order maintenance is not so clear in Taiwan. The neighborhood constabulary was originally conceived as an apparatus of political control, and the work of police patrol was originally defined as a mode of political surveillance.[11] These ideas remain relevant for the way constabulary practice is organized to cultivate civil order into the present. It is a formulation of policing that does not neatly separate into technical means versus policy-defined ends. The police are a generic instrument for cultivating *qing*—the virtual energy that constitutes social relationships. The instrumentality of policing thus conceived embodies a historical conception of the role of police in the political arena and a developmental understanding of the politically significant relationship between order and affect. To gesture briefly toward a vast literature,

China's modern history saw the formation of modern public rationality taken up as a revolutionary project. It was an urgent project, necessary as a defensive reaction against Western imperialism. There was no time to wait for the gradual formation of bourgeois sensibilities within an emergent middle class. This urgency foreclosed any possibility that the nascent republic would draw its political conscience from "private people come together as a public."[12] Modern political conscience would not arise from the inner sphere of bourgeois privacy but be engineered publicly, by the enlightened vanguard of one revolutionary party or another. The resulting modern Chinese concept of *tongqing*—"public sentiment"—situates the formation of modern fellow feeling entirely within the political sphere.[13] The inner feelings of an individual are essentially political, a legitimate object for the agency of external political authorities. There is no autonomous node within the ethical field of subjects-in-relation defined by *qing* available to serve as the seat of a "private" conscience.

As a field of policed order, *qing* becomes relevant to individuals within the fabric of "particularistic" bonds that situate the person as an element in their particular social world.[14] This fabric of particularities is what connects me to Achun, a student to his parents, a lawyer to his wife and another woman as well. As *qing* is taken up by the apparatus of *qingzhi* or *qingbao* (the "*qing*-control" or "*qing*-report/response" systems we call by the English euphemism "intelligence") it becomes a modality of force. *Qing* constitutes an explosive payload, delivered through a banquet toast or courtesy visit that exposes a vulnerable tissue of human care to cold calculations of control. A policing system organized around this means of force can be very efficient. Yet even as it uses *qing* as an instrument of coercive control, *qing* remains a modality of *virtual* force: it targets not the physical substance of human bodies but the social substance of human "mutuality," that is, the fact that human beings "live each other's lives and die each other's deaths."[15] The force that shapes behavior is concern for others, care for those who constitute the core of one's social being.

In a place where this is the core principle of policing, having a banquet is exactly what you would expect the police command to be doing as the foundations of the state shuddered beneath their feet: meeting with the patrons who help keep corporate body and soul together, sourcing shelter for the men standing in the rain outside, cultivating the networks that make the machine work, oiling its gears. And Tiehan, with the effortless spontaneity of a master craftsman who notices something ever so slightly out of whack, gently tapped a potentially errant cog in his machine back into place. *Qing* enables policing to become embedded in social control as a matter of recreational habits, order enforced by a casual remark, a mode of behavior so deeply ingrained that I doubt if Tiehan was even aware of what he was doing beyond upholding the general ethical obligation of a patron to keep his clients in harmonious order.

A Ride in the Dark

Habits of *qing*-based policing are institutionalized in the policing system all the way down to the front lines. The closer we get to street level, however, the more gross and unwieldy become the problems that police are called to handle, and the cruder and more overt their application of *qing* becomes. One autumn evening, during a period when I was deeply submerged in the world of local street policing, I left a police station on patrol with two policemen I counted among my close friends. A couple of blocks from the station we were waved over by Atiao, an entrepreneur active in the social life of the station. He was sitting at a roadside café with a group of enormous men I hadn't seen before. When the car stopped they all rushed over, drunk and ebullient. Atiao jumped into the front seat and three of the burly strangers piled into the back, one of them sitting on my lap. Atiao was ecstatic. He had been coaching an amateur baseball team that had just won their league tournament, bringing him a gambling windfall. One of his coaching innovations had been hiring semipro players to masquerade as amateurs. He was now taking these ringers out to celebrate. The patrolmen drove the packed car to a hostess bar across town, far out of their station's jurisdiction. Atiao would not hear any refusal of his hospitality on that special occasion, and as the baseball players exited the car they carried me with them. We rented an enormous room and began to drink. Other people showed up, and the party became raucous. I ended up sitting next to a man who introduced himself as a criminal detective from the precinct office, who began asking me questions about Acai, a mutual acquaintance of ours who worked in the station.

That was not a happy topic. Acai was an in serious trouble. His wife had been a low-level bookie in a numbers racket known as "Everybody's Happy" (*Dajiale*) when a bet she took hit the jackpot. The higher-level bookie with whom she placed her bets absconded with the winnings. She was more honorable than he and paid off the win with borrowed money. To raise the money she leveraged the family's social network to its limit and made up the difference with a high-interest loan from an underground bank. As these debts began to come due, Acai's family had been all but destroyed. His wife fell into a suicidal depression, they officially divorced, and she went into hiding. The detective expressed sympathy for Acai, saying it was a terrible situation, adding ominously that he too was a "victim" of the disaster. I didn't say much. I knew some things it would have been inappropriate to mention.

Drunkenness made the hired athletes increasingly abusive toward their female attendants. Animosity escalated until one of them punched the woman sitting next to him, knocking her to the floor. The lights came up abruptly and the room flooded with in-house security. In a cloud of tension and Atiao's money changing hands, our group was escorted to the sidewalk. There were about twenty of us standing there, which meant multiple taxis would be required to take us to the next bar. As people sorted out, I was helped into a taxi with three men who had been sitting on the other side of the detective. One of them, a fat muscular older man, had been introduced to me as Big Brother Li. The other two, who had not been introduced, seemed to be his subordinates. I found myself in the back seat sandwiched between Brother Li and one of his subordinates, while the other sat shotgun looking back at me with a blank expression.

As we pulled away from the hostess bar, our taxi did not follow the others toward Taipei's red-light district. It turned the other way and began driving toward an industrial wasteland that marked the outer limit of the greater Taipei urban area. I began to get scared. We drove in silence. The streetlights ended. The landscape outside the window was almost pitch black, temporary factories built of corrugated steel around the network of cement ditches that drain the mountains of the Taipei Basin into the Danshui River. The main channel was a huge canal capable of moving typhoons into the ocean. It was haunted by the memory of bodies dumped there, most recently that of Bai Xiaoyan, a celebrity's daughter kidnapped and murdered with great spectacle in 1997. A few years later Liao Xueguang, a self-styled antimafia crusader newly elected to the national legislature, was taken from his bed at gunpoint one night and left locked inside a dog cage up that road. Like a banquet toast or a home visit, driving people up into the mountains was a conventional way to send a message. The silence in the taxi was almost unbearable, but I had no idea what to say. Then Brother Li reached over and took my hand, held it gently in both of his, and began whispering in Taiwanese into my ear. I couldn't understand what he was saying.

It was terrifying. But, at the same time, I felt some confidence that I couldn't be treated with complete impunity. The network that delivered me to Brother Li would be capable of extracting me if the situation got ugly. I had a phone in my pocket with enough numbers stored in it to find somebody with connections to somebody who could call in a favor with Brother Li. I endured in anxious silence hoping not to escalate the situation into an embarrassing set of phone calls that might lead to a conversation in which the location of Acai's wife became an explicit question. I said nothing, let Brother Li hold my hand and speak his piece, and waited. He fell silent again. Then the car turned a corner and streetlights appeared ahead. We were driving back toward the inhabited area of the city. Brother Li suddenly snarled in Chinese, "Why are you holding my hand, you fucking faggot!" and dropped my hand. His subordinates laughed. We arrived at a desolate tavern and the ride was over. I saw them to the door, excused myself, and went off to find a different taxi back to the police station.

Taiwan's informal economy is enormous. The economic growth of the 1970s and 1980s that lifted the island from third- to first-world status was financed by informal lending practices of the sort at stake in this situation. The security of such loans has no legal foundation; it is anchored entirely by the interpersonal virtues of *qing*.[16] The system of "Black Gold"—as Taiwanese refer to their current fusion of electoral democracy with organized criminal enterprise—situates the work of local police inside a division of social control labor dominated by mafia politicians and saturated with independent security firms operated by people like Brother Li.[17] My ride in the dark was another example of how *qing* technologies operate in order-maintenance work. As in Tiehan's toast, the force of *qing* is the message that we know who you know, and you know what that means. Security and vulnerability are the same thing, seen from opposed perspectives. Acai's wife's bankruptcy, a truly life-defining event, ramified through the field of sociality that mobilized to keep her alive. The force that compelled repayment of her debts was activated *within* these bonds, manipulated instrumentally through the technology of *qingzhi* that objectifies the ways in which people "live one another's lives and die one another's deaths."

When the Sovereign Acts

In retrospect, I estimate my ride in the dark lasted no more than fifteen or twenty minutes. I was treated physically in the gentlest of ways: a man held my hand and whispered in my ear. The whole episode was but a brief detour in an evening's festivities, like Tiehan's banquet toast just a convenient opportunity to pass a message. These messages operationalize the power of *qing* to police and control. They generate force without violence, terror without touching, control through reputation and innuendo. This raises two questions. First, is this really "policing"? Being threatened by gangsters may be a stock element in Hong Kong police films, but it is not a self-evident component of state order. One must look a bit deeper to see the connection. The patrolmen I knew in Taiwan lived in the police station. They worked fourteen-hour shifts five days a week. Their formal duties kept them as busy as any human being I have ever met. And yet, they delivered very few "cases" to the criminal justice machinery. Most of their time was spent mediating and managing conflicts in and around the shadows of legal order. In this work of mediation, law was a flexible resource.[18] The hard lines that could not be crossed were defined by those who kept the shadow economy in order, people like Brother Li. In an informally organized political economy, agents of informal enforcement are the institutional pillars of community order. They are a core element of the regime that secures the city's financial foundations. Policing is unimaginable without them.

This leads to the second question. If we accept that what I experienced was policing, does the way it used affect as its coercive instrument make this style of policing somehow less brutal than modes of police conceptualized as an instrument for allocating physical violence? Certainly the use of *qing* in policing affords a much deeper penetration of the social than overt physical force does. Sending a message through a network that reminds everyone involved to take seriously their mutual implication in one another's security is a mode of intervention that actively consolidates and strengthens the networked qualities of social order. In this, *qing*-based policing seems capable of realizing the totalitarian dream of a truly proactive, "preventative" policing regime. *Qing* is a term that spans the virtual realm of security (as a reflectively conscious emotional state) and the manifest realm of violence (as an embodied affective experience). So long as it remains at the virtual level of security, *qing*-based policing strengthens the bonds connecting people with one another, rather than degrading them the way the application of physical force does. To organize a policing regime around this aspect of *qing* consolidates the foundational significance of virtuous social habits in a way that the punitive application of physical violence can never do.

But the sphere of the political is never free from potential violence. The dispersed capillaries of *qing*-based power—righteous individuals, local bosses, borough chiefs, and a multitude of agencies of other description—cannot be allowed to operate on the basis of any politically autonomous form of virtue. Networks of *qing*-based solidarity that begin to coalesce outside the political designs of the sovereign center are a threat to state security. And when the state security is threatened, the virtual force of casual innuendo gives way to material violence. There have been moments in Taiwanese history, some still in living memory, when the government ruled by naked political terror. In those moments, *qing* provided the axis by which policing was absorbed, whole-cloth, into military operations.

> To clean up residual fragments of seditious organization and eliminate hidden agents of violent disorder, Central Security Command called for a complete municipal inspection. We began by compiling all the information we received from the party, the *qing* apparatus, the military and the police. From this we made a list of suspects, along with their places of residence and habitual activity. At the same time we called a meeting of the municipal administrative officers, all the borough chiefs, and some of the neighborhood chiefs as well. We explained the purpose and direction of our investigation, and asked for their opinions and assistance. Then we imposed martial law on the city. All traffic was halted. At dusk we dispatched combined units of infantry, gendarmes and police to inspect the city in zones. It was very orderly, and very thorough. By dawn we had arrested over three hundred people [who] were taken to military court for a hearing, judgment and formal charges. We carried out the sentences by parading them through the city under military and police escort, to the execution ground, where they were tied up and shot.[19]

Qing is a kind of social knowledge. *Qing*-based policing is founded on the power of this knowledge. The power of knowing who to target, knowing where they live, work, and sleep, of knowing who knows them and knowing who cares. Knowing the hierarchies of patronage and protection organized through the bosses of the neighborhoods and boroughs. Knowing the administrative officials who oversee these clientage networks. Knowing how to act on all this knowledge, how to call on the right people for "opinions and assistance." These inquiries are normally used as stimulating reminders of mutual obligation. But they can occasionally foreshadow an investigation that may end with three hundred corpses tied up outside a city wall. Such is the range of affordances the technologies of *qing* provide the state.

Writing, Ethnography, and Virtual Force

A modern state is a bureaucracy, a system of "rule by writing desk."[20] Bureaus of the state—e.g., the police—operate through written records. Writing is their primary mode of action. The deposition, the evidence, the dossier: these are the vectors of force that compose events within a bureaucratic field and bring a world within the scope of the state's documentary power.[21] Writing is a mode of *virtual* force. Literary representation sits apart from the material world it represents; it floats free in a virtual space enabled by the arbitrariness of the sign. What goes into the dossier is never what actually happened. It *could not be*: it is a representation rather than the thing itself. The art of writing reports is a literary practice shaped by aesthetic conventions of verisimilitude, pragmatic considerations of political prudence, and ethical sensibilities about the qualities and quantities of justice at play in the situation.

There are evident parallels between police writing and ethnography. Indeed, in many places the two are historically identical. The first ethnographers on Taiwan were Japanese colonial officers dispatched to translate local custom into administrative codes. This project was animated by an aspiration to "civilize" the subjects of colonial power at the level of subjective dispositions, making concern with the intimate qualities of human relationships a defining feature in the genre of police ethnography.[22] Such ethnographic sensibilities embedded within police attention remain a noted feature in contemporary police scholarship, even in settings where the colonial legacy has been displaced by entirely republican concerns.[23] All of which is to say, in this context at least, Foucault's historical diagnosis of the constitutive association between "police science" and the human sciences remains a valid and vital point.[24]

If we can see policing as a quasi-ethnographic occupation, can we also accept that ethnography has a police function? At one level, it is not difficult. To the degree that we write in a politically engaged style, hoping our ethnographic truth will enlighten the public sensibilities that inform policy, we embrace the higher aspirations of a broadly republican ideal of police. But, even if this holds true in the abstract, the "street level" practice of ethnography (so to speak) certainly does not look or feel like policing. Indeed, as this volume demonstrates, the relationship between professional ethnographers and the police they study is characterized by tensions and problems that suggest a point of confrontation between distinct, even opposed, enterprises. Academic independence reflects the world from a radically different perspective than does political intelligence. Universities and police interpose entirely different infrastructures of mediation between the production of representation and its practical effects. The virtual force of intellectual comment is qualitatively different from that of bureaucratic command. All of which leads us to feel, perhaps strongly: professors are not police.

But the distinction is not as solid as it appears. Indeed, anthropology teaches us to be suspicious of any claim that invokes essential, strongly felt, ostensibly self-evident differences between a self and its other. Identity and alterity are mutually constitutive ideas; their apparent opposition is constituted on the basis of their underlying relationship. A historical kinship between professors and police illustrates this point. Modern policing and the modern university emerged together, at the same time, in the same process, and, arguably, as parts of the same thing. "Police Science" was one of the inaugural disciplines of modern academia.[25] In the time of their origins, before the bifurcation of modern science and modern politics as distinct vocations, the police and the professoriate were a single community of experts in the cultivation of modern life.[26] To be sure, this was long ago, when neither institution looked much like it does today. The subsequent trajectory of development has led these erstwhile siblings in very different directions, leaving the genealogical facts of their common ancestry obscure.

East Asian modernity has preserved the hybrid formation of the police university as one of its defining institutions.[27] My time in the field has orbited around such institutions. I took my first job after graduate school as a civilian lecturer in the Taiwanese police officers' university (2006–2007). Shortly afterward, I spent five years teaching in a criminology program designed for Hong Kong's "disciplined forces" (2009–2014). I have experienced this engagement with the hybrid field of police-academia as an extended period of anthropological fieldwork. When I first came to Taiwan, in 1997, I was not concerned with police. I set out to study how traditional martial artists understood modern violence. I found a receptive field site for that project inside a neighborhood police station and quickly realized I needed to understand the institution before I could understand the modes of force that circulated through it. So I began to actively study policing. It turned out I had a curriculum ready to hand: my friends in the station had all been to police school. They shared their textbooks with me and introduced me to friends still in school. Through this network I came to know professors in the police university who became my teachers and later colleagues in the academic study of police.

The version of police studies I learned in 1990s Taiwan was a unique disciplinary formation. It was focused by concern with the ongoing democratic transformation, an event overdetermined by the country's longer postwar relationship with the United States. On my bookshelf sit Bittner, Bayley, Manning, Skolnick, Wilson, et al., all the American authors concerned with the defining of the nature of democratic policing. The physical copies of their books on my shelf are photocopied reproductions of copies loaned to me by professors at Taiwan's police university, which were themselves photocopied reproductions of books they had borrowed from the American universities where they were trained. Like Chinese paintings in museums, the texts on my shelf carry an accumulation of collection stamps, chop marks, and personal annotations marking their provenance. These intertextual traces reveal a trajectory of ideas through geopolitical space: the textual vector through which a virtual model of democratic policing—encapsulated in concepts like "problem-oriented policing" and "broken windows theory"—was transmitted. To the degree that Taiwan's democratic police reform was consciously engineered, these books provided the fulcrum by which the system shifted onto its new foundation.

But English-language works of democratic theory are only one brick in the textual edifice of the Taiwanese police. More fundamental are handbooks of institutional procedure. Those are written in Chinese and carry citation chains that stretch beyond contemporary American reform models to the early modern Prussian and Japanese theories of modern government in which Taiwan's police institutions were originally founded. Most illuminating to me were the books of standard operating procedure, in which the abstract goals of the institution were converted into flowcharts and techniques. Here the virtual power of representation converged with the operational routines of the institution. In those handbooks, I discovered how the population registry provided the central organizing device steering the flow of police business through the institution. Every decision-making tree began by establishing the jurisdiction of the police agent over the social field in terms of a registry relationship that attached an individual patrolman to the individual residents of his beat. The labor of maintaining this system of particularistic jurisdictions, the work of keeping registry records up to date, was expected to occupy four hours of every patrolman's standard shift. A—arguably *the*—core task of Taiwanese police was the endless enterprise of writing the neighborhood into the police books.

It is the work of keeping these records that fuses the power of affect with the power of inscription. The project of police registration uses the virtual power of the pen to capture and control the virtual power of *qing*. People are registered not as individuals but as members of families. The fabric of care defined by kinship supplies the basic topography for the police map of society. On top of their family background, individuals acquire a status—one of three grades ranging from normal to suspicious to criminal—based on the quality of their documented interactions with other people. This documentation is done by police. The formal labor of translating interaction into documentary status is the arena in which police agents cultivate skills of political consciousness like those Tiehan has mastered. Elements of this skill are made explicit in the technical instruction of the classroom. A textbook from the police college describes the discipline of neighborhood surveillance as an enterprise aimed at "grasping the subjectivity" of those under jurisdiction. Grasping the subjectivity of an individual or group allows an agent to "easily move their sympathies," as a mode of interpersonal power. Skill in this field of power scales up to policy-relevant concerns through *guanxi* networks that span multiple social spheres and thereby afford police access to the larger arrangement of political sympathies underwriting the social order of their jurisdiction.[28]

Liu Shengzuo, the author of this text, is (like Tiehan) a former officer of the Garrison Command. He teaches "public relations" at the police college, one of the curricular venues through which *qing*-based police skills of political warfare were adapted to the newly democratic milieu. The technical poetry of his description captures and reveals the tactical ethos of Taiwanese policing. *Qing* provides an axial idiom to scale trust from the street-level sphere of interpersonal interaction to state-level concern with collective security. This ethos is visible through a "para-ethnographic" reading of a police textbook,[29] that is, a second-order reflection on the ethnographic sensibilities of the original author. Those sensibilities anchor the coherence of democratic reform as a police project. The lexical capacity of the category of *qing* to link the immediacy of affective experience to intimate knowledge and strategic decision making provided a fixed point on which policing could pivot from enacting a totalitarian ideal to servicing the emergent harmonies of polyarchic balance. In Liu's book, *qing* structures police consciousness simultaneously as gossip, insider information, and political intelligence. The cultivation of *ganqing* networks is instrumental toward building accurate *qingbao*, "intelligence reports," which provide the decisive strategic knowledge required to effectively target points of structural vulnerability.[30]

This calculated intrigue is exposed in the books on my shelf. Reading them is not just an academic exercise. It empowers me. The virtual power of situational awareness—understanding (to a modest degree) what is going on around me—allows me to act as self-conscious agent within the political field I inhabit as participant-observer of a policing regime. Where Tiehan knows what I am doing as a foreign ethnographer attending a banquet, I know what Tiehan is doing as a political handler when he "grasps my subjectivity" with a banquet toast. I know this because I am surveilling him back, by studying the documentary history of his institution. And when Tiehan acts to shock me into immediate vigilance, I react through the highly mediated act of writing about it. Just as Tiehan's police habitus carries a residue of ethnographic sensibilities, my ethnography entails an element of policing e/affect. I bring Tiehan, as a particular individual, into a written record of *qing*: who cares about whom. The covert power of a banquet toast is met and countered, in some small manner, by the overt power of writing about the banquet toast.

Representation is a constitutive element of modern governance. To intervene at the level of representation is to intervene in the substance of governance itself. In the context of police ethnography, there is a tight feedback loop between intellectual reflection and political enactment. Ethnographic studies of policing require a participant-observer-author to dwell in a field of coercive heteronomy. This coercion is strategic, a struggle for a prize. The prize is "authorship," in the sense of a question of who will write social history. Policing through *qing* mobilizes the force of human feeling to impose the state's idea of collective concern onto errant pretensions of individual autonomy. Where policing is overtly political, the field of coercive heteronomy is realized as collectively policed habits of disciplined affect. Its manifest order is politeness, etiquette attuned to a tight closure of the feedback loop by which any particular author produces the ideas that define a collective world. One of the first field interviews I did in Taiwan produced a memorable aphorism. "When you point at someone, be careful," said my interlocutor, holding up a fist with the index finger extended. "Never forget: these three fingers are pointing back at you!" Tiehan reminds me of this every time I see him. To write about police is to represent a corporate body fundamentally and actively concerned with controlling the representations by which their authority to control is legitimated. Police reception of writing about police is never more than one step away from the binary political logic of friend versus enemy, a binary with no place for neutral, "objective" observers. The objectivity of police ethnography is not that of an autonomous author writing dispassionately about an independently constituted world. It is, rather, an expression of the struggle to communicate the experience of human life lived as the object of a political struggle to make the world. To write under such circumstances demands, explicitly and forcefully, that one use words with utmost care.

Conclusion

I have described how a policing regime can use the immaterial or virtual force of affect as an instrument of coercion. This description reflects the continuing relevance of Durkheim's fundamental insight: social institutions like the police cannot be understood by reducing them to the effects of material causes. Defining police in terms of their capacity for physical violence is misleading. Social force is a field of consequentiality in which social actions have social effects. Understanding police force as social force is a sociological project; it must use sociological methods. Durkheim identified these methods in distinction from those of the physical sciences based on the way they treat ideas. In social life, ideas have an ontological status; they do not merely reflect social reality, they constitute it. The pragmatic or performative dimension of human ideas gives social facts a reality that is qualitatively different from physical facts. The idea of *qing*—human affect—as a field of energy in which social identity is formed is consistent with Durkheim's analysis of "the idea of force at its 'birth' . . . when human beings feel themselves transformed and are in fact transformed through ritual doing."[31]

This chapter has explored some of the insights we can gain from studying the culturally specific lexicon of immaterial forces the Taiwanese police use to objectify and control human feelings. The modernizing project that conceptualized police force through the ritualized labor of inscribing *qing* into a population registry successfully channeled this primordial energy into a bureaucratic apparatus of the sort through which modern states participate in "making up people."[32] This leads to a more general insight: treating human mutuality as a policeable object affords coercive technologies that operate on social bonds rather than individual bodies. When used subtly and proactively (the way I have experienced them) these techniques generate a coercive shock that induces people to take their mutual obligation seriously. This is a kind of power that can be used to stress, exercise, and ultimately *strengthen* the moral bonds of collective subjectivity. In places where the overall social order is conceived as a network of networks, *qing*-based policing is an efficient technology for upholding the police responsibility in modern society to secure trust, build community, and prevent crime. But the positive potential of policing mutuality casts its own dark shadow. It is no less fundamentally coercive than policing that targets individuals. This is manifest as the political dimension of *qing*-based policing. When the sovereign source of political order feels challenged, it mobilizes the surveillant capacity of the *qing*-based police apparatus to exercise harsh, brutal, and deadly force onto the collective selves constituted by networks of interpersonal care. Thus even as the functionality of *qing* diverges from the individualistic calculus that denominates coercion in individual bodies, it has its own trajectory of escalation and its own potentials for violent excess.

Notes

1. Bittner 1990. Critical discussion of the "Use of Force Paradigm" can be found in Brodeur 2010 and Jobard 2014.

2. The mayor gave a press conference the next morning refusing to accept the offer. However, the televised event of his submission to the crowd had a tangible effect on police morale.
3. Yang 1994.
4. Masco 2006.
5. Ministry of Education 2015.
6. Kipnis 1997, 10.
7. Ibid., 108.
8. Sahlins 2012, 28.
9. Reiner 2010.
10. Brodeur 1983.
11. Martin 2014.
12. Habermas 1991.
13. Lean 2007.
14. Fei 1992.
15. Sahlins 2012, 28.
16. Winn 1994.
17. Chin 2003.
18. Martin 2007.
19. Jiang Zonglin, former military officer, describing his experience in the pacification of Taichung City after the 228 uprising in 1947, quoted in Li (1998, 187).
20. Hull 2012, 11.
21. Scott 1999.
22. Stoler 2007.
23. Cf. Wender 2008.
24. Foucault 2007.
25. Wakefield 2009.
26. Foucault 2007.
27. Cf. Bayley 1985, 10.
28. Liu 2008, 78.
29. Holmes and Marcus 2005.
30. Liu 2008, 78.
31. Fields 1995, xli.
32. Hacking 1999.

References

Bayley, David. 1985. *Patterns of Policing*. New Brunswick: Rutgers University Press.
Bittner, Egon. 1990. *Aspects of Police Work*. Boston: Northeastern University Press.
Brodeur, Jean-Paul. 1983. "High Policing and Low Policing: Remarks about the Policing of Political Activities." *Social Problems* 30:507–20.
Brodeur, Jean-Paul. 2010. *The Policing Web*. New York: Oxford University Press.
Chin, Kolin. 2003. *Heijin: Organized Crime, Business and Politics in Taiwan*. Armonk: M. E. Sharpe.
Fei, Xiaotong. 1992. *From the Soil: The Foundations of Chinese Society*. Berkeley: University of California Press.
Fields, Karen. 1995. Introduction to *The Elementary Forms of Religious Life*, by Émile Durkheim, xvii–lxxiii. New York: The Free Press.

Foucault, Michel. 2007. *Security, Territory, Population.* New York: Palgrave.

Habermas, Jurgen. 1991. *The Structural Transformation of the Public Sphere.* Boston: MIT Press.

Hacking, Ian. 1999. "Making Up People." In *Historical Ontology.* Cambridge, MA: Harvard University Press.

Holmes, Douglas, and George Marcus. 2005. "Cultures of Expertise and the Management of Globalization: Toward the Re-Functioning of Ethnography." In *Global Assemblages: Technology, Politics, and Ethics as Anthropological Problems,* edited by Aiwa Ong and Steven Collier, 235–52. London: Blackwell.

Hull, Matthew. 2012. *Government of Paper.* Berkeley: University of California Press.

Jobard, Fabien. 2014. "Conceptualizing of Police." In *Encyclopedia of Criminal Justice,* edited by Gerben Bruinsma and David Weisburd, 515–24. New York: Springer.

Keane, Webb. 2003. "Self-Interpretation, Agency and the Objects of Anthropology: Reflections on a Genealogy." *Comparative Studies in Society and History* 45 (2): 222–48

Kipnis, Andrew. 1997. *Producing* Guanxi: *Sentiment, Self, and Subculture in a North China Village.* Durham: Duke University Press.

Lean, Eugenia. 2007. *Public Passions: The Trial of Shi Jianqiao and the Rise of Popular Sympathy in Republican China.* Berkeley: University of California Press.

Lee, Haiyan. 2007. *Revolution of the Heart: A Genealogy of Love in China, 1900–1950.* Stanford: Stanford University Press.

Li, Xiaofeng. 1998. *Jiedu Ererba* [*Interpreting 228*]. Taipei: Yushan Press.

Liu, Shengzuo. 2008. *You Guanxi, Bie Shuo Nin Buhui.* Taipei: Shangyang International.

Martin, Jeffrey T. 2007. "A Reasonable Balance of Law and Sentiment: Social Order in Democratic Taiwan from the Policeman's Point of View." *Law & Society Review* 41 (3): 665–98.

———. 2014. "The Confucian Ethic and the Spirit of East Asian Police: A Comparative Study in the Ideology of Democratic Policing." *Crime, Law & Social Change* 61 (4): 461–90.

Masco, Joseph. 2006. *The Nuclear Borderlands.* Princeton: Princeton University Press.

Massumi, Brian. 2002. *Parables of the Virtual: Movement, Affect, Sensation.* Durham: Duke University Press.

Ministry of Education. 2015. "*Ganqing,*" definitions 1, 2, and 3. *Revised Dictionary of the National Language,* Ministry of Education, Republic of China, http://dict.revised.moe.edu.tw/index.html.

Reiner, Robert. 2010. *The Politics of Police.* New York: Oxford University Press.

Sahlins, Marshall. 2012. *What Kinship Is, and Is Not.* Chicago: University of Chicago Press.

Scott, James C. 1999. *Seeing Like a State.* New Haven: Yale University Press.

Stoler, Ann Laura. 2007. "Affective States." In *A Companion to the Anthropology of Politics,* edited by David Nugent and Joan Vincent, 4–20. Oxford: Wiley Blackwell.

Wakefield, Andre. 2009. *The Disordered Police State.* Chicago: University of Chicago Press.

Wender, Jonathan. 2008. *Policing and the Poetics of Everyday Life.* Champaign: University of Illinois Press.

Winn, Jane Kaufmann. 1994. "Not by Rule of Law: Mediating State-Society Relations in Taiwan through the Underground Economy." In *The Other Taiwan, 1945–92,* edited by Murray Rubenstein, 183–214. Armonk: M. E. Sharpe.

Yang, Mayfair. 1994. *Gifts, Favors and Banquets: The Art of Social Relationships in China.* Ithaca: Cornell University Press.

PART TWO

Observation

FIVE

Predicament:
Interpreting Police Violence (Mozambique)

HELENE MARIA KYED

In urban Mozambique violent acts constitute a routine part of police work, spanning from interrogational beatings and corporal punishment to the rough handling and humiliation of criminal suspects and those regarded as troublemakers. At the neighborhood level such apparently excessive police force is performed not by state police officers but primarily by groups of young civilian men, known as community policing agents. This chapter explores the meaning of everyday police violence used by one such group in Chasana (the name has been changed), a poorer neighborhood of Mozambique's capital city Maputo.[1] The group is the result of an official community policing initiative that was implemented as part of the wider postwar democratic transition in Mozambique that began in 1992, marking a dual shift from war to peace and from a one-party Marxist-Leninist state to a liberal democracy. The initiative aimed to transform the state police from a notoriously violent and militarized force to a service adhering to international rule of law standards by enhancing cooperation between police and citizens. This aim has been supported by laws banning the use of torture and ensuring the legal protection and humane treatment of suspects and offenders. In practice, however, police violence has not reduced. It has continued through a kind of informal outsourcing of police functions to civilian community police groups, who have assumed the de facto authority to use force without any legal mandate. Violence in this context is seen as part of the police job, but it is also justified as responding to popular notions of justice and order. It is even sometimes demanded by neighborhood residents as a means to recover stolen goods, enforce compensation, and discipline misbehaving neighborhood residents. State police actions are here animated by elements of community vengeance and popular justice.[2]

What accounts for these routine forms of police violence in the urban neighborhood of Maputo, and what meanings and justifications underline them? The reproduction of police violence through a community policing initiative challenges a common view held by some scholars of the police and central to most current policies on police reform: closer proximity between police and citizens will reduce police violence.[3] This view, which equates proximity with popular accountability and checks on police power, is based on the notion that violence is categorically evil and destructive or always morally wrong, rather than also socially legitimized in some way.[4] Conversely, routine violence performed by civilian policing actors also defies a reduction of police violence to the state police's legal mandate, which is premised on the Weberian dictum that the state has a monopoly on the legitimate use of force. Whereas this dominant perspective of classic police studies helps to comprehend violence as a core part of the police job and as fundamental to law in modern states, it omits other possible justifications for and meanings of police violence that are external to the modern state.[5] In Egon Bittner's classic definition, the potential and actual use of coercion when deemed necessary by the police to resolve a problem in a given situation is what distinguishes the police from other state professionals and citizens.[6] This discretionary power of the police renders coercive force always potentially legitimate because it is delegated to the police by the state. Consequently, most empirical studies of actual police force have tended either to be purely descriptive, placing force on a continuum between physical presence and deadly force, or to confine evaluations of the propriety of police force to questions of frequency and proportion in specific situations (i.e., force is seen as excessive when it is disproportionate to the problem that it is intended to solve).[7] Other police scholars have focused on the moral dilemmas that arise from the police's particular role in modern states, emphasizing how officers constantly have to use bad means (violence) to achieve good ends (order, security, law).[8] This can be related to a discrepancy between what police officers see as their moral duty to fight crime, for which they have been delegated the authority to use force, and the frustrations that emerge because they cannot achieve such ends within the limits of the law.[9] Whereas this focus highlights morality rather than just legality in the interpretation of police violence, the tendency is to ultimately refer back to the founding claim of modern state sovereignty, which gives the police a mandate to use force in the first place. Violent acts outside the state's delegated mandate, performed by civilian actors, are conversely rendered per se illegitimate by this Weberian framework.[10]

Ethnographies of police and police violence in postcolonial countries challenge this position by showing that the state police do not possess anything resembling a monopoly on legitimate or socially sanctioned means of coercion, but coexist and collude with other enforcers. They have also shown that multiple logics of necessity, morality, and order inform police violence in particular contexts, which include, but are not limited to, the notion of force as central to the state police job.[11] Popular perceptions and particular cultural and historical predispositions of each state also inform the prevalence of violent policing.[12] Consequently, to comprehend the routine performance of violence by civilian policing actors in Chasana, there is a need to contextualize police violence. In doing so, I move beyond fixed legal and moral criteria and begin with open-ended explorative questions: When, how, and for whom is police violence legitimate, and what logics and meanings underlie the justifications for and frequency of violence? These questions can only be answered through an ethnography that knits together observations of police violence with emic views of such violence. Eliciting the meanings of police violence further lays the groundwork for a more in-depth analysis and critique of the enabling conditions of police violence at a structural level. This means asking what makes police violence possible and acceptable within the particular historical and political context. Of particular interest to my endeavor is to understand the reproduction of police violence by civilian actors and what this says more broadly about state and society at the particular moment of postwar democratic transition in Mozambique. Ethnography here poses limits due to its microlevel focus and thus needs to be combined with sociological and historical analysis. Jerome Skolnick and James Fyfe's analysis of the enabling conditions of excessive force in the United States provides a useful starting point, as it highlights different social, political, and historical factors that shape the police culture at given moments. In particular, they argue that police violence along with vigilantism is more likely when the police find the legal system insufficient to deal with order problems and when they face perceived threats and dangers in crime-ridden neighborhoods. Rather than reducing violence to an effect of state law, they link it to deeper disparities in society and to situations "where the existing order is not clearly defined, is undergoing great flux, or favors some groups at the apparent expense of others."[13] What is necessary to add is the significance of popular demands for police violence, which Skolnick and Fyfe leave unanalyzed, and to situate police violence in Mozambique within the particular context of postwar democratic transition.

This chapter begins with the detailed description of two scenes: one that involves a criminal offense and another that does not. Following these scenes, I elicit the different meanings of violence by drawing on emic jus-

tifications and my own etic interpretation. Violence is simultaneously habitual, instrumental, retributive, and empowering. Multiple logics inform
these meanings, ranging from ideas about the police job deriving from a
long history of routine state police violence to popular demands for immediate justice and the emotional desires of policing actors to sustain power
in a context of legal uncertainty and social disparity. The result is an intermediary form of policing between state police action and popular justice.
Key to understanding the enabling conditions of police violence through
this local-level configuration is a deep mistrust in the state legal system. At
a deeper structural level, this does not simply reflect a dichotomy between
state law and popular justice, but also the incompleteness of state formation processes in Mozambican history associated with the failure both to
protect poorer citizens and to assert state sovereignty. In the conclusion
of the chapter, I will address these matters more in depth and discuss the
value and limits of ethnography for interpreting and providing a critique of
police violence.

Scenes of Police Violence

It is an early June morning in 2009 in Chasana, a densely populated and
crime-ridden *bairro* (neighborhood) in Maputo, situated on the frontier of
the inner city and the large poor urban suburbs that surround the city. Two
young community policemen, Julinho and Alfiado, are hearing a theft case
inside a tiny, poorly lit room of the *circulo*—the name given to the local
administration and the ruling party's office in the *bairro*. A man, Simão,
is accused of breaking into a house. João is the victim. A wet, dirty, shiver-
ing cold Simão was brought to the community police office early in the
morning, his hands bound with rope: the "people" around João's house
had caught him, knowing that he had stolen, and had beaten him up and
poured ice-cold water over his head. Then they took him to the *circulo* to
hand him over to the community police. Julinho assures me that "the population sometimes uses this method to punish thieves," referring not to
the beating, which he knows that I am aware of, but the use of ice water.
João, the victim of the theft, does not want to involve the state police or for
the case to end up in court. He just wants the community police guys to
help him get his things back. Simão has already been punished by the people. At the *circulo*, the rope is removed, and Julinho puts proper handcuffs
around Simão's wrists and places him on the floor in the corner. Simão sits
curled up, sweating and looking very nervous. "He is a real thief, this one.
Very dangerous. We know him from before and he was once in prison for

beating up a child," Julinho tells me.[14] At that moment I am thinking that Julinho can sense that I am not comfortable with seeing Simão in this terrible state, so he needs to call him a big thief as a kind of justification, but I am not sure. I nod my head to his comment and just try to be as cool as possible, not showing any particular emotions, neither of approval nor of condemnation. As an ethnographer I want to observe the flow of action, although I know that my presence cannot be ignored, as Julinho's justification to me indicates. During the hearing, Simão quickly admits guilt and explains that he has already resold the goods. So the job for the community police now is to locate the buyer(s). They are determined to get João his things back today. Simão at first does not want to give any names, but Alfiado threatens him with the *chamboko* (a kind of baton or rubber stick). He begs not to be whipped, and at last he says that Paulo, who works at the bakery, bought a DVD player and an amplifier. Acting quickly, Julinho and Alfiado drag Simão to the door and parade him handcuffed to the bakery, passing through the busy market so everyone sees him. Paulo is brought to the *circulo* where he endures fierce questioning. He denies the accusations, but Alfiado is not fully convinced. He takes Paulo by the arm and pulls Simão towards him. They get handcuffed together and then tied to the bars of the only window in the room. This forces them to stand up. They have to wait for other people from the bakery to arrive. Another case is heard in the meantime. The room is hot and reeks of sweat; everyone is crammed together. Two other community policemen, Pedro and Sergio, arrive. Then comes Basil, the sector police officer. He is a civilian state police officer who sometimes works with the community police. He takes over the case when three people from the bakery and Paulo's father get there. They testify to Paulo's innocence and Basil believes them. Paulo is finally released from the handcuffs.

Basil and Alfiado now turn their attention to Simão. They need new names. The men from the bakery are still there and one of them says to Basil: "If you beat him with the *chamboko*, he'll tell you what he sold." Simão shouts in a plaintive voice: "*Chefe* [addressed to Basil], it was not me, what can I do?" But Basil points to the *chamboko* and Simão shouts: "Wait! I will tell you . . . my friends." Basil interrupts him: "I want to beat you first. Give me the *chamboko* [addressing Alfiado]." He tells Simão to lie down and pretend that he is going to sleep, pointing to the floor. Simão, now lying down flat on his stomach, begs him: "I have already been beaten a lot." Basil stands over him with a foot on one of his legs, while holding the *chamboko* and telling him to give names. He beats Simão on the buttocks and between lashes Simão cries out names. When they have six names, the beating stops. Simão is now paraded through the street, in a very bad state. Some people we meet utter words like "thief," "trouble-maker," and "prisoner." Two people on the list are found, and they promise to bring the goods back. It is now late, and the community police are not allowed to keep prisoners. Basil decides to take Simão to the cell of the police station, because "he is a real big thief, this one."

Ten days later, Simão is still in the cell, and five people have already compensated João for the stolen goods, which they had bought from Simão and resold. I ask Basil if a court case will be opened. He explains that this is the norm (meaning that this is the law), but that in this case it is highly unlikely because João is satisfied. He is being compensated, and Simão has been punished. Justice has been done. No one questions the physical beatings and public humiliation of Simão, first by the neighborhood's residents and then by the police. These are unlawful, but legitimate, acts, because Simão was guilty of the crime.

The community police agents who handled this case are part of a group of eleven young men between twenty-five and thirty-five years of age, which began operating in Chasana in 2003. They all come from poorer families, have low education, and had no employment when they first began to operate. They are the result not of a spontaneous vigilante formation but of a community policing initiative introduced by the Ministry of Interior. The idea was to establish community policing councils of socially respected persons in the neighborhood, who would debate crime problems with the police. This would reduce crime and increase the public accountability of the police, which in turn would lessen the violence, corruption, and inefficiency that characterized the state police in Mozambique after the war.[15] While a community policing council was formed, it soon dissolved and was followed by the recruitment of the young men by the local state administrator and the local branch of the ruling Frelimo Party, who provided them with a room within the administration (circulo). The station commander gave them training, batons, and handcuffs. They receive no salary and are not legally recognized, but their tasks are extensive: patrols, investigations, and the resolution of various crimes and social disputes. As is evident in the next scene, they also engage in the disciplining of persons who have not committed crimes.

Pedro and Sergio, two other community police members, come into the room of the circulo with a young man whom they call a Rasta (Rastafarian). Julinho whispers to me that the Rasta, whose name is Jha, was seen by some people at the market selling suruma (a type of cannabis). Jha is told to sit on the floor. Pedro tells him to empty his pocket; out comes a small plastic bag of *suruma*. Pedro and Sergio laugh, shouting: "É surumatico" ("He's a pothead"). During the hearing, Jha argues that he smokes because he is a Rasta. He laughs a bit and seems not to take the community police serious at this point.

Pedro and Sergio want Jha to tell them where he bought the *suruma*. They take turns interrogating him. He is told to go behind the desk in the room, as if put in a little cell. Alfiado, another community policeman, is hard on him: "Tell us where you bought it." Jha finally names some places, but with unclear locations, and Pedro says, "He is lying. This guy is telling stories. He is making a movie. Tell the truth. Give him five *chambokos* to tell the truth." Jha replies, "Beat me. Then you will know I am telling the truth." Alfiado begins to threaten with the *chamboko* and tells Jha to lie down and sleep. There is a lot of pushing to get him to lie down on his stomach so his whole body is stretched out. He struggles and talks all the time: "Let me go. To be beaten is bad. I don't do any crimes. I am a good person." Alfiado stands over him and holds him down with a foot. Jha begs to go to the toilet. Octavio shouts: "Get down now. Sleep. Sleep. Yes, that is right, sleep well. Tell us where you bought it. Now I will get the *chamboko* so you can tell the truth. Sleep, sleep well. I will cripple you. Tell us the person's name." Jha is whipped with the *chamboko* several times. After five strokes I stop counting, because I do not like it. I notice that I blink my eyes hard at every stroke, although I try not to show any reaction, but it is hard to control the body. Jha tries to say where the dealer lives, but the words get disturbed by the strokes. He cries out in pain. Suddenly, between strokes, Basil comes in and the beating stops. They have to attend to the theft case with Simão. I am relieved it is over.

Jha remains in the room until the end of the day. He is not handcuffed. I am amazed to see how Alfiado—who had just beaten him—sits next to him on the table, as if nothing has happened. Before Jha is let go, Basil and Pedro lecture him. Jha explains that he is just a consumer and that this is not a crime like selling is. Yet in an effort to justify the treatment Jha has been through today, Basil and Pedro explain to Jha that any drug is too much and that he could kill himself. Basil says, "One bag of pot, yes, but drugs are never no big deal. Even this little bit gives you problems. When you smoke this, you will get high and not know what you are doing. Do you understand?" Jha: "Yes, I understand." Pedro attempts to give the impression that the police are helping keep Jha safe by taking him in.

Jha is let go. The case is put to rest. As I know from other situations, the community police and Basil do not really go after the drug dealers. This is too dangerous for them because the dealers often carry knives or firearms.

But the police can "educate" the users and "protect" them, the community policemen tell me, because without them the dealers have no customers. Evidently, the law is clear. Jha had not committed a crime. However, it was not legality that was foregrounded, but the demonstration of police authority and capacity to correct misbehaving community members.

The Meanings of Police Violence

The two violent police scenes represent routine aspects of how the community police agents operated in Chasana during the months I spent with them. This covers a wide repertoire of violent methods: beatings during interrogation, rough handcuffing, pushing, parading through the neighborhood, humiliating and degrading remarks, discriminatory searches, threats of brutality, and irregular arrests. During the first two weeks of fieldwork I did not witness any beatings during the interrogations I was invited to follow, likely because they still had to see if they could trust me. However, even on my initial visit I experienced a very rough handling of a drug addict, who was paraded through the streets and handcuffed at the station. This illustrated the ordinariness of violence to my interlocutors. For me it was different. Watching violence was extremely uncomfortable, and I never got used to it, but as it was such an integrated part of everyday policing, which I was trying to understand, I had no choice but to engage with it. To understand the meanings of violence I had to not only tame and hide my own ethical position against violence in conversations but also try as much as possible to control the signs of my physical dislike during observations. I never openly condemned their use of violence, as this would have severely compromised fieldwork, but there was no doubt that the community police agents saw through my bodily reactions that I did not like it. So after some time, we sort of came to an unspoken understanding that I could leave if I wanted to when they were doing the beatings. They simply said, "Doctor, it's time now; the thug is going to 'sleep.'" Although my interlocutors were very aware that physical violence by community police is illegal in Mozambican law, the acts of violence were not hidden or secret. They were the norm of police work, and my task was to try to understand how and why, even if this meant unresolved dilemmas like the participant observer's complicity with violent and illegal acts.[16]

The community police members have to a large extent learned the various violent methods from the state police, especially by working together with sector police officers. They are perceived by the police and largely see themselves as the extended arm of the police. Simultaneously, they perceive themselves as a local structure that does voluntary work for the good of the community. This dual role is reflected in a mixture of case-handling methods. They copy state police practices of interrogation, but they enforce compensational justice, akin to how the quasi-official neighborhood-section leaders and the informal group of local elders, known as *madodas*, handle social disputes. Whereas the *madodas* are not recognized by the state, they frequently advise on social and family matters, informally assisting the local tiers of the state, based on their seniority and respected status. The section leaders are allowed to handle minor social disputes but are no longer part of the official state apparatus as in the socialist period.

This intermediary form of policing is not subject to any regulations or clear lines of accountability, except that the community police are expected to report to the sector police officer and the local administrator on an informal basis. There are no fixed rules and sanctions if community police step out of line. The official community policing initiative has thus turned into a quasi-informal set-up, constituting a de facto police force and a kind of local court that has no legal recognition but has the informal support of the local tiers of the state. Conversely, their continued operation is ultimately dependent on the fact that neighborhood residents frequently bring cases to them. How has this come about, and what makes violence so essential?

During my fieldwork there was widespread consensus among state police officers and neighborhood residents that the community police had drastically reduced crime in Chasana. The majority believed that this success owed to the use of the *chamboko*. Before the community police, people told me, there was no effective police in the neighborhood and violent crime and theft were so rife that people felt unsafe walking around even in broad daylight. Such was a main characteristic of the postwar years of the 1990s, which marked the end of sixteen years of civil war between Frelimo and Renamo and the transition to democracy. Crime not only rose, but former structures of control and order enforcement at the neighborhood level institutionalized by the socialist Frelimo government were also legally dissolved. These included popular vigilante groups and courts, comprising civilians, who policed delinquency and resolved minor crimes, along with ensuring loyalty to the Frelimo party-state. The aforementioned *madodas* supported these structures, and while they persist informally in the neighborhood, the other institutions do not. Simultaneously, efforts to reform the police according to the rule of law, including a prohibition on torture and corporal punishment, did not translate into an effective police force.[17] Instead, the police were associated with corruption and indifference to poor urban neighborhoods like Chasana (the name has been changed). What many people experienced was police absence. The community police group was seen to fill this void. To many state police officers community policing was a means to resolve the problem of an under-resourced and understaffed force. Politically, democratization did open the door for multiple parties, with the former rebel movement, Renamo, becoming the main opposition party, but in practice, the Frelimo party-state continued. Elections did not translate into actual power sharing, and state institutions like police and judiciary continued to favor the Frelimo elite. These matters provide an important context for the local appropriation of community policing by the local branches of the state and the ruling party, but they suffice in themselves to elicit the meanings of routine police violence.

In what follows, I address four main meanings of violence based on emic justifications and on my own etic interpretation that embeds these meanings into the wider context: first, violence as *habitual*, associated with police work and informed by the history of state policing in Mozambique; second, violence as *instrumental* in compensating the victims; third, violence as *retributive*, as a kind of "immediate punishment" to prevent future crimes and to discipline wrongdoers; and; fourth, violence as *empowering*, as a sort of emotional desire for power by otherwise disempowered policing actors. These four meanings convey a mixture of habits, functionality, and emotion and are layered by historically embedded ideas about police work and popular justice.

Police Violence as Habitual: "The Police Job" and Historical Legacies

The community police agents never tried to hide or cover up their beatings even though they are illegal under current law. Violence seemed habitual, an expected and normal part of doing police work. This also explains why they allowed me to observe it. The community police agents operated in the image of what they saw as a proper police force, as an agency associated with the use of force akin to classic definitions of police in modern states.[18] This was partly nurtured by the state police, who trained and instructed the community police on how to use the *chamboko*. This takes place in a context where there has been an extensive colonial and postcolonial history of institutionalized police violence. Flogging as punishment, torture during interrogations, and public beatings and shaming of criminals constituted habitual and, until the ratification of the 1990 constitution, legally accepted policing practices in Mozambique. These practices can be situated in a prolonged history of war and contested state formation, which not only produced a militarized police to defend or constitute regimes but also inserted a kind of war mentality into everyday policing. The national police force was formed during the liberation war, and many current station commanders, including the one covering Chasana, were first trained at the military bases of the liberation fighters. Independence was soon followed by sixteen years of civil war against Renamo. From the beginning, policing was not about law enforcement but about punishing or eliminating "internal enemies" of the nation-state. Internal enemies under the postcolonial Frelimo party-state covered not only those who had collaborated with the colonial regime, such as traditional leaders and political opponents, but also criminals and persons seen as acting immorally (prostitutes, drunks, drug addicts, etc.). These along with customary practices like witchcraft accusations were seen to pollute and threaten the new nation from within. In this way, harsh policing methods came to infuse not only emergency situations but also habitual, everyday ways of dealing with delinquency and immorality. Today, the state police seldom beat people in public spaces, but old habits linger behind the closed doors of the police stations, especially those commanded by older elements of the force like in Chasana. At the same time, they are reproduced in poor urban neighborhoods (and rural areas) in an outsourced form.

In Chasana, the habitual aspect merged with the community police's ideas about popular expectations. Pedro noted: "People expect the *chamboko*." He reminded me that victims and witnesses sometimes ask the community police to use violence as a way "to get the wrongdoers to talk," as in the Simão case, or to make them "feel the pain" of the wrong they have done. Such requests reflect historically embedded ideas about what the police do, but the community police also linked them with recent forms of mob justice.[19] As with Simão, it was not uncommon for criminals to be beaten first by neighborhood residents before they were taken to the community police, who then often continued with more violence and humiliation. On other occasions, the community police members intervened to stop residents from beating a suspected wrongdoer. They even proudly emphasized that the number of lynchings had gone down in the neighborhood since they began their work. When speaking about these matters, the members strongly distinguished their work from popular beatings, which they presented as chaotic and uncontrolled. They highlighted their professionalism, as a group trained by the state police in how much and where to beat so that there were no visible marks or permanent injuries. Pedro explained: "it is better that we beat them, because we know how to do it in the right way, not to kill like the people do."

In this understanding, community police violence is not a straightforward extension of popular punishments but an ordered and controlled version of it. This notion of orderliness draws on images of a proper police force, as an authority in the Weberian sense that substitutes for uncontrolled forms of private vengeance.[20] A core difference is that the violent practices of the community police do not serve law enforcement, but act to compensate the victims, as I address next. In this way, historically embedded state police habits intertwine with current popular demands for justice.

Police Violence as Instrumental: Interrogational Beatings and Compensation to Victims

Interrogational beatings were frequently used to get the "suspects to talk." When I directly asked, these beatings were explained as necessary to effectively resolve crimes, a function that the community police saw as part of their duty as a local police force. This underscores violence as a means justified by serving good ends, characteristic of state police forces elsewhere. However, the frame of reference was not the law but the wishes of the victims. The community police explained: "We always listen to the victims," "we beat the thieves in order to get information out of them so that we can get back the victim's stolen goods," and "when the victim agrees, we stop the beating." Interrogational beatings were justified with reference to popular notions of justice as compensation for injuries and recovery of stolen goods. When I asked neighborhood residents what they saw as "justice," common answers were "The wrongdoer must pay the victim" or "For me, justice is when the person who did wrong brings back the thing that he took. It is necessary to compensate the person he hurt." A legal process was only desirable in exceptional cases, like murder, or *after* a process of compensation to the victim had occurred. Official court processes were associated with prison sentences—if any sentence at all—and with a lack of compensation to the victim.

In this way, interrogational beatings are instrumental in enforcing "immediate justice," which typically means to *avoid* or to substitute them for a legal process. The case of Simão is illustrative: although he ended in a police cell, no one expected or desired a court case because the goods were compensated for and he had been punished. In many cases, the suspects never were handed over to the state police, let alone ended up in court.

This was commonly based on the wishes of the victims, like with João who just wanted his things back.

This function of police violence situates community police practices between popular demands for justice and state police action. Due to the amount of labor they invest in recovering stolen goods, the community police represent a kind of policing that comes closer to aspects of informal social control than to conventional definitions of policing as the bureaucratic administration of state policy. Compensational justice is typical in customary courts, which still function in rural Mozambique but are weak or dissolved in urban neighborhoods. It is clear that the community police draw on principles used by such courts, but they also differ in the proportion and frequency of violence that they apply. It is very uncommon in fact to hear about the use of physical force in customary courts.[21] Rather, interrogational beatings belong to the repertoire of state police practices.

Now the need to beat to enforce compensatory justice still leaves some questions unanswered: How can this justification account for the humiliation that Simão went through when he was paraded through the streets, and why was Jha so badly treated when there was neither a victim nor a real crime at stake? While these questions can be answered in part by referring back to habits, they can also be related to violence as retributive.

Police Violence as Retributive: Crime Prevention and Moral Community

Beatings were not just justified as a necessary means but also as a kind of "immediate punishment." As such, a beating could be an end in and of itself. This challenges classic ideas about police violence as always morally wrong, as simply a bad means to achieve good ends.[22] Even interrogational beatings were frequently described as forms of punishment in their own right. The case of Jha is illustrative: a police interrogation into drug dealing was used as a pretext to beat and humiliate a person regarded as morally out of place, rather than as a means to resolve a crime. The treatment served to educate Jha as a "brother" of the neighborhood. There were also situations where beatings were more directly presented as a pure form of corporal punishment. Simão, who was not a brother but a real dangerous criminal, fell into this category.

Retributive violence to some extent accounts for the apparent excess of resolving violent crime: beatings serve not just to get an offender to talk but also to punish or educate him. There was a preventive rationale to this. Orlando explained, "The person sees that in our neighborhood, we really do beat [criminals], so he won't come back here and steal." This was echoed by neighborhood residents, who, like Mrs. Gino, an older lady, asserted, "When they are beaten, they will think twice before they harm someone again. So you see bit by bit crime went down in our neighborhood." However, retributive violence did not concern crime prevention in the abstract sense of upholding the law. Rather, it concerned the restoration of order and moral community inside the neighborhood. Thus, the emphasis my interlocutors placed on "our neighborhood" was important. Retributive violence *inside* the neighborhood was seen as a substitute for and on other occasions as an addition to an official criminal process, *outside* the neighborhood. This was informed by two popular notions of physical punishment, one associated with moral education and another with bodily pain.

First, punishment as moral education took the form, like with Jha, of educating young men in the neighborhood who had "stepped out of line" and whom the community police took upon themselves to "put back in line." This could be drug users and other youths who drank a lot, gambled, hung out at bars, were involved in smaller fights, or stole from their neighbors or family members. Youths who looked suspicious, dirty, or like Rastafarians were told to shape up and threatened with force if they did not. Most of these youths were known by the community police. Sometimes they were even family members. They were described as brothers. They were counseled, but frequently also beaten. In contrast to "real criminals" like Simão, these youths were told why they were being treated like they were, often, as with Jha, followed by explanations that the community police were doing what they did to protect them from doing harm. Frequently, they were asked to acknowledge that they deserved the treatment for their own good. Romão explained: "We take them in, counsel them, and then they ask for forgiveness. And if they are very young, their family comes and says sorry. But they are also punished, so that we can bring to their attention not to do it again. A few *chambokos* as a way of educating them too."

These forms of punishment can be seen as an expansion of the socially legitimate use of physical disciplining of children within the family, common in Chasana, but they also go beyond this. In a broader sense, the community policemen took it upon themselves to constitute the moral community of the neighborhood.[23] The purpose is not to punish them as criminals but to educate them so as to (re)include them in the moral community. This is nonetheless a moral community that the community police are themselves part of defining by targeting certain youngsters and subjecting them to their disciplinary measures. Intriguingly, moral education was frequently put into a criminal framing. Because Jha was only carrying a small amount of cannabis, he could not be charged as a criminal, but beating him in the first place was presented as a means to catch the real criminals, the drug dealers. Thus, the legal category of crime was used as a resource to perform moral education *inside* the neighborhood. A state legal process cannot substitute for that. Conversely, it is the position of the community police as an informal extension of the state police that enabled them to maintain community order as well as equipped them with the instruments to do so in the first place. This reinforces the point that community policing is not simply an expansion of popular punishments but is mediated by state violence.

The second aspect of retributive violence is related directly to criminal matters. It draws on popular notions of punishment as bodily pain in cases of serious crime related to bodily harm, like rape, stabbings, or murder, or when culprits had repeatedly committed crimes like theft. This was captured in utterances like "They must feel the same pain they caused the victim" or "If a person has raped someone, he must be beaten so that he feels the violence for himself and so that he is not violent against another person again." The community police drew on these notions of punishment as bodily pain when they spoke to me about beating people like Simão. Although Simão had not caused anyone bodily harm, he was defined as a real criminal who had committed many crimes and been to prison. This made him unworthy of inclusion into the moral community. Thus, after he was beaten and publicly shamed, he was taken away to the police station.

Intriguingly, the beatings in such cases were frequently spoken about as an *addition* to how the police and the official justice system worked. Interrogational beatings of suspects before they were handed over to the police were not only seen as a means to resolve a crime but were also regarded as a punishment. Pedro explained:

> We beat them before we take them to the police to make sure . . . for the victim . . . that at least the thug has been given some sort of punishment. You know because when they end up at the station, there is not really any guarantee that they be punished. Here, people know that there will be some form of punishment. Now, at the police station, they just arrive in handcuffs. That's it. And then an official case will be opened that will put them on trial so that they end up in prison. Or they may get lucky, stay for a bit at the station before the police let them go.

Similar opinions were expressed by neighborhood residents. When asked if criminal charges were sometimes desirable, they replied, "If the person is guilty and has committed a lot of crimes, he could go to prison, but first he must be beaten" or "The best is for the thief to be beaten here and then taken to the police station to be charged."

These perspectives reflect a deep mistrust in the current official system to provide justice and protection. Frequently, people complained that when culprits are sent to the police, they are released after a day or two, after which they start committing crimes again. The release of suspects could be the result of the police adhering to the rule of law in cases with inadequate evidence, but many neighborhood residents saw it as the result of bribery or as the system's unwillingness to punish the guilty. Importantly, frustration with unfulfilled state action was also echoed by a number of the state police officers. They frequently said that the law, which now prohibits them from physically punishing the criminals, has reduced their capacity to combat crime. In a conversation with the station commander, I was baffled to hear:

> The people know how to punish the criminals better, so that they won't do [the crime] again. Here, at the police station, we have to follow the law . . . it is very complicated today. It is much easier out there [in the neighborhoods]. They can do more and punish however they like . . . they burn them if necessary. You know, we should reintroduce capital punishment here in Mozambique so that we can see an end to all this crime.

With this view, it is therefore not surprising that the station commander strongly supported the work (and violent practices) of the community police. What these insights reflect is that popular demands for physical punishment and state police ideas regarding the necessity of violence to combat crime have not substantially changed even though the law has. What is at stake is not a simple tension between law and cultural or customary understandings of punishment but also the unfulfilled expectations of state action. Retributive violence as moral education does draw on disciplinary measures within the family, and punishment as bodily pain can be traced back to precolonial practices of traditional leaders. However, equally significant is the historical legacy of violent state policing in Mozambique. This legacy not only shapes how violent acts are performed but also informs popular frustrations with lack of state protection in lieu of increased crime and feelings of insecurity. This has opened a space for community policing agents, whose immediate punishments become both a substitute for and an addition to the current official system as well as a controlled version of mob justice. Taking upon themselves this role simultaneously empowers the community police and makes them vulnerable.

Police Violence as (Em)power(ment): Emotions and Vulnerability

The habitual and functional meanings of police violence still leave open the question of what motivates the community police members to invest so much labor in unpaid police work. I suggest that emotional desires and a sense of empowerment are significant. This adds another meaning to police violence. However, this aspect also needs to be situated in a context of high vulnerability and legal indeterminacy.

Community policing has given the young men, who previously had no occupation or recognition, a sense of worth and self-esteem in the neighborhood. They are proud of their achievements. One member has even become a local neighborhood section leader, and the others have obtained jobs as private security guards. They believe this is because of their community police work. When speaking about their achievements, they frequently referred to their capacity to beat criminals as central. In these talks, I also noted a sense of pleasure and enjoyment associated with the physical work of policing. As Beatrice Jauregui (this volume) notes, not only senses of duty but also sensual desires play a vital role "in the ongoing reproduction of routinized police violence."[24] Orlando explained, "What I really like about this job is to catch the thieves, to run after them and grab them. I do not accept defeat. I always win. You know, I was sort of a jock in school, and you see [pointing to his biceps] I am very strong [laughing]." When I saw them joke about the people they interrogated in a humiliating tone while holding the *chamboko*, I also sensed that they enjoyed being able to demonstrate physical strength over others. These emotional aspects, I suggest, were associated with feelings of strength, courage, and ultimately power. The position the community police had assumed to constitute the moral community of the neighborhood also produced a sense of empowerment. This was evident in one situation where five of the members each beat a young man because he had insulted them in public. After what to me was an excessive punishment, the youngster shook hands with the community police, apologized, and thanked them. The feelings of empowerment such beatings produce may help to explain the apparent excess, the pushing, and the degrading remarks, which go beyond the functional aspects of interrogation and retribution. However, as Skolnick and Fyfe note, excessive force should not necessarily be equated with a desire to have authority over others or with ultimate feelings of power, but is simultaneously a sign of the fear, risk, and vulnerability that police face in uncertain contexts.[25] The community police agents were highly vulnerable actors, even as their work gave them a position of de facto authority. They were simultaneously empowered and disempowered figures.[26] This duality further gives meaning to police violence as both a source of power in punishing wrongdoers and as (oftentimes excessive) acts to overcome vulnerability. This was reflected in their relationship with the state police and the law and in the position they held in the neighborhood and toward criminals.

Community police members often bragged about their physical strength and courage when they compared themselves with police officers, who they presented as more fearful of criminals than they. Pedro repeated often that "we know better how to beat and punish the criminals properly," and he referred to a time when he had rescued an officer from being beaten by an angry mob. Taking the law into their own hands empowered the community police, but this was also intricate. They depended on police protection for the way they (illegally) operated because they have no legal mandate. While infrequent, there were formal complaints about the community police beatings. It was only because the station commander protected the members that just one case ended up in court.

Without arms or protection, the community police were also at constant risk of attack by criminals—twice members were hospitalized due to injuries. They were frequently threatened by those they had arrested, beaten, and taken to the police station. Such risks were used by the members to explain their rough handling of suspects as a kind of self-protection. Pedro explained, "When we make them suffer and show that here we beat, then they will be too afraid to threaten us." Violence in these situations derives from vulnerable job conditions, which cause emotions of fear. Thus, violence becomes a reaction to disempowerment. But how does this explain the treatment of Jha, who clearly did not pose a threat? In his case, I suggest, the excess, beyond the functions of moral education and crime prevention, also conveyed an emotional desire to turn the fundamental vulnerability of the community police as youths who have no secure position into a sense of empowerment. This sense of empowerment is only temporary, and therefore violence is frequently reperformed. This fundamental vulnerability is further compounded by their precarious position in the neighborhood, which was marred by internal community divisions and power struggles.

While enjoying widespread support, the community police guys were frequently criticized. Some neighborhood residents raised complaints about their beatings. Others compared them to criminals and held that they were uneducated and thus knew only how to beat. The community police in short did not enjoy full legitimacy. This too made them vulnerable. The simultaneous support for and opposition to the community police reflected not only different moral views of police violence but also divided ideas about who ought to have the authority to punish criminals. Intriguingly, this division did not boil down to an opposition between state officials, in support of a state monopoly, and neighborhood residents, in support of popular policing. Local state officials, including the Frelimo Party branch and the station commander, supported the position the community police had assumed. That this was because their own authority in the neighborhood depended on the actions of the community police became particularly clear during a local power dispute in 2011.

The dispute began when Armando, a political opposition supporter, raised reasonable complaints about the community police beatings. He demanded that the members and their leader be removed. He got support from the person responsible for community policing at the Ministry of Interior, who was critical of the fact that the community police concept had been used to establish an alternative police force. The local state administrator, with support from the local Frelimo leader and the station commander, maintained that the community police did a good job in combating crime. The result of the dispute was a new community police leader, who worked as a police officer in another part of the city. Later, the local state administrator was also removed because he "preferred to resolve matters locally rather than add them to the system." The young men, however, continued to work as they had done before. According to the administrator, Armando did not care about the community police beatings but wanted to challenge the local state and the Frelimo Party politically. Whether true or not, this allegation reflects how the local tiers of the party-state perceived the community police as central to sustaining their own position. This was also evident during election campaigns where the community police were used as security guards for a group of Frelimo members who campaigned on foot in the neighborhood, putting up posters and visiting individual households. The community police were also encouraged to tear down the election posters of the opposition and threaten Renamo members with criminal charges.[27] So even if the community police, as reflected by the Ministry of Interior representative, could be seen as a challenge to state authority, by constituting an alternative police force, they were instrumental to the local party-state.

At a deeper structural level, local party-state representatives' support for the community police reflects how de jure state sovereignty remains contested in practice and how current laws are seen as insufficient to produce order and sustain authority locally. This has created a space for community policing agents to act as local sovereigns within what could be seen as "microstates." According to Boaventura Santos, microstates are characterized by having their own combination of different local and extralocal historical layers of operational logics belonging to different periods of state formation, including precolonial customary rule. Microstates develop because of the inability of local state institutions to guarantee their own efficiency by relying solely on formal procedures and the codified law.[28] For the community policing agents this scenario gives them a sense of power, but the position they hold is also precarious. The divided opinions and legal indeterminacy also reproduce violence as an effort to continuously restore temporary positions of power.

Conclusion

This text began with observations of police beatings and discrimination, igniting fear, humiliation, and bodily pain in the victims of *ordinary* police violence. The emphasis on *ordinary* denotes frequency, unexceptionality, and routine. In the crime-ridden and poor urban neighborhood of Chasana, violence performed by civilian policing actors is seen as a normal part of "the police job" and is frequently supported and expected by neighborhood residents and local state officials. It also denotes the emotional desires of otherwise vulnerable policing actors for self-esteem and empowerment. The intertwinement of different logics and meanings implies that violence can neither be reduced to the state police's legal mandate to use force or to the moral dilemmas this raises for police officers, nor simply be viewed as a straightforward extension of popular punishments. Police violence is performed by civilian actors who have no legal mandate but who gain legitimacy by both mimicking the state police and enacting immediate justice. The result is an intermediary form of policing between state police action and community vengeance, for which violence is central. This intermediary form of policing raises a more general question about the enabling conditions of (civilian) police violence at a deeper structural level of state and society.

Where does the general question leave ethnography and a possible critique of violence? Eliciting the multiple meanings of police violence is not the same as ignoring or excusing the discriminatory and cruel practices of policing actors. Neither does it render violent acts insusceptible to ethical and moral critique. However, to come to grips with why and how routine police violence is possible and acceptable, there is a need to first complicate it, to see its meanings from different angles and not to reduce explanations to one singular factor or to evaluate it against one particular moral register. Ethnography is central to this endeavor because of the empirical richness and nuances it enables. The ethnographer's task is to go beyond the acts of violence in themselves, not condemning them in the moments of observation but taking the perspectives and logics of local police actors and those they engage with seriously. In my experience this is not an easy task, not only because of my own ethical position against violence or because by not explicitly condemning violent acts, by letting it happen before one's eyes, the ethnographer is somewhat complicit. It is also difficult because of the physical discomfort it aroused in me. However, it is only by exposing the complexities of ordinary violence in particular ethnographic contexts through engaging with violence, I suggest, that it is possible to begin to provide a deeper critique of violence, not in the moment of its enactment but at a structural level. This means addressing the enabling conditions of violence and particularly their relation to power.[29] To do so, ethnography also poses limits due to its microlevel focus and therefore needs to be combined with historical and sociological analysis that situates violence within a wider political context.

In the Mozambican context, a critique of police violence must begin with an understanding of a history of incomplete and contested state formation processes since colonial rule. This history is both one of a state that fails to serve poorer citizens and one that has continuously tried, principally through violent means, to assert sovereignty. First, emic justifications for police violence as instrumental and retributive fall back on a deep-seated mistrust in the official state system to protect poor urban neighborhood residents from crime and to deliver satisfactory justice to them. This reflects both unfulfilled expectations of what the state ought to do in the minds of citizens and a discrepancy between procedural law and popular demands for substantive justice. These discrepancies have a long history in Mozambique, but they also need to be situated within the current political context of transition. Democratization has introduced a range of citizen rights but has also come with increased inequality, unemployment, crime, and corruption as well as a weakening of local order-making institutions. The urban poor continue to feel marginalized vis-à-vis the political and economic elites who are not only able to pay for protection and juridical processes but who also have privileged access to other rights and benefits. Because de jure rights have not translated into actual protection and benefits, the law is predominantly seen as unjust. In such a context, as Daniel Goldstein shows for Bolivia, support for vigilante-style actions and violent punishment can be interpreted as a sign of desperation and frustration in lieu of what is seen as an unresponsive and indifferent state.[30] This goes well beyond a critique of the official justice system, reflecting also deeper power relations and exclusions in society, which affect the security and livelihood of the urban poor. In such a context, the recovery of stolen goods and the immediate punishment of persons who have frequently committed crime become also expressions of survival.

The habitual, routine aspects of police violence find their source less in a critique of an unresponsive state in the present than in a long history of institutionalized state police violence. This brings me to the second aspect of contested state formation processes. Today, the historical legacy informs popular expectations of the police to act forcefully and also underscores state police officers' frustrations with current laws that restrict such violence. However, at a deeper structural level this does not reflect a shift away from a once strong and hyperempowered state. Rather, violence has been institutionalized as the result of continuous efforts to assert state sovereignty in a context where the legitimacy of state law and the claim to a monopoly on force remains contested. This necessarily relies on a theory of violence as a founding element of state law and authority.[31] Since colonial rule, state formation in Mozambique has been marred by alternative sovereign actors, like traditional leaders, liberation fighters, and Renamo rebels, as well as by other normative orders that differ from state law. This has been infused by long periods of conquest and war, with the liberation war (1967–1974) soon succeeded by the civil war (1978–1992). Policing was never only about dealing with delinquency but also about combating enemies in efforts to consolidate power and a singular normative order. The postcolonial party-state's concept of internal enemies, spanning from traditional leaders and insurgents to criminals and persons acting immorally, epitomizes the war mentality that has infused the state police. Internal enemies were treated as unworthy of a due legal process and were subject to harsh punishments, public humiliation, and reeducation, while some traditional leaders were executed. In this context, it is the very limits of state sovereignty that reproduce violent acts as an effort to refound sovereign claims and to overcome alternative notions of order and legitimacy. These practices, which appear as both extrajuridical and outside state law, have been most explicit in wartime and in crack downs on political opposition, but they have also been inserted into everyday policing as routinized violence.

The paradox today is that such routine violence is replayed at the micro-level by civilian actors in an informal and outsourced form as habits passed on by and associated with the state police. In itself this privatization of police violence can be seen as yet another effect of limited state sovereignty, not least because police violence becomes instrumental to the enforcement not of the law but of popular justice. Yet violence here also works to reconstitute the state by other means. The civilian police actors are seen as the extended arm of the state police, and their work also supports the position of local state authorities. As such the community police agents "represent at once the fading of the state's jurisdiction and its continual re-founding through [the] appropriation of private justice and violence."[32] According to Veena Das and Deborah Poole, this apparently contradictory position reflects a core feature of the state in the margins, which they define as the territory of questioned state control (and legitimacy) and as "sites of practice on which law and other state practices are colonized by other forms of regulation" and where there is no clearly defined order.[33]

Viewed in this way the reproduction of police violence through a community policing initiative is not alone enabled by the failure of the official system to provide justice but also by the limits of the state to constitute authority through legal means. At the microlevel, these predicaments empower local policing actors, but at the same time, the very uncertainty of authority also makes them vulnerable, subject to critique and devoid of legal protection. This vulnerability reproduces violence, if not as self-protection then as a way to refound positions of power through violence. As such, it reflects a microlevel mirror of state violence as a means to overcome the limits of sovereignty.

The current democratization process in Mozambique further complicates this picture but also potentially opens up for more popular critique of violence. As in other new democracies emerging from long decades of authoritarian rule, the legacies of routine police violence coexist not only with major legal changes that restrict state violence but also with a growing antiviolent discourse led ahead by human rights and other civil society organizations.[34] This juncture in Mozambique is reflected in split views within individuals, families, the police force, and other state and social institutions about the legitimacy and illegitimacy of violence to produce order and justice. So far only very few prosecutions of police officers using excessive force have taken place, and community police agents have largely acted with impunity. This reflects not only the difficulty of determining when and how police violence can be deemed excessive, as shown by classic police studies,[35] but also the very "indeterminacy of the legitimization of violence itself"[36] in a context where the "existing order is not clearly defined" and is undergoing great flux.[37]

Notes

1. Fieldwork was carried out over sixteen months during 2009 and 2010, with follow-up field visits in 2011, 2012, and 2014.
2. Nina and Schwikkard 1996.
3. See Skolnick and Fyfe 1993; Stone and Ward 2000.
4. Jauregui 2014, 127.
5. This view is strongly inspired by Bittner 1970 and Muir 1977. See also Brodeur 2003.
6. Bittner 1970.
7. Brodeur 2003, 211.
8. Klockars 1980.
9. Skolnick 2011 (1994).
10. Das and Poole 2004.
11. Jauregui 2014, 127; Das and Poole 2004; Pratten and Sen 2009.
12. Pratten and Sen 2009.
13. Skolnick and Fyfe 1993, 239.
14. All the citations from the cases described are from my digital recordings, based on permission from the community police members. They are translated to English from either Portuguese or the local dialect, Shangana.
15. On the community policing initiative in Mozambique, see Kyed 2010.
16. On the question of complicity see Jauregui 2014 and Hornberger (chapter 2, this volume).
17. On police reform in Mozambique, see Kyed, forthcoming.
18. Brodeur 2003; Bittner 1970.
19. During the middle of the first decade of the twenty-first century there was an increase in lynchings reported in the media across Mozambique, and it became part of a wider debate about the deficiencies of the police in protecting poor urban neighborhoods. See Serra 2008.
20. Brodeur 2003, 210.
21. See Kyed 2007.
22. Klockars 1980.
23. Jensen 2007.
24. Jauregui 2014, 130.
25. Skolnick and Fyfe 1993, 18.
26. In this sense, my case agrees with Jauregui (2014), when she challenges Walter Benjamin's notion of police as hyperempowered figures who have almost endless power to make law due to their discretionary power and instead highlights the risks they face in the everyday.
27. On this local political instrumentalization of the community police, see Kyed 2009.
28. Santos 2006.

29. On this point, see also Fassin 2014, 136–37.
30. Goldstein 2004.
31. Benjamin 1986 (1922); Hansen and Stepputat 2005.
32. Das and Poole 2004, 14.
33. Ibid., 8.
34. Caldeira 2002, 97.
35. Brodeur (2003).
36. Jauregui 2014, 127.
37. Skolnick and Fyfe 1993, 239.

References

Benjamin, Walter. 1978 [1922]. "Critique of Violence." In *Reflections: Essays, Aphorisms, Autobiographical Writings,* edited by Peter Demetz, 277–300. New York: Schocken.

Bittner, Egon. 1970. *The Functions of the Police in Modern Society.* Chevy Chase, MD: National Insitute of Mental Health.

Brodeur, Jean-Paul. 2003. "Violence and the Police." In *International Handbook of Violence Research,* edited by Wilhelm Heitmeyer and John Hagan, 207–24. Dordrecht: Kluwer Academic Publishers.

Caldeira, Teresa. 2002. "The Paradox of Police Violence in Democratic Brazil." *Ethnography* 3 (3): 235–63.

Das, Veena, and Deborah Poole, eds. 2004. *Anthropology in the Margins of the State.* Oxford: James Currey.

Fassin, Didier. 2014. *Enforcing Order: An Ethnography of Urban Policing.* Cambridge: Polity Press.

Goldstein, Daniel. 2004. *The Spectacular City: Violence and Performance in Urban Bolivia.* Chapel Hill: Duke University Press.

Hansen, Thomas Blom, and Finn Stepputat, eds. 2005. *Sovereign Bodies: Citizens, Migrants, and States in the Postcolonial World.* Princeton: Princeton University Press.

Jauregui, Beatrice. 2014. "Dirty Anthropology: Epistemologies of Violence and Ethical Entanglements in Police Ethnography." In *Policing and Contemporary Governance: The Anthropology of Police in Practice,* edited by William Garriot, 125–53. New York: Palgrave.

Jensen, Steffen. 2007. "Through the Lens of Crime: Land Claims and Contestations over Citizenship on the Frontier of the South African State." In *The Security-Development Nexus: Expressions of Sovereignty in Southern Africa,* edited by Lars Buur, Steffen Jensen, and Finn Stepputat, 193–211. Uppsala: Nordiska Afrikainstitutet.

Klockars, Carl B. 1980. "The Dirty Harry Problem." *Annals of the American Academy of Political and Social Science* 452:33–47.

Kyed, Helene Maria. 2007. "State Recognition of Traditional Authority: Authority, Citizenship and State Formation in Rural Post-War Mozambique." PhD dissertation, Roskilde University.

———. 2009. "The Politics of Legal Pluralism: State Policies on Legal Pluralism and Their Local Dynamics in Mozambique." *Journal of Legal Pluralism* 59:87–121.

———. 2010. "The Contested Role of Community Policing: 'New' Non-State Actors in the Plural Legal Landscape of Mozambique." DIIS Working Paper, no. 26.

———. Forthcoming. "Post-War Police Reform in Mozambique: The Case of Community Policing." In *Colonial Policing and the Transnational Legacy: The Global Dynamics of Policing across the Lusophone Community*, edited by Conor O'Reilly. Farnham, UK: Ashgate.

Muir, William Ker. 1977. *Police: Streetcorner Politicians*. Chicago: University of Chicago Press.

Nina, Daniel, and Pamela Jane Schwikkard. 1996. "The Soft Vengeance of the People: Popular Justice, Community Justice, and Legal Pluralism in South Africa." *Journal of Legal Pluralism* 36:21–67.

Pratten, David, and Ayetrea Sen, eds. 2009. *Global Vigilantes*. London: Hurst & Co.

Santos, Boaventura de Sousa. 2006. "The Heterogeneous State and Legal Pluralism in Mozambique." *Law and Society Review* 40 (1): 39–75.

Serra, Carlos, ed. 2008. *Linchamento em Moçambique I (Uma desordem que apela á ordem)*. Maputo: Imprensa Universitária.

Skolnick, Jerome H. 2011 [1994]. *Justice without Trial*. New Orleans: Quid Pro Quo.

Skolnick, Jerome H., and James J. Fyfe. 1993. *Above the Law: Police and the Excessive Use of Force*. New York: Free Press.

Stone, Christopher, and Heather H. Ward. 2000. "Democratic Policing: A Framework for Action." *Policing and Society* 10 (1): 11–45.

SIX

Morality:
Understanding Police Training
on Human Rights (Turkey)

ELIF BABÜL

On a rainy November afternoon, a group of eighteen police officers—sixteen men and two women—were gathered around a large u-shaped table in one of the meeting rooms of a downtown hotel in Ankara.[1] On this third day of a five-day-long training for trainers about "The Role of the Police in Preventing Domestic Violence against Women," the participants were doing their best to concentrate on the presentation of Chief Inspector Sertan, who was about to show them the educational film they were supposed to disseminate in their own precincts. Once the film started playing, the postlunch lethargy gave way to an engaged viewing, where the participants' cynical comments and giggles transformed what was meant to be an inspiring portrayal of best practices into the satirical display of the gap between theory and practice in the field.

The film, coproduced by the General Directorate of Women's Status and the Turkish National Police as part of the government's "zero tolerance toward domestic violence" policy, was about how a domestic abuse victim, who comes to the police center to file a complaint, should be treated. In the film, police officers played by professional actors took the plaintiff into a designated interviewing room, assigned a woman police officer to take her testimony, and distracted her young son with toys while her testimony was taken. The prosecutor was notified of the situation immediately. Meanwhile, because the plaintiff was assessed as "high risk," someone from the social services agency was also notified. She was then taken to the hospital for medical examination. After being brought back to the police center, she was promptly transferred to the women's shelter. Before showing the film, Chief Inspector Sertan emphasized that it reflected the institutional ideals and aspired to best practices. Even so, participants continued to crack jokes and make comments about the discrepancy between what they saw on the screen and what happened in real life. One police officer jokingly asked whether the personnel in the film paid for the toys out of their own pockets. Another participant expressed his amazement that there was a woman officer available at the police center. Similar comments were made regarding the ease with which the low-rank officers called the prosecutor without the fear of being told off. And finally, the participants all applauded when someone from the social services agency actually answered the phone.

The program on "the role of the police in preventing domestic violence against women" was one of the many human rights training programs for state officials in which I participated during my research in Turkey.[2] These trainings were conducted as part of a larger "harmonization process" that the country had to undergo in order to attain membership in the European Union (EU)—a goal successive governments have been pursuing since 1987. A long and arduous process, Turkey's candidacy gained official status following the Helsinki summit in 1999. It took another six years to launch accession negotiations between Turkey and the EU. Since 2005, the Turkish government has been continuing negotiations with the Commission for Enlargement under thirty-five chapters, which cover a variety of national policy areas that require harmonization with the total body of the EU law (*the Acquis*).

The Commission defines harmonization as the transformation of a candidate country as it brings its institutions, management capacity, and administrative and judicial systems up to EU standards.[3] Although this standardization scheme features titles ranging from free movement of goods, capital, and workers to competition policy, fisheries, energy, and taxation, those pertaining to human rights and good governance enjoy a special visibility at domestic and international levels, both due to their particular symbolic force and due to Turkey's flawed human rights record. Training programs like the one on domestic violence are one of the principal means of operationalizing harmonization on the ground. They are usually funded by the EU and administered by some form of a joint state-civil society initiative, wherein a plethora of nongovernmental organizations, universities, and think tanks lend technical assistance to various government institutions to build their capacity on a specific topic. Most capacity-building projects include training programs to achieve attitudinal and behavioral transformation of state officials, who are responsible for implementing the abstract legal-administrative reforms at the everyday level.

Drawing from my experience alongside police trainings on human rights, I want to focus in this chapter on how transnational standardization enters into the lives of the Turkish police and shapes the model of policing in the country. Like several other scholars who trace the influence of transnational rights regimes on specific localities,[4] I find it useful to employ translation as an analytic to explore how human rights are rendered relevant to the work of the police in Turkey at this particular conjuncture. Instead of a straightforward conversion of meaning, translation here operates as a creative distortion, where values and behaviors associated with human rights assume different—at times contradictory—meanings to create effect in local settings. The value of ethnography, I argue, lies in its capacity to reveal the rationalities, relationships, and moralities that shape those distortions, which can also shed light on the practices that they inform.

My ethnography of police trainings shows how they operate as sites where human rights standards are translated into standards of professionalism and technical expertise that are supposed to improve policing work in the country. Following these translations and how their audiences receive them exposes the limits of the ethics of profession for instituting a model of policing that is compatible with human rights. In what follows, I present the two principle means through which translation of human rights into an ethics of profession is performed and communicated in trainings: delineation of the field of security as a field of expertise and increasing the bureaucratic prestige of the police. My main argument is that together, these two moves do not restrict but enhance the power of the police in Turkey.

A couple of disclaimers are in order before I proceed. First of all, my ethnographic focus on the discursive and performative spaces of trainings does not necessarily assume that what is talked about in those settings is what the officers actually practice on the street. Noting the critical difference between what people do and what they say they do, I refrain from making a claim that what I have is an account of everyday policing in Turkey. Similar to P. A. J. Waddington's[5] analysis of the police canteen subculture, I believe that the rhetorical performances of officers (both as trainers and trainees) in training programs deserve attention because they demonstrate how performers attribute meaning to their experience and how they sustain their occupational self-esteem. As Didier Fassin[6] argues, although they may not be a direct reflection of how the police behave on duty, these performances are still worth studying because they reveal the underlying set of values, thoughts, and emotions that define certain behavior as moral and ethical, thereby justifying and rationalizing them. The particular setting of human rights training programs also alludes to the institutional logic that governs policing in Turkey and how this logic is then presented to an audience of officers to convince them about the importance of human rights for their line of work.

Secondly, although my ethnographic vignette might seem like a moment where local practitioners resist the imposition of a standard procedure that is foreseen by harmonization, I aim to go beyond a simplistic dichotomy of sincere appropriation versus cynical rejection of human rights standards by the police. Akin to many scholars who work on the everyday operation of the state,[7] I take cynicism not as a form of disassociation but as a mode of engagement with the standards that the officers are introduced to during trainings. The account of the trainees' cynical engagement with transnational standardization and the management of their reactions by the trainers help to understand the local ethos that underlies the institution of policing in Turkey and how this ethos gets transformed in the course of harmonization. What an ethnographic exploration of trainings reveals is that this transformation happens in quite unexpected ways, not necessarily leading to a less violent form of policing.

The above vignette demonstrates how a gender-sensitive approach toward domestic violence got translated into a bureaucratic procedure that the officers are required to follow as professionals—impersonal, neutral operators of a field of expertise—independent of their personal convictions on gender equality or violence against women. Before I get into more detail on how Chief Inspector Sertan responded to the audience's cynical remarks on this bureaucratic procedure, let me give some more background on how human rights trainings are situated within the overall organization of policing in Turkey.

Reforming the Turkish National Police

Unlike many ethnographers of policing, I did not start my fieldwork intending to study the police. It would be fair to say that I rather stumbled upon the police as I was looking for opportunities to participate in human rights training programs directed toward state officials in Turkey. After many unsuccessful attempts to gain access to different training programs administered by various state institutions, I discovered through an acquaintance that an Ankara-based think tank was partnering with the Ministry of Justice and UNICEF to develop a training program on children's rights for the constituents of the newly established juvenile justice system in the country. *Emniyet Genel Müdürlüğü* (Turkish National Police—TNP) was one of those constituents. Contrary to my expectations, the directors of the juvenile justice training program took me in, and for the good part of the rest of my two-year fieldwork I found myself spending long hours helping to develop training materials and the trainers' manual, running test trainings, and attending assessment meetings, most of which took place at the Crime Research and Investigation Training Center (SASEM) and the Police Academy. If it had not been for this unexpected and unplanned ethnographic accident, I would not have realized how heavily the TNP was integrated into the harmonization economy and how central the reimagination of policing was for the agenda of governmental reform in Turkey.

Once in the field, I realized that the TNP was actually one of the most active participants in the harmonization process, taking advantage of lucrative EU project funds, twinning programs, and Technical Assistance and Information Exchange (TAIEX) instruments to organize meetings, workshops, and country visits with the stated goal to "increase (its) organizational and administrative capacity." According to the website of the TNP International Relations Department, between 2002 and 2012 the TNP conducted nineteen EU projects and was the beneficiary of eighteen others. The topic of those projects included border policing and management, asylum and migration, organized crime, human trafficking, drugs, cybercrimes, forensic evidence examination capacity, judicial capacity, use of force, and the accountability of the police.[8] During this period, 568 officers participated in 148 country visits to twenty EU countries. In 2012 alone, 950 officers took part in twenty-two workshops.[9] When I was in the field between 2007 and 2009, the TNP was involved in a number of rights-related training programs focusing on children's rights, women's rights, and the rights of the refugees, working in cooperation with national and international nongovernmental organizations such as UNICEF, the UNFPA, the UNHCR, the Helsinki Citizens Assembly, the Turkish Medical Association, and the Foundation for Women's Solidarity.

The intensity of the TNP's participation in the harmonization process should be understood in the larger context of governmental reform that emerged as a transnational agenda in the post–Cold War era. Following the introduction of the concept of "good governance" by the World Bank in 1989 and the establishment of liberal democracy as the global norm, institutions and mechanisms of governance mainly in places referred to as "the Third World" or "the Global South" became the objects of intervention for reform.[10] This was particularly so for the law enforcement agents, who were "obliged to be violent on behalf of the state."[11] Seen as the primary operators of state violence, discretionary power, and impunity, law enforcement agents were often designated as the quintessential targets of improvement through standardization. In line with this transnational trend as well as the intensification of the EU accession process, the TNP has become the target of reform since the beginning of the first decade of the twenty-first century. At the national level, this period also corresponded to the beginning of the current Justice and Development Party (AKP) rule, where the government allegedly focused its efforts to transfer the ownership of the regime from what it considered to be the republican elites to the real people of the country—a group that it claimed to represent. Reforming the security apparatus of the state to gain its control was one of the first items on the government's agenda toward this end.[12]

In the words of political scientist and security expert Sedat Laçiner, who for a long time taught at the Police Academy, this reform entailed transforming the police from "the guardian of a tyrannical order" to "the defender of law and democracy in a developed country."[13] Contrary to the 1980s and 1990s, during which the institution was heavily associated with corruption, indiscriminate use of force, torture, extrajudicial killings, and forced disappearances, the TNP of the new millennium was to be a bastion of professionalism and technical proficiency, composed of well-educated security experts who performed their jobs in line with human rights and the rule of law. According to another political scientist and a former dean of the Institute of Security Sciences at the Academy, İhsan Bal, the TNP has been going through a "renaissance" since the end of the 1990s, reorganizing itself in line with openness to criticism, auditing, and transparency. As a result of these efforts, police officers were now described as "educated, civilized, polite, and professional people who do not resort to ill treatment" even by the high-profile detainees of the recent controversial *Ergenekon*[14] case that included military generals, newspaper columnists, and elected members of the parliament.[15]

An emphasis on education is perhaps the most important component of this vision of reforming the TNP. Extensive literature on police reform indicates that the assumed correlation between education and reform shapes similar initiatives all around the world. Professionalization and modernization of the police through education is seen as the primary means of resolving the putative dilemma between democratization and security. It is believed that improving the quality of policing would enable the police to effectively tackle with crime while at the same time acting in accordance with human rights standards and the principles of the rule of law.[16] Human rights training often emerges as an important component of the professionalization of the police, where the controversial symbolism of the politics of human rights is carefully managed by reframing them as part of governmental techniques.[17]

In a similar vein, since the TNP's problems were mainly framed as resulting from incompetent management and insufficient legal training of police officers, the remedy was imagined in the form of bolstering the level of education within the police. This was also seen as the way to standardize the application of legal and juridical procedures in order to curb discretion and inconsistency, which were assumed to be among the major factors leading to violation and abuse. To this effect, in 2001 the Police Academy was restructured in the model of a police university. Under this new model the academy included two-year Police Occupational Schools that grant associate degrees for low-level police officers, a four-year School of Security Sciences that grants undergraduate degrees for officers at the commander level (deputy inspector and higher), and Institutes of Forensic and Security Sciences that grant degrees at the MA level for officers who would like to pursue an even higher education. Starting from 1990s, TNP executive officers also sent police officers to the United States and the United Kingdom to learn community policing, citizen-based policing, and intelligence-led policing in order to develop their capacity in the areas of counterterrorism, counterinsurgency, and crowd control.[18]

Due to this institutional background, many project teams running human rights trainings thought that police officers had a higher degree of "readiness to learn." Other state officials, such as judges and prosecutors, were more difficult to convince about the benefits of training. These more "elite" cadres of state officials saw themselves as already well educated, and they were often offended by the EU-initiated efforts to further educate them on human rights and international law.[19] Contrary to these groups, police officers often welcomed opportunities for education, thinking that it might lead to benefits such as occupational specialization, promotion, and salary raises.

During the juvenile justice project team's visit to various stakeholder institutions in preparation for test trainings, the TNP's readiness became quite visible. Unlike visits to other institutions such as the Justice Academy, the Bar Association, and the Education Center of the General Directorate of Prisons and Detention Houses, we were received at the highest management level. The director of SASEM, who was accompanied by a small team of his own, was eager to work with the project and to integrate the final program into the wide array of in-house trainings that were already being offered. He informed us that both high- and low-level police officers were by now very familiar with and responsive toward interactive training methods, that despite the hierarchical setup of the organization most police officers felt comfortable expressing themselves in front of their supervisors. "They are used to participating in training programs without their uniforms," he said, "they participate on a voluntary basis and there is high demand [for trainings] . . . The expectation is that [the juvenile police] will become a specialized unit, so there would be high demand." We left the meeting assured of full cooperation, both for supplying participants for test trainings and for providing the necessary resources and space to hold them.

Redeeming Police Work through Professionalism and Expertise

Receptiveness toward training at the management level did not necessarily render trainings conflict-free zones. On the contrary, it was quite common to come across scenes such as the one I opened this chapter with in almost all training programs, where the police officers partaking in trainings spoke back at what was taught to them. Although they were eager to participate in the programs, practitioners nevertheless expressed doubts about what were presented as "universal standards," claiming that due to inadequate resources, overworked staff, unsympathetic administrators, and incompetent subordinates their implementation was not so easy. One of the two women officers at the domestic violence prevention training for trainers summarized her feelings during the final feedback session in the following words: "My concern with this training is that I'll go to my precinct and tell my colleagues that they can call the social services agency if they assess the plaintiff at high risk. They're going to call and nobody will pick up the phone. I understand that we're raising our standards and raising the bar [for public service]. But we're jumping over a bar and there's nothing to catch us on the other side."

Although they might be read as signs of resistance, the project teams in fact encouraged such responses by intentionally designing the trainings as participatory, interactive spaces that invited the trainees to speak out. All of the training programs I participated in opened with the project managers urging the trainees to dress informally, be comfortable, and speak their mind. They underlined that an ideal training was a two-way exchange of ideas and experiences, not a top-down imposition of content. Active participation in the training—even in the form of questioning it—indicated a higher level of engagement on the part of the trainees, presenting a better chance of influencing their attitude and behavior. In those moments, what fell upon the trainers and the members of the project team was to persuade the participants about both the feasibility and desirability of human rights standards. Institutional trainers such as Chief Inspector Sertan had the advantage of possessing intimate knowledge of the organization and were taken much more seriously by the participants due to their familiarity with everyday police work as well as their higher rank. For example, speaking to the complaints about understaffed police centers that would complicate the implementation of standard procedure for the treatment of domestic violence victims, Chief Inspector Sertan jokingly asked me to cover my ears for a minute. Then he delivered a passionate lecture about how if they called the police officers napping in the patrol cars back on duty and refused to send officers to chase random personal business upon the prosecutors' or the governors' whimsical demands, police chiefs would surely have enough people to run the centers properly. During his lecture, the participants smiled and nodded with a combination of embarrassment and amusement, with the recognition of a common sociality, which confirmed that their trainer was one of them. His access to the world of policing enabled Chief Inspector Sertan to respond to the concerns of the training participants without offending them or causing a backlash—something that was not available to noninstitutional trainers or the civilian members of the project team.

Another equally important feature of Chief Inspector Sertan's response was his framing of the participants' complaints as deriving from institutional inefficiency and lack of professionalism, and in line with the main axes of the larger police reform agenda. In this training, like in many others, the necessity to act in line with human rights standards was portrayed as part of the ongoing professionalization within the TNP. Professionalization of the police meant inculcating an automated persona within each officer, with the intention of mainstreaming their behavior in the office and on the streets toward the general public. When officers became professionals, they would act as cogs in a wheel, as the indifferent operators of a system that was set elsewhere and in line with the government's larger security policy. In a professionalized setting, whether individual officers agreed with government agendas became irrelevant to their implementation of those.

When I interviewed him earlier, Sertan had told me that the main purpose of the training was to "systematize" the officers' approach toward domestic violence across the board and to clarify "the limits of the TNP's professional responsibility" for preventing domestic violence. He repeated these two points throughout the training as well. He said that what was foreseen by the program was "a systematic approach to prevent the police officers' individualistic management of domestic violence cases," which often resulted in covering them up. "It's not their own personal familial problems they're dealing with," he asserted: "Domestic violence is a crime and some crimes necessitate expertise and a multilateral approach." "Expertise, objectivity, not being influenced by anything. Aren't these what we have been taught all along? . . . Here we're going to talk about realities, we will be realistic. We will be professionals. We want to become professionals of this topic. We will develop our skills. If you witness a crime, you have to carry out an investigation; there is no way out of it."

Here, as much as human rights standards meant "doing one's job properly," procedural standardization also meant preventing the overburdening of the police force. One of the phrases Chief Inspector Sertan repeated over and over again was that the police would not do things that are not its business anymore—"*polis artık üzerine vazife olmayan işleri yapmayacak.*" These ranged from functioning like a shelter when the social services agency did not take in victims of domestic violence to acting like a personal bodyguard to oversee the execution of restraining orders and assuming judicial powers to decide whether the perpetrator in a particular domestic violence case was really culpable or not. Within the paradigm of professionalism, problems of misogyny and tolerance for violence against women were put on the same plane with other technical, professional impediments that stem from the lack of clear separation of duty between different state institutions and the absence of coordination among them.

This technical framing of rights-related issues was inherent to the design of trainings. With the realization that human rights was a sensitive and controversial topic, especially for law enforcement agents who are often identified as perpetrators of human rights violations, project teams intentionally adopted an approach that would not alienate their target audiences. Toward this end, the trainers underlined that adhering to human rights standards and the rule of law was not just the right thing to do but also made practical and professional sense. Chief Inspector Sertan used this very same logic when he defended the law that requires the suspects' medical examination before and after detention—a requirement most police officers try to sidestep because they fear it will produce evidence for possible charges of torture and ill treatment. I give a lengthy quote from my field notes to show the unfolding of this instrumentalist logic:

SERTAN: *Arkadaşlar* [friends], I think obtaining a [medical] report is actually in
our interest. I mean we should definitely get reports [for the detainees] before and after detention . . . Because there is nobody who gets arrested according to his or her own will anyway. Have you come across anyone who
gets into a police car willingly, without resisting?

TRAINEES: No!

SERTAN: Do I have the legal right to use force during the arrest?

TRAINEES: Yes, of course!

SERTAN: Of course! The real problem arises not at that point [arrest] but afterward [in detention]. Because we don't get [medical] reports [after the arrest,
before the detention], the bruises that happen during the arrest appear in the
latter reports [causing the bruises to look like they happened as a result of
the illegal use of force during detention]. That's why we shouldn't intervene
in the doctors' business. On the contrary, we should encourage them to report whatever they see . . .

Although many human rights defenders considered medical examination and reporting as an important mechanism to curb police violence and
to fight against impunity, Sertan's rationale for defending medical examination came from an entirely different place. His logic derived from a professional standpoint, which did not necessarily repudiate the use of force
by the police. He argued that medical documentation was actually ben-
eficial for the officers while performing their law enforcement duties, for
which the use of force was necessary. According to this reasoning, medical
documentation did not impede the use of force by the police. On the contrary, it enabled the use of force by documenting that it was used legally.
Rather than curbing the police officers' powers, following the law enabled
effective policing by making the use of force safe. It was thought that this
utilitarian approach would motivate the participants to act according to
law because it would make them realize that abiding by the law "actually
worked." Despite its appeal for the participants, Sertan's advice to obey the
medical examination requirement did not explicitly condemn police brutality. Instead, it led to a utilitarian affirmation of the law, which apparently endorsed police violence under certain circumstances. As the above
quote demonstrates, under these conditions, the training ironically turned
into the mastery of the circumstances that allowed for the legal use of violence cum "force" by the police.

The technical-professional make up of human rights trainings was also
sustained by other topics that accompanied rights-related issues. In the
domestic violence prevention training, sessions focusing on gender equal-

ity and violence against women were juxtaposed with sessions on forensic and administrative procedures, countrywide statistical documentation and analysis of domestic violence, and crime prevention models from select European countries. One of the most important roles of the police in preventing domestic violence was portrayed as the formation of a database for statistical knowledge production that would help assess the prevalence of domestic violence throughout the country. Documentation, data collection, and statistical analysis were depicted as essential for capacity development and as the TNP's "first step toward professionalism." Although these sessions were helpful to convince the participants that fighting domestic violence was part of their crime prevention duties, they also made other "less technical" sessions appear irrelevant. At the final training evaluation session, most participants expressed that they found the sessions on gender equality and violence against women taught by women's rights activists "unnecessary," "too long," and "irrelevant," suggesting to shorten them in the future. Thus, instead of creating gender awareness among police officers, the emphasis on professionalism and expertise provided an excuse for the trainees to refuse to engage with the very modules that would really challenge their gendered worldviews.

Situating the Police within the Bureaucratic Machinery

One of the underlying purposes to reframe police work in light of professionalism and expertise was to improve the prestige of policing as a profession, both in the general public's eye and within the larger bureaucratic machinery. Perhaps the most rewarding aspect of studying the TNP in the context of human rights trainings was to recognize how the police were situated in relation to other government agents that they worked with. In addition to participating in trainings that were exclusive to police officers, a significant portion of my fieldwork also consisted of working with mixed training programs where different groups of government agents were trained together. These mixed trainings were usually designed around a specific service field, in which the participants were expected to coordinate. Juvenile justice training was one of the programs organized according to this principle. Designers of the program, consisting of a team of national and international education consultants, children's rights experts, and legal practitioners put together by the Ministry of Justice and the UNICEF Ankara office, had explicitly planned it as a space of interaction among the people whom they considered to be members of a team. This design was meant to encourage government agents working in the fields of law enforcement, justice, social services, and health care to see themselves as cogs in a wheel and as part of a system that was supposed serve "the best interests of the child." Mixed training was also a way to promote cooperation and collaboration between different government offices, which—again as the opening scene demonstrates—often had negative perceptions of each other. Providing a space in which representatives of different institutions could form face-to-face relationships was the key for building an efficient and effective governmental system.

These mixed trainings elicited diverse responses from their participants. Most state officials who worked in lower level (and what were considered to be less elite) institutions had an especially positive take on the mixed trainings. Working mainly in subordinate positions in relation to other government agents who wielded more administrative power within the bureaucratic chain of command, officials working in fields such as law enforcement and social services saw these trainings as valuable opportunities to make their voices heard. Representatives of the TNP were particularly eager to participate in such trainings, where they could have some valuable face time with the judges and prosecutors that they worked under. Judges and prosecutors who were located in the upper echelons of the bureaucratic structure, however, were more likely to be resentful of being trained together with the people who worked under them.

During the field testing for the juvenile justice training, the hierarchical composition of the participants emerged as a major concern for the project team. This first round of trainings was held with the intention of testing the training material on different groups of state officials in order to get their feedback. Taking advantage of the eagerness of the TNP headquarters, the project team decided to use the Police Academy's facilities to hold test trainings. The plan was to have three separate four-day-long sessions for police officers, probation workers, and judges and prosecutors before bringing them together at a final training program. This way, the merging of the groups would happen gradually, which the team hoped would ease the expected reaction on the part of the judges and prosecutors. Although the team believed that this plan would work, some collaborators from the TNP expressed concern, saying that they did not believe judges and prosecutors would even come to the Police Academy to be trained. What they predicted indeed came true. After waiting for two hours on the first day of the program for judges and prosecutors, the team had to cancel the training because none of the participants showed up.

After some quick damage control, the project team went back to the Ministry of Justice with the proposal to hold the test trainings at the Justice

Academy—the prevocational and on-the-job and in-service training center for members of the judiciary. It worked. Although the participants were in no way thrilled about being trained by a group of trainers that included a young woman inspector with a degree in psychological counseling and a sociology professor who taught at the Police Academy, they nevertheless attended the program for four consecutive days. The tension between the judges and prosecutors and the TNP-affiliated project team members erupted sporadically during the sessions and the breaks. Contrary to Chief Inspector Sertan's striking level of command at the domestic violence prevention training, TNP-affiliated trainers at the juvenile justice test trainings were constantly challenged by the judges and prosecutors on account of their insufficient legal knowledge—even if their session's focus had little to do with the law. It was only during the sessions run by a well-known judge who specialized in juvenile justice—someone whom they considered having enough "juridical capital"[20]—that the participants cooperated with the training.

An encounter that took place on the very first day between an older woman judge, a young TNP-affiliated female project assistant, and a senior male officer is a good example of how members of the judiciary and law enforcement agents related to one another typically. Meyda, a low-level officer who worked at SASEM, had been assisting the project team for some time. For the field testing, Meyda and I were assigned the role of observers. Our duty consisted of attending the test trainings for all three groups of state officials and taking notes on how the participants were reacting to the training material—what was working and what was not. On our first day at the Justice Academy, Meyda and I had taken our usual seats at the back of the room with our training manuals and notebooks, ready to observe. One by one the participants started to arrive. When Judge Neriman, the only woman participant in the training, arrived Meyda's face went white. Turning toward me to cover her face, she said that in the past she had a very unpleasant encounter with this particular judge. "Hope she doesn't recognize me," she whispered. "I look a little different now because my hair was different back then. But I should definitely call Chief Inspector Sami. He was thinking of stopping by today. She would definitely recognize him." It turns out that Judge Neriman was invited to visit a class at the Police Academy a while ago and that she was greatly offended by the standard security check at the gate. "She made such a big deal of it," continued Meyda as she took out her phone to text her boss at SASEM. "You have to show an ID and pass through the toll gates while entering the campus. We were all very respectful, by the way. It's not like she handed her ID herself. We took it from her and we gave the ID to the officer at the gate. Still, she looked furious. She didn't say anything that day. She visited the class and gave a very good presentation. Afterward, when we tried to invite her back, she refused to come."

Not having received Meyda's messages, Chief Inspector Sami arrived a couple of hours later during the lunch break. Judge Neriman recognized him immediately. When Sami walked toward her to pay his respects, she scolded him. "I am very upset with the TNP," she said. "I was invited to give a presentation and then [you subjected me to] all that fanfare at the gate. Show your ID, pass through the tollgate . . . I was very offended, I swear. How could you do that to a judge? [*Vallahi çok gücüme gitti. Bir hakime siz bunu nasıl yaparsınız?*] It probably would have been much less insulting if I had gone to the US embassy to get a visa. I felt as if I was entering in another country. As if it was not my own." Sami listened to Judge Neriman's rant with a worried look on his face, and he tried to interject by apologizing and explaining that security checks were standard procedure. "Don't even start with me," snapped Neriman. "Are you telling me that you treat the governor the same way too?" For the rest of the training, both Chief Inspector Sami and Meyda tried to appease Judge Neriman by smiling and nodding at her when they came across her at the tea counter and the dining hall and by trying to engage her in small talk. By the end of four days, Neriman had eased off. Satisfied with Sami's and Meyda's relentless gestures, she signaled that she forgave them.

Working alongside mixed training activities, I witnessed an elaborate repertoire of deference displayed by the police officers toward the members of the judiciary. While the administrative relationship between police officers and prosecutors displayed a much more direct chain of command, officers were also very careful about how they approached the judges, for whom the prosecutors showed significant respect. Although these well-established/well-rehearsed repertoires of deference were clear signs of how well the police officers "knew their place"[21] within the bureaucratic hierarchy, there were also attempts by some police officers to rework this structure. Certain high-ranking officers who have acquired a level of cultural and juridical capital through their educational pursuits and their involvement in the harmonization economy sought ways to interact with the judges and prosecutors that went beyond deference.

Superintendent Fırat was one of the participants in the final phase of the juvenile justice training program, where five to six representatives from different institutions were brought together for two one-week-long training sessions in order to test how a truly mixed audience would react to the training. He was the highest-ranking police officer in the audience and he had significant experience with institutional capacity-building projects. He was also enrolled in the public law MA program in the Public Administration Institute for Turkey and the Middle East (TODAIE)—an institute of research and graduate education in Ankara that caters to high-level state officials who wish to continue their studies. Unlike other participants representing the TNP, Superintendent Fırat's proximity to the legal field made him eager to relate to the judges and prosecutors more equally. While other police officers enacted standard mannerisms of deference, Fırat took advantage of the tea and lunch breaks to network with the judges and prosecutors and to engage them in heated discussions related to the newly issued Child Protection Law.

In addition to socializing during the breaks, Fırat did not hesitate to speak up during the training either. He made a point by attending the legal-juridical sessions that featured judges or legal scholars as trainers, and he insisted on bringing a "security perspective" to the discussion of the law. During the session on the implementation of the Child Protection Law, he openly challenged the trainer—the same well-known judge at the earlier training for judges and prosecutors—on his remarks on the ban against using handcuffs on children that the law foresees. Arguing against the ban, he said, "When a law is issued on a topic that falls under the expertise of the security forces, they should be consulted. This is how things are done abroad as well. . . . You should let us determine [what is appropriate] here. In the Netherlands, in the US, this issue falls entirely within the field of policing. . . . This is a topic that should be left to the experience and expertise of the police. Can you imagine issuing a law that details the specific angle from which the police are supposed to hit with their baton?"

Echoing the TNP's recent institutional emphasis on professionalism and expertise, Fırat's comments were meant to communicate the basic premise of the police reform in Turkey—that security and policing were legitimate fields of expertise and that the police should be recognized and respected as the professionals of this field. Among many other things, one important outcome of this premise was to imagine law and security on an equal plane, which would give members of the TNP equal standing with their fellow state officials in the judiciary. The underlying assertion in Fırat's comments was that although they might be working in a hierarchical system, the police and the judiciary should be thought of as equals in terms of their respective fields of expertise. The hierarchical setup of the bureaucratic machine should be denoting not an occupational but an organizational hierarchy. In addition to verbally articulating this point, Fırat's attitude and behavior throughout the training also made him an embodiment of this new policing ideal. Relating to the judges and prosecutors as peers rather than supervisors and engaging in policy discussions from a security point of view, he acted as a member of a prestigious profession that rested on a distinct and legitimate body of specialized knowledge.

Conclusion

Fırat's comments and behavior in the juvenile justice training provide a glimpse into what the reframing of police work in terms of professionalization and expertise amounts to—especially with regard to its place in the larger governmental realm as this realm is being reordered in light of EU harmonization in Turkey. The reframing of the policing profession as one of expertise goes hand in hand with the delineation of the field of security as a scientific and specialized body of knowledge that is acquired through education. Although the most emphasized intended outcome of police reform is to standardize policing in order to enable its accountability, what becomes visible through ethnographic engagement is an effect of standardization that is less accounted for—the enhancement of the power of the police.

It is no coincidence that in both juvenile justice and domestic violence prevention trainings the talk of police professionalization and expertise was accompanied by accounts of how powerful the police was in other "advanced" European countries. Just like Fırat's remarks on the authority of the police in security related matters in the Netherlands and the United States, Sertan too repeatedly mentioned how in the United Kingdom and Austria the police had extensive powers that enabled them to fight against domestic violence effectively. As human rights were translated into matters of technical expertise and professionalism that can help police officers do their jobs better, these better-functioning police officers were imagined to become more powerful government agents. The message communicated in all TNP trainings was that human rights and the law did not tie the police officers' hands while fighting crime. On the contrary, human rights and the law were portrayed as "combat multipliers" that can help the police. In a similar vein, police reform via educating officers and standardizing their work was not thought of as limiting but increasing the powers of the TNP.

This ethnographic revelation of the unexpected consequences of human rights training for the police in Turkey compels us to look seriously into the uncanny relationship between audit cultures[22] and governmental authority in general. The good governance framework asserts the improvement of professionalism and expertise through enactments of standardization, effectiveness, and efficiency as a key step for establishing the transparency and accountability of institutions. While the equation of this formula with democratization is rarely contested in places that are on both ends of transnational standardization, the constitutive relationship between capacity/ability and power/authority often gets overlooked. Despite its disregard at the transnational level, a closer look into the operationalization of good governance shows that this relationship is central for persuading the local practitioners. It is this very logic that got activated at the human rights trainings, when the TNP officials considered institutional capacity building synonymous with widening the power and influence of the police.

This particular mindset was not only confined to the training venues. It was—and still is—also manifest in current and past legal regulations as well as the actual practices of policing in Turkey. These manifestations include the controversial 2007 amendments to the Law on the Duties and Authority of the Police that expanded the discretionary power of officers in the areas of stop and search, identity check, fingerprinting, and the use of firearms, all of which could be used on the basis of "reasonable doubt" for crime prevention purposes.[23] The spectacular effects of these expanding powers gained international visibility during the summer of 2013 with the countrywide Gezi protests and during the Siege of Kobanî that primarily took place in the Kurdish regions in fall 2014. In both instances, the riot police used excessive force that included tear gas, water cannons, and plastic and real bullets to crack down on the protestors. In the aftermath of the Kobane riots, Prime Minister Ahmet Davutoğlu announced that a new security legislation was on its way that would grant the police even more extensive authority in the fields of crowd control, intelligence gathering, search, seizure, and arrest.[24] While both oppositional circles and international observers regard these regulations and practices as indicators of the government's growing authoritarianism and estrangement from the EU accession process, government representatives have been emphasizing their similarity to those found in "advanced Western democracies." While the repression of both Gezi protests and Kobane riots were explained by pointing to similar crowd control techniques used against demonstrations in the United States, France, Spain, and Greece, it is said that the latest legislation package follows the German and Austrian models of policing. It should also be noted that all of these regulations and practices coincided with various harmonization activities of the TNP such as the project on "Implementation Capacity of Turkish Police to Prevent Disproportionate

Use of Force," which took place at literally the same time that the Gezi protests were happening.[25]

Standardization in the field of policing in Turkey ironically works to convert police power into something more acceptable. Professionalization and education processes that are supposed to make security experts out of police officers are also imagined to transform the once arbitrary and corrupt power of the police into a rational, calculated, and lawful authority. Reframed as such, acts and discretions that were once considered manifestations of police violence are relabelled as police force—a legitimate mode of enforcement given that it is exercised proportionally according to law. As illustrated by the ethnographic data above, pedagogies of standardization and performances of expertise do not necessarily lead to an endorsement of less violent policing. On the contrary, both Chief Inspector Sertan's comments on the use of force during arrest and Superintendent Fırat's remarks on handcuffing child convicts and suspects indicate an emerging governmental rationality that expands the terrain of violence by rendering it more technical, scientific, and exacting. Standardization and professionalization of policing makes it into a self-referential field where "policing professionalism" (*polislik profesyönelliği*) and "police ethics" (*polis etiği*) become the guiding principles for police officers to decide how, when, and to what extent they can inflict violence. Inculcated as experts in the field of security through proper education and experience, the police are made into both the arbiters and the auditors of this ever-violent field.

The question that follows for both Turkey and elsewhere is how this newfound police power gets appropriated to serve particular political projects. Contestations over the control of this potent force came to fore most strikingly during the summer of 2014 in Turkey, wherein hundreds of police officers were round up due to allegations of misconduct that included illegal wiretapping of top-level officials and fabrication of evidence with the intent to overthrow the government. These "cleansing" operations were part of the government's attempt to regain control of the police force following the dissolution of its alliance with the Gülen movement—a worldwide religious network whose support has been decisive in carrying AKP to power.[26] For the most part of the twelve-year AKP rule, which also corresponded to the period of extensive police reform, the Gülen movement was allowed to dwell within the police as well as the judiciary.

One of the most striking aspects of this recent takeover is the closing down of the School of Security Sciences within the Police Academy in April 2015 with the purported goal to transition into a more "civilian" education for the police. Instead of the four-year specialized training at the BA level in the security field, the new regulation foresees the establishment of new education centers, which will train selected university graduates for one year at the MA level to become commanders (deputy inspector and higher). Meanwhile, the school's current students will be placed within the departments of administrative sciences in designated universities to complete their studies without the guarantee to join the TNP. As the government's most piercing initiative to replace the cadres within the police, it is clear that this radical alteration will have drastic effects on the future of policing in Turkey. The academy being the quintessential symbol and producer of the new and reformed model of policing that is based upon the principles of standardization, professionalism, and expertise, it is certain that this revision will affect the claims for the legitimacy of the power of the police in the country.

Although the AKP government is determined to eliminate large numbers of current and prospective TNP members that are affiliated with the Gülen movement, it does not aim to unsettle the power of the police as such. What remains to be seen at this very critical juncture is how other security paradigms, such as democratic policing or community policing, which are particularly emphasized in the arguments for a more "civilian" police, would interact with the now established paradigm of professionalism and expertise. It is clear that the new police power is here to stay and that it is further ethnographic exploration that will shed light on the details of governmental authority, which this power is yet to entail.

Notes

1. Support for the research that this chapter builds upon was provided by the American Council of Learned Societies; the Social Science Research Council; the Wenner Gren Foundation; Stanford University Department of Anthropology, Clayman Institute for Gender Research, Freeman Spogli Institute for International Studies, Center for Philanthropy and Civil Society, Office of the Vice Provost for Graduate Education, and School of Humanities and Social Sciences. I thank Didier Fassin for inviting me to the workshop on Ethnography and Policing at the Princeton Institute for Advanced Studies, where I presented the preliminary thoughts that became this chapter. I am grateful to all of the workshop participants for their engagement with my work and their helpful comments on it. Both Didier Fassin and Daniel Goldstein provided excellent reviews during the writing process. Special thanks to Hayal Akarsu, who provided me with essential updates on the recent developments in the field of policing in Turkey, especially with regard to the restructuring of the Police Academy.

2. The main body of fieldwork for this research was conducted between 2007 and 2009, during which I worked alongside eleven projects covering torture, violence

against women, children's rights, and maximum security prisons and targeting the police, judges, prosecutors, prison guards, teachers, religious officials, and health care professionals. Although my larger research covered a wider array of state officials, for the purposes of this article I focus on my experience at the police trainings.

3. http://www.avrupa.info.tr/DelegasyonPortal/AB_ve_Turkiye/Muzakereler.html.
4. See, for instance, Englund 2000; Hornberger 2011; Merry 2006; Tsing 1997; Tsing 2005.
5. Waddington 1999.
6. Fassin 2013.
7. See, for instance, Gupta 2005; Ismail 2006; Navaro-Yashin 2002; Sayer 1994; Wedeen 1999.
8. http://www.egm.gov.tr/EN/Pages/the_eu_projects.aspx.
9. http://www.disiliskiler.pol.tr/absube/Sayfalar/default.aspx.
10. Jefferson and Jensen 2009.
11. Martin 2009.
12. One of the most important means through which the AKP government sought to gain control of the security apparatus was by strengthening the police through reform while at the same time eroding the influence of the army, which has a long history of interfering in civilian governance through military coups. Self-declared as "the guardian of the regime," the army emerged as one of the primary targets for the government during its "de-elitization" of the state.
13. http://slancier.blogspot.com/2010/12/cete-bekcisinden-gercek-polise.html.
14. The *Ergenekon* case consisted of a series of trials that started in 2008, where 275 people consisting of current and retired top-level army officials, journalists, and politicians were prosecuted for plotting a military coup to overthrow the AKP government. The final verdict was announced in August 5, 2013. The appeals process began in August 2014 and is still ongoing.
15. http://www.haberturk.com/yazarlar/ihsan-bal-661/506576-poliste-ronesans.
16. Uildriks 2009.
17. DuBois 1997; Hinkley 1997.
18. Piran 2013.
19. Babül 2012.
20. Bourdieu 1987.
21. See Merry 1990; Koğacıoğlu 2008.
22. Strathern 2000.
23. Altıparmak et al. 2007.
24. http://www.al-monitor.com/pulse/originals/2014/10/turkey-police-german-model-judicial-reform-package.html.
25. Babül 2013.
26. http://www.theguardian.com/world/2014/feb/09/turkish-police-fethullah-gulen-network.

References

Altıparmak, K., A. M. Aytaç, O. Karahanoğulları, T. Hançer, and D. Aydın. 2007. "Polis Vazife ve Selahiyet Kanununda Değişiklik: Durdurma-Kimlik Sorma-Arama-Parmak İzi Alınması-Silah Kullanma." Working paper, İnsan Hakları Çalışma Metinleri no. 5, Ankara Üniversitesi Siyasal Bilgiler Fakültesi İnsan Hakları Merkezi.

Babül, Elif. 2012. "Training Bureaucrats, Practicing for Europe: Constitutive Bureaucratic Imaginaries in Turkey." *Political and Legal Anthropology Review* 35 (1): 30–52.

———. 2013. "Gezi Resistance, Police Violence, and Turkey's Accession to the European Union." *Jadaliyya*, October 7.

Bourdieu, Pierre. 1987. "The Force of Law: Toward a Sociology of the Juridical Field." *Hastings Law Journal* 38:805–53.

DuBois, Mark. 1997. "Human Rights Education of the Police." In *Human Rights Education for the Twenty-First Century*, edited by George J. Andreopoulos and Richard Pierre Claude, 310–33. Philadelphia: University of Pennsylvania Press.

Englund, Harri. 2006. *Prisoners of Freedom: Human Rights and the African Poor.* Berkeley: University of California Press.

Fassin, Didier. 2013. *Enforcing Order: An Ethnography of Urban Policing.* Cambridge: Polity Press.

Gupta, Akhil. 2005. "Narratives of Corruption: Anthropological and Fictional Accounts of the Indian State." *Ethnography* 6 (1): 5–34.

Hinkley, D. Michael. 1997. "Military Training for Human Rights and Democratization." In *Human Rights Education for the Twenty-First Century*, edited by George J. Andreopoulos and Richard Pierre Claude, 296–309. Philadelphia: University of Pennsylvania Press.

Hornberger, Julia. 2011. *Policing and Human Rights: The Meaning of Violence and Justice in the Everyday Policing of Johannesburg.* New York: Routledge.

Ismail, Salwa. 2006. *Political Life in Cairo's New Quarters: Encountering the Everyday State.* Minneapolis: University of Minnesota Press.

Jefferson, Andrew, and Steffen Jensen. 2009. "Introduction: Repopulating State Violence and Human Rights." In *Violence and Human Rights: State Officials in the South*, edited by Andrew Jefferson and Steffen Jensen, 1–22. New York: Routledge-Cavendish.

Koğacıoğlu, Dicle. 2008. "Conduct, Meaning, and Inequality in an Istanbul Courthouse." *New Perspectives on Turkey* 39:97–127.

Martin, Tomas. 2009. "Taking the Snake Out of the Basket: Indian Prison Warders' Opposition to Human Rights Reform." In *Violence and Human Rights: State Officials in the South*, edited by Andrew Jefferson and Steffen Jensen, 139–57. New York: Routledge-Cavendish.

Merry, Sally Engle. 1990. *Getting Justice and Getting Even: Legal Consciousness among Working-Class Americans.* Chicago: University of Chicago Press.

———. 2006. *Human Rights and Gender Violence: Translating International Law into Local Justice.* Chicago: University of Chicago Press.

Navaro-Yashin, Yael. 2002. *Faces of the State: Secularism and Public Life in Turkey.* Princeton: Princeton University Press.

Piran, Leila. 2013. *Institutional Change in Turkey: The Impact of European Union Reforms on Human Rights and Policing.* New York: Palgrave MacMillan.

Sayer, Derek. 1994. "Everyday Forms of State Formation: Some Dissident Remarks on 'Hegemony.'" In *Everyday Forms of State Formation: Revolution and the Negotiation of Rule in Modern Mexico*, edited by Gilbert M. Joseph and Daniel Nugent. 367–77. Durham: Duke University Press.

Strathern, Marilyn. 2000. "New Accountabilities: Anthropological Studies in Audit, Ethics, and the Academy." In *Audit Cultures: Anthropological Studies in Accountability, Ethics, and the Academy*, edited by Marilyn Strathern, 1–18. London: Routledge.

Tsing, Anna Lowenhaupt. 1997. "Transitions as Translations." In *Transitions, Environ-*

ments, Translations: Feminisms in International Politics, edited by Joan W. Scott, Cora Kaplan, and Debra Keates, 253–72. New York: Routledge.

———. 2005. *Friction: An Ethnography of Global Connection*. Princeton: Princeton University Press.

Uildriks, Niels. 2009. "Police Reform, Security, and Human Rights in Latin America: An Introduction." In *Policing Insecurity: Police Reform, Security, and Human Rights in Latin America*, edited by Niels Uildriks, 1–20. Lanham, MD: Lexington Books.

Waddington, P. A. J. 1999. "Police (Canteen) Subculture: An Appreciation." *British Journal of Criminology* 39 (2): 287–309.

Wedeen, Lisa. 1999. *Ambiguities of Domination: Politics, Rhetoric, and Symbols in Contemporary Syria*. Chicago: University of Chicago Press.

SEVEN

Experience:
Being Policed as a Condition of Life (Chile)

CLARA HAN

On a warm day, men and women sit outside in plastic chairs taking in the sun, watching and chitchatting, children play in the street, and women sell *anticuchos* (kebabs) in front of their houses, low one-story rowhouses with zinc roofing. I am in the low-income neighborhood in Santiago, Chile, that has been under police occupation for several years. I will call this neighborhood Z. Between 2012 and 2013, I conducted ten months of continuous fieldwork in this setting. By springtime, I've become accustomed to sitting in the storefront belonging to my friend Martita, where we smoke cigarettes, watch people walk back and forth, greet people, and chitchat through the iron rungs of the patio gate. Women down the street are sweeping a church, as part of the state's emergency employment program, administered by an NGO. In the mornings, I might see university students carrying out yet another survey on this neighborhood—on health, on perceptions of security, on crime—resulting in studies that are rarely, if ever, made public. There might also be a chance to see a social worker from the municipality make a visit in the municipal vehicle. Students and civil servants only enter this neighborhood until lunchtime, at which point it is deemed too dangerous to enter. At lunchtime, a neighbor sells *cazuela* from her home; another sells prepared salads of cabbage, beets, and legumes. Another neighbor sells fresh fruit juice, while another goes house to house selling clothes. From Martita's patio, I can smell the tailpipe exhaust of the Special Forces bus. A large military bus, it is constantly next to the house. In front of the bus, Special Forces military police officers stand, watching and listening to the goings on in the street, or distractedly texting on their smart phones. Occasionally, the hum of everyday life is marked by gunfire or the revving of the GOPE armored vehicle, the Special Operations Group military police vehicle that makes rounds within the neighborhood, on the lookout for "delinquency."

The opening scene of this chapter is written in this manner to avoid the tendency of only focusing on spectacular events that seek to grab readers' attention and to make a point that an anthropological examination of policing cannot only be confined to an instance in which the police officer and a person from this neighborhood encounter each other. Policing cannot be seen simplistically as an external force imposed on the neighborhood. Policing in this neighborhood is not simply a "part" of people's lives, it has become a *condition* of life—punishment, its realization and its anticipation; the experience of authority and state institutions; the politics of the family and the neighborhood and the very ways in which livelihoods are secured—all of these aspects of life and more have been shaped by and, indeed, constituted through policing. The approach to policing low-income neighborhoods in Santiago, Chile, is one that draws from the pacification policies pursued in Brazil, and further, its genealogy can be traced in a policing approach rooted in an idea of order maintenance in which the category of the "disorderly" and "delinquent" are cleanly and clearly separated from and opposed to the "law-abiding" and in which criminality is understood to be a tendency of a certain category of persons (the disorderly) and thus in need of surveillance and normative discipline.

In Chile, such clear dividing categories also mean that those from *poblaciones* (low-income neighborhoods) who are injured, humiliated, and killed by police are rarely given a hearing: considered as a priori "disorderly," their punishment can be seen by a mainstream public as not only legitimate but also necessary. In a historical context in which human rights discourse has largely focused on human rights violations of political dissidents, it is extremely difficult to secure legal and political advocacy for those who fall within the category of the "disorderly," both because they are seen as embodying the tendency to be "perpetrators" and because the "disorderly" is that against which the conventional model of politics— both conservative and progressive—defines itself.[1]

In this chapter, I describe three angles by which one can examine policing as a condition of life in this neighborhood: the experience of surveillance, the politics of the family, and the anticipation of police action. As such, I am attempting to widen the framework through which policing is perceived and responded to in ethnography—to better understand policing from the point of view of those whose negotiate a milieu arising from it. An ethnography of this sort, however, propels us into the social categories and relationships in which people live their lives and may provide a needed hesitation in the tendency to gloss low-income *neighborhood* as low-income *population*, as if such ideas can be deployed interchangeably. It also may compel us to reorient ourselves in relation to low-income neighborhoods, not to judge them as places that are "uninhabitable" and from which people desperately seek to escape but to respond to them as a milieu in which people attach importance to place, to flesh-and-blood others, and to things. Finally, it may also compel us to parse out the differences between different modalities of policing—to distinguish among patrols, constant surveillance of occupation, and antinarcotics raids—as well as to pay attention to the circumstances and ways in which people themselves appeal to the police.

Before turning to the ethnography, let me briefly expand on a few key points on the modality of policing in this setting: that of occupation premised on the punishment of the minor offense, particularly petty drug dealing. Legal scholar Bernard Harcourt provided the first and perhaps most pointed critical examination of the "broken windows" order-maintenance approach that emerged in the United States in the mid-1990s and that has been deployed across the Americas.[2] Premised on the idea that small disorders causally lead to crime, the broken windows approach, as is well known, focuses on what had previously been seen as nuisances and places them within a theory of thick propensities, such that those who engage in these disorders reveal a propensity to commit crime and should therefore be punished. Demonstrating that the broken windows approach is not supported by empirical evidence, Harcourt asks why it is that this policy has gained such support across the political spectrum in the United States.

Taking a genealogical approach to this question, Harcourt elaborates how the very category of the disorderly cannot be seen as prior to punishment but emerges from techniques of punishment themselves. And further, order maintenance must be viewed within a wider rhetorical shift to harm arguments across the political spectrum. In debates over pornography, sex work, and drug use, for instance, competing claims of harm have become central axes by which to advocate for or against certain policy positions. Order maintenance is one illustration of this rhetorical shift, in that it justifies punishment in the name of harms done to others (while also eclipsing the harms that police do to those most intensively policed).

In an extremely rich reading of Foucault's *Discipline and Punish*, Harcourt makes clear how in Foucault's work, law and discipline clash and feed off each other in the modern carceral system, which "justifies the power to punish. It makes punishment seem natural, necessary, and preordained."[3] Yet, in contrast to Foucault's focus on the reform of the disorderly, the order-maintenance approach "does not aim to reform the disorderly as much as it does to punish them, exclude them, in the sense of getting them off the street. . . . Order-maintenance policing seems to draw more heavily on both the juridical model and the military form of discipline: the juridical insofar as it utilizes punishment that may seem excessive; the military in the sense that it is normalized along an axis of disorder with a type of military observation, inspection, and exercise."[4] Thus, order-maintenance policing works to create subjects through a set of norms defined by techniques of punishment, while also justifying this punishment in the name of harm.

Let me point out three crucial insights that I draw from Harcourt and that I will take forward into the ethnography. First, the tendency to describe low-income neighborhoods as caught between the "police" and the "gangs" who fight over sovereign right keeps in place the very category of the disorderly created through punishment. In other words, studies that continually emphasize the idea of a clashing over the sovereign power over life and territory only fall within and further ingrain the category of disorderly without questioning it; importantly, by emphasizing this idea, such studies reproduce the state's vision. We should be critically examining the categories—such as "work" versus "drug trade" and "criminal network" versus "police"—through which perceptions of low-income neighborhoods are structured. Second, the clash between juridical power and discipline that has given rise to the modern carceral system remains unresolved in actual policing practice. Policing of low-income neighborhoods has not involved psychotherapeutic treatments but has relied on excessive force. Constant and intensified surveillance in low-income neighborhoods is not only a disciplinary mechanism but also presents the conditions of possibility for the police officer to apply the "rules" as he or she sees fit. Surveillance here does not create regularities but constant irregularity in the name of "regularity" and "order." Third, instead of delimiting an ethnography of policing to immediate encounters with police officers, while important, we can explore the texture of anticipation of police action and how lives are marked by police action.[5]

In the following sections, I describe three different angles with which we can think through policing as a condition of life in this neighborhood. My aim in presenting these three angles is to explore the way people negotiate their milieu in relation to a range of police actions and in anticipation of them and to examine the categories that constitute this negotiation. The first angle examines the ways the categories of disorderly and law-abider constitute the experience of surveillance and examines the existential stakes in these categories. The second angle further complicates these categories by showing how police actions are absorbed into the politics of the family and how the politics of the family are constituted through the anticipation of police action and actual police encounters. Here, the categories of law-abider and disorderly are perhaps less salient than those of family, neighbor, threat, protection, and money. The third angle explores the anticipation of police action and the affects that accompany this anticipation.

Finally, a word about the form of writing. This chapter does not focus deeply or extensively on one single case. I do not pursue detailed discussion of a network of relationships of any individual, as I have done in other writings. Instead, I explore the categories that emerge in talk and actions. This form of writing is in response to the condition of policing—it has demanded experimentation. In what follows, I employ composite figures in some cases and change details of stories, while trying to stay true to insights that emerged in fieldwork.

Surveillance

Several months before I met Martita, her son was killed by the civilian police Tactical Reaction Team of the Antinarcotics Brigade during a drug raid involving several streets in Z.[6] I saw Martita almost every day while working in Z. One week after our first meeting, she made copies of the keys to her house, instructing me to run into her house at any time when I was caught in gunfire on the street. On many occasions, as I ran down the street crouching when gunfire began, Martita held the front gate open for me, her watchfulness somehow helping me to get safely into her house. Upon my making it physically intact to her house, she offered me a cold glass of water, a way of assuaging a racing heart. My fieldwork was not heroic. It was enabled and made possible by the network of embraces of the women in Z. As I spent a part of nearly every day with Martita, which also involved spending time with other women friends and neighbors, the bulk of my field materials are not based on the interview method. Instead, I took extensive notes at the end of the day, detailing as best I could and with the energy that I could muster the conversations that I participated in. This ethnography draws from these notes as well as from the memories that my notes spurred in me as I reread them.

Camilo is Martita's youngest son and had remained in the house with her after his two older brothers moved out after marriage. A few years before Camilo's death, Martita had separated from her husband, and she and Camilo worked to build a fast food storefront selling pizzas, sandwiches, and hotdogs. The Special Forces bus was stationed at a fixed point next to Martita's house, and by virtue of proximity, the officers often bought pizza and sandwiches from their storefront. Sometimes they would ask Martita if they could use the bathroom of her house. (The police officers have eight-hour shifts and have no bathroom.) At other times, they would ask Martita if they could borrow a pot or pan to warm their lunch, using a small portable gas stove. As Martita related, Camilo was *"siempre tirando la talla"* (always joking). And through light jokes ("How many pizzas do you eat a day? You might have to change the size of your uniform") a sort of joking relationship developed between one of the police officers and Camilo. In my conversations with Martita, this joking relationship emerged repeatedly. But, significantly, it emerged in a constellation of other ideas: of being *"sanito"* (healthy, or not involved in delinquency or drug trade); of being engaged in law-abiding work; of a household in which police can enter without the inhabitants fearing arrest. Let us listen to Martita:

> And the micro (the Special Forces bus) of the Carabineros is here all day and night. And they knew my son, they even had conversations with him. And also with me. Sometimes they asked me to use to bathroom. The Carabineros [of the Special Forces bus] even arrived to the emergency room [of the hospital] and there, when they found out that my son had died, they gave me their condolences and came to converse with me. They couldn't believe it. Because they knew how he was. They saw him *sanito* [healthy, but indicating that he was not mixed up with drugs or with illicit economic activities] and they saw him have fun here, they saw him when he arrived. So this police officer said to me, "How could this happen to your son," he said to me, "how could this happen?" What can one do? If justice does not make justice, what can one do?

After Camilo's death, this police officer with "feeling" came round to Martita's house, standing at the gate of her house and engaging in chitchat as a form of company. As Martita related, she took solace in the officer's appreciation of her loss and the feeling of emptiness suffusing her house. Yet, in the months following her son's death, Martita noted a shift in the officer's expressions of concern, from a quiet acknowledgement of loss to a more vociferous concern of Martita's risk of falling into *narco*. As Martita said:

Little by little, he took out the theme, "Hi Señora Martita, when are you going to start working again? I can't wait to have your pizza again." Or, "Señora
Martita, will the Muni [the municipality social program] help you buy soft
drinks? I want to see you working again." Then, once when he came to the
gate [of her house] and it was dark inside the patio, I saw him use a flashlight
to look inside the house. I went out and opened the gate for him, and said,
"Come in. I'm not involved in anything. I have nothing to hide." And he
came into my house and walked around. "See," I told him, "This is Camilo's
bedroom. It has not been changed since the day they killed him. And see,
this is Camilo's car, it has not been touched since the funeral. Look around,
take your time."

Martita relates that the officer was filled with shame at the cordial invitation to inspect and surveil her house, and he apologized for being in-
trusive. Yet he still entered her house and went through each room. She
surmised to me that the officer was troubled by the fact that she had begun
spending most of her time with her friend Blondie. In the months following Camilo's death, Martita spent days in bed in a pitch-black bedroom,
hardly eating. Blondie, having keys to Martita's house, prodded her to get
up, eventually giving Martita the daily chore of picking up her son and two
other children from school. The chore got Martita out of bed, and upon
dropping the children off at Blondie's house, Martita was immediately
invited in for tea, smokes, and a long chat. This police officer, however,
had arrested Blondie's sister for drug trafficking. Because of the severity of
the charges, the sister was sentenced to several years in prison. By virtue of
kinship, Blondie was seen as potentially involved in drug trafficking too
and spending time with Blondie was perceived as a threat of "falling into"
delinquency.

Martita's description reveals how the category of the disorderly is not
only the lens through which the police officer sees Martita but also a lens
she herself attempts to uphold by revealing herself as well as her son as
on "the right side of the law." Her description also reveals how she antici-
pates the police's perception of her relationships: police see those who live
in this neighborhood as having "thick propensities" to crime. Her attempt
to prove otherwise creates possibilities for police discretion to apply the
rules as he or she sees fit: to enter a house and search it without a warrant,
even defiantly prodded to surveil by those who live there. Notice here that
Martita is not contesting the boundaries of the categories of law-abiding
and disorderly as much as she is working to secure her place in relation to
them. Work is implicitly "legal work" and not the illegitimate formalized

work involved in *narco* or thieving. A friendship that keeps Martita alive is perceived as the tentacles of the illicit economy—the network of *narco* in the making—that results in incarceration and violent death. There is a complex of affects surrounding this encounter with the police that rese-cures the boundary between the law-abiding and the disorderly. Resent-ment at being—as people say—"put into the same sack [as those of the de-linquents]"; betrayal in light of the seeming reversal in the police officer's tone, from one in which one's place is secured in the law-abiding category to one in which one must work to secure that place; defiance to show one-self in the eyes of official institutions as belonging to the category of the law-abider.

To appreciate the labor and existential stakes involved in securing one's place within the category of "law-abider," and the way the category of the law-abider is further ingrained in such labor, let us turn to Martita's friend, Blondie. Many years prior, Blondie was arrested and charged for drug traf-ficking in a different city in Chile. It was clear from the charges that Blondie, if convicted, would be sentenced to several years in prison. Blondie was be-ing held in preventive prison before her sentence. But, it just so happened that prison guards did not accompany her and her lawyer as they took the elevator down to see the judge for her sentencing. Her lawyer—sensing an opportunity to evade prison—told her to make a run for it. "This is the only chance you'll have, he told me, go or you'll spend the rest of your good years in prison," Blondie recounted to me, in the voice of the lawyer. Blondie ran. For over a decade, she was living as a fugitive and under a dif-ferent name.

Blondie met Martita when she was living fugitive. Blondie—who during this time was called Stela—was making her living going house to house selling women's lingerie and children's toys. Stela met Martita through sim-ply visiting Martita's house in the hopes of selling lingerie, and they struck up a conversation. Eventually, Martita came into knowledge of Blondie's (or Stela's) state of being *"fuga"* (fugitive). Stela was pregnant when she met Martita, and Martita learned that Stela's pregnancy had resulted from rape. Stela's husband was off and on addicted to *pasta base*, and she had attempted to separate from him several times. But he continued to hound her, following her in the neighborhood and showing up at the small room that she rented. Stela could not go to the police or seek medical help, for she could not risk contact with state institutions and feared institutions that she saw as having an aura of the state (such as a hospital).

Martita took her to a private OB/GYN clinic, paying for the clinic visits herself, and there Stela received her prenatal care. As much as Stela did not want her son and felt that her body "rejected him," Blondie today says that her son is her "reason for living." The birth of Ismael coincided with meeting her second husband Nelson, a much older man who loves to cook and dote on the children. At that time, Stela and Nelson agreed to never let Ismael know of the conditions that led to his birth. Nelson was Ismael's father—not only through the labor of care but through blood. Blondie and Nelson continue to sustain this fiction as part and parcel of their everyday life.

Blondie describes the conditions that allowed her to resume the name Blondie as arising from penal reform. Initiated in 2005, penal reform transformed the penal system from an inquisitorial system to one partially modeled on the United States criminal justice system, in terms of the split between the functions of prosecutor, defense, and judge. "The time passed and the system changed, so my sentence was completed," she explained matter-of-factly to me. It seemed, like others whom I met in Z, that her file had been physically lost when penal reform took place. Yet, like others, she continued to have a criminal record.

With others whom I met in Z, the loss of physical documentation of their sentencing and good behavior in prison made it very difficult to acquire a "certificate of the completion of the sentence" through the civil registry. However, with Martita's help she secured the documentation and gathered the courage to present the documents and herself in the name of Blondie to the office of the Patronato de los Reos (the Patron of the Accused), a state office created in the early 1940s that facilitates social reinsertion through the "cleaning" of one's criminal record (*limpiando los antecedentes*). As part of this contract with the state, Blondie was compelled to demonstrate that she had had an "*oficio*" (or legal work) and was required to present herself to the office and sign each month for two years, thus demonstrating her commitment to the normative order of citizenship. Through a municipal poverty program, Blondie applied for and was granted Capital Semilla funds to establish a modest bazaar in the patio of her house. (These are funds destined to those who meet the point score criteria for vulnerability on their *Ficha de Protección Social* [Social Protection File].)

When I met Blondie, she was working hard to keep her bazaar of children's toys, perfumes, and bath and shower goods viable in these difficult times of occupation. The occupation had stifled the local economy not only through the incarceration of so many who have worked in the "*ambiente*," or drug trade, but also through the pressures created with an incarcerated kin, what women call "a double house." Relatives supply food as well as toiletries not only to their imprisoned kin but also to those with whom he or she shares a cell, creating financial pressures on relatives outside the prison that are enormously difficult to bear. Yet, Blondie's business steadily grew thanks to what she called her "gift"—the twinkle of her eye and her quick wit, her perceptiveness to her customers' needs, and the dogged way in which she found good bargains from wholesalers.

On the day of her last signature, we had a small party with Martita, myself, and Blondie's *travesti* friend Aria. Sitting on stools on the sidewalk in front of the bazaar and enjoying mixed drinks, Blondie said with a twist of humor, "Oh, Stela, you've been such a good friend, but as friends go, our moment has passed." "Ciao, Stela!" Aria exclaimed, blowing her a kiss. The cleaning of the criminal record was one way in which Blondie could stitch her biography together. While Stela was pursued and threatened by the law, Blondie had labored to achieve legitimacy within the category of the law-abider. In so doing, Blondie made the past past, reaffirming the split of the disorderly and the law-abider in relation to her multiple selves, even as her body and the fiction she sustained with her second husband to her son marked her by that past.

Politics of the Family

While the preceding cases described the stakes in the categories of the disorderly and the law-abider and how their distinction is secured, in the case of Celina, we can appreciate the varied ways in which the figure of the police and police action are enmeshed in the life of the neighborhood and absorbed into the politics of the family. Here, we see policing inflected in a different cluster of categories—family, neighbor, money, protection, threat. I came to know Celina through Ruby, who worked for an NGO that administered a state employment scheme providing three-month work contracts to low-income women to carry out janitorial and gardening work within the neighborhood. This scheme—one developed during dictatorship—reduces the official unemployment rate in a municipality by providing work, while institutionalizing low wages and temporary contracts: NGOs are rotated every three months to stay within the bounds of the temporary work contract, thus obviating the NGO—and by extension the state—the requirement to pay into pension and into health care.

Celina had asked Ruby for work in "the programs" as it is colloquially called, as she needed to work within the neighborhood to be able to care for her disabled son. I accompanied Ruby on her home visit. Six months prior, Celina's son Charly had been standing with his friend Micky in front of their house when he was shot in the neck. He is now quadriplegic. Reinaldo, the boy-man who shot Charly, was arrested and put into preventive prison. Later, Celina heard that a hit was put on Micky, and Reinaldo, being a minor, was to carry it out. Reinaldo's mother, Petra, had just been released from a year in the women's prison after being sentenced for drug trafficking. It was unstated in the neighborhood that Petra continued to traffic but did so "*piola*"—quietly—without getting involved in conflicts.

In my subsequent visits to her house without Ruby, however, Celina tells me angrily that Petra had promised to buy her a hospital bed, but the bed never arrived. As an injury from an accident—"Reinaldo wanted to shoot Micky, but shot Charly by mistake"—Celina expected that Petra would make good on her promise, and the fact that the promise did not materialize put Petra's words in doubt that "it was an accident." Celina was approached by the public prosecutor for her testimony, and she agreed to be witness to an attempted murder charge and to assault with a deadly weapon. I sensed this was in part a rebuke to Petra but also to the delicate ways in which silence and impotence keep life intact in the neighborhood. "Imagine it, Clarita, the only one who has helped me is Agnes [the nun from a European country who has worked on a number of social programs for the neighborhood] and now you."[7]

Let me back up a bit to provide some detail on the formation of the neighborhood pertinent to the case I am describing here. The neighborhood was initially settled not through an illegal land seizure, as is the case with several low-income neighborhoods in Santiago, but through *Operación Sitio*, a state housing lottery in the 1950s that assigned plots to individual heads of household who were then living in *campamentos* (squatter camps) in various parts of the city. It continued to grow by the migration of extended kin who settled on streets already "anchored" by kin. Verbal agreements between neighbors to sell houses to these kin means that for many, title to property is in the name of strangers long gone, while the house has been inhabited and effectively owned by kin. Thus, different from the neighborhood where I conducted my previous long-term fieldwork, the "neighbor" emerges through the work of cutting the network of kin. Boundaries become demarcated according to the circumstances. As Isabel, one of my friends in Z, remarked to me, "My daughter asked me, 'Why is everyone related in Z [implying a blood relation]?' 'Well,' I said, 'it just so happens that the people from Z couple (*emparejarse*) with the people from Z. So, we are all related by blood.'"

However, as rancors intensify, potential kin become neighbors as "family" demarcates itself and cuts the network of kin. Isabel is the paternal cousin to Celina and lives just around the corner. We chat as she is hosing down the patio. Charly had just been admitted to the hospital for a necrotic pressure sore. I asked if she knew how he was doing. "I hope he is getting better, but I haven't gone to visit, with all this. You know. I don't want to get involved. But if it happens, well, I would have to side with Celina because after all, Celina is family." A potential demarcation of boundaries of the intimate—defined as family—and "the neighbor" begins to emerge. "This" and "it" may indicate talk amongst "insiders"—for Isabel may have taken it for granted that I simply knew what was happening and knew not to talk about it except obliquely—but it also may indicate the difficulty of accessing context, like shifting sands.

The actions of police officers are enfolded into these demarcations. I arrived at Celina's house shortly after a confrontation with the GOPE, the officers in the armored vehicle that rounds the street, on the watch for acts of "delinquency." She recounted to me with a tightened face that the GOPE drove up to the house, revving in front of the house where Charly was seated in his wheelchair unable to move. Celina ran out of the house. "What is your name, show me your name," she yelled. As Celina recounted to me bitterly, "And this is what he did. He hit his chest and said, "*Soy el teniente, soy el teniente, tal por cual* [I am the lieutenant! I am the lieutenant, (cuss words)]!" El Teniente drove off in the GOPE, but Celina recounts that the GOPE turned the corner and stopped. As she peered down the street, she saw Petra and El Teniente laughing. Petra turned to Celina and made the gesture, a slit across her throat. When Celina looked away, she heard El Teniente laughing, which she took as him mocking her. Yet, rather than spur further stories of police killings, the policeman's laugh is embedded in Celina's recountings of Petra: the damage she has inflicted others and on "her own family." I asked her, "But aren't you worried, scared of El Teniente, what *he* could do?" Celina responded,

My mother is worried. She tells me not to walk alone on the street. But, I'm worried of Petra, that she will do something and the police will cover her, because she has paid them. El Teniente protects her. So whatever she does, she gets off. She was taken to the police station for trafficking the other day, and I thought she would be in prison, but that same night she was out. They say she gave the police what they earned. The police go where money runs [*Los pacos va donde corre la plata*]. I told another *paco* [police officer] that I would tell him where her properties are and the names under which she registered them, but that's only if they give me more protection. Witness protection, that's what they call it. They give you another house.

Celina went to the public prosecutor to file a legal complaint of a death threat against Petra—not against the police. A few days later, Celina returns to the public prosecutor to file another complaint against Petra, for a threat she had heard through rumor. Celina had heard through her cousin who is also in preventive prison with Reinaldo that when Petra had visited Reinaldo, she was goading her son to rape Celina's daughter Esperanza, as payback for the betrayal of testifying against him. Words are spiraling, unmoored. A rumor that invokes the sexual violence toward a daughter seems to cross the boundary of what can be absorbed in everyday life—such as a threats toward a son—and creates a palpable feeling of dread and anxiety that seems to wrap around Celina's actions and movements. Walking in the street with me, Celina is talking of Petra's threats and raises her voice. Women come out of their houses and then see Celina and quickly turn back into their houses, perhaps avoiding getting tangled in an impending confrontation. I think to myself, *I wish she would lower her voice*; my head is pounding. Blondie passes by; she grabs my arm, feigning, "Clarita, I've been looking for you . . ." "Clarita, *ten' cuidado* . . . [be careful]," Blondie says to me.

Because Charly is hospitalized, Celina spends most of her day outside the home and the neighborhood. She cannot be here to, in her words, "accompany" her daughter from one place to another. She says she has a feeling that something terrible might happen, but she can't say what they might do. Celina asks the public prosecutor for police rounds to come to her house. She calls these police rounds *"controles"* (controls). A term borrowed from regular medical checkups (*control médico*), it illuminates the state's form of care: surveillance.[8] These police rounds involve two Carabineros—the military police who carry out the everyday order-maintenance policing. They visit Celina's house in the morning and in the evening. They knock on her door and have her or her daughter sign a roster to affirm that their household has been seen and that any new threats have been registered by the Carabineros. I was at Celina's house during the first few times when the police made their "control." They are dressed in olive green fatigues, helmets, bullet proof vests, and wearing machine guns. One of the Carabineros seems to be much younger than the other. The young officer is holding a large black folder, in which pages of addresses are printed. I'm sitting in the patio of Celina's house with her pitbull Nora. Nora sniffs the young officer's hand, and he smiles, petting the dog. Celina greets the officers, asking them if they would like a glass of fresh squeezed juice. They politely refuse, thanking her for the offer.

While signing her name, Celina tells the officers that she has heard that

Petra's son would be released from prison soon. "Is that true?" The older officer answers, "We are in different units. So, we cannot tell you anything." Celina—"But Petra threatened to kill me, she threatened to have my daughter raped. Can't you help me? I need to know if he is released." The older officer—"As I said, we are in different units. If you've received another threat, you can file it with the *fiscal* [the public prosecutor]." Celina—"So is this all you can do? I can't accompany my daughter twenty-four hours a day. How will she be safe? You can't help me until something happens to my daughter?" The older officer—"I'm sorry, but this is all we are able to do. We don't have information on your neighbor. That is another unit. If you have a problem, you need to speak to the *fiscal*." Celina relents, "Fine, fine. I will talk to the *fiscal*." After the police officers leave, she mutters, "*Huevones de mierda* [fuckers]. They should help me."

Let us notice here the varied encounters with the police that are occurring simultaneously. On the one hand, El Tieniente is embedded in the talk of threat. The fact that his actions come with the stamp of the law not only intensifies the feeling of threat but also imbues the law itself with a feeling of arbitrariness: the law moves where money runs. On the other hand, the police officers who conduct "control" are appealed to for protection and help, even as Celina may know that the officers will do little, if anything, to help her. Here, we can see that the police are not perceived simply as a homogeneous force imposed on the neighborhood, but that their actions are embedded in the *rumors circulating within the neighborhood*.

At the same time, we also see how police action is absorbed into and is a conduit for the politics of the family. By asking for "the control" of her house and in trying to secure the safety of her daughter from the threats of rape that she has heard through gossip, her son Ricky is now in the position of having to flee from the house to avoid arrest. Ricky has had an off and on addiction to *pasta base*. A year earlier, when he was "*metido*" (involved, or in it), he was arrested, charged, and found guilty of petty trafficking of *pasta base*. However, Ricky did not show up to his sentencing hearing, and thus "owes time" (*debe tiempo*). Ricky could be arrested at any moment and thus is constantly moving himself, his girlfriend, and his baby daughter between his mother's and grandmother's houses. Although Celina tells me that Ricky "paid" for what he had done by having suffered from withdrawal from *pasta base*, there are dark undercurrents in their relationship that I perceive but have no way of understanding. When Ricky is in the house when I visit, Celina intersperses her conversation with me with angry glances to him which he responds to with wry laughs.

With the initiation of police controls, Ricky moves to his grandmother's house with his daughter and girlfriend, but after a brief stay, they leave the neighborhood to stay with a distant relative in another low-income neighborhood. I am visiting Celina when he, his girlfriend, and daughter are gathering their things to leave the neighborhood. As he leaves the house, he projects an air of defiant play, drumming the door frame in the rhythm of a song's refrain; it's as if he is affirming that he is not the one being displaced, but is taking command of leaving. Celina reacts to the drumming with a grimace, remarking that it is time that he "made himself independent (*independizarse*)"—that he should be the head of household and live separately from Celina, her daughter, and her youngest son.

Celina's request for police rounds is made to protect her daughter while it simultaneously endangers her son. This differential care of her children seems to stem not only from a general difference in the way daughters and sons are cared for but also from the rancor that Celina and Ricky had built up over the years. Police controls *mark* this differential privileging of intimate relationships within the family. They are not seen as "causing" this differential privileging. Rather, they are rather seen as its expression. Thus, Ricky's response to his and his family's displacement—drumming the door to show defiance to his mother—seems to normalize his displacement within family rancors. It is not that police rounds are seen as an external force that have created his displacement but that police controls are embedded in the affects (the rancors, the care, the anxiety) coursing through this family. Police action is a route through which intimate relationships are negotiated and in which futures of relationships are made possible and denied.

Anticipation of Police Action

In the case of Celina, we see how police action is appealed to and embedded in a complex of affects in which context itself is rendered unstable. As rumors of threats of violence swirl in neighborhood talk, the loss of context is palpable in feelings of dread and anxiety—of the ground dropping away from one's feet. In this final section, I turn to a different angle: not the loss of context through rumor, but the anticipation of police action, which hinges upon projecting into the future that which is familiar. Through anticipation, a field of (precognitive) recognition is already laid out in advance of the encounter, and in relation to which present action is organized.[9] Let me turn to how police action is anticipated and to the texture of that anticipation, focusing on the modality of policing of the *allanamiento*, the drug raid.

In studies of the drugs, police, and low-income neighborhoods in Latin America, the drug trade is primarily described in terms of the ideas of "network" and "membership."[10] Gang membership and criminal networks are thus taken as both the conceptual unit and the empirical sociological unit through which the drug trade is described and viewed. Approaching the underground drug economy through the prism of livelihoods and from the perspective of the household, however, lends us a different set of organizing ideas—the trade is seen not in terms of gang membership or the creation of "networks" but rather in terms of a household *event* that arises in response to moments of need. Participation in the drug economy can be experienced outside of a framework of a sociological unit of "the gang" and understood in terms of time—a transient moment in which women, responding to need, work in the drug economy. This work does not necessarily involve selling drugs—it could involve storing and hiding drugs in their houses or transporting them from one house to another. It is work that can allow a household to pay off debts, to cover costs of a catastrophic illness, or to buy a present for a child, but it involves a whole set of vulnerabilities and anxieties related to police action.

When I met Wanda, her husband was currently incarcerated for theft, and she was struggling with paying the monthly bills. She had to take a taxi to get to the prison to visit her husband every other week. She brought shampoo, soap, and food not only for her husband but also for his cell mates. Wanda had a "double house," supporting households inside and outside of the prison walls. To earn money beyond the emergency employment program where she received half of the minimum monthly wage, Wanda began to sell *anticuchos* (kebabs) on the weekends in the neighborhood, like several of her neighbors who have incarcerated kin.

On my visit to her house with my friend Ruby, who was a former supervisor for the emergency employment program, we discovered that Wanda's electricity had been cut, not by the Chilectra electricity company but by a neighbor from whom she had tethered electricity from for the past year. Wanda had been unable to keep up with her payments to her neighbor, but she also could not keep up with the consumer debt she had accumulated in department stores. We sat in the dark, with the open door bringing faint light into the house. Ruby asked Wanda if things were "critical" in her household. "Are you making it to the end of the month?" Wanda wavered, "Well, I have my debts . . ." She started crying. "I can't make it. I can't. I know that there is that option [referring to the trade]. They said to me that any time that I needed I could do it. That all I need is to store the *merca* [the commodity—drug] in my house. Someone would pick it up. And I know that everyone else on this street is doing it. They all do it. That's how they are able to live. But, I think of what might happen to my daughters. What might happen to my mother and to my sister. When the raid comes, they incarcerate everyone."

Wanda's sense of vulnerability to police action emerges not only from the fact that drug raids occur repeatedly in this neighborhood but also because of how the raid is carried out and who can be charged with a crime. According to the Drug Law 20.000, if a person is accused of drug trafficking, those who occupy the same domestic space and those who are up to second-degree relatives can also be charged with the crime of "omission": of having failed to report the crime of drug trafficking, thus participating in the crime through omission.[11] This means that those implicated in the drug raid are not only those who live within the physical limits of the house, but those within the intimate circle of kin who most likely reside on the same street. Following the pattern of migration to the neighborhood, police raid not just one house but several neighboring houses on the same street, at the same time.

The implication of an entire household as well as an extended kinship network lends the anticipation of the police raid its texture. While for Wanda, this anticipation is experienced through agonizing over whether or not to momentarily enter into the work of the drug economy, a decision that is accompanied by fear, for others such as Maribel, whose relatives worked intermittently worked in this economy, this anticipation is experienced in relation to a precarious future in kinship relationships.

Two years prior to my meeting her, Maribel had been shot in the back and paralyzed from the waist down. Martita, a friend of Maribel since childhood, introduced to me to her and accompanied me to my first visit to her house. Martita asked Maribel to relate to me how she had gotten injured. Maribel related to us that on the evening she had gotten shot, she had received a bit of money from her son and was excited to play the slot machines across the street at her neighbor's storefront. It was a few minutes after playing when she heard the crack of the gun and a bullet piercing her back. Her nephew, she said, had been "playing with the gun" when it went off unexpectedly in his hands. Martita corrected her, "But, he wasn't playing with the gun . . . ?" "No, no, Martita, he was playing with the gun, he was just playing," Maribel responded emphatically. It seemed to me that Maribel needed to keep this action in the realm of accident to keep a future in kinship relationships, even as her talk suggested otherwise.

Maribel turned to me and began to relate to me how her nephew ended up living with her in her house. Four years earlier, a drug raid on her street had resulted in her sister and brother and their spouses being incarcerated. The younger sister, however, had a teenage son and an infant girl who were left alone in the house after the police arrested the adults. As the only remaining adult aunt or uncle on their street, Maribel took both children in and for two years fed them and tried to raise them. But the teenage son, she says, was accustomed to a diet of meat and not just beans. She couldn't buy him the Nike sneakers he was used to having. He was accustomed to living with more economic resources made available by participating in the drug economy. She came home one night and found him dancing on the dining table. She yelled at him with cuss words. Within these tensions, Maribel was shot. Shortly after she was hospitalized, a police officer visited her, not for the injury that she sustained but because he was asking after the whereabouts of her nephew. According to the officer, he had been involved in a theft. Maribel recounted to me that she refused to speak to the police officer, and "the cop leaned over my bed and said, 'But don't you know what he did to you? He did this to you.' That is when I learned that my nephew shot me [she corrects herself]—that he was playing with the gun and it shot me. But still, I couldn't tell the police anything. He's my blood [related to me by kinship]."

Two years after she was shot, Maribel's sister, brother, and their spouses were released from prison. While they were now enrolled in a social reinsertion program of the state, Maribel's sense was that they might have begun to work in the drug economy again. Maribel repeatedly alluded to the possibility of raid indirectly, through the hurt she felt from having her sister's infant girl that she raised for two years abruptly taken away from her. "My sister gets out of prison, and the first thing she does is to take the girl. Do you think I have seen her? I raised her with the bottle, sang songs to her. I was her *mamá*. And do you think they bring her around to see me? Not once have I seen the girl. That hurts. That hurts a lot." She continued, "What will happen if the parents go back to prison? When they come again to *reventar* [raid]? She'll come back to me again. But I have missed her so much." In Maribel's talk of her relatives, the anticipation of the drug raid is now not primarily cast in terms of fear over the vulnerability of the household and the potential consequences in terms of prison time but in terms of the feelings of betrayal, hurt, and loss that permeate her relationships with her kin, and also in the quiet hope that she will be reconnected with the child. That is, in terms of the future in kinship.

Such experiences reveal the fragility of relationships and their capacity for betrayal as they are marked by and weave into the anticipation of the drug raid. The persistent question of "what if, and when" a drug raid will occur cultivates a heightened awareness to the small events in everyday life and organizes a fine-tuned aesthetics of everyday life: the gestures one makes and when, how one speaks and where, the slip-ups, the feelings one gives expression to despite oneself. Yet this aesthetics of everyday life is not necessarily defined by fear. The anticipation of the drug raid—as it draws from bodies marked by pasts and projections of futures—involves the swirl of affects that accompany lives as they are lived, affects that we cannot presume in advance of engaging those lives.

Conclusion

Everyday life is bound up in a temporality of anticipation that emerges from order-maintenance policing. Returning to Harcourt's insights, this approach is premised on an idea of thick propensities to commit crime and is justified through the idea of harm. Through a harm argument, order maintenance recasts nuisance into minor offense, and minor offense is then subject to punishment in order to prevent further, more serious, crime. In his empirical study of New York City, Harcourt demonstrates that while crime has indeed decreased under the "quality-of-life" initiative, there is no empirical support to show that the punishment of minor offenses—such as loitering and panhandling—is what has decreased crime. On the other hand, after adopting this policy of order maintenance, the number of cases of police misconduct in New York City greatly increased.

Fieldwork in the setting of a neighborhood under police occupation allows us not only to perceive actual instances of police misconduct and to document reports of police brutality, but also to perceive the affects that accompany policing in the form of constant surveillance and repeated drug raids and to perceive the way police are inflected in the negotiation of intimate relationships. Here, the police's expectation that persons living in this neighborhood are subjects that need surveillance and punishment to conform to the normative order is a condition not only for affects of dread and anxiety but also for a whole range of other affects—of loss, hope, and betrayal, the affective medium of intimate relationships.

In what way might the descriptions I have offered here be considered an "ethnography of the police"? In this volume, there are several striking ethnographies of police, ranging from studies internal to the institution, as Elif Babül examines in terms of the standardization of policing in order to transform "corrupt" power into legitimate authority (chapter 6) to the ways in which the power and authority of the state is mimicked in social domains outside of the law, as Helene Kyed shows through her description of an intermediary form of (civilian) police violence in Mozambique (chapter 5). This chapter offers an ethnography of *policing* in a neighborhood under occupation and suggests that such policing is tightly aligned with other conditions of life in the neighborhood. From the perspective of the neighborhood, policing cannot be understood as a category apart from these other conditions of life, as much as poverty—if it is not to simply be a category in the service of governmental administration—must be seen within a form of life.[12] The challenge, it seems to me, in the description of policing in this neighborhood is to have a fidelity to that life, such that the complex of emotions—of fear, outrage, love, betrayal—are not crowded out by an overwhelming need to have faith in the law and legal justice when confronted with the violence of occupation. In this sense, as one reviewer has asked of the chapter, "One can imagine not invoking the category of police at all, but the author chooses to. What difference does that make?" In response, I would perhaps say that this ethnography has indeed sought to dissolve a stable category of "police" through the description of clusters of other categories and relations. Yet state disordering by police occupation has a reality in its ongoing and pervasive fraying of the social fabric, which can be perceived through these categories and relations. Indeed, police must be invoked in this ethnography, not simply as a category for (our) thought but in terms of the reality of its force in the lives of the people.

The three angles that I have sketched out here can be seen as lived with simultaneously in a life. Together, they show us how policing involves different clusters of categories—law-abider and disorderly; family, neighbor, protection, threat, money—and that police action is not simply experienced in direct and immediate confrontations but in a temporality of anticipation at the level of households marked by struggles to secure livelihoods in a local economy ever more squeezed by the occupation.

Coming at different angles to an ethnography of policing within a low-income neighborhood, I have sought to depart from a prevailing model of evaluating neighborhoods in terms of "police" versus "neighborhood" or in a related model of "two sovereign powers" in which police and gangs collide in a fight over life and territory. Such models reproduce the very language of the state and may cover over the way in which policing is not just an imposition from above but is a condition of life. In exploring these and other categories and temporalities, we can learn how people negotiate a milieu that arises from policing. In so doing, we also might learn how neighborhoods acquire their specificity, such that "low-income neighborhood" is not a general term to describe the poor—not used interchangeably with the social class marker of "low-income population"—but is an invitation into the various relationships, feelings, and forces that course through the neighborhood and lend it its specificity.

Notes

1. See a related discussion in Caldeira 2000. The literature on citizen security and policies on policing, even those identified as "progressive," rely on the idea of order maintenance in their approach while also drawing from a long-standing theory of the marginality of the poor. Together, the driving set of ideas is that the police are necessary to reinstate the normative order in low-income neighborhoods. Thus, intensive policing is understood here as method through which the poor are brought back into the fold of normative social life. (See, for example, Frühling and Gallardo 2012.)
2. Harcourt 2001.
3. Ibid., 158.
4. See also Foucault 1995; Harcourt 2001, 149–50.
5. I refer here to ethnographies of policing that are situated within neighborhood settings. An ethnography of the institution of the police is a different, and important, project. However, an ethnography of police internal to the police was not what I conducted research on, nor would it have been possible to conduct research among civilian Department of Police Investigation drug squads and military police.
6. I have described Martita's relationship to her son and her loss in depth elsewhere (see Han 2015).
7. Actually, I became the conduit through which help could be given anonymously. Celina's neighbors were very concerned about the material pressures and the need for pain medication, diapers, and antisore cream. However, they could not give these things without positioning themselves within intensifying rancors. So, I became the person they could give things to, and I—by virtue of being an "outsider" and "well-to-do"—feigned that I was giving these things out of charity, when it was the neighbors' kindness concealed.
8. I am not making here a positive definition of care. As I have argued elsewhere, what counts as care itself is contested (Han 2012). And, as others have also shown, care can have both its light and dark sides (Stevenson 2014).
9. Hastrup 2005. Anticipation and loss of context, however, are not opposed. Projecting into the future that which is familiar can also lead to misreading of a context.
10. Arias 2006; Arias and Goldstein 2010; Koonings and Kruijt 2007.
11. Ministerio de Interior 2005.
12. See Das and Randeria 2015.

References

Arias, Enrique Desmond. 2006. *Drugs & Democracy: Trafficking, Social Networks, and Public Security*. Chapel Hill: University of North Carolina Press.

Arias, Enrique Desmond, and Daniel M. Goldstein. 2010. *Violent Democracies in Latin America*. Durham: Duke University Press.

Caldeira, Teresa. 2000. *City of Walls: Crime, Segregation, and Citizenship in São Paulo*. Berkeley: University of California Press.

Das, Veena, and Shalini Randeria. 2015. "Politics of the Urban Poor: Aesthetics, Ethics, Volatility, Precarity." *Current Anthropology* 56 (S11): S3–S12.

Foucault, Michel. 1995. *Discipline and Punish: The Birth of the Prison.* New York: Vintage Books.

Frühling, Hugo, and Roberto Gallardo. 2012. "Programas de Seguridad Dirigidos a Barrios en la Experiencia Chilena Reciente." *Revista invi* 27 (74): 149–85.

Han, Clara. 2012. *Life in Debt: Times of Care and Violence in Neoliberal Chile.* Berkeley: University of California Press.

———. 2015. "Echoes of Death: Violence, Endurance, and the Experiences of Loss." In *Living and Dying in the Contemporary World: A Compendium,* edited by V. Das and C. Han, 493–509. Oakland: University of California Press.

Harcourt, Bernard. 2001. *Illusion of Order: The False Promise of Broken Windows Policing.* Cambridge: Harvard University Press.

Hastrup, Kirsten. 2005. "Performing the World: Agency, Anticipation, and Creativity." *Cambridge Journal of Anthropology* 25 (2): 5–19.

Koonings, Kees, and Dirk Kruijt. 2007. *Fractured Cities: Social Exclusion, Urban Violence, and Contested Space in Latin America.* New York: Zed Books.

Ministerio del Interior. 2005. "Ley 20.000." In *20.000. G. d. C.,* edited by Ministerio del Interior. Santiago de Chile: Gobierno de Chile.

Rodgers, Dennis. 2006. "Living in the Shadow of Death: Gangs, Violence, and Social Order in Urban Nicaragua, 1996–2002." *Journal of Latin American Studies* 38 (2): 267–92.

Stevenson, Lisa. 2014. *Life Beside Itself: Imagining Care in the Canadian Arctic.* Oakland: University of California Press.

EIGHT

Aspiration:
Hoping for a Public Policing (Bolivia)

DANIEL M. GOLDSTEIN

Scholarly research has described the grim realities of life in the contemporary cities of Latin America, the most violent region in the world.[1] Authors have documented the pervasive insecurity of daily life, the lack of effective policing and judicial access, and the popular demand for more and better security in the poor and peripheral urban neighborhoods of Latin America and elsewhere.[2] This chapter, however, does not focus exclusively on people's complaints, nor on the deficiencies in formal institutions or operations of policing, nor on the quotidian realities that insecure societies and individuals face, though all of these enter into consideration. Instead, this chapter offers an ethnographic inquiry into people's *aspirations*. It asks: What hopes do vulnerable and insecure people have for their personal safety and for the world they and their children inhabit? What kinds of institutions and individuals—and more precisely, what kinds of police—do they imagine for themselves and their communities? And what role can ethnography play in studying these aspirations?

This inquiry holds broader implications for the study of the relationship among insecure populations, the police, and the state. Against the vision of a minimal, neoliberal state that outsources its various functions (including policing) to private or nonstate entities, my discussion in this chapter points to the popular imagination as a site of resistance to the insecurity prevalent in societies characterized by austerity and a limited public role of the state. I focus specifically on the police as an object of people's aspirations, the locus of an enhanced security making that they can imagine for their daily existence. Although popular aspirations for a better life can be observed in other ethnographic contexts, a focus on the police—perhaps the state's most quotidian expression in urban areas—clearly reveals the widespread dissatisfaction with the state in matters of security provision and the creative alternatives to the status quo that people can imagine. The analysis calls attention to the hope for a better and more secure life amidst the anxiety and despair of contemporary urban insecurity. These hopes are not, however, without their contradictions: Like other sorts of subjunctive states, the aspirations of local Bolivians for greater security entail a mix of responses to crime or its insoluble menace, revealing the deep ambivalence that people have toward the state, the police, and the possibility of reform.

In what follows, I describe an ethnographic moment in which the idea of what I call *aspirational policing* emerged in my fieldwork. This moment was the product of a seminar I organized with market vendors in the city of Cochabamba, Bolivia, part of what (following Kim Fortun[3]) I identify as a *staged encounter*, an ethnographic technique that uniquely enables the development of insights into processes unfolding at the level of the imaginary, the world of wishes, hopes, and aspirations. I then contextualize this encounter through a discussion of insecurity in Bolivian cities, focusing on the relationships between police and citizens, and particularly between police and Cochabamba market vendors. Here, I introduce the idea of "distributed policing" to characterize the fragmented political authorities and systems of urban regulation that have emerged in Bolivia over the last thirty years. I then turn to a consideration of "aspirational policing," to map out the alternative visions of public policing that Bolivian market vendors imagine to contest the realities of contemporary policing and insecurity. I conclude by discussing the role of ethnography in studying aspirational policing, with special attention to how this kind of work can contribute to a more encompassing "anthropology of the good."[4]

A Staged Encounter

It is a cold, late-summer morning in the *Cancha*, the enormous outdoor market of Cochabamba, Bolivia. Tens of thousands of market vendors (*comerciantes*) make their living in the Cancha, and a good many of them sell in *La Pampa*, the Cancha's oldest and largest commercial sector. Whereas other sectors of the Cancha are laid out in neat and orderly rows, with vendors selling similar items stationed alongside one another, La Pampa is a hodgepodge. The market's rows and aisles are narrow, winding, and dimly lit. Vendors of meat sit alongside vendors of shoes, opposite vendors of school supplies or dinnerware. In addition to the numerous and economically better off vendors who control market stalls inside La Pampa, a great many vendors sell on the streets surrounding the market itself, and these street vendors with their pushcarts and wheelbarrows contribute to the crowding and apparent chaos of the place. The overall sense of disorder colors people's perceptions of La Pampa, which is widely judged to be the most insecure and dangerous sector of the market. La Pampa is reputedly crime-ridden, and vendors are frequently the victims of robberies, muggings, and stabbings perpetrated by those whom they call "delinquents" (*delincuentes*). Crime stories also scare away customers, and the comerciantes fear for their businesses. What's more, public police are virtually nonexistent in the market—in their place, the comerciantes pay private security firms to patrol La Pampa.[5]

This morning I am in church. Well, not church precisely, but the San Antonio church's social hall, right off the Plaza San Antonio at the heart of the Cancha. I am joined by about fifty leaders, mostly men, of the various syndical organizations that comprise the *Federación de Comerciantes de "La Pampa,"* or FCP. Historically the market trade was dominated by women,[6] though in the lean times of the last ten or twenty years, increasing numbers of men have taken up the profession. They also have assumed control of many of the market's trade federations, of which the FCP is one of the largest and most powerful. Security is one of the market vendors' principal concerns. As an anthropologist interested in questions of crime, insecurity, and policing, I have been conducting ethnographic fieldwork in La Pampa, working in close collaboration with the leaders and members of the FCP to understand the problems they face and to explore possible solutions. The federation leaders have been very involved in my research and have proposed that I organize a seminar, a gathering of syndical leaders to discuss their thoughts and feelings about the insecurity they and their constituents daily encounter in their work and their ideas for how to resolve the problems that insecurity entails. It is a brilliant idea, promising to complement perfectly my ongoing participant observation and interviews with market vendors. I wish I had thought of it myself.

The seminar I organized became a path to ethnographic understanding, corresponding with the idea of the staged encounter. Here I draw on anthropologist Kim Fortun's characterization of ethnography as a technology that not only reveals but enables, challenges, and provokes.[7] Ethnography, Fortun suggests, can be designed, in the way one would design an experimental system, creating opportunities for the exchange of ideas and eliciting responses to questions that could not previously be asked. Ethnography here is not merely a method for observing what spontaneously arises but a technology for facilitating the expression of the new and previously unimaginable. It is about, as Fortun says, staging encounters:

—in texts, online, in the street, in conference rooms—that are productively creative, creating space for something new to emerge, engineering imaginations and idioms for different futures, mindful of how very hard it is to think outside and beyond what we know presently.

Ethnography thus becomes creative—setting language games in motion, provoking different orderings of things, having patience for what we cannot yet imagine.[8]

The staged ethnographic encounter is, as this description makes clear, a good vehicle for exploring the abstract and ambiguous. It engenders spaces of emergence, in which the previously unthinkable can be thought, the unimaginable imagined. Through the participation of multiple voices, the staged encounter also allows for the emergence of contradiction, contestation, and refusal, as various perspectives arise and contend with one another. Its spaces of possibility are often future-oriented, allowing people to speculate about what has yet to be, to explore what they fear, or to outline what they desire. As such, the staged encounter is particularly apt for talking about security, which is typically future-oriented, envisioning potential perils, their possible consequences, and the means for confronting them.[9] Creating space for comerciantes to express their fears and visions about security is precisely the goal of my seminar.

On this day, we begin with a round of greetings and expressions of thanks by the federation leaders, both to the comerciantes for attending the event and to me and my research assistants for organizing it (and for sponsoring the lunch that will follow). I offer some words of introduction, which establish the ethnographic objectives of the seminar: "Typically," I say, "there is so much discussion about insecurity, you see it in the newspapers, in the halls of government all the time. But from my point of view, almost nobody talks to the people most impacted by the problem of insecurity, which are the people of the market . . . , no? You all. And from our perspective it is necessary to talk with the people, to understand from them how they suffer from insecurity and what solutions they can propose to solve the problem . . . So our purpose is to gather information. You are the experts in this matter and so we are here to talk with you."[10] We break into groups to facilitate further discussion—one group will focus on the causes of insecurity in the market, one on its effects, and one on possible solutions—and then reconvene as a plenary to share the groups' findings.

At first, there is little surprising in what people have to report. For years I have listened to Bolivian people's complaints about insecurity, about the failures of the state, and especially about the Bolivian National Police, and many of these are echoed in the seminar. One speaker, Don Dario, remarks, "The police are corrupt and work with the delinquents. The big bosses [of the police] work with the heads of the delinquents, the next day they let him go, eight hours after they arrest him . . . The police personnel don't [do anything]." Some people also complain about the work of the private security firms contracted to substitute for the police; says Don Marcos, "the private security that we have does not live up to its mission of preventing crime and being effective." And Don Dario adds, "The [private] security is only physically present to collect their payments." Others, meanwhile, indict the laws, the courts, and the entire Bolivian judicial system; says another comerciante, Don David, "There has never been justice in Bolivia, nor transparency, nor honesty. The justice [system] is vertical not horizontal. Justice does not exist. The legal profession in Bolivia should just disappear. Why? Because they don't make justice, *señores*. There is no security because the justice [system] is corrupt."

I am familiar with comments like these. Bolivians, like people throughout the Global South, denounce police and judicial systems that fail to create what they understand to be security in their communities.[11] But on this day a different kind of exchange occurs. A man named Don José calls for *la palabra* (literally "the word," a way of asking for the floor in a public meeting). "As far as solutions, *compañeros*," says Don José, "I say it is important that we have the private security in the La Pampa market. The people of La Pampa have no confidence in the city police. So the solution is we have to ask that the National Police form a direct relationship with the private security." José's remarks prompt an immediate response from another man, Don Carlos: "Ok, *la palabra*," he says. "What I want to know is, you are asking for a better coordination between the police and private security. But, if there is no confidence in the police, then why do we want more coordination?"

Why indeed? Provoked by this exchange, the seminar erupts into chaos. The polite turn taking that had preceded these remarks has vanished, and people now clamor to express their opinions about possible solutions to insecurity, demanding *la palabra*, shouting to be heard over each other. Don Carlos cries out plaintively, "I'm not trying to invalidate any of these solutions, I'm just trying to add to the plenary discussion!" But the seminar has become a shouting match. Not long after, we adjourn for lunch.

The seminar was inconclusive and, for many of the participants, unsatisfying. But in the exchange between Don José and Don Carlos, I found the expression of a wish, the aspiration for policing and security, in all its many contradictions. I return to the notion of aspirational policing after some necessary contextual discussion.

Distributed Policing in the Bolivian City

Experts debate the causes of high levels of crime and violence in Latin America,[12] but ordinary Bolivians attribute much of their insecurity to the failings of the police, the justice system, and the law. The Bolivian National Police are notoriously corrupt and inefficient, facilities for criminal investigation are woefully inadequate, and judiciaries are understaffed and overburdened with caseloads. As a result, the vast majority of crimes reported to the police, including homicides, go unsolved. Many people decline even to report crimes to the police, for fear of being revictimized by police officers seeking bribes, or out of the belief that to do so would simply be a waste of time.[13] The corruption of the National Police is taken as given by many Bolivians, and comerciantes identify the police as a source of insecurity, rather than a deterrent to it. "Where there is insecurity, there are police," people like to joke, suggesting that the police appear not in response to crime but to demand bribes from citizens and so are themselves the cause of insecurity rather than a solution to it. In the seminar described above, and in individual interviews with comerciantes, complaints about official corruption were a common refrain. Such complaints are not limited to the police but ramify up the levels of the judicial system; said one syndical leader, "It's not just the police, the prosecutors' office is mixed up in it, the district attorney as well." And another added, "The justice system is all on [the delinquents'] side, because they rob and then they hire the best lawyers and corrupt judges [to defend them]." Others also criticize the criminal laws, which they deem to be too lenient and excessively protective of the rights of criminals over the rights of victims.[14]

The absence of a robust state presence committed to making daily lived security for local people is not an unusual scenario under neoliberal democracy in Latin America. Justified in terms of the "decentralization" of the state or the inculcation of popular "participation" in security making,[15] various governmental tasks have been assigned to other entities, including private corporations, nongovernmental organizations, and local communities, which are charged with assuming the responsibilities once performed by the state. Anthropologists like Brenda Chalfin, James Ferguson, and Aihwa Ong have described similar phenomena in Asia and Africa, where neoliberal forms of governance have led to the proliferation of new private *qua* public institutions and authorities, operating parallel to or in combination with the state, which administer, tax, and regulate local populations.[16] In the Americas, these new "sovereigns" are often quasi-legal or entirely illegal entities. In Jamaica, for example, Rivke Jaffe notes the emergence of what she calls a "hybrid state," in which formal state institutions share power with local criminal "dons" to provide security in poor communities.[17] Similarly, anthropologists working in Brazil and Colombia have documented situations in which narco gangs and paramilitary organizations perform critical functions of policing and governance, making them formally illegal yet locally legitimate (if contested) institutions.[18]

In Cochabamba's Cancha market, policing functions are carried out not by the National Police but by private security firms that have been granted authority by the state to police the market. However, this arrangement resulted from a negotiated settlement between the state and comerciantes at the urging of the latter, complicating the picture of a straightforward neoliberal withdrawal of the state. During the 1990s, comerciantes say, armed gangs of delinquents roamed the Cancha, and the National Police responsible for market security were negligent or absent. Market vendors, organized through their syndicates and federations, marched on Cochabamba's city hall in protest, demanding more and better police protection for themselves and their customers. Determined to defend themselves from criminal violence, some comerciantes in La Pampa formed their own patrols to sweep the market in search of suspected delinquents, subjecting criminal suspects to beatings, tortures, and executions (locally known as *linchamientos*, or lynchings[19]). At the same time, private security firms, some operating in direct collaboration with federation leaders, began to appear in the Cancha. These private firms assumed the duties of providing police protection in the market, provoking tensions with the National Police who still held formal responsibility for the zone.

On December 12, 2001, an altercation between the National Police and private security officers turned violent. The police beat and arrested private security personnel; a group of La Pampa comerciantes retaliated by setting fire to a local police substation. Reinforcements were called in and a violent clash ensued, during which a bystander was killed. Comerciantes marched and protested for days following this event, denouncing the police for their impotence and corruption in the face of mounting crime. Peace was finally restored after the Cochabamba *Prefectura* (the state government, under whose authority the National Police were administered) met with commercial leaders to negotiate a settlement. The result was a spatial separation of official and private policing. The Prefectura guaranteed the comerciantes that the private security firms could operate inside the market, while the

National Police would patrol outside but not enter the market itself. For their part, the private security firms agreed to turn over any criminal suspects whom they might apprehend to the National Police for prosecution under the law. Through this settlement, the state agreed to exclude itself from the territory of the Cancha, allowing for the proliferation of private security companies therein. Perhaps realizing its error in ceding control over such a large and vital expanse of urban terrain, in 2005 the Bolivian National Police created an Office for the Control of Private Security, to monitor and regulate the work of the private police. But the effectiveness of this office, like so much else in the National Police force, has been limited.

Today, private firms contract with market syndicates to patrol their sectors and deal with any delinquents they apprehend. These firms are organized like para-police units, with a hierarchy of commanders who supervise platoons of street-level agents. These agents not only conduct daily patrols, always on the lookout for potential criminals; they also are responsible for collecting a daily fee from the men and women who sell on the turf that they patrol.[20] Despite their agreement to turn over criminal suspects to the state for prosecution, most private security officers deal with criminal suspects according to their own codes, usually by administering a public beating or other physical correction to discourage the delinquent from returning to their sector. Although they maintain a jurisdictional separation, many vendors suspect collusion between the owners of the private firms and officers in the police hierarchy, networks that guarantee that peace is maintained and profits are circulated, blurring the lines between the public and private domains.

At the same time as the National Police are notably absent from the Cancha marketplace, other forms of state police are robustly present. Chief among these are the Municipal Police, or *comisarios*, who are tasked with the regulatory functions of market administration. The comisarios police the market against violations of municipal norms and commercial codes. They ensure that vendors occupy only those spaces to which they are legally entitled and do not expand their stalls into public spaces like sidewalks and streets. They confiscate tainted goods and contraband, protect customers from fraud, and enforce the dress code for comerciantes (apron and cap for women, dress pants and shirt for men). The comisarios also police the itinerant vendors (*ambulantes*) who sell illegally in the streets surrounding the market, keeping them constantly on the move to prevent them from blocking traffic or establishing permanent posts in public space. These Municipal Police officers are a constant presence in the market, and a nuisance about which market vendors frequently complain. But crime and delinquency fall outside their purview. The comisarios do nothing to fight crime or to make security in the Cancha, but instead produce additional insecurity by issuing fines and harassing vendors who continually find themselves in violation of the municipality's arbitrary rules for establishing "order" in the market.[21]

Nor has the separation of public and private police jurisdictions solved the problems of insecurity in the Cancha. Comerciantes complain that if the private security guards turn the delinquents over to the public police for prosecution, then corruption, weak laws, and judicial inefficacy result in the delinquent quickly being returned to the streets. Additionally, the public police continue to harbor resentment against the private police, refusing to work with them to improve overall security in the city. The problem is compounded by the fact that nearly all private security firms at work in the Cancha are themselves "illegal"—they have not registered with the Office for the Control of Private Security and operate without the legal sanction of the state. This makes private security officers essentially criminals themselves, and the public police sometimes use this as justification to harass, beat, and arrest private police officers. Private police themselves can be highly abusive, enjoying their authority in the market and mobilizing it to extract resources from comerciantes. Many private security officers are themselves ex-convicts, and comerciantes complain of their gruff manner, disrespect, and overall lack of "education" in dealing with their clients.

The multiple varieties of police practice, spread across a range of state and nonstate actors, represent what I call "distributed policing," the form of policing that typifies the contemporary cityscape. The functions of policing in this context belong not to a single state entity—"the police," as they are often glossed in both popular and scholarly accounts—but are distributed across a range of individuals and institutions, some of them official and legal, others private and quasi-legal, others (like lynch mobs) entirely criminal, all of them doing the work of policing against various threats (real and perceived) to public order and security. Distributed policing exhibits the logics of decentralization, cost-effectiveness, flexibility, and individualization that accompany neoliberal political economy. People and communities are "responsibilized" with creating their own security without relying on state assistance and so make private, corporate, communal, and individual arrangements to perform policing functions. Increasingly, the logic of distribution is coming to characterize policing across a range of neighborhoods: In Cochabamba, rich and poor alike hire private firms and deploy the lynch mob as techniques for controlling crime in their communities.

But the patchwork that is distributed policing does not yield the results that people desire. Instead, it produces a system in which multiple violent actors compete for power, wealth, and legitimacy but ultimately fail to provide the tangible forms of security for which vulnerable populations are desperate. The Cancha exhibits a surfeit of policing forms while still lacking a consistent and reliable police to make security in the market. It is no wonder, then, that ordinary people dream of an alternative.

Aspirations of a Public Police

My understanding of aspirational policing takes as its point of departure the work of other anthropologists concerned with the possibilities of social progress in the wake of neoliberal capitalist democratization. Much of this writing takes as its focus the dispositions of people who have endured the violence of civil conflict, economic restructuring, and social fragmentation. Neoliberalism—"the prevailing approach (for now) to government that supplants regulation by law with market forces, and government functions (especially in the service sector) by private enterprise"[22]—has reconfigured relationships between states and citizens, marked by a shift away from the promises once offered by a liberal politics of governance. The result, some scholars contend, is a sense of deep powerlessness to influence the decisions of government and to have personal efficacy in engaging the precarious conditions in which people daily find themselves.[23] People are alienated in these descriptions of post-Fordist precarity, ground down by the trials of daily life and unable to imagine an alternative or an exit.[24] Ghassan Hage calls this a condition of "hope scarcity," in which working- and even middle-class people feel themselves to be inescapably trapped in insecure economic situations.[25] The objects of many of these accounts of hopeless lives are those whom Hirokazu Miyazaki dubs "neoliberalism's 'losers,'" a tag that accords with what Joel Robbins identifies as contemporary anthropology's "suffering subject."[26]

The hopeless disposition of what we might call the "suffering neoliberal subject" depicted in these writings is at odds with the more hopeful, adaptive character of the urban poor described in other recent scholarship, sometimes identified as "subaltern urbanism." Geographers, anthropologists, and others have written about slum dwellers, market vendors, and other inhabitants of the cities of South Asia and Latin America, to describe their predicaments of poverty and urban precariousness. They cite the flexible and pragmatic nature of these individuals and communities, which are able to respond to the changing realities of urban life while pursuing their

own economic advantage and self-development. Asef Bayat calls this orientation to the world the "habitus of the dispossessed."[27] It is marked by a
high degree of imaginative capacity, an ability to envision alternate worlds
to the precarious reality of the present, and so is deeply transgressive of the
subalternity imposed by global capitalism.[28]

Surely, the depressing hopelessness imputed by Hage and others to the
neoliberal suffering subject is as extreme as the buoyant imagination attributed to the slum dweller of subaltern urbanism.[29] But by staking out
the two endpoints of a possible spectrum of political subjectivities, both
approaches help to define a space for the consideration of aspirational policing. Here I build on work by ethnographers of Latin America who have
found hints of hopefulness amidst the rubble of contemporary neoliberalism and the dispositions it produces.[30] Ellen Moodie, for example, writes
about "democratic disenchantment," the profound disappointment experienced by people in El Salvador after that country's long civil war, upon
discovering that the language of liberal democracy had been hijacked by
rightist forms of market democracy.[31] Amidst worsening crime and pervasive social violence, Moodie documents the stories that people tell about
their encounters with criminals and state authorities like the police, to explore the sense of disappointment that accompanies postwar neoliberal
democratization. In these stories of powerlessness and betrayal, however,
she also finds a "cruel optimism"[32] characterized by both a retrospective
sense of loss and a prospective imagination: "a loss of a never-quite-known
object, a not-yet fantasy of order and democracy with functioning laws
and institutions, a dream of belonging, a yearning for a community of
care and mutual obligation among strangers." The people of El Salvador,
Moodie writes, were not yearning for utopia but something much hum-
bler, namely: "liberal democracy. One of civility and respect in which everyone had equal rights. One that allowed for the possibility of a dignified
existence . . . The stories they shared spoke of betrayal after the peace accords. They had dared to imagine something else."[33]

In her work among residents of the Putumayo region in Colombia, anthropologist Winifred Tate encounters similar kinds of hopeful imaginings
amidst violence and defeat. As in other contexts characterized by conflict, a
partially present state, and the emergence of multiple and competing local
sovereigns, in Putumayo numerous armed actors emerged to challenge the
Colombian state's monopoly on the legitimate use of violence and to compete with the state as legitimate forms of local governance. In her research,
Tate found that Putumayo residents, forced to navigate this complex and
dangerous terrain, articulated a vision of political alternatives through fan-

tasies of liberal statehood and inclusive citizenship. Tate identifies this as a longing for an "aspirational state." It is a practical aspiration more than a utopian one, grounded in historical experience; as Tate observes, it draws on "the conceptual categories of modern liberal democratic citizen-state relations, while at the same time resonating with historic ties of authoritarian paternalistic clientelism."[34] The dream of a liberal state is also a product of dialectical interaction, born of "everyday encounters between the general populace and the violent efforts of those who claim the right to govern them."[35] Although a space formally identified as lacking an effective state presence, Tate shows Putumayo to be a region marked by a hyperpresence of state-like entities, replete with contradictory projects of rule. In such a context, local residents and officials struggle to craft their own political futures by expressing aspirational visions of state-citizen relationships that are markedly different from those that characterize their current reality.

These descriptions of the local aspirations of people living in precarious and insecure conditions offer us a framework for thinking about aspirational policing. As in Tate's recounting of the aspirational state in Colombia, Cancha market vendors' hopes of better policing emerge out of their encounters with the various kinds of distributed policing that characterize contemporary market life and the forms of disorder and violence that this policing entails. Their aspirations do not represent wild dreams of radical inversion, but a desire for an intimacy with the state, a state upon which they can rely for their security needs and which will honor their rights as citizens. So, despite the many deficits exhibited by both the national and the private police in Bolivia, Cochabamba market vendors articulate a vision of what policing could and should be in their environment. Some of the ideas that comerciantes express are practical and immediate; others are more lofty and elaborate. But in general, like the people with whom Moodie and Tate worked, these people's visions are less utopian dreams than a set of aspirations that could conceivably be made to work in the local setting. They express the concrete desire for a liberal state that operates according to a rule of law in the delivery of public policing and a unified citizenry active in demanding the rights accorded them in democratic society.

As I stated at the outset, such imaginings are not without their contradictions. These are perhaps most evident in vendors' evaluations of the National Police. As discussed above, vendors complain of police corruption and inefficiency and bemoan the many and frequent abuses that police officials have been known to commit. At the same time, though, vendors complain of the lack of a public police presence in the market, which, they say, leads to heightened insecurity and a large population of delinquents who prey on vendors and their clients.[36] Despite their own participation in the riots that led to the exclusion of the National Police from the market, many comerciantes still express the wish for their return. One comerciante told me, "Here in La Pampa, we almost never see the police," and attributed his insecurity to that fact. But in the same breath, this comerciante stated that the police are so corrupt that he would actually prefer never to see them. This contradiction—a desire for a greater police presence, even as they fear and hate the corrupt police—is a common refrain among comerciantes in the La Pampa market, as it is in poor neighborhoods worldwide.[37] In another example of this contradiction, vendors point to the sector of the La Pampa market called the *Barrio Chino*, infamous as a hub for the resale of stolen goods and contraband. Many comerciantes regard the Barrio Chino as a locus of vice within the market, a place that attracts all kinds of delinquents and radiates danger into the rest of the market. Despite its criminal reputation, the Barrio Chino is tolerated by both police and market vendors, many of whom profit from the illegal activities that go on there. Comerciantes recognize that this is problematic, and some express the wish that the National Police would establish a police substation (*módulo policial*) in the Barrio Chino. Said another seminar participant:, "A police substation should exist, there should be a substation. Why? To at least bring more control there, no?" This suggestion comes in spite of widespread rejection of the police as an effective instrument of security making.

However, complaints about police corruption and absence are accompanied by expressions of local aspirations, elicited in my research through the staged encounter of the seminar and developed through follow-up interviews with seminar participants. People express their concerns with corruption and judicial inefficacy but also offer solutions on how to fix it, and in those solutions one can detect a deeper longing for a public policing that actually makes them feel secure. On the matter of police corruption, for example, many people offer the suggestion that police be paid a higher salary, with benefits, befitting a public servant with an important job to do. This, they argue, would deter corruption, which is currently very appealing to underpaid police. Officers in the Bolivian National Police currently earn about US$100 a month and must provide their own uniforms, firearms, and other equipment, often including the gasoline for police vehicles. The police also need better training, many comerciantes say, and corrupt police must be severely punished, but above all they need better remuneration. Said one syndical leader at the seminar, "It is not merely training [that they need], it is a good salary. The salary is fundamental. If there isn't a good

salary, nobody is going to work honestly." Notably, many experts on policing in Latin America have made the same proposal, suggesting that raising
police salaries is basic to reducing corruption and promoting the rule of
law in the region.[38] In this case, vendors' visions of better public security
actually coincide with expert recommendations for public policy.

Complaints about the public police contain within them a critique of
distributed policing, as they often imply that neither the public police nor
their substitutes, the private security agents, are adequate to the task of
making security. The failings and abuses of the private police, described
in the previous section, prompt comerciantes to imagine a robust public
policing in the market. Here, important temporal considerations emerge.
Although most comerciantes consider the market to be safer today than
before the arrival of the private firms, crime is still a problem, especially
at night, when the private security goes off duty (round-the-clock private
policing is prohibitively expensive). Unlike the state, whose responsibility
is presumed to be temporally unbounded, private security firms are only
obligated to serve for the hours during which they are paid. In the seminar,
Don Dario put it this way: "We have private security that each of us has to
pay for, but is there a solution for our sector? When many of our *compañeros* leave home at 4:00 a.m. to be in the market, at 12:00 at night they go
home, but at 12:00 at night there is no private security nor any police. . . .
Many of our compañeros are being stabbed, many of our people have been
attacked. . . . The [private] security is only physically present to collect their
payments, [not] at night. . . . because they don't provide twenty-four-hour
coverage." Dario's comment suggests the deep reservations market vendors
have about the security firms, whose explicitly transactional, corporate nature calls into question their dedication to local needs, in much the same
way that police corruption threatens the legitimate sovereignty of the state.
Instead, people long for a police force that doesn't collect funds on a daily
basis the way the private firms do but exhibits a more enduring, temporally
stable commitment to the public and its security.

Comerciantes also envision a more active role for public officials and
citizens, to ensure that the laws are observed and criminals prosecuted
appropriately. In the seminar and in individual interviews, comerciantes
often repeated the desire for formal oversight of the police and security
apparatus. Said one seminar participant, "If there were someone to follow
up [*si hubiera una persona para haga un seguimiento*], a group of people to
follow up on this delinquent, to file the complaint and be constantly there,
pressuring the police, then these delinquents, once they . . . go to the police, they will be processed and not just let go, to return again and commit

the same crimes." Interesting to note is the use of the subjunctive form of the verbs in this quotation, frequently used in Spanish to express conditions of uncertainty, possibility, or desire. Content analysis of dialogue like this, emerging from the staged encounter of the seminar, reveals the conditional, future-oriented temporality through which people are able to conceptualize and speak about their security visions. The engaged oversight proposed here imagines a public authority that in the future would be able to prevent corruption and ensure the enforcement of the law.

The overlapping agencies and discontinuous police jurisdictions in and around the Cancha are a further subject of critique among comerciantes, one expressed as an aspiration for unity in the market. Divided between public and private authorities, the market itself is divided among sectors, syndicates, federations, and other forms of organization that, people say, limit their ability to act in concert to make security. Part of the problem is the multitude of private firms charged with policing the market; these firms work their turfs but ignore problems elsewhere: "We lack unity, because this little group contracts its own security, another group its [private security], but over there they are stealing someone's cell phone, but [the guards say] 'they aren't the ones paying me.'" The critique of divisions between private firms and their contractual nature leads to a broader aspiration for political unification in the Cancha, one not based on capitalist relations of security production. Again one notes the frequent use of the subjunctive mood in these statements. Said another speaker at the seminar, talking about solutions to insecurity: "Our syndical organizations should be unified. . . . I would like us to be able to talk about unity. For me, unity would mean that we are all one market."[39] This in turn leads to an expressed desire for collective action, social empowerment, and civil rights: "Let's behave as actors here," said another seminar participant. "We have to be participants, compañeros, the solution [to insecurity] has to come through us demanding that our authorities take control and asking for our rights."

These comments return us to the exchange between Don José and Don Carlos at the seminar, in which Carlos noted the irony in José's wish for greater coordination between the public and private police. José's statement includes many features of the aspirational policing described above—the desire for an integrated and functional security system, governed by public oversight but respectful of the utility of private security making. Carlos's response to José reveals the contradictions inherent in the security aspirations of many comerciantes, who both want and don't want anything to do with the National Police. But José's wish is a common one among market vendors, who see the proliferation of distributed policing forms and the absence of a public authority as detrimental to their overall security. Though they despise the National Police as they are currently configured—corrupt, inefficient, and unconstrained by a rule of law or a sense of public responsibility—they nevertheless long for such an authority, a public police force that operates effectively to control crime and protect the citizens. This public police can take many forms in this imagination and can even include the private police (José: "we have to ask that the National Police form a direct relationship with the private security"). Several speakers at the seminar noted that greater coordination between public and private police would mean that private police could hand over captured delinquents to the public police, with the expectation that they would be prosecuted under the law. Coordination might also mean that the public police offer training courses to the private security guards, to improve their capacity to enforce the law. And others demanded that the public police treat the private police with respect, asking "that the state recognize the [private] security officer as a public functionary." These suggestions represent a significant departure from the ways in which policing is currently organized in the Cancha and embody the vision of a new way of organizing, of creating security in the public market.

Conclusion

My consideration in this chapter of aspirational policing is intended to be optimistic—a contribution to an "anthropology of the good," to follow Robbins.[40] In examining local aspirations for policing, security, and their entailments, I am calling attention to the ways in which people living in contexts characterized by precarity and insecurity imagine for themselves a better world, one characterized by honesty, justice, and security in its broadest sense. Theirs is a vision of social inclusion, in which the police are public servants committed to fostering security for the law-abiding majority; in which citizens are united, have rights, and can influence their government; in which an understanding of the "public" is broadened to include other sets of actors in whom the people place their trust. This positive imaginary is not without its contradictions: Even as they dream of a progressive political future, the comerciantes of the Cancha have also been known to lynch criminal suspects, to advocate for a more heavy-handed state that uses violence (including the death penalty) in managing delinquency, and to tolerate various forms of abuse if they feel these are more likely to produce security. But these are familiar themes in the study of crime and policing in Latin America, part of the interdisciplinary construction of the suffering subject in the insecure city. This chapter has tried to move beyond that framing, to examine something else that exists simultaneously alongside these more negative visions.

The concept of aspirational policing owes its novelty to what Didier Fassin has identified as the dearth of ethnographic studies of the police and policing.[41] Ethnography is uniquely able to reveal questions that remain invisible to other techniques of investigation. In this, I mean more than the rather obvious assertion that long-term presence and intimate engagement with a particular population enables the ethnographer to observe things that otherwise would be obscured. As I have discussed, I echo Fortun's call for an ethnography that is designed to challenge and provoke, an ethnography that is creative not only in how it is rendered on the page but in how it produces the knowledge about which it reports. The encounter I staged in the social hall of the San Antonio church established a space in which the aspirational expressions of an imagined policing could emerge. These aspirations may have appeared through other forms of inquiry, but the face-to-face encounter of the seminar enabled a dialogical exchange through which new and possible futures could be voiced. These futures also contained contradictions, as the confrontation of Don José and Don Carlos illustrated. But the seminar, much to my surprise, was a feat of ethnographic engineering through which new insights—what in this chapter I have called "aspirational policing"—could be born.

The staged encounter of the seminar sat well with other ethnographic techniques, suggesting that such staging may be one element among many that can be combined as part of an overall ethnographic design. For example, the ideas that were first articulated during the seminar were elaborated through other forms of conversation and observation: my subsequent interviews with seminar participants allowed me to deepen my understanding of the ideas that emerged during the seminar event, and in further participant observation I was alert to signs of their reappearance. The dialogues of the seminar were taped and transcribed, allowing me to conduct content analysis of what occurred. This included linguistic analysis: As I noted above, the repeated use of the subjunctive by speakers in the seminar when describing their visions (e.g., "If there were someone to follow up/*si hubiera una persona para haga un seguimiento*") pointed to the conditional, future-oriented, and aspirational nature of individuals' comments.

Ethnography, unlike other forms of inquiry, requires the researcher to be highly tolerant of ambiguity. Especially in consideration of the possible, the potential, and the aspirational—referring to future moments that cannot be grounded in solid "data" but depend entirely on accessing individual and collective imaginations—ethnography demands patience and a willingness to suffer the unknown and the impossible. Elsewhere I have called for an "uncertain anthropology," one that requires us to "to live with the ambiguity of multiple and overlapping possibilities that are shifting, temporary, and uncertain."[42] Luckily, as Fortun notes, anthropologists are good at tolerating the unknown: "we have an affordance for unimaginable futures."[43] Ethnography allows us to grasp the diffuse and sometimes hopeful dispositions of those caught in the webs of contemporary urban insecurity, providing an alternative to the often nightmarish renderings of crime and policing that other forms of research reproduce.

Notes

1. The material contained herein is based upon work supported by the National Science Foundation under grant number 0540702. Any opinions, findings, and conclusions or recommendations expressed in this material are those of the author and do not necessarily reflect the views of the National Science Foundation. My thanks to Didier Fassin for inviting my participation in the workshop at the Institute for Advanced Study where I first presented the ideas contained in this chapter, and for his comments on this draft. I also thank Julia Hornberger and the other participants in the workshop for their helpful feedback on these ideas.
2. Bergman 2006. I have documented this in my own work in Bolivia (Goldstein 2012).
3. Fortun 2012.
4. Robbins 2013.
5. A much fuller discussion of these issues can be found in Goldstein 2016b.
6. See, e.g., Seligmann 2004.
7. Fortun 2012.
8. Ibid., 459.
9. Pedersen and Holbraad 2013.
10. All quotes from the seminar are transcribed from recordings of March 15, 2007. Some quotes also appear in Goldstein 2016b.
11. For more about these issues in the Bolivian context, see Goldstein 2012.
12. As Albro (2015) has noted, the reasons behind rising crime rates are many and varied, and include widespread economic and social inequality; lack of economic opportunity; weak state institutions, including the police and the judiciary; legacies of past social and military conflicts and lingering authoritarian values; urban segregation; and the militarization of society provoked by the war on drugs, among other things.
13. This fact suggests that reported levels of crime, high as they are, actually underrepresent the problem nationwide.
14. I have written about this in detail; see Goldstein 2012.
15. Marquardt (2012) describes popular participation and citizen security in Peru. The language of "citizen security" is a common public discourse in Latin American security policy, something that I have reviewed elsewhere (Goldstein 2016a).
16. Chalfin 2010; Ferguson 2006; Ong 2006.

17. Jaffe 2013.
18. On Brazil, see Penglase 2014; on Colombia, see Civico 2012. A more general survey of the relationship between violence and democracy in Latin America can be found in Arias and Goldstein 2010.
19. See Goldstein 2004.
20. I present a fuller ethnography of private security firms and their operations in Goldstein 2015.
21. Extensive discussion of these issues can be found in Goldstein 2016b.
22. Greenhouse 2010, 1.
23. Writings on "precarity" in the neoliberal context convey a similar sense of hopelessness and alienation, often with good reason (e.g., Allison 2013). Alternatively, see Miyazaki 2004.
24. See the descriptions in Muehlebach 2013.
25. Hage 2003, 20.
26. Miyazaki 2010, 239; Robbins 2013, 448.
27. Bayat 2007.
28. In this, subaltern urbanism resonates with Crapanzano's (2004, 6) concern with the "transgressive possibility" of the imagination. On hopefulness and the idea of "wishful images," see Bloch 1995 (1959).
29. Ananya Roy (2011) has written persuasively about the limitations of a subaltern urbanism.
30. Gordillo 2014.
31. Moodie 2010.
32. Berlant 2011.
33. Moodie 2010, 168.
34. Tate 2015, 110.
35. Ibid., 111.
36. The Bolivian government recently conducted a very interesting survey on questions of insecurity, though the reliability of the data is open to question; see ONSC 2012.
37. E.g., see Fassin 2013.
38. See, for example, the essays in Uildriks 2009.
39. Spanish: "nosotros debemos tener nuestras organizaciones sindicales en unión . . . entonces yo quisiera que nosotros podamos hablar sobre la unidad, para mi unidad quiere decir que somos un solo mercado."
40. Robbins 2013.
41. Fassin 2013, 32.
42. Goldstein 2012, 255.
43. Fortun 2012, 458.

References

Albro, Robert. 2015. "Violence and Everyday Experience in Early Twenty-First Century Latin America." In *Religious Responses to Violence: Human Rights in Latin America Past and Present*, edited by Alexander Wilde, 63–92. Notre Dame, IN: University of Notre Dame Press.

Allison, Anne. 2013. *Precarious Japan*. Durham: Duke University Press.

Arias, Enrique Desmond, and Daniel M. Goldstein, eds. 2010. *Violent Democracies in Latin America*. Durham: Duke University Press.

Bayat, Asef. 2007. "Radical Religion and the Habitus of the Dispossessed: Does Islamic

Militancy Have an Urban Ecology?" *International Journal of Urban and Regional Research* 31 (3): 579–90.

Bergman, Marcelo. 2006. "Crime and Citizen Security in Latin America: The Challenges for New Scholarship." *Latin American Research Review* 41 (2): 213–27.

Berlant, Lauren. 2011. *Cruel Optimism*. Durham: Duke University Press.

Bloch, Ernst. 1995 [1959]. *The Principle of Hope, Vol. 1.* Translated by Neville Plaice, Stephen Plaice, and Paul Knight. Cambridge, MA: MIT Press.

Chalfin, Brenda. 2010. *Neoliberal Frontiers: An Ethnography of Sovereignty in West Africa.* Chicago: University of Chicago Press.

Civico, Aldo. 2012. "'We Are Illegal But Not Illegitimate': Modes of Policing in Medellín, Colombia." *PoLAR: Political and Legal Anthropology Review* 35 (1): 77–93.

Crapanzano, Vincent. 2004. *Imaginative Horizons: An Essay in Literary-Philosophical Anthropology.* Chicago: University of Chicago Press.

Fassin, Didier. 2013. *Enforcing Order: An Ethnography of Urban Policing.* Cambridge, UK: Polity.

Ferguson, James. 2006. *Global Shadows: Africa in the Neoliberal World Order.* Durham: Duke University Press.

Fortun, Kim. 2012. "Ethnography in Late Industrialism." *Cultural Anthropology* 27 (3): 446–64.

Goldstein, Daniel M. 2004. *The Spectacular City: Violence and Performance in Urban Bolivia.* Durham: Duke University Press.

———. 2012. *Outlawed: Between Security and Rights in a Bolivian City.* Durham: Duke University Press.

———. 2015. "Color-Coded Sovereignty and the Men in Black: Private Security in a Bolivian Marketplace." *Conflict and Society* 1 (1): 182–96.

———. 2016a "Citizen Security and Human Security in Latin America." In *Routledge Handbook of Latin American Security Studies,* edited by David R. Mares and Arie M. Kacowicz, 138–48. London: Routledge.

———. 2016b. *Owners of the Sidewalk: Security and Survival in the Informal City.* Durham: Duke University Press.

Gordillo, Gastón R. 2014. *Rubble: The Afterlife of Destruction.* Durham: Duke University Press.

Greenhouse, Carol. 2010. "Introduction." In *Ethnographies of Neoliberalism,* edited by Carol Greenhouse, 1–10. Philadelphia: University of Pennsylvania Press.

Hage, Ghassan. 2003. *Against Paranoid Nationalism: Searching for Hope in a Shrinking Society.* Annandale, Australia: Pluto Press Australia.

Jaffe, Rivke. 2013. "The Hybrid State: Crime and Citizenship in Urban Jamaica." *American Ethnologist* 40 (4): 734–48.

Marquardt, Kairos M. 2012. "Participatory Security: Citizen Security, Participation, and the Inequities of Citizenship in Urban Peru." *Bulletin of Latin American Research* 31 (2): 174–89.

Miyazaki, Hirokazu. 2004. *The Method of Hope: Anthropology, Philosophy, and Fijian Knowledge.* Stanford: Stanford University Press.

———. 2010. "The Temporality of No Hope." In *Ethnographies of Neoliberalism,* edited by Carol Greenhouse, 238–50. Philadelphia: University of Pennsylvania Press.

Moodie, Ellen. 2010. *El Salvador in the Aftermath of Peace: Crime, Uncertainty, and the Transition to Democracy.* Philadelphia: University of Pennsylvania Press.

Muehlebach, Andrea. 2013. "On Precariousness and the Ethnographic Imagination: The Year 2012 in Sociocultural Anthropology." *American Anthropologist* 115 (2): 297–311.

Ong, Aihwa. 2006. *Neoliberalism as Exception: Mutations in Citizenship and Sovereignty.* Durham: Duke University Press.

ONSC (Observatorio Nacional de Seguridad Ciudadana). 2012. *Trabajando por la seguridad ciudadana: Primera encuesta de victimización, prácticas y percepción sobre violencia y delito en La Paz, El Alto, Cochabamba y Santa Cruz. Primeros resultados 1(1).* Equipo Técnico del ONSC, Ministerio de Gobierno, Estado Plurinacional de Bolivia.

Pedersen, Morten Axel, and Martin Holbraad. 2013. "Introduction: Times of Security." In *Times of Security: Ethnographies of Fear, Protest and the Future,* edited by Martin Holbraad and Morten Axel Pedersen, 1–27. London: Routledge.

Penglase, Ben. 2014. *Living with Insecurity in a Brazilian Favela: Urban Violence and Daily Life.* New Brunswick, NJ: Rutgers University Press.

Robbins, Joel. 2013. "Beyond the Suffering Subject: Toward an Anthropology of the Good." *Journal of the Royal Anthropological Institute* 19:447–62.

Roy, Ananya. 2011. "Slumdog Cities: Rethinking Subaltern Urbanism." *International Journal of Urban and Regional Research* 35 (2): 223–38.

Seligmann, Linda J. 2004. *Peruvian Street Lives: Culture, Power, and Economy among Market Women of Cuzco.* Urbana: University of Illinois Press.

Tate, Winifred. 2015. *Drugs, Thugs, and Diplomats: US Policymaking in Colombia.* Stanford: Stanford University Press.

Uildriks, Niels, ed. 2009. *Policing Insecurity: Police Reform, Security, and Human Rights in Latin America.* Lanham, MD: Lexington.

PART THREE

Description

NINE

Sense and Sensibility:
Crafting Tales about the Police (Thailand)

DUNCAN McCARGO

Elinor, this eldest daughter, whose advice was so effectual, possessed a strength of understanding, and coolness of judgment, which qualified her, though only nineteen, to be the counsellor of her mother, and enabled her frequently to counteract, to the advantage of them all, that eagerness of mind in Mrs. Dashwood which must generally have led to imprudence. She had an excellent heart;—her disposition was affectionate, and her feelings were strong; but she knew how to govern them: it was a knowledge which her mother had yet to learn; and which one of her sisters had resolved never to be taught.

—Jane Austen, *Sense and Sensibility* (1811)

Captain Daeng, the duty investigator, takes me along to the juvenile court with a seventeen-year-old suspect.[1] He was arrested at a friend's house by a group of detectives and is charged with possessing 125 amphetamine tablets. In the statement the police wrote that he ran into the house where he was arrested, but actually they made that up: they burst into the house without a warrant. Under a newly enacted law, youth suspects must be taken to court within twenty-four hours, under provisions designed to protect their safety, and to ensure they are not tortured, abused, or incarcerated in the wrong sort of places.

The lad sits in the back seat of the pickup truck since I am in the front seat blocking his exit; otherwise he would have been put in the tailgate lock-up. Captain Daeng had asked his colleagues how to handle the situation, since according to the new regulations he is not supposed to handcuff juveniles. Another officer tells him to keep the lad handcuffed, and then take the cuffs off right in front of the door of the court, to reduce the chances of him running away. If the suspect runs away, the investigator will be held responsible.

The suspect's mother is waiting at the court and has brought some land documents she hopes to use to bail him out. But since he is charged with possessing a large quantity of drugs it will be very hard for him to get bail; they don't usually bail suspects caught with more than fifteen tablets. I talk to a couple of court officials and ask permission to attend the short hearing. To my surprise, I am taken back to meet the judge who will preside over the case, who is very friendly and open. The judge explains the proceedings and his concern to ensure that juvenile defendants have not been abused by the police and that their rights have not been infringed.

However, when I attend the hearing a few minutes later the judge does not ask about the circumstances of the arrest—which was actually illegal, since the police had no search warrant. He asks if the lad has been properly treated, has been abused or tortured. But these questions miss the point. The hearing lasts a couple of minutes. A court-appointed lawyer sits in the room; he was there for the previous case and seems to be on some sort of daily retainer. The lawyer says nothing useful and fails to ask whether the arrest was legally made—surely the key question?[2] Captain Daeng tells me later he was very relieved. Then we take the lad around to another building within the complex and hand him over to the custody of the court. Oddly, this is Captain Daeng's responsibility, not the court officials'. The officer presiding over the incarceration block sits under a remarkable old black-and-white picture of the king, dressed in judge's robes.

The judge and the court-appointed lawyer must be well aware that many—if not most—drug suspects are arrested illegally. Was the judge ready to turn a blind eye to illegal arrests (presumably as a necessary practice to curb the drug trade), so long as the police do not torture or abuse those they arrest? The court lawyer apparently had no interest in rocking the boat. The handcuffing episode involved a similar compromise; so long as the suspect is not handcuffed when he enters court premises, correct procedures have been followed, and nobody will worry—let alone inquire—about whether he was handcuffed en route to the hearing.[3]

This episode was from a typical day's fieldwork at a Bangkok police station, where I have been conducting ethnographic research for a couple of weeks. I am following the work of police investigators, officers who are responsible for processing charges and preparing cases for court. They are extremely overworked and enjoy low status in the Thai police force, partly because most of them are university graduates, rather than insiders who have attended the police academy. In theory, lower-ranking policemen should act as drivers for investigators and as custodians for any suspects being taken to court, but in practice the investigators often have to perform these roles themselves. The detectives who make the actual arrests almost never go to court; the investigators frequently have to create legal paper trails for dubious arrests in which they played no direct role. Most investigators are buried in bureaucratic work and feel frustrated, dreaming of transferring to less demanding branches of the police or of passing the challenging entrance examinations to become prosecutors or judges. The poor treatment of suspects reflects coded hierarchies that are all-pervasive in the Thai criminal justice system, and Thai society more broadly.

Captain Daeng is the most likeable and decent investigator at his station: he is young, somewhat idealistic, and tries hard to treat everyone fairly. But on this occasion he colludes with an illegal arrest by the detective team and compounds matters by illegally handcuffing the juvenile suspect. Especially after my personal chat with the judge before the hearing, I was sorely tempted to say something in court to call attention to the irregularities in this case. But my position as a participant observer made speaking out fraught with risks: that would probably be the end of my fieldwork at the station and would imperil any future access. My own collusion echoed that of Captain Daeng, who also said nothing about the circumstances of the youth's arrest. I have become more than an observer; I am now a party to the illegal arrest. Did I allow my sympathy for Captain Daeng to cloud my moral judgment? Would allowing my sympathy for the defendant to jeopardize my research access have been a smart move? By allowing my sympathy for Captain Daeng to outweigh my sympathy for the defendant, did I engage in an act of strategic complicity?

During the juvenile offender incident, I was at least not called upon to do anything. The moral and ethical dilemmas increased when I was put on the spot by my police informants. This happened routinely during drug and gambling raids, since despite frequent encouragement to do so, I never grabbed any of the suspects myself. I was regularly teased by the detectives for failing to apprehend anybody. At one station, I became familiar with a range of scam activities, including drug-dealing *tuk-tuk* drivers working in cahoots with the police to entrap foreign visitors, fake "guides" who "helped out" tourists caught up in sting operations for a fat fee, and cut-price long-distance bus companies that made most of their profits stealing from their passengers' luggage. I soon realized which officers were linked to these scams and provided protection for the criminal gangs in the area. When I found myself imploring some tourists to steer clear of a fake guide who was touting for business right inside the police station, I knew it was time to move on to another fieldwork site. My solution to the problems I was facing was one of exit, rather than voice or loyalty.

Understanding Ethnography

A minimal definition sees ethnography simply or primarily as a method or set of methods. In this essentially technical understanding, ethnography is simply one piece of equipment in the social scientist's toolbox. Others, those who see social science as a vocation rather than a mere occupation, are inclined to view ethnography in rather more exalted terms—as a way of life, a way of being in the world. Among those supporting this view is Edward Schatz,[4] for whom ethnography should ideally constitute a sensibility. "Sensibility" means different things to different people, but for me it is above all a word that evokes the romantic movement of the late eighteenth and earlier nineteenth centuries—a susceptibility to feelings, emotions, and intuition. Jane Austen's first published novel offers a wry reflection on the term, contrasting "sensibility" with its close relative, "sense." This chapter argues that ethnography is neither an item of research gadgetry nor a mode of intuition. Rather, ethnography might best be seen as an additional "sense"—one that involves knowing how to govern our strong and excellent feelings, as well as our weak and base urges. The contrast between sense and sensibility is illuminated nicely by Jane Austen. The younger sister in the novel, Marianne Dashwood, is the more attractive figure: too easily smitten with her unsuitable suitor, she resembles an ethnographer who struggles to maintain the necessary degree of detachment from those she studies.

> Marianne's abilities were in many respects quite equal to Elinor's. She was sensible and clever; but eager in every thing; her sorrows, her joys, could have no moderation. She was generous, amiable, interesting: she was every thing but prudent.[5]

Sensibility is a learned way of being, seeing, and apprehending, involving the cultivation of sensitivity and the refinement of emotional response. Marianne's sensibility is an enormous asset, the fount of her charm, and her way of being in the world. But sensibility, accompanied as it is by naïveté, optimism, and an unquestioning confidence in one's own world view, is also a liability. Sensibility could amount to a form of self-romanticization.

Marianne's elder sister Elinor Dashwood epitomizes the notion of sense. Elinor is also strongly intuitive, but she is also hard-headed, wary, and less susceptible to becoming carried away. She is always grounded in a set of clear-sighted understandings. Initially, Elinor seems a rather cool character, toward whom the reader may feel a tad indifferent. But over time, Elinor grows on us, as we begin to see that Marianne's sensibility is a mixed blessing: on balance, sense trumps sensibility. In part, this is also a matter of birth order: Elinor is a first child,[6] who has to make her own way in the world and cannot afford the luxury of fanciful follies. As she explains to Edward Ferrars:

> I have frequently detected myself in such kind of mistakes, in total misapprehension of character in some point or other: fancying people so much more gay or grave, or ingenious or stupid, than they really are, and I can hardly tell why, or in what the deception originated. Sometimes one is guided by what they say of themselves, and very frequently by what other people say of them, without giving oneself time to deliberate and judge.[7]

Like sensibility, sense is something learned over time. But an important difference between sense and sensibility is that practitioners of sense are reflexive learners, constantly trying to spot their own mistakes, and are highly skeptical about what other people tell them. Those who lean toward sensibility may just be more engaging as human beings, but they are less discriminating.

Either sense or sensibility could form the basis of an intellectual—or ethnographic—vocation, but there are different birth-order vocations. Jane Austen writes of the younger sibling in the novel that "Marianne Dashwood was born to an extraordinary fate. She was . . . to discover . . . her most favourite maxims."[8] As David Shapard notes, Marianne's "faults stem from bad doctrine, [and] her fervent adherence to that doctrine and refusal to acknowledge its deficiencies is at least partly the product of her youth and circumstances."[9] *Sense and Sensibility* can be read as a warning against methodological determinism: Austen urges the reader not to become excessively attached to a particular approach to life—in short, not to permit being too "feelingly sensible" to assume the quality of dogma. By extension, the best ethnographers need a balance of sense and sensibility, even though the former may be better developed.

The danger sensibility poses for ethnographers is not simply one of becoming too sympathetic to their informants and becoming ethically or analytically befuddled in consequence. It is true that through overattachment to their own opinions and maxims, ethnographers certainly run the risk of losing the plot of their projects. But a parallel and perhaps greater danger is that adopting ethnography as a vocation allows the ethnographer to assume moral superiority over those who prefer other research methods, not to mention those who happily spend their lives without conducting research of any kind. Another of Jane Austen's novels warns against the dual temptations of pride and prejudice. Perhaps the gravest objection to the notion of an ethnographic sensibility is that it lacks humility and so makes the ethnographer still more susceptible to falsehoods. If ethnographic sensibility is essentially a form of emotion, it needs to be balanced by an ethnographic sense that is firmly grounded in capacities of perception. I do not believe that a preference for sense over sensibility represents a masculine favoring of reason over emotion: these are choices that go far beyond matters of gender.

Ethnography and Me

I conducted intensive participant-observation research at two Bangkok police stations during the first part of 2012. This fieldwork formed part of a larger project into politics and justice in Thailand; my initial focus was on police investigators, the officers who are responsible for sending criminal cases to court. I wanted to understand how people were arrested in Thailand and how the police collaborated with prosecutors and judges. But I soon discovered that most arrests are made by teams of plainclothes detectives (*seupsuan*) rather than uniformed investigators (*sopsuan*), and my police station fieldwork quickly broadened out to cover both branches.[10] As a result, I became deeply interested in the day-to-day work of detectives. This aspect of my unfolding project led me to accompany detective teams on a prostitution raid, several drug raids, a number of gambling raids, and an illegal alcohol raid. I also spent many hours observing how suspects, crime victims, and witnesses were dealt with in police stations. An important focus of my fieldwork was on deprived inner city areas, primarily the "congested communities" (slums) that adjoin some of Bangkok's most glitzy shopping areas and expensive condominium blocks, often alongside filthy *khlong* (canals) or railway lines, or underneath expressways.

If I felt completely comfortable with (and sympathetic toward) criminals and other troubling characters, I would need to desensitize myself to what I was seeing and experiencing. I do not have the right kind of personality to socialize for hours in the company of those with whom I have little in common. I speak a rather formal, academic Thai, which well befits a middle-aged university professor, and I would be very reluctant to adopt a different mode of self-presentation. I have always done my Thai fieldwork—which has included several spells of extended participant obser-vation—without compromising my own sense of myself: I have never tried to be cool, gregarious, or tough, for example. I don't even pretend to like spicy food or hot weather. My informants and collaborators have to take me as they find me. During this project, I continued to find it disturbing to spend an evening accompanying detectives making a dozen illegal and arbitrary arrests in some of Bangkok's most deprived slum communities. Some of the detectives I came to know best were themselves very critical of their own routine "raids" and ritualized evasion of officially laid-down procedures. How was I to respond?

On another occasion, my presence seemed to complicate a detective captain's decision making. My field notes read as follows:

> A quick visit back to the detective room around 9pm. Two *tang dao*, Burmese migrants, have been brought in. One has a valid passport and visa, the other, his wife, no paperwork at all. The captain asks me what they should do. I say that of course legally the wife should not be here, but actually the labor of these people is badly needed in Thailand; and we all know that if she is sent home she will come back in the next few days anyway. But one of the other detectives is very adamant that she should be sent back and tells the captain this. This detective tells the husband to "find some work out of sight of the police." The woman is crying. There is brief talk that somebody at the police station wants a housekeeper and might hire her. She used to earn 7,500 a month. Would she work for 4,000? She does not look happy, and the idea is dropped.
>
> The captain apologizes to me for sending her back to Burma and asks me to understand his position. Personally he sympathizes with their situation but has to follow the law. The other detective says the police always make human rights their basic principle. I tell them *"pom mai wa arai"* (I am not saying anything).

Should I have answered the captain's original question so frankly? I was very tempted not to offer a comment, but I had been sharing a lot with these people for several weeks at that point, and to dodge the question would have been to engage in deliberate evasion. But having offered my opinion in the first place, should I have retracted it so readily, or stuck to my original arguments? Ought I to have challenged the other detective's far-fetched claim that they were always primarily concerned about human rights? I am not sure how far cultivating an ethnographic sensibility should involve suppressing my own anxieties and scruples in favor of sympathizing with those who engage in criminal acts and abuses of power. Again, the captain in this case was one of the friendliest and most open officers in the station. For a second time, I found dealing with a sympathetic informant in some ways more difficult than dealing with a less sympathetic one.

How best could I turn a collection of similar field note vignettes into a book? The safe option would be to do exactly what I did here: to frame these stories within an analytical discussion that locates the tales within a broader context and also explores my ethical dilemmas as a researcher. I am about to suggest some alternatives to this approach, alternatives that foreground an emphasis on ethnographic sense and pursuing heightened perceptions.

Immersion versus Sensibility

A classic summary of the notion of "ethnographic sensibility" appears in an essay by Ellen Pader, from a methods textbook originally published in 2006. For her, this sensibility involves learning how to give more equal weighting to local knowledge, expert knowledge, and the researcher's knowledge. The overall goal of the textbook, summarized in a chapter by the editors entitled "Doing Social Sciences in a Humanistic Manner," seems extremely laudable.[11] But Pader's ideas about sensibility hinge mainly on "ways of seeing" that make the invisible visible—understanding, for example, why people from other cultures are often very happy to share intimate sleeping space with family and friends.[12] She argues for *"listening* and *looking* at a profoundly close and detailed level."*[13] In the end, Pader's claims for ethnographic sensibility are modest and understated: they amount really to a plea for more ethnographic sense. Ethnographic sense is at its core a matter of heightened perception, an ability to notice much more than normal people. Ethnographic sense is not simply a technique but a form of mental facility.

By contrast, Edward Schatz has argued that "political ethnography" goes beyond participant observation and immersion in fieldwork, though these are extremely important starting points. Properly understood, ethnography also involves a "sensibility" that amounts to more than simply the sum of ethnographic parts[14]: "It is an approach that cares—with the possible emotional engagement that implies—to glean the meanings that the people under study attribute to their social and political reality."[15] For Schatz, this kind of sensibility involves paying close attention to the people being studied, without falling prey to overly simplistic distinctions such as those between insiders and outsiders. Nevertheless, Schatz suggests that it is very difficult to conduct such research without an essential stance of sympathy toward those being studied:

> Imagine a hypothetical researcher who, though intending to conduct an ethnographic study, does not enjoy spending time with particular individuals (local strongmen, perpetrators of violence, corrupt police officers and extreme ideologues come to mind, though this is at root a normative question). Since an ability to sympathize lies at the core of ethnography, conducting a study that relied on ethnographic contact with such individuals would be practically and sometimes ethically difficult.[16]

There's the rub: for those who conduct ethnographic research with the police, encounters with potentially unsympathetic informants such as unscrupulous or abusive officers, not to mention drug dealers and other criminals, are a daily reality. We are likely therefore to gravitate toward more agreeable informants—such as "good" police officers who see or present themselves as struggling against the system, or officers with some international or academic exposure—rather than typical officers who are thoroughly and unapologetically acculturated into institutional norms. By bringing our moral preferences to bear on what we encounter, we risk developing a limited and problematic understanding of police work. But by suspending our moral preferences we risk forsaking our true selves in pursuit of research objectives, funding opportunities, good stories, and opportunities for professional advancement. For many researchers, the outcome is some version of what Beatrice Jauregui terms "strategic complicity."[17] As she starkly declares: "When you study and work with police in any 'policed society' . . . you are complicit with their violence."[18]

I would concur with Schatz that ethnography is rather more than method or process; I have always shared Weber's belief that science (in my case, political science—for want of a better term) is not simply an occupation but a vocation. But this vocation resides not in some slightly masonic notion of a "sensibility" to be attained by the elect insider but in the combination of work and passion that helps yield ideas: "Yet ideas would certainly not come to mind had we not brooded at our desks and searched for answers with passionate devotion."[19] It is surely this Elinorean conjunction of an excellent heart, strength of understanding, and cool judgment to which Weber is referring, not to Mariannean excesses of sympathy. In other words, an ethnographic sense is a much more desirable companion than its flightier if more striking younger sibling, an ethnographic sensibility.

To my mind, an ethnographic sense involves a heightening of the five senses. In particular, it is about finding new and different ways of seeing and listening, ways that allow us all the more usefully to brood at our desks. As Cedric Jourde writes, ethnography helps us to "see" the ambiguities that surround empirical realities,[20] allowing us to spot what he terms "Unidentified Political Objects" that might otherwise escape our notice, and to understand the discrepancies between conventionally understood realities[21] and the way they are experienced by ordinary people. In the end, doing ethnography is about flinging wide open what Aldous Huxley called "the doors of perception," so as to let in more light—rather than an immoderate and self-congratulatory sympathy for our subjects that could actually blur our vision. I do believe that political ethnography is more than a methodology, if somewhat less than a whole way of life; accordingly, I would like to develop an "ethnographic sense" to enable me to maintain sufficient critical perspective on my work, without falling into an unreasonable preoccupation with my own role as a researcher.

The "sensibility" that Schatz identifies as a prerequisite for serious ethnography can all too easily blur into an emotional sympathy for those alongside whom ethnographers work. Arguably, it might best be resisted in favor of a more critical ethnographic "sense," one that is based upon empathy rather than sympathy: what Jauregui refers to as "critical empathy," the conjoined twin of strategic complicity.[22] The ethnographer of sense, unlike the ethnographer of sensibility, requires above all an ability to govern her feelings. At the same time, the ethnographer of sense does not need to apologize for her otherness and need not feel guilty about being a privileged outsider or an observer. As Jane Austen insisted, reserving a coolness of judgment is perfectly compatible with having an excellent heart: one does not negate the other.

Max Weber wrote in his "Politics as a Vocation," "Politics is a strong and slow boring of hard boards. It takes both passion and perspective. Certainly all historical experience confirms the truth—that man would not have attained the possible unless time and again he had reached out for the impossible."[23] Like politics, political ethnography is the art of the possible. The best results are likely to be achieved through the requisite combination of passion and perspective, rather than an excess of sympathy or of self-congratulation.

Conclusion

There is no reason why ethnographic research could not be written up in very readable forms. But sensibility may prove difficult to communicate to others without descending into clichés. As Marianne Dashwood explained about her inability to praise a beautiful landscape, "I detest jargon of every kind, and sometimes I have kept my feelings to myself, because I could find no language to describe them in but what was worn and hackneyed out of all sense and meaning."[24] Ethnographic sense should also be evident in the way I write up my fieldwork: avoiding jargon, engaging the reader's interest, but resisting the temptation to tug at her heartstrings. John Van Maanen, whose best known work is an ethnographic study of policing, distinguishes between realist, confessional, and impressionist tales, three alternative ways of writing up ethnographic research.[25] Realist tales perhaps correspond best to notions of ethnography as a more neutral "method," and confessional tales—where the researcher is always present, rather than a disembodied voice—come closer to ethnography as sensibility. Most interesting are the impressionist tales, deliberately crafted writings that, properly done, may transform mere fieldwork into a kind of art form. While Van Maanen later added some additional categories to his original three,[26] most of his new categories appear primarily to be elaborations of the impressionist form, appropriated for slightly different purposes.[27] As he explains:

> Impressionist tales typically highlight the episodic, complex, and ambivalent realities that are frozen and perhaps made too pat and ordered by realist or confessional conventions. Impressionist tales, with their silent disavowal of grand theorizing, their radical grasping for the particular, eventful, contextual and unusual, contain an important message. They protest the ultimate superficiality of much of the published research in social science, ethnographic or otherwise.[28]

For many academics, especially those writing on contemporary social and political issues, the appellation "journalistic" is the one they fear most. To be viewed as a journalist is to be written off as superficial, sensationalist, atheoretical, lacking a broader intellectual agenda—and, perhaps most fatally, lacking methodological rigor. Van Maanen's category of impressionist tales runs many of the same risks as engaging in "journalism": academics are rightly wary of being labelled merely "impressionistic." But the gap between accessible academic writing, creative nonfiction, and higher journalism is a blurred one. There is a rich middle ground that includes fieldwork-based journalism (much of it book-length) and crossover academic work, a terrain staked out in publications such as the *New York Review of Books*, where intellectually inclined journalists jostle for space with popularizing scholars. Many academics really want to reach a wider audience and see their names in the newspapers—but fear the associated label of journalist. Similarly, journalists envy the higher status of academics—which comes with writing "proper" books—but are wary of the pomposity and irrelevance they associate with the academy.

The self-aggrandizing notion of an ethnographic sensibility appears to inhabit the social science imagination primarily as a defense against the merely journalistic or impressionistic, since an ethnographic sense—with its heightened powers of perception and an associated acuity of expression—is much harder to distinguish from a journalistic nose for detail. Yet to write about ambiguous matters on the basis of extensive ethnography—as with my research on the Bangkok police—should not require any special aptitude. Writing based on ethnographic sense relies on thick description, but a thick description that is filtered and ordered by sharp-eyed reflexivity, while not overburdened with confessional agony. Humanizing social science means adopting those writing styles preferred by the majority of humans—which means writing more like a storyteller or a journalist and less like a social scientist. While Van Maanen sees the impressionist mode as a rejection of superficiality, writing in such a way about crime or policing can easily generate accusations of sensationalism and questions about accuracy, methodological rigor, and research ethics.

An example of a popular work of impressionist sociology that generated this kind of controversy was Sudhir Venkatesh's 2008 book *Gang Leader for a Day: A Rogue Sociologist Takes to the Streets.* There is no bibliography or footnotes, and discussions of methods are scant: "Whenever possible, I based the material on written field notes. Some of the stories, however, I reconstructed from memory."[29] Venkatesh generated considerable media attention for his book, which was published by Penguin and sold in airport bookstalls. It was not, however, always appreciated by his fellow academics: one typical critic argued that he put forth a disturbing "hero social scientist narrative," driven mainly by a desire to advance his own career.[30] Whether or not such criticisms are fair in the Venkatesh case, ethnographers who try to popularize their research run the risk of lionizing their own roles and diminishing the social and political nuances of the stories they tell. Rebekah Nathan's *My Freshman Year: What a Professor Learned by Becoming a Student* (2005), also published by Penguin, aroused far less controversy. While drawing on ethnographic research by this fifty-something anthropology professor who enrolled as an undergraduate student on her own campus, the book relies mainly on more conventional methods such as interviews and surveys. Nathan announces early on that "As a reader,

you will find that some topics . . . receive short shrift."[31] These topics include dating and sexuality and alcohol and drug use. By selecting out these
sensitive personal issues, Nathan avoids both ethical problems and any
risk of sensationalism. But the resulting sanitized account of student dorm
life lacks both authenticity and analytical force: if Venkatesh delivers a bit
too much authenticity, Nathan fails to fulfill on the promises of her book
title, as though fearing to tread too far along the lowbrow path. Nathan
also appears to have faltered in her enthusiasm for ethnography: during
her first semester she made only occasional visits "home" (to her comfortable house close to the campus), but the second semester she was spending
most nights there typing up her notes, only returning to her dorm each
morning.[32] A strength of the book is Nathan's refreshing frankness about
the limitations of her approach.

For political scientists, unlike anthropologists and sociologists, ethnography is a minority pursuit and an unfashionable one at that. Working in
the more eclectic British tradition of political studies, I have been able to
spend entire years conducting fieldwork in Thailand on three separate occasions since completing my doctorate—but I would be hard pressed to
name many United States–based political scientists who have done anything similar. Crucially, I gained my PhD from the University of London's
School of Oriental and African Studies, at a time when the informal injunc-
tion to "know your patch" was still audible in the corridors, and cultural
fluency was considered at least as important for the budding social scientist
as a good nose for causal inference. The recent efforts of Edward Schatz,
Dvora Yanow, and others to rehabilitate political ethnography as a project
have been commendable. But the challenge for political scientists remains
how to find the right language, tone, and narrative approach for their ethnographic endeavors, maintaining disciplinary credibility while avoiding
the self-regarding assumptions of both area studies and anthropology.

One example of a political science book driven by a strong "ethnographic sense" that adopts a highly impressionist style is Timothy Pachirat's *Every Twelve Seconds*, based on undercover fieldwork in a Nebraskan
slaughterhouse. Pachirat limits literature review and theoretical discussions
to his introduction and conclusion, and even these are pretty scant. The entire book has only fifty-odd footnotes and no in-text referencing. For more
than 200 pages,[33] the reader is simply taken inside the slaughterhouse and
forced to see through Pachirat's unflinching eyes. The thick description is
reflexive and critical, not merely realist—yet for many pages at a time we
can easily forget that we are reading an academic book, much of which
derives, almost verbatim, from a Yale PhD dissertation in political science.

Rather than providing a linear analytical argument, intermittently illustrated by "docile, heavily policed" informant quotations or extracts from field notes, Pachirat adopted "a writing strategy molded largely by the requirements of narrative, rather than analysis."[34] He reserves his boldest move for the final sentences of the book's introduction: "The detailed accounts that follow are not merely incidental to or illustrative of a more important theoretical argument about how distance and concealment operate as mechanisms of power in contemporary society. They *are* the argument."[35] Pachirat's radical embrace of the notion that narrative *is* argument takes the ethnographic "sense" to its logical endpoint: it's all about ways of seeing and ways of describing what we see. This is a decisive break with the approach taken by most ethnographers of policing, including Didier Fassin,[36] whose writings typically intersperse inductive ethnographic stories and critical reflections within the same articles or chapters. Pachirat's narrative descriptions are illustrated by a stunning series of diagrams that plot the workings of the slaughterhouse in meticulous detail. Nevertheless, Pachirat does have an analytical argument, closely linked to a political project that is sketched out in the book's closing pages:

> These conclusions signal the need for a context-sensitive politics of sight that recognizes both the possibilities and pitfalls of organized, concerted attempts to make visible what is hidden and to breach, literally or figuratively, zones of confinement in order to bring about social and political transformation.[37]

For Pachirat, the ethnographer has an important role as the trespassing narrator of hidden transcripts and the revealer of secrets.[38] He argues that his book offers "footholds" for gaining access to these zones of confinement. Whether or not Pachirat's notion of a "politics of sight" seems completely persuasive,[39] his book certainly offers a blueprint for writing up ethically challenging immersion fieldwork in order to do full justice to the principles of ethnographic sense.

Following Pachirat's footholds as a guide, I should perhaps have written this chapter entirely differently, making my argument by narrating stories about working alongside Bangkok detectives, instead of by examining different approaches to research and writing. At the same time, Pachirat's apparent rejection of broader social, historical, and political explanations for the interactions in which he participates can only go so far. Without the framing that he provides in his opening and concluding chapters, *Every Twelve Seconds* would be a very different book—and one that advanced no real argument, explicitly or implicitly. In the end, I am not willing to give up on all discussions of history, society, and politics that provide a context and a framework for the ethnography itself. The idea of such a radical way of writing ethnography is alluring but ultimately unconvincing. My work on and in Thailand is grounded in many years of formal and informal study, which cannot be quietly stripped from the tales that I have to tell.

Writing about the police would seem to lend itself to general audiences, for whom fictionalized accounts of the work of detectives and forensic investigators have an endless appeal. But how to make ethnographic research as readable as crime fiction? Peter Moskos makes a serious attempt in his well-crafted account of a year working as a rookie cop in Baltimore's drug-plagued Eastern District.[40] Moskos is upfront about his approach: "Some will criticize my unscientific methods. I have no real defense. Everything is true, but this book suffers from all the flaws inherent in ethnographic work and some, perhaps of gonzo journalism. Being on the inside, I made little attempt to be objective."[41] Most of his chapters contain only a page or two of notes,[42] and the book is written from the stance of a researcher who willingly—sometimes almost uncritically—embraces the culture and social norms of the Baltimore police department. It seems apparent that Moskos had very little difficulty working as a cop in one of America's toughest urban police districts; he is the epitome of sense and the polar opposite of sensibility. At times, Moskos appears not so much to be lionizing his own role as a researcher, or exposing the police to sustained critical scrutiny, as simply lauding the fine work done by his fellow officers.[43] But his stance has the advantage of giving him a distinct, down-to-earth point of view: whatever Moskos's shortcomings, he is never pretentious, let alone precious.

How could Jane Austen offer a guide to writing about ethnographic fieldwork with the Thai police? The answer should by now be clear. Austen enables us to understand the shortcomings of "sensibility": an immoderate, imprudent, and oversympathetic mode of thinking and writing. She expresses a strong preference for "sense," a warm engagement with our subject matter that spills over into a playful and ironic writing style characterized by intense acuity—but with an associated distaste for verbosity, pomposity, and jargon. By keeping Austen's warnings in mind, by aiming for some version of Van Maanen's ideal type of the impressionist tale, by using Pachirat's well-crafted empirical footholds to help with our ascent, and by heeding Moskos at least in his ebullient refusal to become overly defensive, it ought to be possible to reach the goal of writing a political ethnography of policing that general readers will find readable and important. But the answer is that there are no easy answers, no perfect model or paradigm from which to work. The kind of ethnography that informs science as a vocation is a singularly unscientific one.

Notes

1. I gratefully acknowledge funding for this project from a Leverhulme Trust Major Research Fellowship, 2011–14, F00 122BC.
2. While the legality or otherwise of the arrest seemed a key question to me, this was obviously not a major concern for the court.
3. Lightly edited fieldwork notes from early 2012.
4. See the introduction to Schatz 2009.
5. Austen 2011 (1811), 8.
6. In the interests of full disclosure, I should mention that I am the eldest of three.
7. Austen 2011 (1811), 176).
8. Ibid., 706.
9. Ibid., xxxiv.
10. Very little serious academic research, ethnographic or otherwise, has been published on the Thai police, even in Thai. For a rare exception using an ethnographic approach, see Haanstad 2008.
11. Yanow and Schwartz-Shea 2014. Unfortunately, the editors discuss this humanistic enterprise in rather high-blown terms, with very little of the sense of irony that best distinguishes the humanities from the social sciences.
12. Pader 2014, 199–203.
13. Ibid., 204.
14. Schatz 2009, 5–10.
15. Ibid., 5.
16. Ibid, 7.
17. Jauregui 2013, 143–48.
18. Ibid., 148. Jauregui favors a very broad definition of "violence," which goes beyond physical coercion (2013, 148n1).
19. Weber 2009, 136.
20. Jourde 2009, 211.
21. Jourde 2009, 215–16.
22. See Jauregui's chapter in this volume (chapter 3).
23. Weber 2009, 128.
24. Austen 2011 (1811), 186.
25. Van Maanen 2011.
26. Ibid., 166–72.
27. Jauregui, in chapter 3 of this volume, argues for the need to go beyond such impressionist approaches in order to write with critical empathy.
28. Van Maanen 2011, 119.
29. Venkatesh 2008, 285.
30. See Claire Potter, "Puff the Magic Sociologist: Sudhir Venkatesh, Gang Leader For A Day, A Rogue Sociologist Takes To The Streets," April 7, 2009, http://chronicle.com/ blognetwork/tenuredradical/2009/04/puff-magic-sociologist-review-of-sudhir/.
31. Nathan 2005, 4.

32. Ibid., 16.
33. Pachirat 2011, 20–232.
34. Ibid., 18.
35. Ibid., 19.
36. Fassin 2013.
37. Pachirat 2011, 255.
38. See Scott 1992.
39. I was not convinced that much would be accomplished by building glass-walled slaughterhouses, for example—see Pachirat 2011, 253–54.
40. Moskos 2008.
41. Ibid., 6.
42. The exception is his chapter 7, a history of drug prohibition that seems to have only a tangential connection with the rest of the book.
43. For example, his insistence that there is no culture of police corruption and that the vast majority of police officers are "clean" (2008, 78) reads like the argument of one who protests too much.

References

Austen, Jane. 2011 [1811]. *Sense and Sensibility*, edited by David M. Shapard. New York: Anchor Books.

Fassin, Didier. 2013. *Enforcing Order: An Ethnography of Urban Policing*. Cambridge: Polity.

Haanstad, Eric. 2008. "Constructing Order through Chaos: A State Ethnography of the Thai Police." PhD dissertation, University of Wisconsin, Madison.

Jauregui, Beatrice. 2013. "Dirty Anthropology: Epistemologies of Violence and Ethical Entanglements in Police Ethnography." In *Policing and Contemporary Governance: The Anthropology of Police in Practice*, edited by William Garriott, 125–53. New York: Palgrave Macmillan.

Jourde, Cedric. 2009. "The Ethnographic Sensibility: Overlooked Authoritarian Dynamics and Islamic Ambivalences in West Africa." In *Political Ethnography: What Immersion Contributes to the Study of Power*, edited by Edward Schatz, 201–16. Chicago: University of Chicago Press.

Moskos, Peter. 2008. *Cop in the Hood: My Year Policing Baltimore's Eastern District*. Princeton: Princeton University Press.

Nathan, Rebekah. 2005. *My Freshman Year: What a Professor Learned by Becoming a Student*. New York: Penguin.

Pachirat, Timothy. 2011. *Every Twelve Seconds: Industrialized Slaughter and Politics of Sight*. New Haven: Yale University Press.

Pader, Emily. 2014. "Seeing with an Ethnographic Sensibility: Explorations Beneath the Surface of Public Policies." In *Interpretation and Method: Empirical Research Methods and the Interpretive Turn*, edited by Dvora Yanow and Peregrine Schwartz-Shea, 2nd ed., 194–208. Armonk, NY: M. E. Sharpe.

Schatz, Edward. 2009. "Introduction: Ethnographic Immersion and the Study of Politics." In *Political Ethnography: What Immersion Contributes to the Study of Power*, edited by Edward Schatz, 1–22. Chicago: University of Chicago Press.

Schatzberg, Michael. 2009. "Ethnography and Causality: Sorcery and Popular Culture in the Congo." In *Political Ethnography: What Immersion Contributes to the Study of Power*, edited by Edward Schatz, 198–200. Chicago: University of Chicago Press.

Scott, James C. 1992. *Domination and the Arts of Resistance: Hidden Transcripts*. New Haven: Yale University Press.

Van Maanen, John. 2011. *Tales of the Field: On Writing Ethnography*. 2nd ed. Chicago: University of Chicago Press.

Venkatesh, Sudhir. 2008. *Gang Leader for a Day: A Rogue Sociologist Takes To the Streets*. New York: Penguin.

Weber, Max. 2009. *From Max Weber: Essays in Sociology*. Abingdon: Routledge.

Yanow, Dvora, and Peregrine Schwartz-Shea. 2014. "Doing Social Sciences in a Humanistic Manner." In *Interpretation and Method: Empirical Research Methods and the Interpretive Turn*, edited by Dvora Yanow and Peregrine Schwartz-Shea, 2nd ed., 433–47. Armonk, NY: M. E. Sharpe.

TEN

Detention:
Police Discretion Revisited (Portugal)

SUSANA DURÃO

From time to time, the police, for the purpose of conveying a kind of satisfaction to society faced by the occurrence of so many crimes, arrest a *fadista* [a *fado* singer]. What we have to ask is: Why not arrest all the *fadistas*?

—Ramalho Ortigão and Eça de Queiroz, *As Farpas* (1878)

Why do some police officers obtain more power and freedom than others? Why are they authorized to deploy certain idiosyncratic and sometimes adventurous styles of performing their duties not only on the streets, but also bureaucratically? How do they "force" law enforcement while simultaneously knowing and even taking into consideration specific legal and administrative limitations? And just what do they achieve by it all?

In this chapter, I will debate these questions on the basis of ethnographic notes written after one of the longest shifts I have ever participated in at a neighborhood police station located in West Lisbon. During a twelve-month period of in-depth fieldwork at the station, and having already engaged in Portuguese policing issues for over a decade, I followed two of the five groups of approximately twelve officers as they went about their six-hour shifts (which rotated every four days). For two months, I frequently had the opportunity to participate in the routines of two officers who occasionally during their regular shifts were assigned by the station's captain to carry out "undercover police operations," as they were called in 2004.

This text explores and analyzes the details of one specific detention: a young man accused of dealing small amounts of hashish by these two plainclothes officers. The two first conduct an improvised street investigation and then go through the bureaucratic process of charging the man.

The chosen example illustrates the human and professional investment of officers who aspire to achieve a successful arrest by any means—even if it involves the disproportionate and apparently unjustifiable use of police force and results in a legally questionable case, facts that both the officers and I are well aware of. As such, this text examines the maneuvres of what I term an *improbable detention* and the intricate material conditions and meanings of this kind of adventurous and to a certain extent simultaneously controlled police style of action. The detention also reflects the career expectations, personal recognition, and promotion ambitions within the wider context of the Portuguese urban national police force, the *Polícia de Segurança Pública* (PSP).

This episode (and others of its kind) leads us to the theoretical question of police discretion and the limits of the police mandate in democratic states—a classical debate in the social sciences and critical criminology.[1] My aim is to go beyond the a priori normative social thinking that frames the idea of discretion—often delimited as positive or negative, justifiable or unjustifiable, legitimate or illegitimate—and to consider, in police terms, whether it is proportionate or disproportionate.[2] The idea is to rethink police discretion in light of ethnographically grounded anthropology. I contend that the social theory of policing will benefit from an anthropological definition of discretion that takes into account the logics and emotions displayed by certain people in the course of everyday political expressions of enforcement. As such, we must recognize that police discretion may frequently appear to be in tension with the application of official policies and the freedom of the police may at times seem at odds with the oversight of the institution but, in practice, these contradictions actually represent two sides of the same coin, as first considered by Didier Fassin. I seek here to argue that the anthropological analysis of a small-scale event with the complex usage of tactical improvisations led me to question discretion from an anthropological standpoint and therefore challenge the persuasive construction of critical social theories that defend the state and the police as violence (as expressed by Walter Benjamin) *or* the state and the police as law (as described by Edward P. Thompson).

In the first part of this text, I demonstrate how the detention of a youth by the police was conducted by a duo of officers, Duarte and Cruz, and was even imagined and desired before it took place. I narrate how despite the officers' mixed feelings of adventure, enthusiasm, jitters, and anger when it becomes apparent that the youth's detention is not justified (for lack of sufficient material evidence as required by the law or for failure to catch the youth in the act), they continue working to *make* a case. They deliberately force the detention not only because they are in charge of the situation and can improvise but also because they feel empowered and never suspect that they might have no freedom or superior and administrative support to do so. In the second section of this text, I analyze this kind of officer discretion and frame it within the wider context of police station organization and the changing Portuguese preventive politics for policing over recent decades. Finally, I return to the theoretical issue of policing powers and strive to point out how I believe anthropology, through inductive ethnographic approaches, can contribute to a better understanding of discretion through underlying connected dimensions often forgotten by scholars such as human desire, ambition, and emotion. A description of the long shift follows.

An Improbable Detention

At the station, one detainee cries with his head between his hands. He is seated on one of the uncomfortable metallic chairs in a row in the atrium of the station, which had recently been painted in blue and white, police colors. One police officer stands guard. A young man has entered the web of the criminal justice system. Luis is in his late twenties, white like the majority of residents in this area, and unemployed. He was detained during the work shift of the two officers in charge of his case, Duarte and Cruz. His detention was neither a planned action such as the result of a stop and search operation nor a case of *in flagrante delicto*. The youth was suddenly surprised in the streets by a uniformed officer who took him to the station after an improvised sequence of undercover observations led by Duarte and Cruz, both of whom were in plainclothes that day. The pair reached the conclusion that the youth was dealing small amounts of hashish and decided to exaggerate their report to transform it into an offense for the judge. However, they would still have to face a very real problem: in the course of events, it became impossible to find any material evidence proving their "theory," and without any warrant, they could not reveal in writing all the informal improvisation and discretionary tactics that led them to make the arrest. I spent the entire day, from around 6:30 a.m. to 4:00 p.m., with these two officers moving around the neighbourhood, allegedly trying to find out information and build a case. We returned to the station with Luis, who, in the eyes of the officers, was a true *mitra*.[3]

It was while I was observing Luis as he sat handcuffed in the atrium around 2:00 p.m. that I heard that his own father had tried to talk to Duarte, seeking to make a deal with the officer, who nevertheless decided to proceed with the report. Inside the station, it becomes obvious to me that not all officers agree with the situation. I hear some of Duarte's colleagues referring to him as an "old-timer," implying that he is inflexible and wants to enforce the law at any cost. In the meantime, in a busy atmosphere of changing shifts, I see two other officers hovering close to the detainee, trying to reassure him that "this is a simple process." Suddenly, I recognize one senior officer known by many for being a reasonable and understanding cop talking discreetly with Duarte. I cannot hear their conversation, but I learn afterward that he was trying to convince Duarte to let the youth go and drop the case, arguing that there was no solid basis for reporting it to the judge. An instant later, visibly disturbed, Duarte passes by me. Standing by my side he whispers in my ear: "Here, there's an impressive lack of professionalism; we (referring to him, his partner Cruz, and possibly the station captain) cannot count on them (their peers)," after which he disappears into an office presumably to write up a report. The captain never leaves his room; throughout the entire situation, he never interferes. At one point, I look over to the front of the station, through the glass of the doorway, and see some young women from the detainee's neighborhood gathered; others remain seated on the sidewalk, agitated, wanting to be heard by the police. The officer standing guard at the entrance allows an adolescent mother carrying her baby in to fill up a water bottle. Viewing the scene, I hear one of the officers beginning the afternoon shift, and certainly unaware of all the facts, comment with contempt: "Perhaps they all live from drugs." From the point of view of the youth, his relatives, and his friends, this arrest represents a factor of institutional intimidation.

How did this ambiguous and nonconsensual detention first occur? I will narrate the sequence of events conducted by Duarte and Cruz and explain all their efforts and commitment to making the arrest and the report happen while tracing the improvised set of choices and the anxious rhythm of the entire shift.

Before going into detail, it is important to bear in mind that the station is located in an area of Lisbon characterized by the police as a mix of a wealthy middle class and a poor unemployed population renowned for its networks of families, generations of which have made a living selling drugs on the streets since the 1980s. As I detailed on another occasion, most of the routine of patrol work is divided between protecting the inhabitants of the middle-class neighborhood from trouble and identifying and following the moves of residents, especially youths, in the poorest areas.[4]

For some weeks, I had shadowed and participated in the routines of Duarte and Cruz as they patrolled the streets. These two were the first to welcome me after two months spent struggling in a markedly masculine environment. Out of sixty police officers, there were only three women, a number that reflects the low percentage of female representation in the police force as a whole. Recognizing their curiosity in me, I decided to start doing the rounds in their group where I would extend my interpersonal relationships. Duarte and Cruz both considered themselves as the best prepared and most able to engage in police work at the station. The station's captain apparently shared their opinion. Unlike all the other station officers, they occasionally went about their duties in plainclothes. Aware of their ambition to go beyond the "nothing to report" attitude, as it is termed in these circles, the captain decided to give them this chance. Duarte and Cruz would be assigned to apply their "police intuition," as they call it, walking the streets looking for relevant information, signs of criminal or illicit activities, and eventually doing "some good," that is, handling a true and reported occurrence with an explicit preference for making arrests.

In fact, the captain revealed his displeasure at the lack of interest and motivation in the majority of "his men" on the streets. Nevertheless, he also wanted to "make his mark on the station and the police institution," he once confessed to me. I remember one day how he approached me and some officers as we were about to leave on car patrol and said loudly so as to be clearly heard: "My hope is that the presence of Susana here makes you eventually produce results, that you guys feel ashamed about doing nothing." And there I was with Duarte and Cruz willing to "do true police work," as they stated. Furthermore, in order to understand the extent of this motivation, we must take a step back and reconsider the sequence of events that day building up to the contested detention.

That particular morning, Duarte, Cruz, and I left the station at 7:00 a.m., had some coffee, and took up position on a corner not far from the station "observing concrete points" where we might witness evidence of drug dealing. "Plainclothes detectives are in the area," Duarte suddenly announces after receiving a call from a friend at the Criminal Investigation Division. "We'd better be going; they don't want us here in their way." The plan changes, but Duarte sees a youth getting into his old, rundown car. Showing him his badge, the officer joins him while signaling for us to get in. This is a type of improvisation that most captains would not dare dream of, I remember thinking. The nervous youth is told to take us to another spot in the neighborhood, which is also known for drug dealing. After passing by in the car several times, observing movements, both officers agree that their interest is focused on one particular café. The driver is dismissed, and we stand briefly on one corner. In a flash, Cruz and I see Duarte going to talk to a woman standing at the doorway of a building, the rear of which faces the café entrance. Duarte comes back and explains to us: he has managed to get access to the fourth floor apartment (another moment of absolute improvisation: getting inside without a warrant). While we make our way up the stairs, Cruz confides, hopeful and excited: "We go about with our hands out begging. The informants are our eyes. However, today we really got lucky!" Inside, Duarte presents us both as police and something amazing happens, according to these two: it turns out that the big back window looks out right over the café they are eager to observe. For more than half an hour, they stand at the window, just watching. "That one is certainly a dealer," I hear them comment. They are speaking about Luis, I learn later. They also invite me to watch: "See?" But all I see is the indiscriminate movement of men standing outside or entering the café. Eventually, looking at his watch and seeing that the end of the shift is approaching—it is almost 1:00 p.m.—Duarte decides it is time to go. Before this, he explains to the woman that they will look for her again. Sensing her fear, Duarte improvises again, saying, "They are a bunch of layabouts." Cruz seconds the assertion, applying a moral tone: "And if they come here to sell, someday they'll be robbing in the area." She admits they are both right, manifesting indignation but also the fear that her husband and daughter might find out about this arrangement of theirs. Duarte leaves behind a gym instructor's card, improvising once more, trying to cover their police tracks, and promises to come back.

Having seen nothing, I assume that the shift is about to end as we leave the building, but Duarte suddenly challenges Cruz to go and arrest the youth, the one they are convinced they saw dealing. This will turn out to be the crucial moment of improvisation. I see them rapidly discussing that the best approach is to call for back-up from whoever is on patrol car duty (since they do not want to be seen in plainclothes by the locals and thus saving themselves for future undercover services). By phone, Duarte informs Caetano, a timid rookie who is on duty, and describes the suspect as a white "dude" in a beige jacket, aged twenty. I hear him specifically warning Caetano about a crack in the wall where the drugs seem to be hidden. After no more than fifteen minutes of anxious waiting, the call gets returned, but with bad news: they have the suspect at the station, but no drugs, that is, no criminal evidence. Duarte is extremely disappointed. We make a fast-paced return to the station.

Back at the station, the atmosphere is busy due to the shift change. After booking the suspect and searching him, Duarte and Cruz concur: the detainee has money on him (over €100), but only a small quantity of hashish (no more than a gram, below the legally stipulated five-gram limit for ten days of consumption) and no previous criminal record. At first, Cruz hesitates; however, Duarte is determined to proceed. Cruz is vexed and cannot accept that their colleagues were unable to find the drugs. Suddenly, without thinking, as if driven by impulse, Cruz returns to the "crime scene" in a police car accompanied by me. When we arrive at the café, he searches the minuscule hole in the wall and finds nothing more the glares of the area's male residents. I see that Cruz is practically beside himself with rage. In his impatience, he risks both exposing himself and revealing the hideout used. Stoop-shouldered, he decides to return, silently, to the precinct.

Both Duarte and Cruz try to find a quiet spot and a computer where they can concentrate, avoiding the constraints and protests of others at the station. The process of writing up their report ends up taking around three hours and nevertheless becomes renowned as one of the swiftest arrests ever made. The text goes through three different versions as well as a thorough review by the captain (inside his office, so it was impossible for me to see his reactions). Even though Cruz deals only with the simpler forms, he ends up signing the arrest report, which, I learn afterward, will guarantee him some prestige and the kind of recognition Duarte has already attained. Never read his rights (in violation of the law), Luis ends up being transported to the metropolitan police command where he will spend the afternoon and the night in a jail cell prior to appearing in court the following morning. It is noteworthy that the officers draft the report based on two main improvised arguments. Firstly, they try to prove that Luis is a known hashish dealer in the area, identified by the frequent and regular work of police who patrol the neighborhood (even though he has no criminal record). Secondly, they try to argue that the money (€100) is evidence of his illegal drug selling activity, as no unemployed person would carry around such an amount in his pocket.

Nearly 4:00 p.m., Duarte, Cruz, and I have lunch at a local restaurant where, in one of the back rooms, the tired officers recover the privacy of common citizenship. Duarte shares his plans for the next shifts: he wants to go into the cafés in an attempt to identify the traffickers themselves and maybe also return to the woman's home to observe. Cruz expresses how he wants to learn more with the help of Duarte, whom he considers almost a detective. But the planned stakeout never actually takes place, and the story of these plainclothes officers comes to an end here. Soon others will fill their shoes. Not that both are not already accustomed to these discontinuities in station work. In the next few days, Cruz will join a group training in the new information technology system that the police force is implementing. Alone, Duarte starts wearing the dark blue uniform and joins car patrol activities. However, within a week, Duarte is summoned to the Criminal Investigation Division, the career move he was waiting for. Years later, I learn that Cruz received public praise published in the service orders (written by that same captain) and was duly commended for his "dedication." While considered one of the station's best officers, he still awaits his turn for promotion to the Criminal Division, a dream that never comes true for most officers.

Some weeks later, I try to track down what happened to Luis, but nobody at the station seems to care much. When asking Duarte for his opinion, he agrees that he supposes the detainee must have been released by the judge immediately after appearing in court. Without evidence or a sustained investigation, the case was unlikely to proceed. He eventually admits, "After all, that was an improbable arrest, but at least we take that kind of opportunity to learn and to train true police work."

Contextualizing Discretion

Would the improbable and ambiguous detention of the youth have ever occurred if I had not been there? Did my presence influence the course of events? The same doubts plagued me before. Once I was with Duarte as he tried to find a dealer and decided to enter an apparently abandoned building. Gun in hand, he said that I should stand behind him; he would protect me if anything went wrong. Knowing from experience the relative lack of risk to police life in the area, and the sheer unusualness of officers drawing their guns, I asked myself: Is this real or is this to impress me? These are difficult questions to answer. All participant observation in policing deals with a high degree of performativity that, at times, attempts to hide the intrinsic ambiguity of this work.[5] Moreover, when we are watching the watchers, we are certainly also being watched and guessed by them all the time.[6] I think that to a certain extent, my presence and my curiosity about their street work did stimulate something in Duarte and Cruz. In fact, I learned about "cop work" with the help of this pair, and they may perhaps have been eager to share their unusual tactical know-how with me and to prove, through action, their sarcastic dismissal of the intrinsic boring vein to patrol work—surely an aspect deserving more theoretical attention.[7]

Despite these ambiguities, it still remains intriguing to encounter the dexterity required to conceive of a detention a priori, as described, and transform into a crime report what had first been a police desire. Accordingly, we may also consider the social politics of discretion. On the one hand, by this episode, I wish to demonstrate that proactive practices are a timeless resource encapsulated into the tactical repertoires of captains and officers (not dependent on consensus or mere individual motivations). On the other hand, I argue that discretionary styles are deeply embedded in singular historical and sociological arrangements.[8] In fact, the tension between the possibility to improvise and moderate or more open criticism of it, as I narrated previously, is connected to the wider context of policing in Portugal during the three decades of democracy through to the first decade of the twenty-first century.

During the period of my fieldwork, encountering a neighborhood station's officers working in plainclothes was not so common. The very allocation of some selective officers to do such work would be locally and carefully administered by the captain, occurring without the full knowledge of superiors even though everybody knew about such occasional practices inside the force. The main reason for keeping these activities relatively discreet was that the police stations had become deeply identified with a new philosophy emerging in the late nineties—proximity policing. Although in practice a minority of patrol work—focused on domestic violence victims, schools (mostly public), retail commerce, and the preventive safety of the elderly—the station proximity teams began to prove so popular in Portugal that they got confounded with the main work of the stations, its legitimate essence. This produced a popular and political idea that stations should be in fact citizen/client oriented, consigning to invisibility the majority of the anonymous work on urban safety.[9]

While the idea of proximity policing was gaining public support, behind the scenes, the professionalization of criminal investigation within the force (as well as within *Guarda Nacional Republicana*) was gaining ground, creating an entirely new division (with their own stations) that consolidated new competences hitherto the exclusive domain of the judiciary police. Along with other forms of reorganization, the founding of a new specialized division also served to consolidate and monopolize policing investigation by removing it from the stations whose performance levels had been deemed amateur. Moreover, under the new law for the organization of criminal investigation, station captains could not openly encourage their constables to go out in plainclothes. This new trend of policing professionalization was also fed by a legal and regulatory process led by the *Inspeção Geral da Administração Interna* (the ombudsman) that was intensely active in those years before it subsequently lost substantial governmental support. New forms of external accountability of the police institution—governed by the spirit of subordination of the Portuguese Constitution to the Convention on Human Rights, which was internationally required as a prerequisite for Portugal to join the European Union in 1986—certainly contributed if not to inhibiting street police discretion then at least to enveloping it in a blanket of cautious local acts. Every effort was thus made to spare the national administration of the police force and clearly then the central governments of any bad propaganda that might affect the public image of an ideal of democratic policing close to the people. Since the late eighties, a new public image of the urban police aimed to erase from public opinion and common sense their association with violent police practices and militarism, themselves both associated with the security forces throughout one of the longest dictatorial periods of history, from 1926 to 1974.[10]

While participating in these police station routines, I was able to confirm how some of the old discretionary dynamics remained intact even if they were now reconfigured within a professional discourse deployed by some professionals on specific occasions, as I detail in the ethnographic description. One of the most decisive facets explaining the resilience of these historical practices comes with the endurance of the old station service regulations, a manual dating to 1961 (adapting the original from 1940). Certainly these old regulations, applied as an organizational guide, could not compete with the modern penal laws and codes enacted in the intervening period, but they still had an important impact on some aspects of station management and policing, in particular in allocating zero restrictions to station captains in how they managed their subordinates. Nonetheless, even though the urban force was becoming progressively and entirely civil, according to the old regulation the police remained classified as a "military organism that prevents and represses criminality."[11] In sum, this regulation empowered the discretion of commanders based on a text that praises a dictatorial and military ethos dispensing with citizen control and accountability. Through interviewing many retired officers and senior police station chiefs, I learned about the long existence of this same style of proactive teams, the so called *saltos* (jumps) that, following the democratic changes in 1974–75, would be renamed the station's *furões* (ferrets). I heard many accounts as to the way certain senior officers would wear plainclothes and apply their discretion to gain favors, confessions, or detentions within a universe of generalized suspicion in which anyone might be a snitch and inform the regime's political police. In those days, as the cited regulation stipulates, the urban police had to send secret reports of a "political and social nature" to the national police command.

Coincidently, with the investment in criminal investigation and policing professionalization, stations also fell under the influence of a new wave of management, policing planning, and reporting of results—with the annual open crime statistics report one of the most mediatized. Even though Portugal still officially remained one of the safest countries in Europe, all governmental plans proved sensitive to the transnational issue of security and therefore insisted on the issue in their respective political agenda.[12] During my fieldwork, I was able to grasp how, on several occasions throughout any month, the station's captains would experience pressure and thus foster environments propitious to police occurrences and reports "happening." It was neither clear nor openly revealed just what pressured the captains and officers to engage in such activities. During my fieldwork at the stations, I realized that the practice of large-scale regulatory and traffic control operations, with some involving all the units in Lisbon's metropolitan command, was beginning to become a constant station activity. This was perceived in general terms by local captains as an incentive to engage in proactive tactics. Accordingly, the concept of the so-called "stop operations" became common in several other domains of law enforcement, especially the small but collective anti–drug dealing operations and raids, many launched by station personnel with the help of the anticrime squads that were then gaining increasing professional autonomy in the urban force in a process similar to, but on a smaller scale than, that described by Didier Fassin.[13] It is noteworthy that at the station level, crime statistics were not seen as a policy for reducing or preventing crime. "That was the case before when captains worked with situational maps," as I was told. Officers do however often disagree. For the more optimistic, these statistics constituted a tool that forced officers to be proactive (whatever that means), while for the more critical, the pejoratively termed "stats" instead became a way to reduce the visibility of officers who considered their role to involve regulating social life through establishing local relations and tempered interactions with the citizens. At the aforementioned station, the principal captain belonged to the first group while his lieutenant, a woman, belonged to the second.

However, the pressure that commanders specifically felt to produce more results also had other sources. A new generation of high ranking and well-trained police arrived at the stations over the course of the 1990s; they were deemed elite specialists in police sciences and internal affairs. The command activities previously held by officers from the chief career level (an intermediate status) were progressively replaced by the "academic cops," as they were labelled. Most had never served on the police force and arrived at the stations with little or no actual experience of street work. During my fieldwork, I observed how they had to (and still have to) prove they were up to doing the job. The performance of these new hierarchical superiors fell under the scrutiny of the senior officers who had preceded them, many of whom had qualified through serving in the armed forces. On the other hand, the results presented by the new captains were immediately translated into an internal negotiation over the human and material resources that remained very unevenly distributed across the 300-plus urban stations for Portugal's relatively small conurbations. This was certainly a time for competition among captains and among stations, even though they were not always able to motivate their own officers. Internally, each precinct's reputation became defined by their respective statistics— particularly when announced by the local captains at the monthly metropolitan command meetings. I tried, but never did get permission, to participate in these, the top meetings of the force.

As such, everyone at the station had to deal with this pressure for results, frequently a synonym for the production of extra occurrences—and the usage of discretionary methods—despite flouting the internal dynamics of the force (the separation between proximity policing and specialist criminal investigation operations). Ironically and sometimes bitterly, many officers referred to the situation as "the politics of the numbers" and not as a proper policing policy. However, constables like Duarte and Cruz, along with some others, also grasped the present moment as an opportunity and a means to imagine how they might gain better control over their jobs and careers. As becomes clear from the final part of the long shift description the "station ferrets" police in plainclothes may use detentions as a means of proving and consolidating their know-how through improvisational street-crime investigation. Thus, discretion here is seen as containing a clearly pedagogic angle. The officers who turned in what were considered "good service" standards (such as detention reports) more frequently gained greater opportunities from the outset to stand out in a professional career that otherwise had very poor prospects of any specialization. Specialized patrols therefore tended to be perceived as a form of promotion.[14]

Undertaking work in an improvised criminal domain represents a point of departure from the anonymity of patrol work, especially whenever officers gain the trust and confidence of their superiors. This is one way in which more ambitious officers set about defining their places within the networks of formal and informal knowledge built up within the large national police force context and, as Duarte once encapsulated it, is "a sea of opportunities for those who know how to exploit them." The benefits may emerge immediately in terms of police station duties. Whoever produces more arrests to a greater or lesser extent becomes more authorized—by both their superiors and their colleagues—to withdraw from other tasks and duties normally falling to any officer. Captains are well aware that while younger constables should have "fire in their bellies," few of them are able to withstand the ardors of patrol work and the resultant bureaucratic paperwork. As such, those who stand out in such tasks tend to get rewarded while also recalling the contrast with the boredom and randomness of foot patrols.

The proactive detention that I have described is a good illustration of how discretion works qualitatively. Only ethnographically may we encapsulate the process and the dynamics of that described by the officers themselves as the politics of numbers. A proactive detention at the local station level may constitute an end in itself and not necessarily lead to a legal arrest, as Duarte does end up admitting. This thus explains why forcing law enforcement is not perceived as an illegitimate step to those participating in such actions, but rather something that is done cautiously, discreetly, and contextualized within the macropolitics that prevail throughout the entire urban police force. Those officers participating in these processes never perceive this as resulting from an order but instead as a personal opportunity to carefully implement "true police work" tactics. Thus, occurrences and reports also constitute the means by which captains and officers can achieve singular gains.

There is certainly no originality in positing how arrests may represent one of the more central features of discretion. In his in-depth ethnography of Baltimore police, Peter Moskos dissects what he calls a US police culture of detention based on the politics of the war on drugs, the police position within the criminal justice system, and the cult of guns among both police and dealers. From the point of view of Baltimore street officers, the arrest constitutes a *message* against criminals and drugs.[15] Comparatively, I would choose not to follow the steps taken by Moskos to analyse the Portuguese context and would also like to adopt a different theoretical angle. First of all, some reflection on the empirical findings: in the United States, paid court appearances provide a fundamental motivation for arrests—"court is like our heroin," some officers said to Moskos—contrary to what happens in Portugal, where going to court is seen as part of the police *mission*, non-paid extra work, frequently occurring when off duty, and rarely compensated for by the captain. In addition, as I tried to illustrate, processing an arrest in a Portuguese station is both difficult and hard to justify, and thus proving only relatively occasional. Commonly, officers do not detain individuals for minor charges that will eventually be considered too fickle by the attorneys and judges. When I did fieldwork, loitering, prostitution, and the possession of soft drugs for personal usage were not deemed felonies per se and, to the police, were relatively indifferent indiscretions.

Furthermore, in Portugal, detentions do not merely form the "arrest quota" of each officer, a policy measuring the aggressiveness of individual officers (as Moskos reveals); they become a factor in the performance of both stations and their captains—a kind of bonus. Likewise, what seems a small ingredient changes the entire equation: from an "arrest-based philosophy" (in the US) to a "keep-to-the-minimum-arrest philosophy" (in Portugal). In the situation I described previously, the problem was not about how many arrests each officer should make but about not having registered a single detention in a month's work at the station. Duarte and Cruz were striving to come up with the only possible arrest, through improvisation. Thus, from a theoretical point of view, policing productivity, or the so-called "politics of stats," does not amount to one single reality and may indeed take on plural logics, motivations, and consequences in different places around the globe. High-arrest officers—those Moskos calls "urban cowboys"—are a rarity in local neighborhood Portuguese stations. One of the main causes stems from the improbability of justifiable arrests occurring. Importantly, discretion proves not a question of good or bad policing, legal or illegal, and serves to complement individual benefit with more collective gains—which finally implies shifting from individual-based analysis toward an anthropological politics perspective.

Rethinking Discretion

Having considered what motivates, enables, and authorizes police discretion to become cooperatively and creatively applied, we now need to revisit how the police, as a state institution and in its relationship with the law, have been critically interpreted before proposing a new theoretical way to position discretion.

The French sociologist Dominique Monjardet has warned that there are no grounds for imagining police work in perfect harmony, as institution tends to operate through a triple determination: the state police represent an instrument of power (receiving orders) and render a public bureaucratic service (required by all) while also constituting a profession (with its own corresponding interests). As such, the author determines how policing is set in motion from different and simultaneously combined sources: by the "call" from the senior officer, by the "orders," or by the "initiatives" of the agents themselves.[16] I have written elsewhere on how these different dispositions to policing activity are incorporated into practices that result in

different street-political impacts, developing dissimilar police-citizen relations in space and time in accordance with the different service and tasks
related to the knowledge displayed by officers.[17] One problem remains,
however. The detention of the youth narrated in this text certainly does not
stem from an emergency call but also does not prove strictly dependent
on either some mere order or the initiative of Duarte and Cruz. Rather, it
represents a combination and articulation of both the latter factors and
ultimately of police government and policing autonomy. Perhaps counter-
intuitively, a fruitful combination of discretion and applying policies
proves precisely a high degree of police tactical improvisation, which, after
all, makes up an intrinsic characteristic of police work.

Therefore, as Didier Fassin suggests, there is in practice no contradiction between the two opposite theses of insularity and manipulation that
account for the relationship between the police and the state. Inspired
by the analysis of Jean Brodeur, the author explores the tension revealed
by the two major and opposite theories on this matter, the Weberian and
the Marxist, and shows how that tension gets dynamically revealed in policing praxis. The Weberian *doxa* advocates how police officers engage in
police actions perceived within an insular framework. In other words, they
represent part of a *state within a state*. Weber simultaneously details the historical and political processes leading to law enforcement becoming the
favored tool for managing social problems and bringing about a singular
level of governmental manipulation of the police. In Marxist versions, officers are portrayed as the *armed wing of the state*, or those employed to reproduce the existing social orders. Some authors have demonstrated how unproductive maintaining this dichotomy proves.[18] Furthermore, in Fassin's
case, inductive ethnographic approaches to French anticrime squads prove
essential to demonstrating that articulation: "Officers choose to do what
they are ordered to do not by fortuitous chance but because of the *predictable convergence* between their expectations and government objectives."[19]
In the situation I have described, and on many other occasions observed in
Portuguese stations, there is always an element of this predictable convergence: applying discretion represents one course of action for officers and
local captains to be taken into consideration by chiefs and other branches
of the force; through cooperating with the agenda of their superiors, the officers as well as the captains hope to gain something in return.

Accordingly, a more structural and critical theoretical condition for understanding the police use of force and violence needs revisiting. Among
several debates, I opt here to focus on the arguments of two different so-
phisticated and critical theories—E. P. Thompson and Walter Benjamin.

Following Thompson's views, the rule of law has long established its own ways to control violence in general and policing activity in particular, at least in democratic societies. However, in drawing upon Benjamin's conceptions, as several anthropologists have recently done in several contexts, the police may be seen as the exact means and the end of institutionalized violence: the state *as* violence.[20]

It is worth detailing these arguments. In one of his later texts, the 1975 *Whigs and Hunters*, the already well-known Thompson argued for a liberal and legalistic version of Marxism incorporating a minimal historical conception of the "Rule of Law." In that short essay, he distinguishes between states whose rulers had unfettered discretion from states whose rulers were constrained by legal rules. Rule of law is "little (or nothing) more than a rule of equal application of the legal rules, which limits ruling power."[21] Deeply criticized by some of his fellow Marxists, Thompson further insisted, in the 1980 "The State of the Nation," that the rule of law is an "unqualified good," a necessary condition not only to ensure just legal rules but also at least in some way to control its opposite: unbridled power. In sum, law matters and situates itself beyond legal injustice and the mere instrumentalization conducted by the ruling powers.

Countering any natural and positive perspective of law, Walter Benjamin had written several decades earlier about the law and state *as violence*. From his historical-philosophical view, Benjamin condemns to ignominy the authority of modern institutions such as the police where he finds that the separation between law-making and law-preserving violence has been suspended. Ultimately, his position stands opposite to Thompson's view when he states that "the assertion that the ends of police violence are always identical or even connected to those of general law is entirely untrue. Rather the *law* of the police really marks the point at which the state, whether from impotence or because of the immanent connections within any legal system, can no longer guarantee through the legal system the empirical ends that it desires at any price to attain."[22] In this view, the benevolence of the law completely vanishes, and violence becomes the greedy desire of the state to dominate. It is a perspective reminiscent of Derrida's claim that the contemporary police do not merely represent a force of the law, but rather *"the force of law,"* representing the original violence of state law.[23] According to Benjamin, military and police institutions not only *preserve* but *make* the law on the use of violence for legal ends and consolidate the authority to decide on those ends within wide limits. Coincidently, I refer to how Benjamin reduces those wide limits to the "right of decree" and not to the rule of law. From his perspective, power, more than any gain in property, is that guaranteed by all laws on making violence. Likewise, Benjamin finds his home in the radical Marxism that Thompson tries to temper several decades later.

Benjamin's radical position was certainly attuned to the times of conflict he experienced as a German Jew living between the two world wars. To some authors, such as Joseph Masco, a critique of capitalist progress itself proves implicit to Benjamin's dark thinking, emphasizing the very idea of policing as a means of protecting the class system from any ongoing revolution—the police being the counter-revolutionary force par excellence. For Benjamin, the immanent fear of revolution always speaks louder and determines that "law and order" is guaranteed by force to the detriment of citizen protection. Nevertheless, as Masco firmly underlines, for Benjamin a "transition from law making to law preserving is embedded in everyday life, which produces an unending negotiation between citizens and the state over the terms of order."[24] That argument would seem a suitable starting point for Foucault's theories, which conceive of policing beyond the police as extended micropractices sometimes visible by their absence.[25]

It is the persistence of a dual and absolutist condition of thinking about *all* policing (as previously analyzed by Fassin) that is at stake: whether by choosing between police government and insularity power or by defending the rule of law against the state as violence. Inductive ethnographic descriptions such as the one I recount in this text allow for the analysis of mixed forms of action that can be simultaneously conceived of as more or less controlled and accountable discretion, or at least not illegal (from the perspective of police officers and judges), and as the explicit effects of the contemporary government of injustice (from the perspective of the detainees, their relatives, and their friends). This means that the presence of *more eyes and different eyes* in the action returns different meanings to whatever happens.[26]

In this case, officers in no way receive simple authorization to take justice into their own hands and on their own initiatives. I expect the reader may apprehend the ways in which proaction works according to certain limits, that enable the improvisation to be witnessed and accompanied by police outsiders like myself and justified (in a semi-judicial tone) by the legal and bureaucratic apparatus. In sum, officers do not confound law making with law preserving in any given moment of the course of events. Nevertheless, those improvisations are not entirely submitted to the rules that frame legal and ethical police conduct. Instead, they are able to play with a repertoire of authorized and known underhanded tactics that are simultaneously historically and sociologically contextualized and certainly neither entirely unpredictable nor fully predictable. Importantly, we are thus clearly not in the domain of "police fictions" or "ghostly and spectral police power," or at least any of those described for other contexts by Jean and John Comaroff.[27]

This finally helps one understand why in the aforementioned episode the forced detention of one (or any) youth considered a drug dealer may even be imagined and desired before actually happening, which in the end conforms to a policy. When Duarte and Cruz tell me they "really" want to work, they are imagining how determined they are to arrive at the station with an arrest, and their arrest—Luis—is viewed indifferently (not necessarily by all officers) as but one small dealer among many others. To sum up, within the contemporary dynamics of the Portuguese officers working at police stations, their shared desires and emotions play an important role in the dynamics of law enforcement and tactical repertoires.[28] The ethnographic *momentum* reveals how emotions are not merely a product of a situated action after the fact; officers are constantly in (e)motion. This makes improvisation more desirable at least to those who reject standing idly by and cannot imagine work without being provoked by the streets. In this situation, the "police results" are produced by officers who feel satisfaction but also frustration when playing out an adventurous style within certain limits and framed institutional conventions.

Conclusion

This text examines the details and mismatches of an improbable and forced detention made by two officers with the consent of their captain, all three of whom act in the interstices of the freedoms and constraints that exist within the contemporary environment of Portuguese police stations. This proves a fine example of how a *predictable convergence* between macro and micro, administrative powers and local pressures operates through specific and selected policing practices as well as desires. There is no denying that European and US governments have sought to instrumentalize the police, their statistics, and their actions in recent decades, but as Fassin points out, "correspondingly, the police are becoming more insular, by taking responsibility for what is imposed on them. The more officers operate in an insular fashion (through the use of their discretionary powers), the more they reinforce the logic of instrumentality (placing themselves in the service of power)."[29] As such, policing improvisations are not merely the result of organizational and individual *ilôtage*. Nor are they a product of a moral discipline imposed by any power or any clear governmental agenda.

It is worth noting that the actions described are based on historical legacies and repertoires that are constantly recreated through action. This transpires in the irony displayed by the famous late nineteenth-century chroniclers of Lisbon city life, Eça de Queiroz and Ramalho Ortigão, who comment on the random arrests of *fado* singers by a police force pressured to present "results." Ever since the 1980s and through to the first decade of the twenty-first century, police attention has very much been focused on a population somehow related to small-scale street drug dealing, often legally and financially insignificant in scale. This phenomenon has simultaneously been accompanied by a new cycle of governmental and police attention more specifically directed at the undocumented and racialized poor and migrant neighborhoods generically identified with crime.[30] As such, the simple discretionary detention is an illustrative moment of what may be seen as a complex and never complete process of the period of democratization of the country and its urban police force.

Finally, we must not overlook the imagined future ahead of those motivated officers and captains who take responsibility for what is imposed on them. Aiming for advantages in the era of "stats" and the politics of numbers, they reveal that they are attuned to the new policing projects, the imagined future. This case exemplifies the awe that some police officers experience with respect to the rising importance that has been placed on the professionalization of criminal investigation, a new branch of the force. This also conveys how, governed by their own desires and emotions, some officers intuitively grasp the macro governmental and organizational politics occurring without necessarily being aware of what is happening and without actually being trained to do so. In sum, in anthropological terms, discretion must be viewed not only in terms of power and violence, as in fact it is, but also in terms of desire and ambition, with its feet in the past and its eyes on the future.

Notes

1. As argued by Herman Goldstein in his classic paper "Police Discretion: The Ideal versus the Real" (1973), discretion is the positive exercise that portrays police officers as something other than automatons, whose personal judgment is essential to determining whether or not to invoke criminal process. Some other authors portray discretion as something police officers may have and with which they negotiate their often violent actions on the margins of the law even if the structure of the

244 / Susana Durão

argument does not differ greatly (cf. Manning 1978). Discretion is usually described as a singular and independent police power.

2. "Proportion" is a term expressed in professional police writings and training manuals. The ideals of a moral action that deploys the exact use of force demanded by each situation was a regular claim made by the more academic and legalistic captains during my fieldwork.

3. "*Mitra*" has many meanings, but mainly serves two. First, it is a noun that identifies someone who has a lifestyle somehow related to illegal or criminal activities: officers say, "The drug dealer is a true *mitra*." Second, it is used as an adjective, a means of depreciating someone; they say, "The dealer is such a *mitra*." This second sense more probably corresponds to the way Van Maanen describes the "asshole" deployed in North American police contexts (cf. Van Maanen 1978a). *Mitra* is a noun born in the past and from the period of the authoritarian Estado Novo (1933–1974) regime. It was originally an establishment for confining street populations such as beggars and homeless persons. The word survived the democratic transition, which marked the end of the institution, and since the 1980s, it has become part of the inner informal lexicon identifying street dealers and other kinds of petty criminals. See more in an article on this issue (Durão, Gonçalves, and Cordeiro 2005).

4. See Durão 2010. Note that this process has been described in a more detailed way for the policing in the Paris banlieues by Fassin (2013).

5. According to Peter Manning (1978), modern police organizations have an impossible mandate to manage: "what has happened as a result of their inability to accomplish their self-proclaimed mandate is that the police has resorted to the manipulation of *appearances*."

6. I am here referring to the famous text by John Van Maanen, "On Watching the Watchers" (1978b).

7. Cf. chapter 12 by Didier Fassin in this volume.

8. Proaction, by definition, differs from police prevention or from police reaction. Proactive strategies are means of discovering crime as it happens. This is the argument put forth by Donald Black (1978).

9. That confusion between police stations and proximity policing, as representing the most modern policing techniques, in the sense of democratic and moderate, has been in the political crosshairs of left-wing governments but has proven its resilience over time. The Ministry of Internal Affairs, responsible for the first generation of the project (since 1995), established the ambiguity that would only be reinforced one decade later in the project's second generation, which was instituted by police leaders (since 2007). The ministry defined proximity as "A policing orientation strongly focused on knowledge and inclusion in community life, adopted [by stations] as opposed to the previous strategy of retraction and concentration in big police divisions." See Costa 2002.

10. I have written about this historical process in the book *Patrulha e Proximidade: Uma Etnografia da Polícia em Lisboa* (Durão 2008) and in the text "Policiamento de proximidade em Portugal: Limites de uma metáfora mobilizadora" (Durão 2012).

11. *Regulamento para o Serviço das Esquadras, Postos e Subpostos*, Ministry of Internal Affairs (1961).

12. As stated in note 10, I have written about this on other occasions.

13. See Fassin 2013.

14. See Reiner 1985.
15. See Moskos 2008, specifically the pages that deal with the analysis of the arrest as message (83–86); collars for dollars (121–23); the arrest-quota (153–54); and officers as urban cowboys and the politics of stats (136–45).
16. Cf. Dominique Monjardet in *Ce Que Fait la Police: Sociologie de la Force Publique* (1996).
17. See Durão 2008; Durão 2010.
18. Here I follow the argument of Didier Fassin (2013, 183–86) and the way he reads the entanglement between policing instrumentalization and insularity based on the assumptions of Jean-Paul Brodeur (1984), then complemented by the arguments of Patrice Mann (1994). Brodeur also argues that, even at best, formal requirements, as in the cases of countries with strong police centralization (which is the case of both France and Portugal), the assumption of service cohesion remains problematic. Additionally, the police hierarchy experiences all sorts of pressures. Both theses (insularity and instrumentalization) seeking to report on the entirety of police reality stem from confusion between simplifying procedures and illustrative demonstration.
19. I follow Fassin's arguments (2013, 186, emphasis added).
20. In the foreword to the edited volume of the William Garriott book, *Policing and Contemporary Governance* (2013), John Comaroff repositions Walter Benjamin among the main authors, along with Marx and Foucault, who have contributed to establishing an anthropological perspective on policing.
21. This was very well discussed by Daniel H. Cole in his essay "'An Unqualified Human Good': E. P. Thompson and the Rule of Law" (2001, 177, 185).
22. This is argued by Benjamin (1978 [1922], 287).
23. Cf. Jauregui 2013, 127.
24. This is argued by Masco (2013, 266).
25. Foucault develops this perspective in his famous book *Discipline and Punish* (1995 [1975]).
26. To know more about what may be called "critical perspectivism," see the written debate engaged in by Didier Fassin and Clara Han in *Social Anthropology* (2013).
27. Cf. Jean Comaroff and John Comaroff (2014).
28. Eventually, my argument touches on that of Shearing and Ericson (2005). The authors stress the requirement of individual decision and the unusual practice of improvisation in policing. They do not believe, therefore, that such an activity, always in the making, is produced from a preordered and cohesively ruled world. Offering theoretical substance to the concept of "style" and "strategy," these authors see in the stories of officers and detectives their narratives of everyday life, tropes, metaphors, parables, poetic social concerns, and ways of driving generators for action; but never closed into some simple guides. The stories shared between police officers, seen from Wittgenstein's line of thinking, are previous vocabularies that help them create styles and family resemblances between different actions. However, I would stress, as Fassin does, the liaisons between rules, values and the emotional dynamics present in everyday life policing.
29. See note 13.
30. Some authors, myself included, have written about this in Frois 2008.

References

Benjamin, Walter. 1978 [1922]. "Critique of Violence." In *Reflections: Essays, Aphorisms, Autobiographical Writings*, edited by Peter Demetz, 277–300. New York: Schocken.

Black, Donald J. 1978. "The Mobilization of Law." In *Policing. A View from the Street*, edited by Peter K. Manning and John Van Maanen, 167–86. New York: Random House.

Brodeur, Jean-Paul. 1984. "La Police: Mythes et realités. " *Criminologie* 17 (1): 9–41.

Cole, Daniel. 2001. "An Unqualified Human Good: E. P. Thompson and the Rule of Law." *Journal of Law and Society* 28 (2): 177–203.

Comaroff, John. 2013. "Foreword." In *Policing and Contemporary Governance: The Anthropology of Police in Practice*, edited by William Garriott, xi–xxi. New York: Palgrave Macmillan.

Comaroff, Jean, and John Comaroff. 2014. "Ficções policiais e a busca pela soberania: Distantes aventuras do policiamento no mundo pós-colonial." *Revista Brasileira de Ciências Sociais* 29 (85): 5–21.

Costa, Alberto. 2002. *Esta (Não) é a Minha Polícia*. Lisbon: Editorial Notícias.

Durão, Susana, C. Gonçalo Gonçalves, and G. I. Cordeiro. 2005. "Vadios, mendigos, mitras: Prácticas classificatorias de la policía en Lisboa." *Política y Sociedad* 42 (3): 121–38.

Durão, Susana. 2008. *Patrulha e Proximidade: Uma Etnografia da Polícia em Lisboa*. Coimbra/São Paulo: Ed. Almedina.

———. 2010. "The Social Production of Street Patrol Knowledge: Studying Lisbon's Police Stations." In *Police, Policing, Policy and the City in Europe*, edited by M. Cools, S. Kimpe, A. Dornaels, M. Easton, E. Enhus, P. Ponsaers, G. V. Walle, and A. Verhage, 79–112. The Hague: Eleven International Publishing.

———. 2011. "The Police Community on the Move: Hierarchy and Management in the Daily Lives of Portuguese Police Officers." *Social Anthropology/Anthropologie Sociale* 19 (4): 394–408.

———. 2012. "Policiamento de proximidade em Portugal: Limites de uma metáfora mobilizadora." In *Polícia, Segurança e Ordem Pública: Perspectivas portuguesas e brasileiras*, edited by Susana Durão and Marcio Darck, 101–34. Lisbon: Imprensa de Ciências Sociais.

Fassin, Didier. 2013. *Enforcing Order: An Ethnography of Urban Policing*. Malden: Polity Press.

Fassin, Didier, and Clara Han. 2013. Debate Section, *Social Anthropology* 21 (3): 371–88.

Foucault, Michel. 1995 [1975]. *Discipline and Punish: The Birth of the Prison*. New York: Vintage.

Frois, Catarina, ed. 2008. *A Sociedade Vigilante: Ensaios sobre a identificação, vigilância e privacidade*. Lisbon: Imprensa de Ciências Sociais.

Garriott, William, ed. 2013. *Policing and Contemporary Governance: The Anthropology of Police in Practice*. New York: Palgrave Macmillan.

Goldstein, Herman. 1973. "Police Discretion: The Ideal versus the Real." In *The Ambivalent Force*, edited by Arthur Niederhoffer and Abraham Blumberg, 148–56. San Francisco: Rinehart Press.

Jauregui, Beatrice. 2013. "Dirty Anthropology: Epistemologies of Violence and Ethical Entanglements in Police Ethnography." In *Policing and Contemporary Governance: The Anthropology of Police in Practice*, edited by William Garriott, 125–56. New York: Palgrave Macmillan.

Mann, Patrice. 1994. "Pouvoir, politique et mantient de l'ordre: Portée et limites d'un débat." *Revue Française de Sociologie* 35:435–55.

Manning, Peter K. 1978. "The Police: Mandate, Strategies, and Appearances." In *Policing: A View From the Street*, edited by Peter K. Manning and John Van Maanen, 7–31. New York: Random House.

Masco, Joseph. 2013. "Afterword." In *Policing and Contemporary Governance: The Anthropology of Police in Practice*, edited by William Garriott, 263–68. New York: Palgrave Macmillan.

Monjardet, Dominique. 1996. *Ce Que Fait la Police: Sociologie de la Force Publique*. Paris: Editions La Découverte.

Moskos, Peter. 2008. *Cop in the Hood: My Year Policing Baltimore's Eastern District*. Princeton: Princeton University Press.

Reiner, Robert. 1985. *The Politics of the Police*. Sussex, UK: Wheatsheaf Books & Harvest Press.

Ortigão, Ramalho, and Eça de Queiroz. 1883. *As farpas: Chronica Mensal da Politica das Letras e dos Costumes* 4 (3) (May 1871). Lisbon: Typografia Universal, 1871–1883.

Regulamento para o Serviço das Esquadras, Postos e Subpostos. 1961. Aprovado por despacho do Ministro do Interior.

Shearing, Clifford, and Richard Ericson. 2005. "Culture as Figurative Action." In *Policing: Key Readings*, edited by Tim Newburn, 315–37. London: Willan Publishing.

Van Maanen, John. 1978a. "The Asshole." In *Policing: A View from the Street*, edited by Peter K. Manning and John Van Maanen, 221–38. New York: Random House.

———. 1978b. "On Watching the Watchers." In *Policing: A View from the Street*, edited by Peter K. Manning and John Van Maanen, 309–49. New York: Random House.

ELEVEN

Alibi:
The Extralegal Force Embedded
in the Law (United States)

LAURENCE RALPH

In February 2015, national news outlets broke the story of a "domestic black site" in Chicago. In an abandoned warehouse on the south side of the city, police officers overstepped their legal jurisdiction in several ways. They kept criminal suspects out of the official booking database, beat them severely, shackled them for hours on end, and denied their access to lawyers. At least one man was pronounced dead after he was found unresponsive inside an interrogation room. Although the Chicago police department has issued a statement, claiming that police officers have abided by all laws "pertaining to any interviews of suspects or witnesses," skeptics claim that interrogating criminal suspects in an abandoned warehouse was a calculated effort to hold people outside of the system. In making their case, cynics point to the fact that Chicagoans who are questioned inside this particular location (an off-the-books site called the "Homan Square facility") do not appear to have a public, searchable record indicating where they are, as happens when someone is booked at a precinct. Moreover, a number of attorneys have stepped forward, claiming that for years, the facility has been a public secret.

"This Homan Square revelation seems to me to be an institutionalization of the practice that dates back more than 40 years," said Flint Taylor, the civil rights lawyer most associated with pursuing the Area 2 police commander Jon Burge (who will become a focal point of this chapter). "Back when I first started working on torture cases and started representing criminal defendants in the early 1970s," Taylor continued, "my clients often told me they'd been taken from one police station to another before ending up at Area 2 where they were tortured. . . . That way, the police prevent their family and lawyers from seeing them until they could coerce, through torture or other means, confessions from them."

Insofar as it relates to the longer history of police torture in Chicago, the constellation of issues surrounding a hidden interrogation facility points to the central question of this chapter: Why do the police ever resort to extralegal violence if they are legally granted a monopoly on its legitimate use?

Scholars have long questioned the police's use of extralegal force. The use of force outside the bounds of law has threatened to undermine police authority, dating back to the inauguration of the very first department in 1844.[1] In early studies, scholars lamented the fact that typical social science methods are highly inefficient at capturing use-of-force incidents because, oftentimes, no one (except for other police officers) is around when these violations take place.[2] In this chapter, I argue that these twinned ideas—(1) that there is a lack of knowledge about extralegal force because (2) the phenomenon is difficult to study—serve as an alibi that perpetuates the use of extralegal force by the police. These explanations can prevent the comparison of similarities by singling out incidents of extralegal force, either at the level of the individual or the department for which a particular police officer works.

Stated differently, the assertion that extralegal force is "exceptional" betrays a certain faith in policing—a faith that is premised on a very particular Weberian idea of "the State." Only two sentences are essential to summarize this conviction: "As the everyday embodiment of State authority, the primary objective of the police is to minimize crime and capture dangerous subjects. Society would be less safe without the police."[3] Yet victims of police violence contradict such beliefs. As one man who had been interrogated at the Chicago Police Department's secret facility stated, "It's very, very rare for anyone to experience their constitutional rights in Chicago police custody, and even more so at Homan Square."

It is this faith in policing that perpetuates a public secret in policing scholarship. Namely, the scholarship itself is allowing a social problem to masquerade as a methodological one. I am arguing that incidents of extralegal force, when identified by scholars, often reify the figure of the rogue cop and the notion of the corrupt police department. In the wake of the US Department of Justice's findings of discriminatory practices toward African Americans by the Ferguson Police Department, it is critical to point out that no matter how welcoming revelations of police violence may be, these archetypes are still problematic. They presume that if you sanction the rogue cop or the corrupt department, the use of extralegal force will no longer be an issue. But what if extralegal force is an embodiment of an idea—an idea that as a police officer, one must do whatever is necessary to solve the case and capture a criminal? And what if this idea is foundational to how a police officer conceives of his occupation? Taking these questions seriously means that examining extralegal force as if it is an exceptional phenomenon fails to account for the cultivation of collective identity within the police.

How to Study Extralegal Force

In this chapter, I will develop a framework for examining the process through which the use of extralegal force is enacted as well as the purposes it may serve by investigating the proceedings from civil suits against the notorious police commander Jon Burge, which were filed between 1990 and 2010, when Burge was incarcerated. In addition to courtroom transcripts, I mine the affidavits from police officers that worked for Jon Burge as well as witnesses who were knowledgeable about his torture operation. A Chicago law firm, the People's Law Office, has represented the majority of Burge's torture victims. Over the past twenty years, the state of Illinois has paid nearly $100 million in legal fees and settlements to these victims in civil suits. The People's Law Office has donated court proceedings from these suits to the University of Chicago, and they are housed in an archive at the university's Center for Human Rights. Legal documents, such as these, are among the few sources of data that draw from internally provided information (i.e., information among officers within the precinct where the torture was said to take place).

Even if we concede that the civil suits concerning police torture are statistically rare because, as Didier Fassin mentions, filing charges against an officer and having those charges culminate in a trial is actually "an exceptional event,"[4] that fact should not diminish the analysis. To acknowledge the exception and to exceptional*ize* are not one and the same. Following Fassin, I will examine these civil trials to glean insight on the specific circumstances that give rise to the use of extralegal force in policing. Instead of asserting that the civil cases I reference are *exceptional*—and thereby isolating Jon Burge and the Chicago Police Department from the more fundamental issue of why police officers may use extralegal force in the first place—I examine the extent to which they are *exemplary* in order to glean insights about the occupation of policing itself.[5]

In this regard, several findings are relevant to my analysis. Early work on policing by William Westley[6] noted that: (1) the police often employ moral claims to justify the use of extralegal force; (2) the justification of extralegal force arises through the practice of policing; and (3) the police show little interest in criminals whom they do not have to use force to contain.[7] Perhaps there is no facet of policing where the methodological alibi provides cover for the use of excessive force more than in the interrogation room, where all of Westley's longstanding findings are in play. Interrogations are highly stressful situations where the pressure to solve cases can incentivize police officers to extend the use of extralegal force. Since the trajectory of a police officer's career can depend on not disclosing information about the practice of violence in interrogations, the testimony from retired police officers proves critical to my analysis. This testimony illuminates key elements of how extralegal force is commonly practiced. But before we dive into the affidavits and court proceedings, some clarification on the "extralegal" is in order.

Scholarship conceives of force as being spread across a continuum. This broadly encompasses the physical presence of the beat cop to the global force of military occupation. For a long time, scholars of policing have thought that the police continuum of force ceases where the military one starts (with lethal force involving a growing number of casualties).[8] This shift along the continuum of force has also been thought to entail an accompanying shift in disposition. The police have long been presumed to abide by an ethos of minimum force, while military officers understand that any means may be necessary to destroy an enemy's powerbase. Thus, when I refer to extralegal force in this chapter, I am referencing instances when the police have adopted a military ethos, pursuing means of enacting violence and obtaining information that have been traditionally reserved for war. Indeed, the "militarization of policing" and the "policification of military intervention" have had a profound impact on the continuum of force as we know it today. It is worth mentioning, in this regard, that Cook County, where the Homan Square facility was located, has received more than 1,700 pieces of military equipment from an often-criticized Pentagon program that sends used resources from the Afghanistan War to police departments across the United States.

While this continuum of force may serve as a suitable reference point, ultimately we will see that it is too narrow to help us fully understand the examples of extralegal force (and particularly police torture) brought to bear in this chapter. This is because it does not account for another spectrum that exists within the interrogation itself (a spectrum that extends from psychological pressure to various forms of physical violence); a close look at police torture thus demonstrates the overlap between the police and the military. In what follows, I develop a middle-level theory on the relationship between extralegal force and police interrogations that conceives of shared secrets as fundamental to policing and to our scholarly understanding of it. The aim of this chapter is not to contest the validity of the police use of extralegal force (i.e., to examine whether such-and-such instance was actually a violation of law) but to contribute to its understanding by developing an interpretive framework that considers the social factors that enable excessive violence on the part of the police.[9]

The Methodological Alibi

In *Defacement*, Michael Taussig[10] demonstrates the intimate relationship between knowledge and power, offering an analysis of the role of secrecy in social life. Since the social sciences are rooted in the Enlightenment project, he argues, the goal of these disciplines has been to explain the social world in terms of historical origins and social functions. Taussig complicates the study of origins and functions by critiquing the kind of inductive reasoning that moves from the particular to the general to the universal. In this way he upends the basic assumption that the goal of the social scientist is to build a system of knowledge that better approximates reality. The public secret, by contrast, pushes us to think about moments of affective communication that exceed rational explanation. The people that Taussig describes, in his characteristically eclectic way, participate in a subterfuge, pretending not to know things that they in fact do know.

For a long while scholars have professed not to know the extent of extralegal force or be able to measure it, but, so often, these claims disguise what is generally known by making it seem exceptional. It is this conceit, I argue, that helps sustain the practice of excessive force on behalf of the police. To put it another way, explanations of how little is known about the extralegal use of force work by mystifying much of what draws police officers to extend their power beyond its rightful domain. Consider the claim articulated in Brodeur's influential work:

> The research agenda on the use of violence fails to provide explanations and remedies for the highest profile abuses, with the exception of sensationalized instances of the most excessive brutality against individuals (e.g. the beating of Rodney King in Los Angeles and the Abner Louima incident in New York) and of police shootings of innocent persons (e.g. the killing of Amado Diallo, which also occurred in New York; in France, police killings of ethnic youths have sparked devastating riots).[11]

Here, I want to focus on the seemingly innocuous claim that the Rodney King and Abner Louima beatings, the police shooting of Amado Diallo, and the riots in France are "the most excessive" incidents of the police use of force. This assertion is actually a presumption that sees these incidents as exceptional, rather than regarding them as tips of a metaphorical iceberg that signal a more foundational problem.

Notice how Jean-Paul Brodeur's analysis inadvertently positions the social scientist as someone who "knows what not to know," creating an "epistemic murk" around what the excessive use of force actually reveals. More specifically, the explanation that these so-called extreme cases of police violence can provide a remedy to the problem presents itself as a revelation, yet uncannily neutralizes the phenomena in question by drawing our attention to its rarity. The claim explains police violence by explaining it away. It shuts down the analysis of extralegal force in the name of the analysis itself.

What I want to show, alternatively, is how police officers learn what not to know about the enactment of extralegal force. This, I argue, is how extralegal force becomes embedded within the law. In what's to come, I focus on the common terror and desire entailed in the occupation of policing that sustains secrecy around torture in an infamous Chicago precinct as police officers learn what not to know.

Learning What Not to Know

In 2004, Flint Taylor, a lawyer representing one of Burge's torture victims, tried to convince an African American beat cop who worked under Jon Burge's command, Barry Mastin, to give a sworn statement concerning the public secret that some detectives tortured detainees, but Mastin promptly denied this request. "It's been thirty years," Mastin reasoned, "I'm retired and trying to put all that stuff behind me. Nothing is going to happen to Burge and those guys, anyway."[12]

Mastin's refusal to come forward even after thirty years shows how silence—and the act of silencing people—socializes institutional relationships. In fact, at the Area 2 police headquarters, the inaction associated with learning what not to know is a crucial aspect of how relationships between police officers were formed. As such, they were all complicit in the abuse of criminal suspects, and thus accountable to each other in order to protect the collective self.

At first glance, this idea of protection seems to harken back to what is sometimes referred to as the "blue code" or the "blue wall of silence," concepts that refer to the unspoken rule believed to exist among police officers in which they implicitly agree not to report on their colleagues' errors or crimes.[13] The problem with these concepts, as we will see, is that they imply nonaction. Yet, in reality, there is an enormous amount of work entailed in keeping silent. A police officer might, for example, avoid particular areas of the precinct where he suspects a criminal suspect is being beaten. Or if an officer happens to hear screams emanating from an interrogation room, she might resist the urge to barge in and opt to leave her workplace instead. Furthermore, these concepts assume a consensus among police officers not to report misconduct, but they do not often account for the internal fissures and hierarchies that emerge among members of the same police force.

Walter Young was another African American police officer at Area 2 who worked under Jon Burge's command. Although Taylor was unable to get Mastin to testify against Burge in 2004, he did secure the testimony of Young and two other police officers. Like Mastin, Walter Young was not personally involved with interrogating criminal suspects, but he often overheard Burge and the officers that worked closely with him (a group that Burge referred to as his "A-Team"). Young witnessed members of the A-Team on numerous occasions speak about giving suspects a "Vietnam Special" or "the Vietnamese Treatment."[14] (This language is telling not merely because it mimics the military ethos that any means are necessary to contain "enemy" combatants, but also because Jon Burge served as a military policeman in Vietnam, even earning a Purple Heart, prior to becoming a police detective in Chicago).

Because Young was aware that police misconduct was prevalent in his precinct he stayed out of the station as much as possible, sometimes even taking his work home rather than facing the prospect of having to witness the use of extralegal force.[15]

"And when you thought some stuff was going on," Flint Taylor asked him during the 2004 trial, "what would you do?"

"Vanish."

"Vanish?" Taylor responded, inquisitively, before reminding Young that, on a previous occasion, he described having an "ostrich-type of approach" to the way he thought about policing at Area 2. Was this still a fair characterization of how he felt, Taylor wanted to know.

"Right," Walter Young responded in an affirmative manner. "I would bury my head in the sand," he said. "See and not see."[16]

Part of the reason that officers who were suspicious of police violence did not blow the whistle on Burge was because they came to learn that taking action against him had serious implications for their careers. As some of the few black cops within the Chicago Police Department in the 1970s and 1980s, they did not want to become more marginalized within Area 2 and subject to any more undue discrimination than they had already encountered. The racial discrimination they experienced had implications for their social mobility.

Retired officer Sammy Lacey explained: "Well, the only thing I can say —and this is why I consider that it was totally racist—is that every time Burge would give us our detective division evaluations, we would always be rated low."

It did not matter what they did. They could make an extraordinary amount of arrests. Still, Burge would always counter by telling them that they did not solve any homicide cases. Lacey would even remind Burge that he was their commanding officer, and he did not assign homicide cases to them. Burge simply replied nonchalantly, "Well, that's your problem."

Lacey then testified that this was precisely the reason why all the black detectives felt that they were constantly on "the chopping block."[17]

Since they knew they were being discriminated against, some of the black officers tried to file a formal complaint against Burge. But they quickly learned why registering a complaint was not a feasible solution to their problem.

"It was 1983. Me, Doris Byrd, and Jack Hines, we kind of got upset that we were not being assigned any homicides, and we went to then Commander Leroy Martin, who is also African American, and explained that Jon Burge would not assign us homicides."[18]

Initially Martin was sympathetic with them, even going as far as to say that he would start an investigation. But the next day they were called into Commander Burge's office and he gave them "the hoopla" about going outside of the chain of command. "And at that time I said I would never evade the command structure again."[19]

Sammy Lacey's testimony demonstrates that even though black police officers in Area 2 were the furthest away from Burge's inner circle (and thus, we might assume, felt less of an obligation to him), they had a heightened sense that he was responsible for their careers. And so it was that even when they did not choose to "put their head in the sand," as Walter Young described it, and filed formal complaints, Burge made sure they walked around "blind."

Walter Young explained that in Area 2 there was a case management sergeant who assigned different cases to police officers. When a crime was reported this sergeant classified them in two different types: (1) *blind cases* where the probability was that it would not be solved and (2) *hot cases* that were likely to be solved because the offender was known.

Young explained: "Say if Joe Willie Stupid went out and rob somebody and then knocked his girlfriend in the eye. His girlfriend would get pissed off. She would get on the horn and call the station and say, 'Remember that guy who committed the robbery? That was Joe Willie Stupid. He is here.'"

Young explained that the sergeant would contact the A-Team and send them to arrest the person who committed the crime.

"He would hold these calls and give those type of calls to the A-Team," Young explained.

Upon hearing this explanation, Taylor clarified Young's testimony by asking if there was a distinction between certain detectives in terms of who got what kind of case.[20]

"Basically no black detectives were on the A-Team," Young replied, before confirming that it was the A-Team that received the cases with the names on them. "We got the blind cases," Young said.[21]

The A-Team was set up by Commander Burge to settle hot cases. It was common knowledge that these officers were among the most privileged, since when Burge chose to go out in the field he would usually go with them.[22] But the A-Team's reputation for solving cases was not only based on the fact that the ones they handled were the easiest to solve. They were also known for using extralegal force to coerce a confession.

An in-depth examination of what took place in Area 2 headquarters helps illuminate exactly why it is not sufficient to make the extralegal use of force seem exceptional. Even if the argument could be made that one "bad apple" police commander orchestrated torture, cops of all ranks helped sustain excessive police violence by learning what not to know. Such an understanding points us to examining the occupation of policing in conjunction with instances of extralegal force. Here we see how police officers were made accountable to each other. Those who did not have the privilege of being in Burge's good graces (or on his A-Team) learned that they would be rated low if they did not accept the command structure that was in place. Filing complaints about how the cases were allocated proved futile. So did appealing to a higher authority for a more equitable distribution of cases. While it may seem that the everyday nuances of how cases were managed does not necessarily have much to do with police torture, Walter Young's testimony makes clear that accepting the current structure meant learning how to disappear (or "vanish") when there was a possibility that one could witness extralegal violence.

Epistemic Murk

Now that we understand what it means to learn to know what not to know, I want to examine how this institutional practice creates epistemic murkiness that embeds excessive police violence within interrogations at Area 2.

Doris Byrd, one of the four black officers—and the only black female—who worked at Area 2 in the 1980s, recalls hearing "screaming and other unusual noises" coming out of interview rooms while Burge's elite unit, the A-Team, was interrogating people. In a sworn affidavit, she discusses how, because they viewed her as a potential ally, black suspects would report that the white officers in her precinct had physically abused them.[23]

"And did they tell you," Flint Taylor inquired, "the kinds of techniques that were used . . . against them?"

"Yes," Byrd answered, before mentioning the telephone books that suspects talked about being beaten with, the plastic bags they said they were suffocated with, and the black box with which they described being shocked.

Byrd's testimony implicitly references Andrew Wilson's murder trial in 1989. When Andrew Wilson told a jury about "the black box," a field telephone that police officers had repurposed into a torture device, this was the first time that torture allegations against Burge came to light. Wilson said that Burge cranked the generator, sending 9,200 volts of electricity into his body: "He put it on my fingers," Wilson explained, ". . . one [of the clamps] on one finger and one on the other finger. And then he kept cranking it and cranking it, and I was hollering and screaming. I was calling for help. . . . My teeth was grinding. Flickering in my head. Pain . . ."

"It hurts," Wilson continued. "But it stays in your head, okay? It stays in your head and it grinds your teeth . . . it grinds, constantly grinds, constantly. The pain just stays in your head. . . . And your teeth constantly grinds, and grinds, and grinds, and grinds, and grinds, and grinds."[24]

Here, it is important to note that despite the allegations of torture that first surfaced during Wilson's trial, Burge was able to torture many more criminal suspects over the next decade. A large part of the reason was that police officers who were suspicious of Burge refused to step forward.

"And I take it," Taylor continued to question Byrd, "you would have been willing to tell them what you told me if, in fact, somebody from downtown came and tried to conduct a legitimate investigation about what was going on there?"

". . . I would have to think twice about that," Byrd responded, "because when Laverty spoke out, they didn't do very much for him."

Frank Laverty was a white detective at Area 2. When the son of a black officer was accused of a crime he did not commit, Laverty revealed that members of Burge's elite unit kept secret "street files." The files sometimes allowed Burge's men to enact vigilante justice—in this case, by framing the son of a cop who in their opinion had "crossed the line." It was from watching what happened to Frank Laverty after he exposed the truth that other officers in Area 2 came to know "what would happen to you if you stepped on Burge's toes," as Doris Byrd put it.

Byrd said that one day she was in a conference room with other officers, and Laverty was in there as well, looking for a file. Laverty, preoccupied with rummaging through a file cabinet, had his back turned when Burge entered the room. The police commander drew his weapon and pointed it at the back of Laverty's head.

"Bang," Burge said.

Taylor asked if Byrd took that as a warning of what would happen if police officers came forward and broke the "code of silence."

Yes, Byrd replied, before stating that Burge "squashed" Laverty's career by placing him in the Recruit Processing Department, "never to make rank."

Byrd went on to explain that the reason she was talking to the People's Law Office now was because she was retired and had secured her pension: "And if they haven't taken Burge's, they sure as hell won't take mine."

Through Doris Byrd's testimony we see how learning what not to know cultivated spaces of ambivalence—what I have been calling epistemic murkiness—such that the direct knowledge of torture was obscured. Jon Burge ensured the details of his torture ring were mystified by excluding from his inner circle people like Laverty whom he did not trust, and then by ostracizing them or issuing warnings until they excluded themselves. Byrd mentioned that even if someone tried to conduct an investigation about extralegal force she might not have participated because of the implications it would have had for her career. Thus, on the one hand, someone in Byrd's position would not have direct knowledge of torture or be able to validate it directly because she would not be privy to Burge's secret "street files." But additionally, she knew where not to look to avoid being in conflict with Burge. After all, she saw that Frank Laverty's career suffered from trying to expose the police use of extralegal force. The point is that being excluded at Area 2, and excluding oneself to protect career ambitions, created a space for torture to become part of the everyday practice of eliciting confessions at Area 2.

The Public Secret

In 1993, the People's Law Office received a series of anonymous letters written by someone who claimed to have inside knowledge of Area 2 police headquarters. The self-proclaimed "insider" described the awareness within Chicago's government of Burge's illicit activities: "You must remember that they all knew, as did all the state's attorneys and many judges and attorneys in private practice. . . . Mayor [Jane] Byrne and States Attorney [Richard M.] Daley were aware of the actions of the detectives."[25]

Over the years, many people who have wanted to bring allegations of police torture to light have argued that part of the reason why Burge was never prosecuted criminally was that the local authority for the initiation of criminal charges in these cases, the Cook County State's Attorney, was Richard M. Daley, who was later elected Chicago's mayor, serving from 1989 to 2011. Had he investigated Jon Burge, they argue, it would have come to light that he was aware of the public secret of police torture.

At one point, while addressing lawyers at the People's Law Office, the police insider suggested that Wilson's legal team check in local taverns around his precinct, claiming that they would easily find people who would attest to the fact that Burge liked to "brag about everyone he beat." Had Taylor ventured to the pub, he might have overheard a conversation like the one Burge had with Eileen Pryweller, the sister of a police officer under his command.

In an affidavit for a civil case against Jon Burge in 2004, Pryweller testified that in January 1987, while sitting at a bar in her brother's basement, her sibling Bobby and Jon Burge proceeded to tell her about the hazards of being a cop in urban Chicago.

"I think God couldn't have found a worse hell for what they described," Pryweller said. According to her, Burge and her brother said that they beat criminal suspects, threw them against walls, burned them against radiators, smothered them, poked them with objects. They even said that "they did something to some guys' testicles."[26]

It was a jumbled conversation, she said, that started off with a rant in which they denigrated African Americans and the communities in which they lived, calling them "violent" and "filthy." But after a while, the conversation got more specific.

"Oh, and this guy, this skinny little nigger boy, I got him," her brother said, before describing torturing him, and smothering him. "He said he used handcuffs on him so that he was helpless," Pryweller stated.[27]

Upon hearing these stories, Pryweller asked her brother and Burge about how they could get away with these extreme methods of interrogation. Burge replied that he "can make anybody confess to anything."

Pryweller said that Burge's admission devastated her, especially when he claimed that police officers have "a right to do this" and that "there are no attorneys in the room." Burge went on to explain that he has a "strong relationship" with the judges and the State's Attorney's Office and that they all work together.[28]

Eileen Pryweller's testimony resonates with other evidence that Burge was prone to "show off" while torturing criminal suspects.[29] After receiving an anonymous tip, lawyers at the People's Law Office found the transcript of another suspect, Melvin Jones, who described what happened to him while in custody at Area 2. In the transcript, Jones stated that upon his arrest Burge put an electrical device on his foot. He started screaming, before telling Burge that he was not supposed to be hurting him.

After hearing this comment, Burge looked over to the other officer in the room. "You see anything?" he asked. The officer looked up at the ceiling. Then Burge said, "You see. It's just me and you. No court and no state are going to take your word against a lieutenant's word."[30]

Later in the transcript, Jones says that Burge asked him if he knew a man who went by the moniker of "Satan."

Jones had heard of Satan and knew he had a reputation for being "tough," but did not know him personally. Burge then informed him that Satan had the same "treatment" that he was about to receive and that he "crawled all over the floor."

Pryweller's and Jones's testimonies are significant because they demonstrate how the faith in police officers helps to conceal the forms of torture they enact. We see here that part of the torture that Burge inflicted entailed a psychological warfare in which he confessed his secret to the person he was about to torture. Burge's not-so-well-hidden secret was that he was fully aware that torture was illegal, but he was equally aware that no one could stop him. It is through this revelation that Westley's longstanding arguments are supported. Burge employs moral claims (like African Americans are "violent" and "filthy") to justify the use of extralegal force. As Westley suggested, Burge also seems not to be interested in criminal suspects that he does not have to use force to contain. Such observations can help us understand his seemingly reckless behavior. These common findings, which arise from the occupation of policing (and not merely the proclivities of a particular man), may be why he humiliated the people he tortured and why he was so preoccupied with the memory of watching a man named Satan crawl "all over the floor."

On Revelations

In this chapter, I have tried to highlight the sounds, the sights, and the feeling of torture, rather than merely explain its history or social function. I have also demonstrated that embedded in the way extralegal force has been enacted is also a series of revelations that uncover the public secret.

What makes the secret of police torture in Chicago "public" is that there is no direct connection between Jon Burge and the people he tortured that allowed him alone to hide his affairs and in this way keep his secret safe. His secret was not merely his. This secret was propelled by the people he threatened and by those who, in receiving these threats, learned where not to look. Throughout the decades that Burge enacted torture, there were many people who exposed him for who he was and what he was doing. But these exposures—these revelations—only produced more mystery. Those with the power to stop Burge likely asked themselves: Can I really take the word of a confessed killer like Andrew Wilson or a hardened criminal called Satan over a well-respected police commander and decorated army veteran? Perhaps it should not surprise us that the answer to this question would be negative. Recall Taussig's assertion that revelations often fail to undermine the power and mystery with which actions (such as torture) and people (such as Burge) are imbued before their exposure.

This is because police officers pretend not to know that suspects are being tortured. City judges and lawyers pretend that if torture is taking place, it is toward a greater good. These judges and lawyers also pretend not to know that the officers actually do know that torture is taking place. And police officers pretend not to know that the judges and lawyers also know about torture but are pretending not to know. The whole thing appears to be some elaborate deception. But at whose expense?

In Taussig's scheme, revelation and secrecy are mutually constitutive, and the interplay between them is infinite. Any attempt to explain the public secret only exposes another myth beneath the one previously revealed. For him, the point of it all is that exposure cannot destroy the mystery entailed in the public secret. By contrast, many communities in Chicago that have been subjected to extralegal violence wish to dwell in the space that revelation affords. They hope to demonstrate that the rational explanation that there is a lack of understanding about the police use of extralegal force actually exposes an entrenched myth: government officials have an unfounded faith in the law.

That said, I will end this chapter with a town hall meeting on Chicago's west side to help demonstrate the urgency of revelations for poor communities of color. This town hall meeting illuminates what Fassin has referred to as a "divided social world,"[31] in which black Chicagoans who experience police violence on a regular basis confront politicians who may not share this reality.

Below the police camera on a street in west Chicago, surveillance technologies with all-seeing eyes operate like police officers incarnate.[32] And in the spotlight created by one of these police cameras—or "blue lights" —Mr. Otis paces frantically. A longtime resident of west Chicago in his late sixties, he has a tight grip on the community newspaper, which features an article about Burge's trial. Underneath the article is a photograph of a slain teenage boy. Glancing at the paper, then shaking his head, Mr. Otis gives me a version of the report that differs from the one captured in print:

"Police say the boy ran from them, ducked and dodged through an alleyway when he saw them. When the officers cornered him, they say he pointed a gun at them, so they shot to kill. And believe me, they succeeded. But get this: the kid was shot in the back. The boy's mamma says he was scared stiff of the police. A couple days ago, before he was shot and all, she said some cops told the boy, 'we're gonna get you.' So now she's trying to sue the city. She says the police planted the gun. She says the police want to turn her son into a criminal, you know, justify the shooting—make it seem okay."

It is September 2009, just months before local elections. Shortly after discussing the newspaper article of the slain boy, Mr. Otis informs me of a meeting that will take place later that evening, where residents plan to voice their grievances about police violence. Hours later, we walk in to the House of Worship on Oliver Street and sit together in the musty basement room. Unlike the community meetings on housing evictions, which are dominated by the area's fierce cadre of older women and always spiked with an undercurrent of long-lived injustice, there are a number of young adults and teenagers in the pew, many of them family members of the thirty-three people killed by the police thus far into the year.

Eric Childs, a west Chicago resident and local political activist, calls the meeting underway. The audience numbers more than one hundred people, a boisterous crowd. In the front row is another noticeable group—twenty city council members, most of them seeking election.

"He wasn't a gang banger," one mother says to the audience and the panel of politicians. "He wasn't a thug." This woman, Felicia Allen, reaffirms a common refrain: an assurance from mothers and fathers and sisters and brothers, each testimony at sharp odds to police reports and most media coverage.

"Tell them about the killer *po*-lice," Eric Childs interjects from the audience.

"The police, they threaten them," Allen says in response. "They say they're gonna kill them. So yeah, they run when they see them. My boy was running 'cause he was scared."

Felicia Allen, of course, does not know what her son was thinking while sprinting from the police for the last time.[33] But she wants to sever any presumed connection he has to local gang activity. She means to dispute the claim that he was merely some kid who aimed a gun at a police officer, thereby subjecting himself to legal return fire. Her words serve to expiate his guilt. Like many other residents in attendance, she cites a longstanding tradition of police torture of the kind that Jon Burge signifies.

Even though Jon Burge hasn't been an officer of the law since 1993, his name is still frequently invoked on the west side of Chicago. Of the thirty-five families that testify at this meeting, twenty-one of them specifically mention Burge or the people he tortured. One woman says, "because of Burge, Chicago police officers know they can get away with murder." She elaborates, "Crooked cops are still protected by a crooked system." A few other people turn "Burge" into a verb while referring to an excessive use of police force—my son was "*Burged*," they say. Others who address the audience mention youngsters like Marcus Wiggins, the thirteen-year-old who testified in 1991 about how Jon Burge supervised his electric shock:

"They started—my hands started burning, feeling like it was being burned. I was—I was shaking and my—and my jaws got tight and my eyes felt like they went black. . . . It felt like I was spinning. . . . It felt like my jaws was like—they was—I can't say the word. It felt like my jaws was sucking in. . . . I felt like I was going to die."[34]

At the House of Worship, everyone with a badge is understood to have the same impunity that Jon Burge wielded for decades—the impunity that carried him to his retirement down South all the while collecting his pension. Everyone without a badge is a potential Wiggins, or Aaron Harrison, Lester Spruill, Sam Mitchell, or any one of the others killed by Chicago cops.

"They act like the judge, jury, and executioner," Lester Spruill's baby sister says.[35] "How many families have to be destroyed? How many more people have to die? They treat us black folk like criminals. Make laws to criminalize us, like we aren't taxpayers. I tell you what: we're paying them to kick our ass, is what we're doing. We're paying them to kill our children."

"Go ahead and tell them about the killer *po*-lice," Eric repeats.

The shared testimony at the town hall meeting is meant to expose the public secret of police torture in Chicago. In Eastwood, the public secret that the police constantly enact their own form of justice through extralegal force is invoked through and by offering different accounts of police shootings. Residents like Mr. Otis supplement the version of the shooting that a newspaper might take for granted by citing instances where the police threatened a teenage boy just before he was killed. In this way, they link enactments of violence that would normally fall within the legitimate continuum of force (such as shooting someone with probable cause) to a wider history in which the police have illegally coerced confessions out of criminal suspects. Jon Burge and the people he tortured figure prominently in their narrations because they represent the hidden truth that Benjamin famously articulated: through enactments of extralegal force, the police actually create law in the name of preserving it (i.e., "They act like the judge, jury, and executioner"). Hence, the notion of the public secret can help us understand the gulf between how black Chicagoans experience extralegal force and how it is generally understood in the scholarship on policing by pointing us to the consequences of learning what not to know and the epistemic murkiness that such willful ignorance creates.

Conclusion

They are located about every half mile. Lampposts on which cameras encased in domes of plastic have been mounted high above the street. Inside the dome, a florescent blue light flashes—a siren that can be seen but not heard. In west Chicago it is said that the persistence of that silent blue light, its relentlessness, can transform a person.

If ever a mechanism of policing exemplified how misleading the notion of "objectivity" can be when it comes to solving crime it would be Chicago's blue light system. Objectively speaking, there could never be irrefutable evidence to show that blue lights are an effective crime deterrent. Many criminologists have lamented the reasons why this is true: (1) the blue light system has been implemented with no "control" neighborhoods, and so in high-crime communities, there are few areas left without cameras to compare against areas that have them; (2) many blue lights have malfunctioned, and there is no system for identifying which cameras are working properly; and (3) there are not enough police staff to monitor the cameras that actually do work.

While they cannot be seen as objective crime deterrents, blue lights can help accomplish another task: to reaffirm, and preserve, the power of the law for the law's own sake. To put things another way, the blue light system signifies objectivity but cannot be objective, leading residents to regard it as just another practice of deception and secrecy. Such tactics of surveillance, which reside on a seemingly harmless side of the continuum of force, are connected to the opposite end where torture resides when Chicagoans point out that certain mechanisms of policing cannot achieve their stated aims. Do they not have a point? When looked at in conjunction with the revelation of a "domestic black site," for instance, the blue light—and the faith in the law that it embodies—can be regarded as a pretext for a wider desire for social control at the expense of particular populations.

This chapter contributes to the anthropology of policing by demonstrating how ethnography can help scholars understand why the use of extralegal force cannot exclusively be seen as an act committed by a rogue cop or a corrupt department against a particular person. Torture must also be regarded as an act endured by people and their families, friends, and neighbors. I've shown that functional explanations of the police's use of extralegal force often conceal what makes a police officer enact torture when trying to solve a case. We saw, further, that some of the enticements that motivated Area 2 police officers to either engage in torture or ignore it were the ambitions to move up in rank and to develop a reputation, as well as the need to rationalize illegal behavior as a way of finding meaning in their vocation. Since these enticements are not unique to Chicago-area cops, comparative ethnographic studies should examine how the incentive structures embedded in police work produce the use of extralegal force.

If such approaches are not undertaken, scholars of policing can run the risk of masking the occupational incentives to enact extralegal force through a methodological alibi that focuses on what cannot be known about police violence. This stance is the scholarly equivalent of burying one's head in the sand. Hence, I have argued that instead of seeing extralegal force as exceptional based on what scholars do not know, or can never know, an alternative approach is to develop a framework for investigating the circumstances that make the use of extralegal force both predictable and appealing. In Chicago, such an approach opens us up to a world of sadism that is not merely about punishing a criminal for an act that transgresses the law, but dwelling in a space of revelation that peels back the secrets that seldom gain public recognition and, in so doing, exposes the cruelty of a society to itself.

Notes

1. Westley 1953.
2. Brodeur 2003, 217; Adams 1998, 68.
3. These two ideas are common in the social scientific literature on policing in a number of different countries. See Bayley 1983; Bittner 1970; Elias 1996 (1989); Lofthouse 1996; Waddington, Jones, and Critcher 1989.
4. As Fassin (2013, 124) points out, a number of steps have to be taken in order for an instance of police violence to be tried in court: (1) the victim has to file a complaint, (2) a grievance has to be recorded, (3) a lawyer has to take up the case, (4) there has to be an investigation, (5) a dismissal has to be avoided, (5) there has to be a trial, and (6) a verdict has to be issued. As we saw with the Eric Garner case in New York, even when there is clear evidence of police violence (in this instance, a video recording of an officer choking an unarmed citizen), this is an extremely high bar to pass.
5. Fassin 2013, 124.
6. Westley 1953.
7. Bittner 1970; Brodeur 2003, 211.
8. According to Brodeur (2003, 208), the entire spectrum of the police use of force is as follows: (1) the *physical presence* of the police officer; this is followed by (2) the *verbal or visual commands* of the police officer or signified by the flashing lights of his squad car; (3) *neutralizing agents*, such as tear gas that are employed to stabilize a crowd; (4) *physical contact*, such as wrestling a criminal suspect to the ground in the midst of an arrest; (5) *impact techniques*, such as using a Taser gun or rubber bullets on a criminal suspect who is deemed to be unruly; (6) *lethal force*, such as choking or shooting a criminal suspect when that suspect threatens the life of an officer.
9. Fassin 2013, 137.
10. Taussig 1999.
11. Brodeur 2003, 215.
12. Goldston 1990.
13. Chin and Wells 1998.
14. During the trial, Burge would admit that he was familiar with electrical devices operated by a crank because he used field telephones in the army, but stopped short of saying that he had actually witnessed any acts of torture in Vietnam. See Conroy 2000, 76.
15. *Patterson v. Burge*, 328 F. Supp. 2d 878 (2004).
16. Ibid.
17. Ibid.
18. Ibid.
19. Ibid.
20. Ibid.
21. Ibid.
22. Ibid.
23. Ibid.
24. Conroy 2000, 69.

25. Goldston 1990
26. *Hobley v. Burge et al.*, 445 F. Supp. 2d 990 (2006).
27. Ibid.
28. Ibid.
29. Ibid.
30. Conroy 2000, 159.
31. Fassin 2013, 114.
32. The ethnographic aspects of this chapter are based on my ongoing ethnographic fieldwork in urban Chicago. I have been conducting research in Chicago since 2007.
33. In *Enforcing Order*, Fassin (2013, 114) likewise describes several scenes of young people fleeing from police custody. One of the most striking is of a nineteen-year-old high school student who drowned while trying to evade police capture. The teenager's father mourned his son's death while recalling his own fraught relationship with the police during World War II. Fassin's example resonates with my own study because, in both cases, we see how not only a fear of the police is transmitted through generations, but also the banality of deaths in the course of policing.
34. *Wiggins v. Burge*, 173 F.R.D. 226 (N.D. Ill. 1997).
35. Cf. Benjamin 1978 (1922).

References

Adams, Kenneth. 1998. "A Research Agenda on Police Use of Force." In *Use of Force by Police: Overview of National and Local Data*, edited by Kenneth Adams, Geoffrey Alpert, Roger Dunham, Joel Garner, Lawrence Greenfeld, Mark Henriquez, Patrick Langan, Christopher Maxwell, and Steven Smith, 68. Washington, DC: National Institute of Justice.

Bayley, David .1983. "Police: History,." In *Encyclopedia of Crime and Justice*, edited by Sanford H. Kadish, 1120–31. New York: The Free Press.

Benjamin, Walter. 1978 [1922]. "Critique of Violence." In *Reflections: Essays, Aphorisms, Autobiographical Writings*, edited by Peter Demetz, 277–300. New York: Schocken.

Bittner, Egon. 1970. *The Functions of the Police in Modern Society*. Chevy Chase, MD: National Institute of Mental Health.

Brodeur, Jean-Paul. 2003. "Violence and the Police." In *International Handbook on Violence Research*, edited by Wilhelm Heitmeyer and John Hagan, 217. Dordrecht: Kluwer Academic Publishers.

Chin, Gabriel, and Scott Wells. 1998. "The 'Blue Wall of Silence' as Evidence of Bias and Motive to Lie: A New Approach to Police Perjury." *University of Pittsburgh Law Review* 59: 233.

Conroy, John. 2000. *Unspeakable Acts, Ordinary People: The Dynamics of Torture*. Berkeley: University of California Press.

Elias, Norbert. 1996 [1989]. "Civilization and Violence: On the State Monopoly of Violence and Its Transgression." In *The Germans: Power Struggles and the Development of Habitus in the Nineteenth and Twentieth Centuries*, edited by Michael Schröter, 171–203. New York: Columbia University Press.

Fassin, Didier. 2013. *Enforcing Order: An Ethnography of Urban Policing*. Cambridge: Polity Press.

Goldston, Michael. 1990. *Special Project Conclusion Report*. Chicago: Office of Professional Standards.

Lofthouse, Michael. 1996. "The Core Mandate of the Police." In *Policing Public Order: Theoretical and Practical Issues*, edited by Chas Critcher and David Waddington, 39–51. Aldershot: Avebury.

Taussig, Michael. 1999. *Defacement: Public Secrecy and the Labor of the Negative*. Stanford: Stanford University Press.

Waddington, David, Karen Jones, and Chas Critcher. 1989. *Flashpoints: Studies in Public Disorder*. London: Routledge.

Westley, William. 1953. "Violence and the Police." *American Journal of Sociology* 59 (1): 34–41.

TWELVE

Boredom:
Accounting for the Ordinary in
the Work of Policing (France)

DIDIER FASSIN

Boredom may lead you to anything.

—Fyodor Dostoyevsky, *Notes from the Underground* (1864)

The police are confronted with a major paradox that has received little attention in criminology despite its crucial importance in understanding the way they practice their activity as well as the incidents that occur in this context. On the one hand, the imagination and the representation of police work are associated with action, crime, flurry, high-speed chase, arrests in the act. Crime novels as well as films and television series convey this image of constant excitement and riveting adventures. The officers themselves often admit they had this image in mind when they decided to enter a career in law enforcement. On the other hand, the everyday reality of patrols is a monotonous and tedious routine, which basically consists in driving around neighborhoods expecting calls that rarely come and, if they do, often turn out to be mistakes or pranks. On the average day and even more so on the average night, little happens, time goes by slowly, and most crimes committed are not accessible to the agents who arrive too late to catch the criminal or often learn about it long after it took place. As a result of this lack of available offenses and due to the pressure of expected arrests, they are forced to take proactive measures, which frequently involve stop and frisks of individuals who happen to be present in public spaces, generally on the basis of their physical appearance rather than suspect behavior. This paradoxical contrast between an imagined world of enthralling action and a concrete reality of minimal activity obviously departs from the commonly shared assumptions concerning law enforcement that are rooted in the accumulation of crime-related news reported by the media, from local newspapers to cable news, not to mention tabloids and reality series, which feed the discourse of urban insecurity and legitimize law and order policies.

Both the representation of police work as exciting and its actual weari-some content have been described in various studies, although it is clear that the former varies with time (the explosion of television series on crime, detective movies, and police channels in recent years is a sign of a renewed interest) and the latter differs according to places (inaction is logically more common where crime and misdemeanor are less prevalent as well as where inhabitants do not trust law enforcement agents). But the tension resulting from their concomitance and contradiction has seldom been analyzed by criminologists.[1] Yet the gap between imagination and re-ality has important consequences for the ways officers carry out their duties and more broadly act and think with respect to themselves, their public, and society. How do they experience the paradox of a job, the practice of which corresponds neither to the image people have of it nor to the fantasy they themselves once had about it? How does this experience influence their daily activity, their reaction to events when they occur, their attitude toward their public when nothing happens, the manner in which they en-vision their profession and life? These are the questions that arose from an ethnography conducted in France's largest police district, which is located in the Paris region, from 2005 to 2007, that is, in the interval between the two most recent periods of major urban unrest in the country sparked by the deaths of several young men as a result of interactions with the po-lice in housing projects. The agglomeration comprises a population of a little less than 200,000 inhabitants. The unemployment and poverty rates, the proportion of immigrants and foreigners, the number of so-called sen-sitive urban zones, and the level of criminality are higher than in the rest of the Paris region, a fortiori of the average of the country. Even in this supposedly heated context there was not much to do for the police—and therefore to see for the ethnographer. In fact, at the climax of the riots, there was less action than usual due to the curfew and the massive presence of police forces: once in while, a car was set on fire, but by the time law en-forcement agents arrived at the scene, nothing would be left but a smolder-ing carcass surrounded by distant bystanders watching in the dark. For the most part, days and nights went by without incidents.

In the following pages, I will, first, discuss how boredom in law enforce-ment practices came to my attention and relate it to various approaches in the social sciences; second, attempt to describe boredom in the activity of a special unit, suggesting that this very depiction presents some specific difficulty; third, analyze some of the consequences of boredom on patrols, particularly in the production of incidents; and fourth, propose a broader interpretation of what boredom reveals about law enforcement in poor urban areas.[2] The general argument is that although this aspect of police work, especially on patrol, has not been ignored by criminologists, little emphasis has been put on its meaning and implications.

Uncovering and Exploring Boredom

Although the dullness of patrolling may seem manifest in retrospect, it took me a long time to acknowledge it. This belated awareness was probably due to my expectation of thrill, which had been enhanced by the sort of performance the officers I accompanied put on for me as well as for themselves through the hasty pursuit of unlikely fugitives and long stakeouts for elusive perpetrators. Moreover, when a day or night had passed without any significant incident, they would often narrate in my presence supposedly engrossing anecdotes about events that had precisely happened during a previous shift. The illusion of action could thus be maintained toward their colleagues as well as toward me despite all evidence to the contrary. Actually I was perhaps myself reproducing a similar pattern with my family and friends after my diurnal and nocturnal rides around the city, overstating the allegedly exhilarating moments I had lived through.

At some point, though, it became obvious that the boredom I felt was shared by my law enforcement companions. Ethnography was definitely irreplaceable in this regard. A journalist invited to go out with a brigade for a shift or two or a sociologist conducting a series of interviews with officers are much less in a position to realize how empty and tiresome police work can be: in the first case, a few runs may give the illusion of thrilling moments; in the second one, compelling narratives can be a good replacement for lacking adventures. Through observation over long periods, ethnography allows for the actual experience of unending weariness. By emphasizing the importance of ethnography, I nevertheless do not want to minimize the role of other forms of knowledge, such as statistics: the count of the time spent carrying on various tasks during patrols has allowed for an objective measurement of inactivity.[3] But ethnography adds a subjective comprehension to it. Only after I became aware of the succession of eventless days and nights and experienced the overwhelming impression of endless patrols was I able to go beyond the power of imagination, the play of performance, and the charm of stories. Ultimately, despite the fact that no one ever really admitted it, I came to comprehend that ennui was the dominant affect for both the observed and the observer.

Boredom is therefore the subject of this chapter. Although it has been rightly argued that "because of its reputation as an inconsequential emotion, the significance of boredom has often been minimized if not ignored," it is certainly not a topic foreign or even new to the humanities and the social sciences.[4] From Kierkegaard, for whom the aesthetic life is characterized by resistance to boredom, to Heidegger, who places boredom at the heart of his metaphysics, philosophers have considered it a fundamental existential feature of human experience.[5] More recently, literary studies have proposed to historicize this affect, for which the very verb "to bore" only appears in the second half of the eighteenth century, with Patricia Meyer Sparks examining the emergence of boredom in the post-Enlightenment literature, while Elizabeth Goodstein encompasses a much longer temporality tracing its trajectory back to Pascal but focusing on the post-Romantic period.[6] Interestingly, these perspectives, whose authors enter little in dialogue with each other, are symmetrical if not opposite: for philosophers, boredom is a universal character of the human condition; for literary scholars, it is an affect linked to the social transformations associated with modernity. To differentiate the two stances, Reinhard Kuhn has proposed to speak of ennui for the universal experience and boredom for the modern sentiment.[7] Although his linguistic distinction has not been adopted by most authors it underlines this dual dimension.

Sociologists, for their part, have recently reclaimed the legacy of two major thinkers: Georg Simmel, who, as the founder of the sociology of culture, considered that the acceleration of urban life leads to a paradoxical adjustment of individuals who tend not to react to its multiple stimulations, thus adopting a form of emotional detachment; and Henri Lefebvre, who, from a Marxist perspective, insisted on the invasion of our world by a quantity of information and sensation that produces an atrophy of experience and a sense of emptiness.[8] Finally, anthropologists themselves have begun to explore the subjective dimension of boredom and its sociocultural signification in various contexts of rapid social change related to neoliberalism, from Ethiopia to Romania, from Australia to Colombia, with a special emphasis placed on excluded groups and precarious lives.[9] Thus the growing literature in the social sciences and the humanities does not lead to a unified theory or even concept but instead illustrates a series of tensions between the existential and the historical, the cultural and the social, a mood of the elite and an affect of the marginalized, a tragic feature of modernity or collateral damage of neoliberalism. These tensions are telling of the indefinite character of boredom and its potentially unlimited expansion through the human condition.

It is quite possibly this indetermination that has contributed to the lack of interest in boredom shown by criminologists.[10] What could they make of a notion that seems to oscillate between metaphysics and phenomenology, critical theory and social anthropology? To characterize more precisely what is meant here by boredom and how it can contribute to the comprehension of police work is therefore not a futile exercise. The etymological origin of the English word "boredom" being unclear, one can refer to the German noun *Langweiligkeit*, meaning literally "long time," which also echoes the French expression "trouver le temps long," finding that time passes slowly. Understood in this way, boredom would thus simply mean the experience of the slowness of the passing of time. Students in class, clerks in their office, workers on the assembly line, scholars attending a lecture can have this experience. No transcendence here, no civilizational process, no side effect of modernity or neoliberalism. Rather: a common, mundane, ordinary experience. It is in this experience, cleared from grandiose perspectives, that I am interested. Neither universal condition nor historical sentiment: a simple fact of life—and work.

However, boredom in policing presents a unique character. Whereas the routine of bureaucratic activities renders monotony and weariness predictable, the presumed thrill of police work makes them unexpected—by the public as well as, more importantly, by the officers themselves. The specificity of the case of law enforcement is that there is a complete but often denied discrepancy between the experience of boredom, which is encountered in numerous professions, and the representation, imagination, and expectations of police work, which is definitely specific. This cognitive dissonance is, I contend, a crucial element to comprehend what Egon Bittner called the "functions of the police in modern society."[11] It gives important clues to understand both the way in which officers act in their everyday work and the role that they are given by the state.

Almost Nothing Happens

March 20, 2007, 2 p.m. I join the anticrime squad day shift in the small closed space that serves as office, cafeteria, and locker room. The ten-by-fifteen-foot rectangle is cluttered with a desk, several chairs, a small table for the coffee machine, and half a dozen lockers. A French flag conspicuously hangs in front of the opaque window. Two large posters adorn the empty space on the walls, one showing a gleaming Ferrari on which a man bends suggestively with his hands on the roof so as to be searched by two female officers wearing provocative miniskirts and low-cut shirts as their uniform, the other one promoting the action movie *Zero Tolerance* with the caption "A film doped with testosterone." Several xenophobic stickers with stylized representations of Arabs in traditional clothes and the slogan "Against racism . . . Stop immigration" are posted on the metallic doors of the lockers. Perhaps the most remarkable decoration is composed of photographs of Detective Vic Mackey, the main character of the television series *The Shield*.

This fictional character is the leader of the Strike Team, an experimental unit of the Los Angeles Police Department devoted to aggressive antigang operations. The scenario of the drama is inspired by the real Rampart Division of the same department, whose members were involved at the end of the 1990s in criminal activities, including beatings, unprovoked shootings, bank robbery, framing of suspects, and covering up of evidence, causing one of the most serious scandals in the history of the police in the United States. The television program had started a few years before and had become an immediate success among the members of the anticrime squad: Vic Mackey and his colleagues were their heroes. The officers could easily identify with the characters since they shared many common features. Not only did they wear plainclothes and drive unmarked vehicles, but more importantly they also had a substantial degree of autonomy in comparison with the other units. They were assigned specific objectives, used heterodox methods, and only reported to their sergeant, who himself reported directly to the commissioner instead of the lieutenants, as was the case for uniformed officers who likewise patrolled the streets. To be recruited in the special unit, officers were supposed to have worked in law enforcement for at least eighteen months, to have passed a basic fitness test, and to have gone through a psychological evaluation, but the most determinant factor was the assessment by the leader of the squad. Although the level of brutality, racism, and illegality in the practices of the unit was significantly lower than in the television series, the solid reputation of the aggressive behavior of its members led most officers working in the district not to apply. The composition of the anticrime squad thus reflected a dual process of self- and hetero-selection by the agents and by the sergeant, respectively: the affinity manifested by the former toward the bellicose style of the brigade met the logics of cooptation by the latter.

The first anticrime squads were created in the mid-1990s within the context of a growing concern regarding urban violence, increasing implementation of law and order policies, and the aggravation of socioracial segregation and socioeconomic inequality. They operated mostly in disadvantaged neighborhood in the banlieues, that is, the outskirts of major cities, where they were supposed to intervene more rapidly and more effectively, thus allowing for criminals to be caught in the act. Being confrontational, they were often involved in incidents with the inhabitants of housing projects, particularly the youths of immigrant families. A chief of police described them to me as "a necessary evil" very appreciated by their superiors because they "produced numbers." He was referring to the politics recently established by the minister of the interior that imposed arrest quotas higher than the actual level of criminality, with the result that officers felt legitimized to harass and even provoke certain publics. A high-ranking official of the Ministry of the Interior told me that "when they step in, anticrime squads often cause rather than solve problems." Indeed, these units have been involved in most incidents that have resulted in the deaths of young men in the past two decades. However, their creation was not related to a rise in crime, but quite the opposite: most serious crime, including homicide and robbery, had almost continuously decreased. More than anything else, the shift in emphasis to law and order, from the mid-1980s on, with a marked accentuation in the first decade of the twenty-first century, was the combination of a growing sense of insecurity within the general population and right-wing politics exacerbating security issues, the two fuelling each other.

Let us return to this day in March 2007. When I arrive, the crew with which I am to go out on patrol is not all present: one of the two officers has been summoned by the disciplinary board following a complaint filed by a citizen who accuses him of brutality. Having therefore to wait, his colleague talks with a female agent at the entrance of the garage where the vehicles are parked. Among others, they broach the subject of "insulting and resisting a representative of the public authority," an offense that has boomed in recent years. The young woman proudly asserts that she has never been confronted with any such case, which she explains by her conciliatory attitude toward the public. After one hour, the other officer comes back from his hearing, visibly confident in the decision of a commission well known for siding with the personnel. The two men take the car and drive to the gas station a mile away. When they get there, they realize that they have forgotten their credit card. They head back to the precinct, look for the card, go to the station a second time, fill the tank of the vehicle, and return to the precinct to give the card back, and ninety minutes after the beginning of their shift they begin their patrol.

With no specific goal, they drive around the housing projects at a slow pace, scrutinizing the surroundings and paying visits to the parking lots. At some point, they receive a call from dispatch: a helicopter has been seen flying over the jail of the district, which could signal a possible breakout. Our vehicle immediately speeds up, lights flashing and sirens wailing, and gets onto the highway where it soon reaches ninety-five miles per hour. As we try to pass a car whose old driver has not seen or heard us, we come very close to the guardrail, scaring the man, who almost causes an accident as he pulls back to avoid our vehicle. Ten minutes later, when we arrive near the prison, several other police cars are already there. We learn that the helicopter was in fact transporting a patient to the nearby hospital. Obviously disappointed by this false alert, the officers, after having exchanged a few words with their colleagues, start cruising again across another housing project. Feeling hungry, they stop at a fast-food restaurant for a good moment and while eating their hamburgers start a conversation about the new guns they have just received.

Back in the car, they decide to follow a white van, which they suppose belongs to a Roma person. Without any legal justification, they stop him, check his identification, search him and his van, question him harshly to know what he is doing and where he is going, and, not having found anything suspect, end up letting him go. Back in their vehicle, they head for a housing project, driving slowly around the apartment buildings, unkindly commenting on their inhabitants, mostly migrant families from North and Sub-Saharan Africa. As they pass by a construction site in the center of the city, they call the precinct to verify whether the bulldozer they see is the one that has been reported stolen: it is not. Later they are informed that a young woman has just had her cellphone taken by youths wearing hoodies. The officers head for a nearby housing project and observe from a distance a group of adolescents, all wearing hoodies, who glance at them with hostility. They visit the victim, deliver a few comforting words, and tell her to lodge a complaint the next day. On their way back to the precinct, as the shift is ending, they see two Arab men sitting in a car in the parking lot of another housing project. They check and search them and the vehicle and find under the carpet a small quantity of marijuana obviously corresponding to personal use. They hesitate a moment and finally decide not to arrest them; it is almost 9 p.m. and were they to question them and file the paperwork, the officers would have to put in overtime. When they arrive at the station, their night shift colleagues mock their excessive zeal: the members of the other units have already finished their day and gone home.

The seven hours of the afternoon and evening patrol have thus been unproductive. The following eight hours will be even more eventless. During the first thirty minutes, the officers chat over a cup of coffee. They talk about a video showing a scene of police brutality filmed by a passerby, which generates a series of jokes, and evoke a man they seem to know well who has been stopped and searched in vain the night before, leading the sergeant to declare that had he been present he would have found something to have the man's suspended prison sentence revoked. The three crews ultimately go out on their patrol. I am with three young officers. We are informed that a fight has occurred in front of a movie theater. When we get there, everything is calm. The agents stop and check the identity of adolescents who have just come out of the cinema, writing their names down in a notebook. Then they return to their car and resume their patrol. After one hour of eventless cruising, the radio announces that an alarm has gone off in a house on the other side of the agglomeration. This time I notice that our car reaches one 110 miles per hour on the road that bisects the city: exactly twice the speed limit. When we get to the address ten minutes later, another police car is already there. In the houses nearby, people are watching through their windows. A neighbor gets out and says that he is the one who called the police but explains that the alarm has actually been going off since the morning. Aggrieved, the agents realize that they should have been alerted almost twelve hours earlier and that their intervention was doomed to fail. On their way back to the station, they follow and pull over an old car, whose occupants they suspect of being Roma people. While they check and search the driver and the vehicle, they make derogatory remarks, accusing them of being profiteers and deceivers, but cannot find any element that could justify an arrest. As they return to their vehicle, they continue denigrating these "manouches" (gypoes) until a call from dispatch mentions a brawl in an illegal settlement of Romanians in the countryside. When we arrive on the premises via a muddy path across fields, an ambulance is already there, taking a wounded man to the hospital. The officers ask the persons present whether someone wants to file a complaint, and rather than look for witnesses and take their statements, they quickly leave what they see as a hostile environment and head for the station where they eat their night meal. It is almost 1 a.m. by then. There will be no other events during the second half of the night spent, like so many others, cruising the agglomeration waiting for a call and not even having a nighthawk to stop and frisk.

Writing about the Eventless

Reading about this series of events, one might have the impression that after all the two shifts have been relatively busy. It is indeed an effect produced by the description itself, which Michael Banton, who is perhaps the first anthropologist to have underlined the temporal dimension of police work, noted in his 1964 ethnography: "The account given here emphasizes some of the more demanding and puzzling tasks, but underrates the routine, the waiting, the boredom, the paperwork."[12] Actually it is much easier to write about what happens than about what does not. The eventless resists the narrative. It can only be rendered through the arduous depiction of dullness and monotony. And not only is it simpler to tell stories in the various styles identified by John Van Maanen, but it is also more gratifying for the author.[13] The "tales of the field" are rewarding for the officers, whose bold feat is thus celebrated, as well as for the ethnographer, whose rhetorical bravura contributes to the success of his works. By contrast accounting for an eventless shift and the sort of weariness that seizes its members simultaneously depreciates the work of the police and the work of the observer.

But let us recapitulate what went on that day in March 2007. During the seven hours of the day shift, the police had an erroneous call regarding a possible evasion from the prison, a fruitless check of the vehicle of a Roma person, an unproductive intervention concerning a cellphone theft, a vain verification by radio of a construction machine, and an ineffective check of two Arab men and search of their car. As for the eight hours of the night shift, they stopped and frisked a group of adolescents possibly involved in a fight with no one injured, hurried to a scene of a burglary that might have occurred twelve hours earlier, pulled over a car suspected of belonging to a Roma family only to insult its occupants, and visited a settlement of Romanian travelers where a man had been stabbed without being able to find a witness or have a complaint filed. Not only did the crews return to the precinct empty-handed, but the time spent in the various episodes mentioned represented a total of approximately eighty to ninety minutes for each shift, including the rush to the scenes. Which means that five and a half hours in the afternoon and evening and six and a half hours during the night were eventless, spent talking over a cup of coffee, a fast-food meal, or a late cold dinner, chatting in the office while waiting for a colleague, laboriously getting gas at the station, and most of the time randomly patrolling the agglomeration in cars filled with two or three officers—plus an ethnographer in one of them—expecting calls from dispatch while wearily scrutinizing unfamiliar surroundings, tediously commenting on current events, or openly uttering their ideas. As Peter Moskos notes: "Most police officers—whether out of a desire to express themselves or the simple boredom of being confined in the intimate space of a squad car for eight hours—speak extremely candidly."[14] This candor goes from political opinions to racist prejudices, from discussions about new weapons to complaints concerning their job.

At this point, I should add that the day I chose for this account of the ordinary activity of law enforcement was particularly lively. Most of the time, especially during the night shift, there would be only one call from dispatch or even none. One evening, for instance, we have been patrolling for half an hour when the radio announces that gunshots in a nearby park have been reported. We rush to the location. When we get there all is calm. One of the two officers asks a passerby who is walking his dog if he has heard or seen anything. The man says he has not. In the meanwhile the other agent calls the precinct to get more detail about the incident. He is told that they have gone to the wrong side of the park. The two men resume their patrol around the area in search of possible clues—in vain. There will be no other calls during the shift. There will not even be a suspicious vehicle to pull over or a dubious individual to stop and frisk. It is a cold winter night and few people are outside. Almost the totality of the eight hours is spent in idleness. Boredom progressively overwhelms the shift. At the beginning of the night the conversation is about the pregnancy of the first officer's wife and the health of the second one's newborn. Little by little the dialogue dries up, though, and the warm comfort of the vehicle induces a sort of torpor that cozily lingers until the return to the precinct slightly after midnight for the ritual prandial break.

If we consider the discrepancy between the tedious routine and the imagined life of the police, a question comes up: How do they fill the gap between the two? As exemplified in the previous descriptions, the most common strategy consists in the transmutation of any event into an enthralling adventure. Every time a call from dispatch is heard, the officers feel entitled to rush toward the location they have been indicated, speeding far beyond the authorized limit, lights flashing, sirens wailing, and tires screeching—their haste sometimes leading them to the wrong address, as I observed on several occasions. Even more breathtaking is the chase of another vehicle that is speeding, has run a red light, or has not stopped when requested to pull over, since in such cases it turns into a gripping race against a real adversary rather than a mere race against time—although in most cases, the other car or motorcycle is much faster than theirs and they know it perfectly well from the start. These practices are strictly forbidden by their hierarchy because of the danger to which they expose both the police and their public: two-thirds of law enforcement agents who die in the line of duty do so as a result of car accidents, and although statistics about individuals run over under these circumstances are not made public it is probable that they are even higher since pedestrians are more vulnerable than car occupants.[15] However, for the officers, driving at an extreme speed through the city in the middle of the night and even the day to get to the scene of an often minor or nonexistent incident or in the pursuit of a car they know they will never catch up with is an exhilarating experience that exceeds all possible risk incurred and restores something of the lost meaning of the job.

In his study of the signification of the idea of and the desire for adventures in the modern world, Georg Simmel considers two elements to be fundamental: first, such adventures must be delimited periods of time sharply contrasting, by their intensity, with the normal process of life; second, they must nevertheless be related to this life in a way that allows the individual to make sense of them.[16] The rushes of the police across the agglomeration correspond to such a definition: they are brief moments of utmost intensity that disconnect the officers from their routine and connect them with their imagined mission. For a few minutes, however disappointing the ultimate outcome may be in terms of efficacy regarding the prevention of crime or the arrest of criminals, the agents pretend to experience what they dreamt of when they chose this profession and what they still fancy while watching films, series, and videos. The warnings of their superiors—who anyhow do very little to enforce their prohibition of such excesses—are negligible in comparison with the pleasure of these engrossing instants when the officers can fugaciously identify with a heroic image of the police.

In fact, contrary to what is often heard from trade unionists and read in criminological works, fear is not the emotion experienced in such moments: instead, it is excitement. I have often seen officers being affectively transfigured by the perspective of an operation that would disrupt the monotony of the patrol: their affect was never fright or anxiety; it was always thrill and eagerness. And when it appeared that the call was a hoax or an error, or that the suspect was out of reach or simply innocent, the frustration and disappointment were mitigated by the good time they had earlier speeding through the streets of the city. Actually the anticrime squad could even sometimes experience this form of exaltation by proxy. On weekend nights, when activity was resolutely inexistent and boredom was at its height, they would go to a place in the margins of the city where crowds would gather to watch so-called "runs," that is, races on a portion of road momentarily transformed into a track where cars would reach high speeds within a few seconds.[17] Such races were of course illegal but hundreds of spectators attended and dozens of vehicles were parked on the shoulder. The plainclothes officers driving their unmarked car tried to blend in with the crowd, although it was probable that some in the public immediately recognized them. They would stay for a half hour or so, pretending to observe the course of events while merely enjoying the spectacle of the race. Their passive presence at this illegal performance seemed peculiar. When I asked them about it, they told me that it would have been too complicated to organize an operation considering the size of the public. But my question was inadequate: they were not passively present but actively watching.

Yet the sum of all these moments when something happened, either real events, however derisory they were most of the time, or occasional performances, through which they lived by proxy, occupied at the most one-fourth and sometimes as little as one-tenth of the shift. How, then, did the officers spend their five or six hours of patrolling the streets in the expectation of a call from dispatch? One major difference between France and the United States is that in the latter the agents are most of the time alone in their car, whereas in the former they usually go by three and more rarely two. Although the situation is objectively much more dangerous for the police in the US inner city than in the French banlieues, it would hardly be imaginable for those operating in the latter context—and certainly unacceptable for their unions—to reduce the size of their crews. The advantage of this plethora of personnel—the official discourse of professional organizations as well as the government being that, on the contrary, there is a shortage of law enforcement agents—is not so much perceptible in terms of gain in security or even efficacy as it is in terms of occupying time. Spending days or nights in a car without any other activity aside from watching through the window in search of an improbable crime being committed or, more reasonably, of a potential suspect to be stopped and frisked or pulled over and searched is rendered much more bearable in the company of one or two colleagues, especially since crews are generally composed by affinity. Thus the work organization consisting of placing three officers in one car when one would suffice in terms of efficacy against crime and management of risk finds one rational explanation in diminishing the psychic pressure of the emptiness of time.

Chatting is indeed the main activity during a shift.[18] Possible topics are obviously infinite, but they can be classified in three principal categories.

The first one relates to the private life of the officers: conversation extends from wives, children, and pets to gardening, do-it-yourself projects, and, most of all, video games. The second one pertains to current events: it can be political or other news heard on the radio or on television, but officers seem especially attracted by amateur footage about police work or youth illegal prowess watched on the Internet. The third one deals with their professional world: it includes personal matters, such as the transfer to another district closer to one's home, or collective subjects having to do with the evolution of the job and the relationships with others, whether superiors, magistrates, journalists, or the public. The most frequent topics fall under the last category and almost always take the form of a complaint. A summons by the disciplinary board for acts of brutality, a witness confrontation by the prosecutor for a discrepancy in the report of an incident, or the liberation by a magistrate of a suspect retained in custody for lack of evidence are occasions to deplore the loss of trust in the police. More generally officers reproach their superiors their absence of support, the judges their bias against them, the media their partiality, the public its hostility. These grievances are usually incremental, each member of the crew adding his anecdote or comment to the collective expression of discontent. Seldom does one of them attempt to contradict the flow of protests by evoking some real issues at stake that can explain the increasing mistrust of the institutions and the population toward law enforcement agents. This litany is only interrupted on rare occasions by calls from dispatch and, most of all, by decisions to stop someone in the street, pull over a car, or go to a train station or another public place to check the identity of the persons present, these activities being generally oriented by racial profiling and justified in terms of statistical discrimination: "we focus on blacks and Arabs because there is more criminality among them" is the usual argument.

But the comprehension of boredom among the French police should not be restricted to the world of labor. It should be extended to the after-hours when most officers, instead of heading back home, go to the small poorly furnished apartment they share with colleagues in a similar situation. Indeed, because the institution is "national," the recruitment of its agents is carried out for the whole country. Officers choose their post according to their seniority, which implies that the new recruits get the least valued districts, namely in the banlieues, with their poor neighborhoods and housing projects. Four out of five come from rural areas and small towns and are propelled in this environment that is foreign to them and distant from their home. Instead of moving closer to their workplace, they rent in the area an apartment, where they can spend either nights or days depending on their shift, impatiently waiting for the forty-eight-hour break that will allow them to join their family two hundred miles away. Not only does this residential alternation add to their fatigue and irritability but it leaves them during long hours in an empty, insipid, lifeless, provisional space where they only eat, sleep, watch television, and play video games in the company of colleagues with whom they have to get along. Only after fifteen or twenty years of this exile in what they see as hostile territories will they be able to work in the area where their family lives and where, often, they were born. When the officers are posted far from home, ennui thus exceeds working hours to infiltrate their resting time.

What Boredom Does

The gap between the idealized world of the police and its wearisome reality is experienced with a particular intensity by the anticrime squads. Indeed, more than other units, they are supposedly characterized by their propensity for action. They were created to catch criminals in the act, and their reputation is based on their capacity to intervene rapidly and effectively. Since burglaries are one of the most common serious crimes, generating anxieties in the public and impatience among politicians, I asked various officers how often they had caught a burglar in the act and every time obtained the same response confirming the rarity of such events. One of them was more precise: "It's simple," he said. "I've been in the squad seven years, and it's only ever happened to me once. And even then the stupid asshole had got himself shut into the house and couldn't get out. All we had to do was pick him up!" Despite this obvious discrepancy between the assigned mission and the actual results, the attitude of the agents regarding this disappointing deficit of efficient activity remains ambivalent.

On the one hand, they perpetuate the myth of their relentless engagement against crime. Their performance in the neighborhoods, combining toughness often coming close to mere harassment of project youths and reactivity as they speed up through the city in search of minor offenses or evanescent offenders, serves to preserve this glorious image—toward the other officers, their superiors, the public, but also themselves. On the other hand, they permanently complain about their working conditions, their lack of resources, and more generally their disillusionment concerning the content of their activity. They frequently comment that had they known what the job really was they would never have chosen it, and some evoked their transfer or even resignation—a threat seldom concretized, as they benefited from life employment security and had limited professional alternatives. Certainly, as P. A. J. Waddington writes, "police are not un-usual in saying one thing and doing another."[19] Yet this ambiguous situa-tion, which makes them appear to be what they are not, contributes to the discomfort of many. Boredom, simultaneously lived and denied, is at the heart of police disenchantment.

Distancing myself, in my earlier comments, from the philosophical, lit-erary, and even sociological approaches to boredom, I have emphasized both its ordinary dimension in everyday life and its specific manifestations in the case of the police. Rather than a state of being that would be in-herent to the human condition, a feeling that could be linked to modern sensibility, or a fact associated with the acceleration of time and the ac-cumulation of information in contemporary society, I have considered it to be a mundane reality that connects expectation and experience, activity and temporality. However, I would like to return to the distinction pro-posed by Heidegger between three forms of boredom: one can be "bored by something"; one can be "bored with something"; one can live through a "profound boredom." My argument is that, freely interpreted, this differen-tiation can help analyze the officers' various relationships to work, job, and life, respectively, as observed through ethnography.

At the first level, the police are merely bored by their activity or the lack thereof. This boredom manifests itself in the slowness of time, the re-current checking of the watch only to realize that there is still a long way to the break or the end of the shift. It can be corrected by the occurrence of events, which are either reactive when initiated by a call or proactive when the decision is taken to stop a passerby or pull over a vehicle.[20] At the second level, officers become bored with their profession and institu-tion. This boredom translates into the dialogues in the car expressing dis-enchantment regarding the former and resentment toward the latter. Anger can also be turned against the justice system and its magistrates accused of leniency; against the public and more specifically the segment they usually have dealings with, that is, the poor, the minorities, and the immigrants; and finally against society as a whole, all this animosity being closely re-lated, according to them, to the lack of recognition law enforcement suffers from. The remedy to this discomfort is transfer to another district, in the minimalist version, and resignation from the job, in the maximalist reac-tion. More often, though, officers turn cynical.[21] At the third level, agents may experience a profound boredom, with a sense of emptiness that ex-tends from their activity to their entire existence. The ultimate expression of it is suicide, even though it would be simplistic and inaccurate to link such an event only to the profession. The annual number of officers committing suicide is twenty times higher than that of agents being killed in the line of duty, which seems to have been until recently the main concern of both the media and the unions. But no data are available to establish a thorough comparison in terms of risk between the police and the rest of the population, since the Ministry of the Interior has censored the publication of the only investigation conducted on this subject by the French National Institute for Health and Medical Research.[22] Notwithstanding these uncertainties, it is reasonable to suggest, on the basis of collected testimonies, that there is a relationship between the experience of being an officer and the possibility of committing suicide, as is the case for certain other professions. Considering these three levels, there is thus a gradation not only in depth but also in meaning, as the agents may be bored by what they do, with what they are, and, ultimately, regarding what they live for.

Yet what boredom does should not be analyzed only through the experience of the police: tedium has also major implications for the relationships officers have with their public. The rare events that occur during the shift, whether spontaneous or provoked, take a more dramatic turn because they take place in a context of inaction contributing to emotional excess in the interventions and a cynical attitude toward the population. The combination of excitement caused by the perspective that something may happen and of resentment toward the public exacerbated by the ongoing conversation among officers increases the probability of a disproportionate reaction and of an aggressive attitude. A minor offense or a simple check can thus degenerate into a brutal arrest. But this disparity between the act or the situation and the response by the police is more than a qualitative question of intensity in the individual behavior of the agents. It has also a quantitative dimension in terms of the number of officers involved. Because the various crews patrolling in the area are confronted with the same lack of activity, a call from dispatch often brings two, three, or four vehicles to the premises, representing five to ten agents, sometimes for a mere altercation between two youths. The imbalance may then provoke a sense of entitlement to the use of force. The power of numbers thus induces a feeling of superiority and sometimes a spiral of violence. Many incidents, some of them leading to the death of a suspect or mere witness, result from this qualitative and quantitative excess directly related with the experience of boredom—even if it is not their only explanation.

Recent political developments aggravated this trend. As part of law and order policies implemented in the past three decades, especially after 2002, more pressure has been exerted on the law enforcement institution.[23] The problem that it faced, though, was that with less serious crime and more special units, its efficiency would have been expected to decrease. To solve it, the minister of the interior, who was preparing his future presidential campaign as the candidate of the "tough right," instituted what he called a "culture of results," concretely translated into quotas of arrests. Eager to show his determination through flattering statistics, he asked his administration to establish these quotas at a level substantially higher than what could possibly be achieved under normal circumstances. In order to reach their objectives, the police had therefore to shift their activity from reactive to proactive, which meant more stops and frisks of individuals and more pulling over and searching vehicles. Two offenses were notably concerned because they were considered easy to "get": breaches of drug laws and breaches of immigration laws. The two corresponding groups were marijuana users and undocumented foreigners. Although the former could be found across the lines of race and class, the youths belonging to minorities and living in poor neighborhoods were the main target, and although immigrants had diverse geographical origins, only people of color were checked.[24] Both practices were illegal with regard to the criteria for stops, frisks, and searches defined by the code of criminal procedure: the officers and their superiors knew that under the law such practices were only permitted if there was a suspicion of crime having been committed or on the verge of being committed. In fact, the new politics implicitly legitimized racial profiling. The dual contradiction between the expectation of action and the reality of inaction on the officers' side and between the decline in serious crime and the necessity of flattering statistics on the government's side had indeed been resolved at a cost: an increase in discriminatory practices and, ultimately, in social tensions. The 2005 riots were the culmination of this deleterious political process.[25] Actually, during my fieldwork, officers would often complain about the politics of quota, the perverse effects of which they were knew too well—not that they felt sorry for those they harassed, but they considered that it diverted them from more meaningful activity.

Beyond the microsociology of the patrol, boredom should thus be analyzed in light of the macrosociology of policing. It may be a common characteristic of law enforcement everywhere, but its intensity and its consequences, its meaning and its functions vary across time and space. They depend on local variables, such as the frequency of crime and the trust of the population, but also on historical contexts and political choices. Prima facie, one could view boredom as the sign of a well-policed society: driving around with little to do would suggest that the presence of law enforcement agents both discourages criminals and reassures honest citizens. Yet studies suggest that it is not the case, that patrols have little effect on crime control and people's sense of security.[26] Without noticeable practical or symbolic effects, patrols remain, however, the central piece of law and order policies. Inaction can thus be manipulated—and boredom instrumentalized.

Conclusion

Police work relies on a collective deception actively kept alive by the officers, their institution, the media, politicians, and society as a whole. The image of the "cop" thus coproduced is associated with action, thrill, and danger, whereas the reality of the job is made of inaction, routine, and weariness. Boredom is a major feature of urban policing. Monotony is the rule, adventure the exception. It is the case in France as it is in the United States and elsewhere, and it has crucial consequences on police practices, including the production of violence and deviance. Because this reality is ignored by the population and disavowed by the agents, the illusion can be maintained, serving to justify the need for more forces and more repression. It can even be obscured by politics of quota artificially exaggerating statistics and deceptively feigning action. It then becomes an instrument of power.

Probably more than other approaches, ethnography allows for the uncovering of this public deceit.[27] Not only is a long presence in the field necessary to become aware of what is precisely obscured to the observer, including the ethnographer who may often be afflicted by the same ignorance or even denial as his interlocutors, but the commitment to the everyday and the ordinary, which is part of the ethnographic ethos, makes possible this paradoxical discovery of the obvious. Nourished by the hours of shared ennui in the company of members of units allegedly devoted to the most intrepid operations aimed at catching criminals in the act, the description of police work accounts for the overall deficit of activity, the excesses of the rare interventions, and the massaging of data under the pressures of quotas. Ethnography thus provides clues to interpret how these various dimensions of law enforcement are linked.

But the study of police practices can also illuminate more general issues regarding the object and the method. On the one hand, long neglected by the social sciences, boredom gains thickness under the ethnographic gaze. Its metaphysics incorporates the mundane. Its phenomenology acknowledges the political. Boredom does not only have causes; it has also consequences. On the other hand, the lack of interest in boredom in criminological research, or perhaps the difficulty to perceive its significance in law enforcement, invites a broader reflection on what remains unseen or unsaid by social scientists themselves. Part of it is due to their own blindness, and it pertains to their capacity to recognize what is meaningful. But part of it is due to their muteness, and it concerns their ability to write about the insignificant, what cannot be narrated and can hardly be described. Blindness and muteness reflect both aspects of the ethnographic experience, fieldwork and writing. But in the end what can—or should—be rendered visible or expressible under the ethnographic gaze remains an open question.

Notes

1. This is not to say that criminologists, whether sociologists, political scientists, or legal scholars, are not aware of this dimension of police work. For instance, in his pioneering study of a law enforcement department conducted in the 1950s, William Westley (1970 [1950], 35) notes: "Hours will go by without absolutely nothing happening, and then everything will break loose. This is the action to which the men look forward through the monotonous hours of driving up and down the streets." However, the significance and implications of this inactivity are rarely examined as such. A review of the classics on law enforcement shows that none of them includes the word "boredom" in its index until Richard Ericson's (1982) important book on policing in Canada.
2. The scenes described in this chapter are drawn from my monograph on the ethnography of policing in the banlieues of Paris (Fassin 2013 [2011]).
3. There exists an important literature characterizing and measuring what officers actually do during patrols. Despite considerable differences depending on places, it is generally acknowledged that little time is effectively devoted to crime related activity (Manning 1977, 100).
4. In their study of an American Indian reservation, Lori Jervis, Paul Spicer, Spero Manson, and the AI-Super PFP Team (2003, 38) add that "despite its ubiquity in contemporary cosmopolitan societies, boredom has generally been considered an ordinary, trivial, and inevitable state of being."
5. The difference between the two philosophers being that for Kierkegaard, boredom is at the center of one of the three possible sorts of good life he conceives (the aesthetic life, as opposed to the ethical and the religious ones), while for Heidegger (1995), boredom is crucial to all human experiences but can correspond to three different depths and meanings (becoming bored by something, being bored with something, and profound boredom).
6. These authors propose a dual approach of literary texts: whereas Patricia Meyers Spacks (1995) considers from a cultural perspective both the appearance of the affect and the way it is described and interpreted, Elizabeth Goodstein (2005) adopts a social reading that inscribes the emerging malaise within the changes in society and in relation to the reflexive experience of the authors, paraphrasing Robert Musil's major work for her own title.
7. Reinhart Kuhn (1976) is generally credited for being the pioneer in the literary studies of boredom but also criticized for not having established the historical and national dimension of this sentiment.

8. Kevin Aho (2007) proposes a thorough analysis of Simmel's work, in particular his 1903 essay "The Metropolis and Mental Life," while Michael Gardiner (2012) rehabilitates Lefebvre's *Critique of Everyday Life*, recognizing however that the French thinker did not theorize boredom as such.

9. Daniel Mains (2007) studies jobless and futureless young men in urban Ethiopia, Bruce O'Neill (2014) homeless people in post-Communist Romania, Yasmine Musharbash (2007) Aborigines in an Australian settlement, and Juan Orrantia (2012) survivors of a massacre in Colombia. All of them explore boredom in the everyday life of ordinary people, mostly in the lower segments of society.

10. Ironically, the only article explicitly on boredom in a criminology journal is a critical analysis of the discipline emphasizing its "institutionalized boredom" due to "rationalized methodologies and analytic abstraction." Calling for "cultural criminology" in way of rebellion against this paradigm, Jeff Ferrell (2004, 287) sees in it the "possibility of intellectual excitement."

11. In this seminal work initially presented as a report ten years earlier, Egon Bittner (1980 [1970]) proposes an influential thesis according to which the functions of the police may be extremely diverse but have in common that they may require the use of force.

12. Having studied both Scotland and US police, Michael Banton (1964, 85) presents, in his pioneering work, a detailed description of a day in the work of various patrols.

13. Based on his own ethnographic work, John Van Maanen's famous *Tales of the Field* (1988) distinguishes three main rhetoric forms: the realist, the confessional, and the impressionist.

14. After having gone to the police academy, Peter Moskos (2008) spent a year in a Baltimore precinct, about which he wrote his PhD dissertation.

15. According to the statistics gathered by police officers themselves, 63 percent of all deaths in the line of duty since 1971 are caused by car accidents (http://www.victimesdudevoir.info/Stats.htm).

16. In his essay on the life of Casanova, Simmel (1997, 225) thus suggests that "something becomes an adventure only by virtue of two conditions: that it itself is a specific organization of some significant meaning with a beginning and an end; and that, despite its accidental nature, its extra-territoriality with respect to the continuity of life, it nevertheless connects with the character and identity of the bearer of that life, in the widest sense, transcending, by a mysterious necessity, life's more narrowly rational aspects." In other words, the adventure is an intensification of the present that synthesizes various aspects of life within certain temporal limits.

17. This illegal street racing has been popularized among the youth by the *Fast and the Furious* series of action films, whose original movie in 2001 has been followed by seven sequels and which became the biggest franchise of all time for Universal Pictures, which distributes it.

18. A thorough discussion of storytelling in the police is found in Merlijn van Hulst's recent revisiting (2013) of the "canteen culture." My findings indicate, however, that more than to the narrative dimension of verbal activity among law enforcement agents, researchers should pay attention to the argumentative aspect as it is developed in their litany of complaints.

19. In his famous essay on police canteen subculture, P. A. J. Waddington (1999, 289) underlines the importance of not inferring police acts from police words.

20. In his description of the everyday work of law enforcement patrols, Albert Reiss

(1971) analyzes the tensions between reactive and proactive interventions. In the French case, the scarcity of the former renders the latter necessary, especially under the pressures of quota.

21. In his essay on police cynicism, Joel Caplan (2003, 304, 306) considers it to be a "necessary survival skill," which has positive effects on the practice of crime fighting. For him, "policing is essentially a sequence of potentially hazardous encounters with the public, interrupted by stretches of boredom," and this tension between action and inaction renders suspicion helpful.

22. According to the official statistics, the annual number of suicides among law enforcement agents was on average forty-six in the first decade of the twenty-first century, which represented a moderate decrease by comparison with the previous decade when it was fifty per year (http://www.laurent-mucchielli.org/public/La _prevention_du_suicide_chez_les_policiers.pdf). The figure repeatedly mentioned by journalists and trade unionists, according to which the rate of suicide is 32 percent higher among police officers than in the general population, does not take into account the fact that the demographic composition by age and sex of the two groups is very dissimilar.

23. The recent history of law enforcement policies in France has been studied by Christian Mouhanna (2011) in a book with an evocative title: "The police against citizens?"

24. The selection of publics via racial profiling in the case of these two offenses, which the police consider "adjustment variables" that help them to reach their quota, allows for the convergence of two apparently contradictory logics of their profession: the exercise of their discretionary power and the compliance with the government's policy (Fassin 2014).

25. The unrest triggered by the deaths of two adolescents of immigrant origin in a housing project near Paris have interestingly been analyzed in comparative perspective with similar events determined by similar circumstances in the United Kingdom by David Waddington, Fabien Jobard, and Mike King (2009) and in the United States by Cathy Schneider (2014).

26. Both facts have been established since the famous Kansas City Experiment in the 1970s (Kelling et al. 1974), and even if this study has generated debates, the lack of criminological and psychological efficacy of patrols is generally acknowledged (Reiner 2000).

27. A parallel can be made between the idea of public deceit proposed here and the notion of public secret developed by Michael Taussig (1999).

References

Aho, Kevin. 2007. "Simmel on Acceleration, Boredom, and Extreme Aesthesia." *Journal for the Theory of Social Behavior* 37 (4): 447–62.
Banton, Michael. 1964. *The Policeman in the Community*. New York: Basic Books.
Bittner, Egon. 1980 [1970]. *The Functions of the Police in Modern Society*. Cambridge, MA: Oelgeschlager, Gunn & Hain Publishers.
Caplan, Joel. 2003. "Police Cynicism: Police Survival Tool?" *Police Journal* 76:304–13.
Darden, Donna, and Alan Marks. 1999. "Boredom: A Socially Disvalued Emotion." *Sociological Spectrum* 19:13–37.

Ericson, Richard. 1982. *Reproducing Order: A Study of Police Patrol Work*. Toronto: University of Toronto Press.

Fassin, Didier. 2013 [2011]. *Enforcing Order: An Ethnography of Urban Policing*. Cambridge, UK: Polity Press.

———. 2014. "Pouvoir discrétionnaire et politiques sécuritaires: Le chèque en gris de l'État à la police." *Actes de la Recherche en Sciences Sociales* 201–2:72–86.

Ferrell, Jeff. 2004. "Boredom, Crime, and Criminology." *Theoretical Criminology* 8 (3): 287–302.

Gardiner, Michael. 2012. "Henri Lefebvre and the 'Sociology of Boredom.'" *Theory, Culture & Society* 29 (2): 37–62.

Goodstein, Elizabeth. 2005. *Experience without Qualities: Boredom and Modernity*. Stanford: Stanford University Press.

Heidegger, Martin. 1995. *The Fundamental Concepts of Metaphysics: World, Finitude, Solitude*. Bloomington: Indiana University Press. 1st German ed. 1983.

Jervis, Lori J., Paul Spicer, Spero M. Manson, et al. 2003. "Boredom, 'Trouble,' and the Realities of Postcolonial Reservation Life." *Ethos* 31 (1): 38–58.

Kelling, George, Tony Pate, Duane Dieckman, and Charles Brown. 1974. *The Kansas City Preventive Patrol Experiment*. Washington, DC: The Police Foundation.

Kuhn, Reinhart. 1976. *The Demon of Noontide: Ennui in Western Literature*. Princeton: Princeton University Press.

Mains, Daniel. 2007. "Neoliberal Times: Progress, Boredom, and Shame among Young Men in Urban Ethiopia." *American Ethnologist* 34 (4): 659–73.

Manning, Peter. 1977. *Police Work: The Social Organization of Policing*. Long Grove, IL: Waveland Press.

Moskos, Peter. 2008. *Cop in the Hood: My Year Policing Baltimore's Eastern District*. Princeton: Princeton University Press.

Mouhanna, Christian. 2011. *La police contre les citoyens?* Nîmes: Éditions Champ social.

Musharbash, Yasmine. 2007. "Boredom, Time, and Modernity: An Example from Aboriginal Australia." *American Anthropologist* 109 (2): 307–17.

O'Neill, Bruce. 2014. "Cast Aside: Boredom, Downward Mobility, and Homelessness in Post-Communist Bucharest." *Cultural Anthropology* 29 (1): 8–31.

Orrantia, Juan. 2012. "Where the Air Feels Heavy: Boredom and the Textures of the Aftermath." *Visual Anthropology Review* 28 (1): 50–69.

Reiner, Robert. 2000. *The Politics of the Police*. Oxford: Oxford University Press.

Reiss, Albert. 1971. *The Police and the Public*. New Haven: Yale University Press.

Schneider, Cathy. 2014. *Police Power and Race Riots: Urban Unrest in Paris and New York*. Philadelphia: University of Pennsylvania Press.

Simmel, Georg. 1997. "The Adventure." In *Simmel on Culture*, edited by David Frisby and Mike Featherstone, 221–32. London: Sage Publications. 1st German ed. 1958.

Spacks, Patricia. 1995. *Boredom: The Literary History of a State of Mind*. Chicago: University of Chicago Press.

Svendsen, Lars. 2005. *A Philosophy of Boredom*. London: Reaktion Books.

Taussig, Michael. 1999. *Defacement: Public Secrecy and the Labor of the Negative*. Stanford: Stanford University Press.

van Hulst, Merlijn. 2013. "Storytelling at the Police Station: The Canteen Culture Revisited." *British Journal of Criminology* 53:624–42.

Van Maanen, John. 1988. *Tales of the Field: On Writing Ethnography*. Chicago: University of Chicago Press.

Waddington, David, Fabien Jobard, and Mike King, eds. 2009. *Rioting in the UK and France: A Comparative Analysis.* Cullompton, UK: Willan Publishing.

Waddington, P. A. J. 1999. "Police (Canteen) Subculture: An Appreciation." *British Journal of Criminology* 39 (2): 287–309.

Westley, William. 1970 [1950]. *Violence and the Police: A Sociological Study of Law, Custom, and Morality.* Cambridge, MA: MIT Press.

INDEX

"academic cops," 235–36
Acai, 98–100
accountability, 23–35, 37, 39
Achun, 93
"adjustment variables," 290n24
affect, 62–64, 95, 101, 105–7, 176, 180; *ganqing* and, 92–95; how it can serve the interests of police, 91–94; nature of, 91, 108; order and, 96; power of inscriptions and power of, 105; virtual force of, 91, 107 (*see also* virtual force). *See also* boredom; critical empathy; *qing*
affective distance, 9
affective feelings. See *ganqing*
African American police, 253–58
African Americans, 16, 17n2; extralegal force against, 15–16, 27, 257, 262–64 (*see also* Burge, Jon). *See also* racial discrimination; racism
Agnes, 172
Albro, Robert, 201n12
Allen, Felicia, 263
ambush marketing, third-party. *See* FIFA Soccer World Cup
anticrime squads, 235, 239, 273–75, 280–81, 283
Arabs, 274, 276, 278, 282
Arendt, Hannah, 55
Aria, 171
armed wing of the state, police as, 239
arrest-based philosophy, 238
arrest quotas, 238, 286

aspirational policing, 184–85, 189, 193–95, 198–201; contributing to "anthropology of the good," 185, 199. *See also* Cancha
aspirations of a public police, 193–99
Atiao, 98
Aurora Avenue, 25, 27, 28, 30, 31, 34, 38
Austen, Jane, 207, 210–12, 221

Bal, İhsan, 144
Bangkok police stations, 212–14
Banished: The New Social Control in Urban America (Beckett and Herbert), 31, 32, 36, 38
banishment, 32, 38, 39
Barrio Chino, Bolivia, 196
beatings, 190, 248, 252–53, 259; by neighborhood residents, 116, 118, 123–24 (*see also* community police); by private security officers, 190–92; retributive, 116–18, 120, 122, 124–29; in secret locations, 248. *See also* interrogational beatings; violence
Beckett, Katherine, 23
Behar, Ruth, 64
Benjamin, Walter, 239–41
biopolitics, 4
Bittner, Egon, 18n13, 114
Black Lives Matter, 17n2
black market. *See* black money
black money, 68, 71, 74–75, 77
blacks, 282. *See also* African Americans; South Africa

black sites, domestic, 248, 265. *See also* extralegal force; Homan Square facility

blind cases, 255–56

Blondie (aka Stela), 168–71, 174

blue light system (cameras), 262, 264–65

blue wall of silence/blue code, 253–54, 258. *See also* Burge, Jon; impunity

Bolivian National Police, 188–91, 195–96, 198–99. *See also* Cancha

boredom: criminological perspectives on, 273; forms of, 284–85; meanings of the term, 273; philosophical perspectives on, 272; sociological perspectives on, 272–73

boredom in law enforcement practices, 269–70, 287–88; almost nothing happens, 273–77; consequences, 283–88; uncovering and exploring, 271–73; writing about the eventless, 278–83

Brodeur, Jean-Paul, 239, 245n18, 252, 253, 266n8

brotherhood. *See* kinship

Brown, Michael, 15–16, 27

bureaucratic machinery, situating the police within the, 150–55

Burge, Jon, 256–62, 264, 266n14; Andrew Wilson and, 257, 259, 261; A-Team (for settling hot cases), 254, 256, 257; background, 254, 255; Chicago government's awareness of the illicit activities of, 259; civil suits against, 248, 250, 253, 259; Doris Byrd and, 257, 258; Eileen Pryweller and, 259–60; Frank Laverty and, 258; homicide cases and, 255; legacy, 263; Melvin Jones and, 260; Michael Taussig and, 261; police officers' reluctance to testify against, 253, 254; racism, 255, 260; reasons police did not blow the whistle on, 254–59, 261; Richard Daley and, 259; Sammy Lacey and, 255; Walter Young and, 255–56

Byrd, Doris, 255, 257–58

Byrne, Jane, 259

Caetano, 230

Caldeira, Teresa, 182n1

cameras, police, 262, 264–65

Camilo, 166–68

Cancha, 185, 195, 198; a staged encounter in, 185–89 (*see also* Cochabamba: seminar with market vendors in). *See also* Cochabamba; distributed policing

"canteen culture," 289n18

car chases, 279–80

Carlos, Don, 188, 200

Celina, 171–76

Chakkar Rasta Thana (CRT), 66–83, 87n39; personal policing and fictive kinship, 73–77

Chalfin, Brenda, 189

chamboko (baton/rubber stick), 117, 119, 121–23, 126, 129

Charly, 171–74

Chasana, Mozambique, 113, 115, 116, 118, 120–24, 126, 132

Chhottu, 70, 75

Chicago Police Department, 248, 250, 251, 253–55, 258, 259, 261–66

Childs, Eric, 262–64

Chile, being policed as a condition of life in, 162–66, 180–82; anticipation of police action, 176–80; politics of the family, 171–76; surveillance, 163–71, 180

civilian community police. *See* community police

civil suits against the police, 248, 250, 259

Cochabamba, Bolivia, 185, 190, 192, 195; distributed policing in, 189–93; seminar with market vendors in, 185–89, 196–200. *See also* Cancha

code of silence, 258. *See also* blue wall of silence/blue code; Burge, Jon

coercion, socially sanctioned, 37, 114–15

Colombia, 194–95

Comaroff, Jean, 242

Comaroff, John, 242

comerciantes (market vendors), 185–92, 195–99

comisarios (Municipal Police), 191–92

community police, 30, 113, 114, 116–28; attacked by criminals, 130; criticisms of, 130–31; impact on crime, 121; overview and nature of, 113, 118, 120–32, 135, 158; power and empowerment of, 129–32; violence perpetrated by, 114, 116–

23, 127–32, 135–36. *See also* private security officers

community policing councils, 118

community policing initiative, 113, 114, 118, 121, 135

complicity, 42–45; multisited research and, 44; objective vs. subjective, 43; with police violence, 120, 133, 215, 253; the relationality and temporality of, 55–59; "studying up" and the question of, 52–54. *See also* strategic complicity

conversation among police officers, topics of, 281–82

copyright infringement. *See* media piracy in Johannesburg

corruption, 188–90, 195–99, 223n43, 263

corrupt police departments, 249

counterfeit goods, 49. *See also* media piracy in Johannesburg

Counterfeit Unit of Commercial Crime Unit of South African Police Service, 45, 49, 51–52

Crapanzano, Vincent, 53

crime prevention, moral community, and retributive police violence, 125–29

critical empathy, 216; defined, 63; ethnographic kinship and, 40n6, 62–65, 77–84; intimacy and, 63, 66; nature of, 216; of police officers for the people they police, 42, 50; sensibility of, 63–64, 84, 216. *See also* empathy

cruel optimism, 194

Cruz, Officer, 226–32, 236, 238–39, 242

cynicism, police, 290n21

Daeng, Captain, 207–9

Daley, Richard M., 259

Dario, Don, 188, 197

Das, Veena, 135

David, Don, 188

Davutoğlu, Ahmet, 156

deaths: of police officers, causes of, 280, 284–85. *See also* lethal police violence; lynchings and lynch mobs

decree, right of, 240

democratic disenchantment, 194

democratic reform and democratic policing, 105, 106

depression, 284–85. *See also* boredom

Derrida, Jacques, 240

description, 10–11, 14, 15, 17n6, 218, 219, 234, 241, 278, 287. *See also* ethnographic sense; ethnographic sensibility; staged encounter

detention, 225–26; an improbable, 226–32. *See also* discretion

Diallo, Amado, 252–53

discipline, physical, 126–27. *See also* physical punishment

discovery (ethnography), 6–7

discretion: contextualizing, 232–38; proportionate vs. disproportionate, 226, 244n2; rethinking, 238–42; social politics of, 232–33

distributed policing, 185, 189–93, 195, 197–99

"domestic black site," 248, 265. *See also* extralegal force; Homan Square facility

domestic violence, 139–40, 142, 146–50, 152, 155

drug dealers, 119, 125, 127, 215, 225, 227, 230, 231. *See also* drug trade, illegal

Drug Law 20.000, 178

drug raids, 166, 176, 178–80, 209, 212, 235

drugs, war on, 237

drug trade, illegal, 125, 164, 168–72, 177–79, 208, 209, 228–31. *See also* drug dealers

drug users and drug possession, 119, 120, 126, 207–8, 219, 225–26, 230–31

Duarte, Officer, 226–32, 236–39, 242

duplicity and complicity, tension/dance between, 10, 35–36

Durkheim, Émile, 107–8

DVDs, pirated, 46–50, 57

Eça de Queiroz, José Maria de, 225, 243

education: moral, 126–27. *See also* human rights, police training on

emotions: police violence, vulnerability, and, 129–32. *See also* affect; *ganqing*; *qing*

empathy, 50, 52, 75; and identification with the police, 83. *See also* critical empathy

empowerment. *See under* police violence

Erickson, Kai, 34

Ericson, Richard, 245n28
Esperanza, 174
ethical dilemmas, 24–30, 37, 39
ethical human, ethnographer as, 33–36
ethical relations between fieldworkers and
    those they study, 26–27
ethical treatment of research subjects, 37
ethics, 95; of mutuality, 53; of profession,
    141; violence and, 120, 133
ethnographers: responsibilities, 37. *See also*
    police ethnographers; *and specific topics*
ethnographer-subject relation, 28
ethnographic encounters, 24–26
ethnographic sense, 212, 214–20. *See also*
    sensibility (and sense)
ethnographic sensibility, 103, 106, 212–16
ethnographic virtue, 51–52
ethnographing the police, 1–16. *See also*
    specific topics
ethnography, 201; defined, 3; dimensions,
    3–4; Duncan McCargo and, 212–14;
    heuristic properties, 5–7; how police
    ethnography can enrich our compre-
    hension of, 9; of policing, what we can
    learn about, 5; understanding, 210–12.
    See also specific topics
Ethnography and Policing Workshop at
    Princeton Institute for Advanced Stud-
    ies, 85n1, 158n1
European Union (EU). *See* harmonization
Every Twelve Seconds (Pachirat), 219–21
excessive use of force, 129–30, 135–36,
    156, 165, 251–53, 263. *See also* Burge,
    Jon; police brutality; police violence;
    torture, police
executions. *See* lynchings and lynch mobs
expertise, redeeming police work through,
    146–50
extralegal force, 52, 249–50, 265; circum-
    stances that make it predictable and
    appealing, 265; definition and scope
    of the term, 251; as "exceptional," 249;
    how to study, 250–52; investigations of,
    258, 265; methodological alibi for the
    use of, 251–53, 265; moral claims used
    to justify the use of, 260; negative con-
    sequences of exposing the use of, 258
    (*see also* Burge, Jon); scholarship as al-
    lowing a social problem to masquerade
as a methodological one, 249; used to
    coerce confessions, 256. *See also* Burge,
    Jon; torture, police

family, politics of the, 171–76
Federación de Comerciantes de "La Pampa"
    (FCP), 186
Ferguson, James, 189
Ferguson Police Department (Missouri),
    249
fieldwork, 24. *See also specific topics*
FIFA Soccer World Cup (2010), 45
Fırat, Superintendent, 153–55
first information report (FIR), 67–68
force: nonphysical dimension of, 91 (see
    also *qing*; virtual force); police "force,"
    37, 114. *See also* coercion, socially sanc-
    tioned; excessive use of force
force of law, 240
Fortun, Kim, 186–87, 200
Foucault, Michel, 4, 18n14, 164–65
Frelimo Party, 118, 121, 130, 131
Frelimo party-state, 121–23
French police, 280–82. *See also* anticrime
    squads; boredom in law enforcement
    practices; Paris
Fyfe, James, 115, 129–30

Gable, Eric, 24
ganqing (affective feelings), 92, 94–95, 106;
    defined, 92, 94–95; etymology of the
    term, 94; nature of, 95
Garner, Eric, 15, 27, 266n4
Geertz, Clifford, 54
gender roles, 79
Gezi Park protests, 156
"going native" problem, 34
Goldstein, Herman, 243n1
guanxi, 92–93, 106
Gülen movement, 157, 158

habitus of the dispossessed, 193–94
hamraahi (traveling companion), 75–76
Harcourt, Bernard, 164–65, 180
harmonization, Turkish National Police
    (TNP) and the process of, 140–43, 153,
    155, 156; defined, 140
Harrison, Aaron, 263
high-arrest officers, 238

Hines, Jack, 255
Homan Square facility, 248, 249, 251
honesty, 33–34
Hong Kong, 96, 101, 104
hope scarcity, 193
hot cases, 256
human rights, police training on, 139–42,
    155–58; redeeming police work through
    professionalism and expertise, 146–50;
    reforming the Turkish National Police,
    142–46; situating the police within the
    bureaucratic machinery, 150–55
humor, 64, 68, 80, 129, 147, 171. *See also*
    jokes

immersion fieldwork, 214, 220
immersion vs. sensibility, 214–16
immigrants, 286
impressionism and impressionist tales,
    217, 218, 221
impunity, 1, 135–36, 143, 149, 263. *See
    also* blue wall of silence/blue code
Indian police: ethnographic kinship and
    critical empathy, 77–84. *See also* Chak-
    kar Rasta Thana; Uttar Pradesh (UP)
    police
Indian Police Act (1861), 85n4
informants, 75, 93, 209, 211, 213–15, 220,
    230
intellectual property (IP), policing of, 43,
    45, 49–52, 56, 58. *See also* media piracy
    in Johannesburg
intelligence, police, 49, 93–94, 96, 97, 106.
    See also surveillance
interpretation, 6, 7, 10, 13–15, 122, 252,
    287. *See also* Mozambique
interrogational beatings, 113, 117–20, 122,
    124–25, 127, 129, 254, 257; epistemic
    murkiness that embeds, 257–59. *See
    also* beatings
intimacy, 62–66, 76
intimate relationships, 176, 180
Isabel, 172
Ismael, 170

Jackson, Michael, 57–58
Jaffe, Rivke, 190
Johannesburg, policing media piracy in,
    45–48

jokes, 9, 47, 80, 139–40, 167, 189, 277. *See
    also* humor
Jones, Melvin, 260
José, Don, 188, 200
Jourde, Cedric, 216
journalism, 217–18, 221
Justice Academy (Turkey), 151–52

keep-to-the-minimum-arrest philosophy,
    238
King, Rodney, 252–53
kinship: ethnographic, and critical em-
    pathy, 77–84; personal policing and
    fictive, 73–77
Kipnis, Andrew, 95
Kobanî, Siege of, 156
Kurdish riots in Turkey, 156

Lacey, Sammy, 255
La Pampa, Bolivia, 185–86, 188, 190, 196
Latin America, 194. *See also* Bolivian Na-
    tional Police; Chile
Laverty, Frank, 258
law: police creating law in the name of
    preserving it, 264; rule of, 240. *See also
    specific topics*
Leo, Richard, 34
lethal police violence, 27; minorities killed
    by police, 15–16. *See also* lynchings and
    lynch mobs
Li, 99–101
liberal democracy, 194
litigation. *See* civil suits against the police
Los Angeles Police Department (LAPD),
    274
Louima, Abner, 252–53
Luis, 227, 230–32, 242
lynchings and lynch mobs, 123, 136n19,
    190, 192, 199

Malinowski, Bronislaw, 1
Manning, Peter, 17n5, 17n6, 244n5
Maputo, Mozambique, 113–14, 116. *See
    also* Chasana, Mozambique
Marcos, Don, 188
Marcus, George, 44, 53–54
Maribel, 178–79
market vendors (*comerciantes*), 185–92,
    195–99

Marquardt, Kairos M., 201n15
Martin, Leroy, 255
Martita, 162, 166–69, 171, 178
Marxism, 240
Masco, Joseph, 241
Massumi, Brian, 91
Mastin, Barry, 253, 254
media, police in the, 17n3. See also *Shield, The*
media piracy in Johannesburg, policing, 45–48; moral laundering, 48–51. *See also* intellectual property
Meyda, 152–53
Micky, 171, 172
militarized police, 113, 123, 165, 234, 251, 254
military ethos, 234, 251, 254
military operations, 102; contrasted with police work, 96, 240, 251
military police, 162–63, 174
minorities: killed by police, 15–16. *See also* African Americans; Arabs; racial discrimination; racism; Roma people in France
Mitchell, Sam, 263
mitra, 227; meanings, 244n3
Monjardet, Dominique, 238
moral community. *See under* police violence
moral education, physical punishment as, 126–27
moral laundering, 48–51; defined, 50
Moskos, Peter, 221, 237–38
Mozambican National Resistance (Renamo), 121–23, 131, 134
Mozambique: democratic transition, 113, 115, 121, 122, 133, 135; history, 133–35; politics, 113 (*see also* Frelimo Party). *See also* police violence
Mozambique Liberation Front. *See* Frelimo Party
Municipal Police (*comisarios*), 191–92

Nathan, Rebekah, 218–19
Neighborhood Corrections Initiative (NCI), 24–26
neighborhood surveillance, 105–6. *See also* surveillance
Nelson, 170

neoliberalism, 189–90, 192–94, 272–73
Neriman, Judge, 152–53
Nyamnjoh, Francis, 53

objectivity, ideal of, 84, 264
Ong, Aihwa, 189
order, affect/*qing* and, 91, 96–98, 100, 101, 108
order maintenance/order management, 91, 93, 98, 100–102; political intervention and, 96
Ortigão, Ramalho, 225, 243
Otis, Mr., 262, 264

Pachirat, Timothy, 219–21
Pacific Highway. *See* Aurora Avenue
Pader, Ellen, 214
Paris, 270, 275–77. *See also* boredom in law enforcement practices
"personal" policing, 73–77, 81, 84
Petra, 172–75
physical punishment: and physical pain, 127–28; popular notions of, 126–28
picket duty, 70, 75
piracy. *See* media piracy in Johannesburg
plainclothes officers, 212, 225, 227, 229–34, 236, 274, 281
police: distancing oneself from the, 42–43; as object of people's aspirations (*see* Cancha). *See also specific topics*
Police Academy (Turkey), 143–45, 151, 152, 157–58
police brutality, 149, 180, 252, 274–75, 277, 282, 285. *See also* Burge, Jon; excessive use of force; police violence; torture, police
police cars, time police officers spend alone in their, 281
police crews, sizes of, 281
police ethics, 157
police ethnographers, roles of, 29–36; conflicting, 37; disjunctures, challenges, and, 36–38; position of the police and of the ethnographer, 26–29
police ethnography, 17n8, 180–81; how it can enrich our comprehension of ethnography, 9
"police job." *See under* police violence
police life, exciting imagined life and popu-

lar media portrayals vs. the tedious reality of, 269–70, 279. *See also* boredom in law enforcement practices
police officer: becoming a, 42; being mistaken for being a, 42
police professionalism, 157
police university, 104
police violence, 23, 113–16, 132–36; epistemic murkiness that embeds, 257–59; as habitual/as part of "the police job" (and historical legacies), 113–16, 122–24; as instrumental, 124–25; meanings of, 120–22; as (em)power(ment), 129–32; prosecution of, 135 (*see also* civil suits against the police); as retributive, 125–29; revelations of, 248, 249, 261–64; scenes of, 116–20. *See also* beatings; Burge, Jon; lethal police violence; torture, police
Polícia de Segurança Pública (PSP), 226
policing: defined, 4; types of, 4 (*see also* "personal" policing). *See also specific topics*
political ethnography, 214–15
politics and political ethnography, 216
Poole, Deborah, 135
population registry, 91, 105, 108
Portuguese national police. See *Polícia de Segurança Pública*
positivism, 7
power, 105; virtual (*see* virtual force). *See also under* police violence
Prithvi, Constable, 66, 69, 75–76
Private Security, Office for the Control of, 191, 192
private security firms, 186, 188–90, 192, 197–99. *See also* Cancha
private security officers, 129, 190–92, 197; altercation between National Police and, 190–91. *See also* Cancha; community police
proactive detention, 237. *See also* proactive vs. reactive interventions
proactive vs. reactive interventions, 31, 101, 108, 232–35, 284, 286, 290n20
professional, ethnographer as, 29–31
professionalism: norms of, 31; redeeming police work through, 146–50
proximity policing, 233, 236, 244n9; defined, 244n9

Pryweller, Eileen, 259–60
public actor, ethnographer as, 31–33
Public Administration Institute for Turkey and the Middle East (TODAIE), 154
public-private partnerships, 49, 51–52
public secret, 249, 252, 290n27; of police torture, 248, 253, 259–61, 264. *See also* secrets
punishment. *See* physical punishment; retribution, police violence as
Putumayo, Colombia, 194–95

qing (affect), 91, 95, 97–98; definition and nature of, 91, 95, 96, 101, 102, 108; force and, 97, 100 (*see also* virtual force); how it can serve the interests of police, 91–94; police as instrument for cultivating, 96; terminology, 97. *See also* affect; *ganqing*
qingbao (intelligence reports), 106
qing-based policing, 91, 94–98, 100–102, 105–8; vs. materialist model, 96
qingzhi ("*qing*-control"), 96
quotas of arrests, 238, 286

racial discrimination, 6, 8, 11, 16, 84, 85, 120, 132–33, 249, 282, 286; against African American police, 254–55
racial prejudice, 7, 279
racial profiling, 282, 286
racism, 5, 8, 9, 27, 255, 259–60, 274, 279
registry-based police techniques, 91, 105, 108
Reinaldo, 172, 174
relationships: between fieldworkers and those they study, 26–27; intimate, 176, 180; of police officers with each other, 253; of police officers with the public, 285
Renamo, 121–23, 131, 134
representation, 107
research subjects: need to situate one's, 37; overidentification with, 34
results, culture of, 286
retribution, police violence as, 116–18, 120, 122, 124–29
rhetorical decisions, 11
Ricky, 175–76
ride-alongs, 24–26, 34, 35. *See also* Aurora Avenue

riots, 17n1, 156, 196, 252–53, 270, 286
Romanians, 277, 278
Roma people in France, 276–78
Ruby, 171, 172, 177

Sami, Chief Inspector, 152–53
Sanders, Mark, 55–56
Santos, Boaventura de Sousa, 132
Schatz, Edward, 210, 214–16, 219
Schwartz-Shea, Peregrine, 222n11
science, police, 103, 104
Seattle Police Department (SPD), 24–26.
    See also Aurora Avenue; Neighborhood
    Corrections Initiative
secrecy, 265; learning what not to know,
    254–56; role in social life, 252. See also
    Burge, Jon
secret facilities. See black sites, domestic;
    Homan Square facility
secret police, 18n13, 96
secrets: revelations that uncover public,
    248, 249, 261–64; shared secrets as fun-
    damental to policing, 251–52. See also
    Burge, Jon; public secret; torture, police
secret "street files," 258
self-other opposition, 103–4
senior superintendents of police (SSPs),
    68, 69
Sense and Sensibility (Austen), 207, 210–11,
    221
sensibility (and sense): of critical empathy,
    63–64, 84, 216; vs. immersion, 214–16;
    meanings of the term, 210; understand-
    ing ethnography and, 210–12. See also
    ethnographic sense
Sertan, Chief Inspector, 139, 142, 147–49,
    152, 155, 157
Shapard, David M., 211
Shearing, Clifford, 245n28
Shield, The (TV program), 274
sight, politics of, 220
Skolnick, Jerome, 115, 129–30
Soccer World Cup, 45
South Africa: "studying up" and the ques-
    tion of complicity in, 52–54. See also
    Johannesburg, policing media piracy in
South African Federation against Copyright
    Theft (SAFAC), 46, 48, 58
South African Police Service, Counterfeit

Unit of Commercial Crime Unit of, 45,
    49, 51–52
Spruill, Lester, 263
staged encounter, 185–89, 196, 198, 200.
    See also Cochabamba: seminar with
    market vendors in
state agents of coercive force, role of police
    as, 37, 114–15
State Route 99 (SR 99). See Aurora Avenue
state within a state, police as a, 239
"station ferrets" police, 236
station officer (SO). See Yadav, Y. K.
Stela. See Blondie
stop operations, 235
strategic complicity, 64, 209, 215, 216. See
    also complicity
"street files," 258
"studying up" and the question of complic-
    ity, 52–54
subaltern urbanism, 193, 194
suffering subject, 193
suicides among law enforcement agents,
    284–85, 290n22
surveillance: in Chile, 163–71, 180; in
    Taiwan, 93–96, 105–6, 108. See also
    intelligence
surveillance tactics and technologies, 4,
    262, 265

tactical complicity, 43, 44, 54. See also
    complicity
Taiwan, 91, 104–5; a banquet toast, 92–
    100, 106–7; economy, 100. See also
    affect; qing
Taussig, Michael, 252, 261
Taylor, Flint, 248, 253, 254, 256–59
Thai police, 222n10; crafting tales about
    the, 207–10. See also Bangkok police
    stations
Thompson, Edward P., 239–40
Tiehan, 93–94, 97–98, 100, 106–7
tongqing (public sentiment), 97
torture, police, 248–51, 265; epistemic
    murk around what excessive use of force
    reveals, 257–59; how police officers
    learn what not to know about enact-
    ment of, 253–58, 264; the public secret
    of, 248, 253, 259–61, 264 (see also pub-
    lic secret); revelations that uncover the

public secret of, 261–64. *See also* Burge, Jon; extralegal force

Trivedi, Arjun, 67, 78, 79, 81; beatings by, 87n41; first information report (FIR) against, 67–68; land dispute case, 74, 86n20; overview, 67; party, 66–68, 77, 78; Y. K. Yadav and, 67–68, 74, 77–79, 87n41

Truth and Reconciliation Commission (TRC), 53, 55

Turkey: Crime Research and Investigation Training Center (SASEM), 143, 145, 152; Justice Academy, 151–52; Justice and Development Party (AKP), 144, 157, 158; Police Academy, 143–45, 151, 152, 157–58

Turkish National Police (TNP), 139; reforming the, 142–46. *See also* human rights, police training on

uncovering (ethnography), 5–6

undercover operations, 225, 230. *See also* plainclothes officers

United States: police culture of detention, 237. *See also* Chicago Police Department; extralegal force

university, police, 104

Uttar Pradesh (UP) police, 62–64, 76–77, 80, 82, 83; a Christmas story with the, 66–73. *See also* Chakkar Rasta Thana

Van Maanen, John, 17nn6–7, 217–18, 221, 244n3

vendors, market. See *comerciantes*

Venkatesh, Sudhir, 218

victims, interrogational beatings and compensation to, 124–25. *See also* civil suits against the police

vigilante justice, 115, 121, 134, 258. *See also* lynchings and lynch mobs

Vikram, 70–71, 75, 76, 83

violence: state-sanctioned, 23; against women, 139–40 (*see also* domestic violence). *See also* beatings; police violence

Virendra, 68–69, 71

virtual force, 91, 96, 97, 101; writing, ethnography, and, 102–7

Waddington, P. A. J., 141

Wanda, 177–78

Washington State Department of Corrections (DOC), 24–26

Washington State Route 99. *See* Aurora Avenue

weapons. See *chamboko*

Weber, Max, 73, 215, 239

Westley, William, 250–51, 260

whistleblowers. *See* extralegal force: negative consequences of exposing the use of

Wiggins, Marcus, 263

William P. Stewart Memorial Highway. *See* Aurora Avenue

Wilson, Andrew, 257, 259, 261

Wittgenstein, Ludwig, 245n28

World Cup, 2010 FIFA Soccer, 45

writing, 10–11; as a mode of virtual force, 102–3 (*see also under* virtual force); police writing and ethnography, 103

Yadav, Y. K., 66–71, 73–78, 82, 87n39; Arjun Trivedi and, 67–68, 74, 77–79, 87n41; Constable Prithvi and, 66, 69, 75; CRT police and, 79

Yanow, Dvora, 219, 222n11

Young, Walter, 254–56

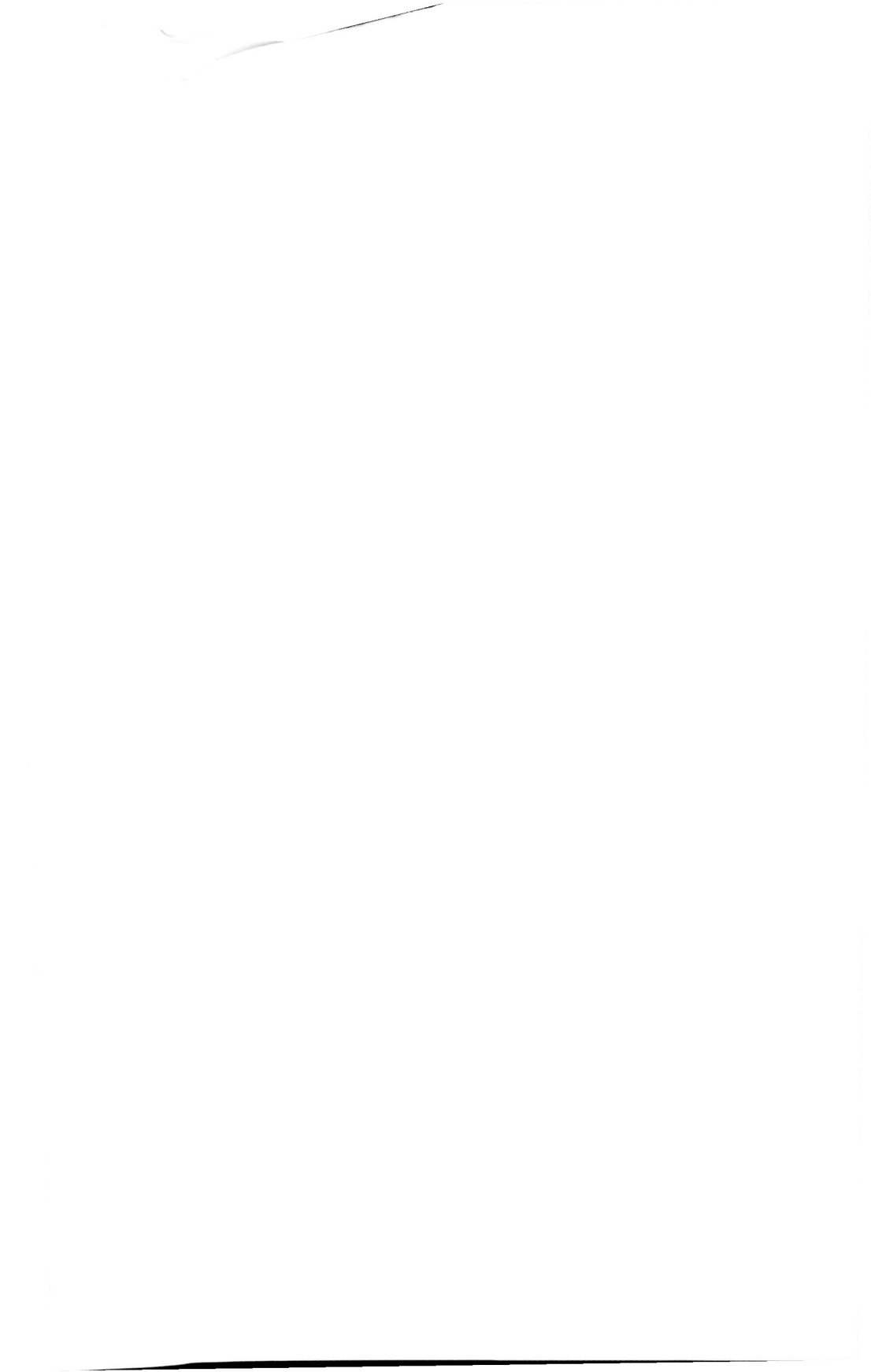

www.ingramcontent.com/pod-product-compliance
Lightning Source LLC
Chambersburg PA
CBHW050900050426
42334CB00052B/978